A LEADER MUST BE A LEADER

Encounters with Eleven Prime Ministers

A LEADER MUST BE A LEADER

Encounters with Eleven Prime Ministers

Hon. Jerry S. Grafstein, Q.C.

mosaicPRESS

Library and Archives Canada Cataloguing in Publication

Title: A leader must be a leader : encounters with eleven prime ministers / Jerry Grafstein.

Names: Grafstein, Jerry S., 1935- author.

Description: Includes index.

Identifiers: Canadiana (print) 20190083751 | Canadiana (ebook) 20190083786 | ISBN 9781771614085 (softcover) | ISBN 9781771614092 (HTML) | ISBN 9781771614108 (Kindle) | ISBN 9781771614115 (PDF)

Subjects: LCSH: Political leadership—Canada. | LCSH: Political psychology—Canada. | LCSH: Prime ministers—Canada. | LCSH: Prime ministers—Canada—Biography.

Classification: LCC JC330.3 .G73 2019 | DDC 320.01/9—dc23

Published by Mosaic Press, Oakville, Ontario, Canada, 2019.

We acknowledge the Ontario Arts Council
for their support of our publishing program

Funded by the Government of Canada
Financé par le gouvernement du Canada

MOSAIC PRESS
1252 Speers Road, Units 1 & 2
Oakville, Ontario L6L 5N9
phone: (905) 825-2130

info@mosaic-press.com

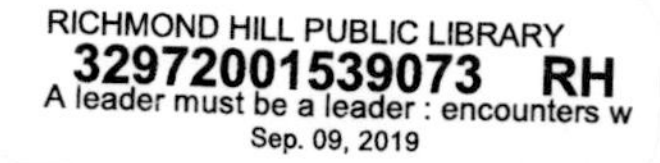

"We accept in the fullest sense of the word the settled and persistent will of the people. All of this idea of a group of supermen or super-planners... making the masses of the people do what they think is good for them, without any check or correction is a violation of democracy."

– Winston Churchill, House of Commons, Nov. 1947

Table of Contents

Dedication

This book is dedicated to Roy Faibish whose ideas on politics, the meaning of history and political leadership remain as insightful as they were inspirational.

And to Keith Davey, a master of politics, who studied political leadership at close hand and freely passed on the lessons he learned suffused with his special brand of the joy of politics.

A Leader Must be A Leader

Encounters with Eleven Prime Ministers

This book essays political leadership in modern Canada. Based on impressions and personal encounters with each of the last eleven Prime Ministers, their followers, reflections on their paths to power, and their legacies still being written on the pages of history - all in the context of their times as observed through the eyes of an insider, political activist and participant.

A Leader Must be A Leader

Encounters with Eleven Prime Ministers

"The two most important days in your life are the day you are born and the day you find out why."
– Mark Twain

I have been privileged to observe the last eleven Prime Ministers of Canada and interact with each of them since my first political experiences in the late '50s and early '60s. What follows are my reflections and personal impressions on leadership and their leadership as Prime Ministers[1] for almost three score years. For the record, I have included my take on their legacies.

Factors of Leadership

Like all politicians have, I became obsessed with the factors that made a leader a leader early on. Was leadership a natural or learned skill set? What unique amalgam of oratory,

[1] Each leader who aspires to lead Parliament indeed any politician in Canada should read and reread '*The Will of the People: Churchill and Parliamentary Democracy*' by Martin Gilbert (Vintage Canada, 2006).

ambition, character,[2] persistence,[3] doggedness, detachment, decisiveness,[4] empathy, intelligence, optimism,[5] personality, experiences, energy, memory, common sense, ideas, judgement, temperament, robust health,[6] and most especially, self-awareness of one's persona, separate wannabee leaders from the pinnacle of leadership?

Beyond a leader's inherent aptitudes for leadership is the ability to be, or exhibit, empathy, if not compassion, with members of the public. Words are the leader's tools of the trade. Body language in the age of visuality is equally important. Perception becomes reality. To speak and invoke inspiration or have the gift of persuasion to groups, large and small, spontaneously or with careful forethought is a necessary

---

[2] In 1934, Ivan Maisky, the recently appointed Soviet Russian Ambassador to England, met with Winston Churchill for the first time. Churchill was then an outlier of the Conservative Party in his 'wilderness years'. A few days later, Lord Beaverbrook (William Maxwell Aiken, Canada born publisher of *Daily Express* group of newspapers and later a Cabinet Minister under Churchill during World War II) wrote Ivan Maisky about Churchill the following, "*I send you a strong recommendation of that gentleman. ... In character he is without a rival in British politics. I know all about his prejudices. But a man of character who tells the truth is worth much to a nation.*" – '*The Maisky Diaries: Red Ambassador to the Court of St James's, 1932-1943*', edited by Gabriel Gorodetsky (Yale University Press, 2015, pp. 50).

[3] Winston Churchill ran for election to House of Common in England, the mother of all Parliaments, eighteen times. He was unsuccessful in five of those election campaigns.

[4] Considered by many as a crucial, concise, practical guide to political leadership, read '*Churchill On Leadership: Executive Success in The Face of Adversity*' by Steven F. Hayward (Prima Publishing, 1997).

[5] Leaders like the Roosevelts, Reagan, and Churchill were all incredibly optimistic.

[6] All eleven Prime Ministers enjoyed robust health and were disciplined in their culinary habits during their time in office. Jean Chrétien had a heart operation but quickly recovered while in office.

talent.[7] Of course, per force, a leader needs to be a quick study, well informed and a good listener – a quick and thoughtful responder. A major criterion of leadership is to attract a loyal team that are skilled and comfortable in a team environment under the public's glare.

Keeping a cool head when other lose theirs in a crisis is the epitome of leadership. No leader is perfect. He[8] must know how to pace himself, and how to organize his time to allow him to reflect.[9] Mistakes are often made in haste. How to recoup is a necessary skill. For this, he needs a tight rapid response team he trusts to get at the facts of any surprise, for in these modern times, there are many swift changing parts at home and abroad. The public has access to more platforms of news and is bombarded with information and the wide range of issues from 'natural disasters' to 'identity' to 'nuke' weaponry that is both constant and astonishing. So, a leader and his team must keep up with fast breaking news, separating facts from fiction or opinion.

Most politicians aspire to leadership, but so very few achieve their goal. Usually a long preoccupation and a lust for 'making

---

7 Just when you think you have read all books on the facts of Winston Churchill's political and writing career along comes another volume: '*Churchill – Walking With Destiny*' by Andrew Roberts (Penguin Random House LLC, 2018). On page forty-nine, Robert sums up Churchill's "five elements to great oratory" – appreciation of words, sound and cadence, accumulated argument, analogy, and emotion and passion of the speaker.

8 For concision, I have used the masculine.

9 John Diefenbaker loved to fish for a change of pace. Mike Pearson took time to watch sports programs. Pierre Trudeau understood the need for down time to reflect. He regularly visited a Prime Ministerial retreat outside Ottawa at Harrington Lake as did Brian Mulroney. Jean Chrétien took Trudeau's advice and followed suit when he was Prime Minister. John Turner loved to spend vacation time at the Lake of Woods and a family vacation home in Nova Scotia when a minister. Stephen Harper practiced with a small band when he could.

a difference' in the public area or self-aggrandizement compels some to study, practice, prepare, and reach for the political mountaintop, master or mistress of all they perceive. Most leaders have a deep vein of narcissism. But do they possess that special, elusive alchemy, the 'royal jelly'?[10]

Each successful leader is a master of the 'dark' arts of politics, and as Churchill once wrote, needs, at times, to be a 'butcher' to chop errant supporters especially his Cabinet, whilst he keeps his own counsel. To be a skillful self-promotor and propagandist while appearing sincere and authentic, even reticent, is an essential talent to become a leader and practice leadership.

While the public understands ambition, it usually prefers those who do not appear power hungry.

Leaders will find their groove like a championship golfer. Once in that groove, some leaders, unsure of their own talents, demonize their political predecessors 'who always leave a mess' and are quick to 'project' blame for their mishaps on the 'others'.[11] Other leaders disdain this narrative and eschew this line of politics, believing their own merit and ideas will win the day.

A Leader's Coterie

The leader's coterie quickly learns to align their 'echo chamber' with their leader's policies or stances to spread his 'word'. A leader of necessity to be a leader needs to attract a tight circle of followers and acolytes, as he practices perfecting his style. Can his coterie avoid the public eye? Rarely. If they don't, the leader

---

10 Donald MacDonald, when he briefly sought Liberal leadership, withdrew wisely assessing himself, saying he did not possess the 'royal jelly'.

11 'Transference' as first defined by Freud, then applied in political theory, is the redirection of repressed or flawed behaviour unto another political actor.

usually suffers. It is tempting for them to bask in the reflecting light of their leader's halo.[12] Yet, they both conspire to transmit nuanced propaganda if not 'fake' news to justify their hold on power for the 'people', or they place a brighter gloss of 'values' on their inexplicable behaviour to distract public attention from other potent mistakes of other issues while they seek to recoup. Leaders are driven by the belief that such conduct is permissible for they are offering a 'better' way forward for the nation. The 'people' are the object of their narrative. Words are coined like the 'average Canadian', the 'working Canadian', the 'forgotten Canadian', and recently, the favourite, the new sweet spot, the 'middle-class'[13] to focus on this torqued market once empowered. Every leader, or his followers, are loath and reluctant to take responsibility for his own flaws or their mistakes, but rather light an incendiary torch to his adversaries to distract attention while seeking to maintain public empathy, if not sympathy, and supporter affinity.

Chief of Staff

Many Prime Ministers get off to a rocky start as the Prime Minister's election crew is suddenly confronted by a constant avalanche of problems and tasks that assail a Prime Minister

---

12 "*The last temptation is the greatest treason: to do the right deed for the wrong reason.*" – '*Murder in the Cathedral*', T.S. Elliot

13 Pollsters who undertake daily and strategize polls for leaders look for the 'soft spot' in public opinion. American leaders of late have focused on the 'middle-class' as their key target market. The Americans divined this demographic. This is now mimicked in Canada. The problem of course is who are the members of the middle-class? And should their needs be a leader's paramount pre-occupation? Is designating the 'middle-class' for preferential treatment a 'class' argument like Marxists who relished 'class' warfare, or at least divisions amongst the so-called classes?

once he accedes to office. One important key to this dilemma are the skill sets of the Prime Minister's Chief of Staff formerly called Principal Secretary.

John Diefenbaker never truly solved this endemic problem in his office. Mike Pearson appointed a youthful Jim Coutts who quickly grew in the job and matured later when Pierre Trudeau, after disastrous mistakes in his first period in office and some turnovers, appointed Jim, his Principal Secretary, in 1974 for the balance of his term in government.

Joe Clark's office disorganization caused him problems from the outset of his short administration especially his first trip abroad with luggage woes, and never fully recovered. John Turner's advisors were visibly divided from the outset and this damaged his Prime Ministership. Brian Mulroney had his problems at the outset of his administration, as did Jean Chrétien. When Chrétien appointed Jean Pelletier, his long-time friend and law school classmate, former Mayor of Quebec City, defeated Liberal candidate and shrewd political organizer, his office began to purr like a well-oiled machine. Pelletier became Chrétien's alter ego and brought judgment and gravitas to every problem, large or small.[14]

Paul Martin's office failed to reach out beyond his tight knit entourage and assay the problems from within the Party and without to his detriment.

Stephen Harper had a turnover of Chiefs of Staff and suffered as a consequence.

Justin Trudeau's office was stable at the outset.

---

[14] Jean Pelletier for his outstanding service to Jean Chrétien was appointed Head of Via Rail and then summarily dismissed by Chrétien's successor Paul Martin. For over a decade, Pelletier fought in the courts for damages for his job loss, damages to his reputation, and costs. Ultimately, he was vindicated in the courts with a healthy judgement on all three claims.

Taking The Office

A leader must also be a strategist and a tactician in the day-to-day onslaught of crises under the watchful eye of the media. As Churchill once wrote, "*I could never be responsible for a strategy which excluded the offensive principle. A leader must know where and how to take the offense.*" A leader must know how to leave issues alone until he contributes to resolutions.

One common trait in a leader's longevity occurs when he displays restraint and yes, humility. It is tempting for leaders to fall in love with public adulation and forget that public admiration is transitory at best. To refrain from gloating about political victory or political successes is the mask a true leader devoted to the public interest should seek to wear.[15]

Ronald Reagan once queried how a politician could enter and maintain public office without being an actor. Reagan, like Lincoln and both Roosevelts, was a master of story-telling and could spin narratives to explain his actions. Obama loved telling stories about himself. So, telling stories is part of the art of leadership.

Charles de Gaulle wrote in his memoirs on leadership, "*There can be no prestige without mystery, for familiarity breeds contempt.*" De Gaulle relished keeping his own counsel and his distance from even his closest confreres.[16]

---

[15] Churchill personified this approach to politics when he was gracious to his political opponents both on the opposite side and adversaries within his own party. He used the word 'magnanimous' in victory. Churchill never held grudges. Churchill recalled his 'wilderness years' from 1929 to 1939 when he was cast off from higher office and shunned by friends and foes alike when he opposed 'appeasement', the conventional sentiment in the U.K. at the time. He readily forgave his foes and was gracious to his enemies.

[16] Winston Churchill could not figure out what was on Franklin Roosevelt's mind. Churchill, when he and Roosevelt met in Cairo during their meeting

A leader, like a good chess or bridge player, should be able to think two or three steps ahead of his opponents, even his own advisers, and never disclose what he is really thinking. To reach out and garner advice from a larger range of voices who he trusts beyond his own circle and know when, where, and who to seek such advice broadens a leader's perspectives. Group think is an anathema to rational decision-making.

The Leader's Entourage

The leader of necessity runs his entourage like a modern enterprise. The 'nuts and bolts' are vital to success. The choice of the traditional 'bag man', the leader's key money raiser, is an essential ingredient in the leader's operation, who in turn, requires good astute ties to the financial community and is careful to avoid conflicts of interest and flying under the radar. In addition, a leader now needs a modern fundraising crew to ply the cyberspace to organize and gain their own adherents in the social media. In this modern era of legal issues drowning politics, a key legal adviser and a rapid response legal team also remains imperative. His election campaign chair must be on the ready at all times. Key strategists are also essential who can debate, devise, and agree on the steps forward with the leader's assent.

Ever Present Polling

Pollsters who provide daily glimpses of public opinion is now deemed requisite for the leader to nuance his message. Focus groups

---

in 1943, arranged for their visit to the Sphinx. Churchill considered that Roosevelt, like the enigma of the Sphinx, kept his own counsel. As one historian wrote, "*...he [Roosevelt] was as inscrutable as the Sphinx at his core, he remained shrouded, unknowable, dispassionate.*" – '*1944 FDR and The Year That Changed History*' by Jay Winik (Simon and Schuster, 2015).

complete the leader's arsenal to test and shape his message. The social media now plays a powerful role in the leader's interactive tool box. Still, public events, large and small, are necessary to allow the leader to read public opinions and keep in touch with his vital supporters. No doubt, Prime Ministers' pollsters have taken on a sinister role with little, or no, transparency.

Truth and Propaganda

There is a paradox between advocating truth and facts versus palpable fiction.[17] Orwell wrote how autocratic regimes burnished their propaganda machinery. To persuade the public is not necessarily successful based on the presentation of only a careful construct of facts. T.S. Elliot wrote, "*We tend to substitute emotion for thought*". The leader should be able to turn on the emotions tap to reach out and persuade the public and his followers. Leaders should be able to seize a 'teaching moment' to instigate a redirection in public opinions. Hierarchies surround power. C.S. Lewis considered how these relationships interact to gain loyalties. How 'men not yet bad will do very bad things to gain access to the inside, to be close to power'. At times, this emotive passion is difficult to abate. It lies buried in the human condition.

Luck

Above all, a leader needs luck to be successful. Techies glued to social media are now essential and leaders now respond quickly to erupting issues. Patience while waiting for a favourable climate

---

[17] A leading poet of the 20th century, Zbigniew Herbert, a Pole who refused to leave his native land while in the grips of communism, wrote that 'truth' is 'beauty'. Facts are important. Words are important. "*A bird is a bird... slavery means slavery...a knife is a knife...death remains death...*" (1983).

to move towards a leader's goals is just good politics. Timing remains everything in politics.

Reacting To The Unexpected

Sometimes the unexpected can tell more about the instincts of a leader for leadership. When Pierre Trudeau attended a St. Baptiste Day parade in Montreal, he was pelted by separatist extremists in the crowd below. Rather than be pulled to safety, he insisted on keeping his place cementing in the minds of the public, a man of courage and strength. Strong elements within a leader attract followership. Sometimes unpredictable events can be a teaching moment. When Trudeau was accosted during the FLQ crisis and the War Measures Act was hastily imposed, he was asked by a TV reporter what he intended to do next, Trudeau replied, "*Just watch me*". It was another teaching moment.

Crisis Management

No better insight to a Prime Minister's skill is crisis management. Quickly getting the facts, organizing a quick response team, and arriving at a solution or solutions all in public view is an essential attribute of leadership.[18]

A Leader Must Be A Leader

'*A leader must be a leader*', a phrase I helped coin with Terry O'Malley (the master creative director at Vickers and Benson) in

[18] Required reading for a superb analysis of Presidential crisis management is chapter twelve in *Leadership in Turbulent Times*, Doris Kearns Goodwin, Simon Schuster, New York, 2018. Kearns recounts how Theodore Roosevelt handled a crippling national miner's strike and Franklin Roosevelt on the economic crisis he inherited in 1932 to gain public confidence in his rapid moves the first 100 days in office.

1979 for the faltering Pierre Trudeau, when in his lackadaisical meandering campaign for election as Prime Minister ran out of steam in 1979. Preoccupied with family issues and episodic energy, his appetite for politics and most importantly, his groove, suffered as Trudeau lost to the unlikely leadership Joe Clark in the 1979 national election. Trudeau had dithered too long, and he gave up his majority.[19] Joe Clark gained power, though Trudeau led the Liberals in the popular vote in the 1979 national election results. Still, an instinctive leader cannot easily give up. His drive and ambition, like an alter ego, did not allow him to go quietly into the twilight zone. His major political ambition had not been achieved. So it is with almost all political leaders. Once in the public limelight, in the public arena, it is hard to return to the shadows, away from public attention.

A Prime Minister's Powers

What is often overlooked by Canadians and observers is the almost absolute power a leader in Canada gains once he reaches

[19] In 1979, Pierre Trudeau sensed he was losing the election. For a while, well before the election, he was ahead on the polls. He had waited too long. I helped organize a rally at Maple Leaf Gardens as a finale to the campaign televised by Peter Raymont's documentary on Trudeau believing economics was always a key to any campaign. Trudeau's heart was not on the economic message. Rather, he felt the repatriation of the Constitution would be a rallying call on his last stand. So, refusing to follow the advice of his campaign advisors, he concluded his speech with words to this effect, "*... as for the Constitution, we will bring it home.*" Peter's documentary captured the disappointment in the faces of his advisors including me. The following day, I went to visit my mother who was avid fan of Pierre Trudeau and followed the campaign. "*What do you think?*" I asked her. She said, "*You know I like Pierre Trudeau. He is a good man. But I didn't understand what he talked about bringing home the Constitution. Is that some kind of breakfast cereal?*" I knew then we would lose the election.

the pinnacle of politics – the Prime Ministership. He chooses the head of the state, the Governor General, and the Lt. Governor of each province. The Prime Minister is the absolute master of his Party, his Cabinet, the elected members of his Party, the government bureaucracy, and all government agencies. Most of his appointments, in the thousands, serve at his 'pleasure', by order in council and can be removed without notice or cause. He appoints or 'green lights' Party officials, both elected volunteers and paid. He chooses not just the Chief Public Servant and the members of the Privy Council's office, but the members of the Prime Minister's Office. He appoints all senior federal bureaucrats at the Deputy and Assistant Deputy levels and all ambassadors, consultants, boards and heads of all government agencies and Crown Corporations, the heads of RCMP, all intelligence agencies, the heads of the armed services, and senior assistants. He 'green lights' the Speaker of the Commons to run for Speaker, appoints the Speaker of the Senate, the Government leader of the Senate, 'green lights' Parliamentary officers and he appoints all Senators, all federal judges especially the Chief Justice and Supreme Court of Canada and Chief Justice of Courts of each province, Chairs of each Committee of House, and now, in part, the Senate. He 'green lights' all senior political staff of his own, all ministers and, in some cases, M.P.'s. He chooses his election campaign committee and pollsters. He chooses the party media team and party fundraisers. He chooses his House leadership, his whip, and their assistants to corral his members to vote. He can decide what out of country trips an M.P. takes on public business and to mete out rewards for foreign travel. He approves the national caucus chair, and if he chooses, 'green lights' each chair of the committees of the caucus and the appointment of chairs of each committee of the Commons who serve at his pleasure! Sometimes he decides the appointment of a Chair over his party members' objections. He retains the right to kick members out of his caucus and invite others to join.[20]

The Cabinet

The first difficult task confronting a new Prime Minister is the selection of his Cabinet. The Cabinet under Parliamentary democracy is an essential linchpin to government. Ministers, in recent times, especially since John Diefenbaker, not only represent their regions but also reflect the diversity of the Canadian population. Justin Trudeau took the next major step appointing a Cabinet with gender parity.

Each Minister has extensive legislative duties and discretionary power. On his appointment, a thick book prepared by the PCO/PMO[21] setting out his duties, range of activities, and an up-to-date review of all direct matters directly affecting his department people, is presented for his close study and consideration. Of late,

---

[20] The powers of the Prime Minister, his government, and all Parliamentarians was seen by the public as not held sufficiently in check by the opposition or the media. Witness the rise of independent Parliamentary officers to check egregious government and officials conduct. These independent officers include: Auditor General, Chief Election Officer, Commissioner of Lobbying, Conflicts of Interest and Ethics Commissioner, Information Commissioner, Parliamentary Budget Officer, Privacy Commissioner, and Public Sector Integrity Commissioner. Each of these Parliamentary officers has full legislative powers of investigation and public action after reporting their findings whether on their own accord or by request of the public under separate acts of Parliament. These reports are geared to curb egregious conduct and excess use of powers. Prime Ministers, Governments, Members of Parliament, and public servants have felt the sting of their reports. In the main, it is left to the electorate to correct carefully documented abuses of power.

[21] Two secretariats report directly to the Prime Minister, the Prime Minister's Office (PMO), the political arm of the Prime Minister, and the Privy Council Office (PCO), the public service arm of the Prime Minister.

each Minister receives a letter from the Prime Minister setting out his priorities. These have been made public.

The Prime Minister also appoints all Ministers and Chairs to various Cabinet Committees. By convention, all Cabinet deliberations are held in the strictest secrecy so that any decision appears to the public to be unanimous. That allows for full and open debate within Cabinet on any and all issues. Only when the archives of Cabinet deliberations are made public years later can we learn what went on.

The Prime Minster chairs the Cabinet and the Priorities and Planning Committee that deals with the day-to-day issues presented in Parliament.

By practice, one Minister is named the 'political minister' for his province and gains oversight and responsibility for all political activities within his region.

Still, the Prime Minister's leadership reigns supreme. Any continued grumblings in Cabinet is usually a harbinger of Prime Minister loss of Cabinet confidence. It was the Cabinet loss of confidence and not the caucus that led to Diefenbaker's fall from power.[22]

The Trappings of Office

Becoming a leader can be a powerful boost to any leader's ego. The constant armed guards, the protective limousines,

[22] When and how to remove a Cabinet Minister or change Cabinet are delicate and yet, vital decisions to maintain public confidence. For an excellent consideration of the nature of Cabinet deliberations under adversity, read *Ministers At War: Winston Churchill And His War Cabinet* by Jonathan Schneer (Basic Books, 2014). *All Behind You, Winston: Churchill's Great Coalition 1940-1945* by Roger Hermiston (Aurum Press, 2017) is another excellent historical analysis of cabinet deliberations under Churchill and is a must read as well.

the ready availability of helicopters or jets to take the leader quickly to any destination, the constant saluting by guards and military can inflate anyone's sense of self-importance. The Prime Minister's daily calendar carefully husbanded by his senior office demonstrates the importance placed on every minute of his time on official work. Yet a mindful leader needs to insist that his schedule allow adjustment for careful reflection and downtime as events swirl around him.

Prime Ministers and Public Policy

Awesome in scope and reach, and yet rarely understood, the Prime Minister also determines the policies of his government, the timetable and agenda, the legislation, and regulations put before Parliament while in office. No one democratic leader in the world has this capacious range of powers. He chooses his spokespersons to the media. He decides where and when to travel and who should represent him abroad when he chooses not to travel. He sets foreign policy by his own travels. Long established historic buildings can be renamed on a gulp of public opinion or change its use. All Ministers' policy speeches and their Parliamentary Assistants require his approval since he appoints them all. The national budget with last minute additions and subtractions require his prior consent. Until recently, he remained only accountable to the 'confidence' of his elected caucus. The Canadian Prime Minister cannot be fired as leader by the caucus alone. It now requires his Party in convention to do so. Still, he decides how to raise party funds and allocates how they are to be spent.[23] The Canadian Prime Minister is more powerful than the

[23] Another reminder of the limited access to the Prime Minister is the now thousands of emails he receives each day. Each Prime Minister handles this aspect of his leadership differently. Normally, each letter and email

British, Australian or New Zealand Prime Ministers under their respective Parliamentary practices and mandates.[24] However, elected members in the caucus in each Parliamentary democracy can triggers a change in leadership.

Perhaps most important is the power to 'make war' and send Canadian forces abroad at the risk of their lives on forceful missions, peacekeeping, and peace-making engagements. This unlimited power in practice is the Prime Minister's decision alone to make. Parliament usually follows his lead or silently acquiesces.

Polls As A Check on Prime Ministerial Power

Still, the public via the incessant political polls, can act as a quick if temporary 'check and balance' on the Prime Minister's lead on issues large and small opposed by Opposition and abetted and amplified by the ever-present echo chamber of the ubiquitous

receive a response. The days of a Prime Minister responding to each missive personally is over. Diefenbaker and Pearson both responded to some personal correspondence from close friends and outside advisor. Pierre Trudeau would respond to my notes and memos himself as did John Turner. Turner would personally pen notes of condolences or thanks. Reagan and Obama would be given a small sample of letters to respond to personally. These would be publicized from time-to-time.

[24] Of course, the American President is the leader of the most powerful nation in the world, but the President is constrained by a large array of explicit legislative 'checks and balances' in Congress, the Judiciary and the Constitution, unlike the Canadian Prime Minister whose powers cannot be attenuated, except periodically by the Judiciary when it opines on the Constitution (though at times beyond the scope of the intent of the Constitution), and occasionally, by the spotlight of the media and of course, by the polls. The Opposition in Parliament, rarely covered in a major way by the media, has only episodic success in changing a Prime Minister's chosen course of action, mainly supported by a twitch in the polls.

social media, and with decreasing influence, the traditional press gallery power composed of press, TV and radio. The print media power now is diluted by the TV and radio scrums after question period, and the social media.

Canada's Fragmented Political Power Structure

Canada owns a highly decentralized power structure divided between the federal and provincial powers. Of late, Prime Ministers have stealthily accumulated powers from the provinces. The Prime Minister must be able to gather the disparate strands into organized ideas and themes to maintain national unity on key issues, large and small, of national interest while paying at least lip service to endless provincial demands for a larger share of the national pie. There is validity to provincial claims that result in greater calls for a greater allocation of the taxpayers' dollars. Regretfully, accountability continues to be blurred between levels of government, especially which level is accountable for which taxpayers' dollars when tax measures are blended. The theory of responsible government is blurring. The greatest distortion lies between the needs of the cities compared to the provinces because of increasing growth of cities as the divide between 'urban' and 'rural' continues to accelerate. This dysfunction continues to widen as cities grow even larger with inadequate financial resources to cope with their crushing needs. Citizens cannot easily allocate responsibility for the expenditure of tax payer's dollars to the appropriate level of government to hold them accountable.

Prime Minister as a 'Butcher'

A Prime Minister must be a good judge of character and capability, especially in his immediate circle, and of course, his Cabinet and his caucus (all of whom he must approve or reject for egregious conduct) and be an acute delegator via his key appointments. He must be prepared to make changes when their judgment falters, or his! Churchill offered that a Prime Minister must at times be a 'butcher' to chop Cabinet Ministers or other senior officials who disrupt his administration. When to do so, is a delicate choice a Prime Minister alone must make.

Of course, the Cabinet, the caucus, the opposition, the media, public opinion, and most of all polls all act as a check of the Prime Minister and his entourage, his inclinations and his reach for unlimited power and public support. The oversight by Parliament on the power of the public purse has been diluted as a check on the Prime Minister's executive power by budget omnibus bills and complexity that time limits Parliament's ability to debate each budget item, especially when larded beyond legislative reach by other bills that cannot go through public scrutiny because these bills are attached to one budget vote based on 'confidence'. Parliament, as a check and balance, on executive action continues to weaken as the Prime Minister's powers are enhanced. The practice of Prime Ministers appearing alone, almost as if they were the President of the U.S.A., weakens the concept of government by Cabinet in our Parliamentary system.

Leaders and Followers

Leadership is a collage of primary and secondary colours in the eye of the beholder – a palimpsest that covers over the deeper darker tones. Leadership, as perceived or desired by followers, takes the hue of colours that are visually attractive. A leader paints in bolder colours to justify what he is selling, while glossing over or muting the lesser darker colours and his deficits. Followers become instant apologists for their choice of leader. Their choice of leader can do no wrong. Their followers provide alibis for his or her and their gaffs to justify their followership. One draws from leaders what one seeks. A follower cannot help but nuance and alibi the undesirable aspects of their leader especially their patent mistakes and inadequacies. They are often in denial for their own sake or loath to admit their own judgment is flawed. They minimize the leader's mistakes; they look for scapegoats. The political herd gathers around to protect their leader even when it is clear he may be leading his party over a precipice. Distractions are sought or in the most egregious cases, they may even 'wag the dog' to deflect public attention.[25] Weak embattled leaders use 'transference' reflexively to blame others or to weather their own gaffs. The mind accepts only what it chooses and desecrates or demonizes the 'other'. Loyalty can become toxic.

Leadership idolatry is an easy trap to fall into. The most difficult task for a loyal party follower is to dissent when the leader takes a wrong turn or two. Remember it was Abraham who destroyed his father's factory making clay idols. Belief in a higher spirit should be one's guide.[26]

Succession

Perhaps the fatal flaw in most leaders, who came to cherish the exercise of power and are naturally inflated when basking in

[25] Bill Clinton, mired in his impeachment in Congress, belatedly bombed targets in war torn Yugoslavia at the behest of Tony Blair. This strategy was called 'Wag The Dog' by skeptical observers.

[26] Charles Krauthammer, a brilliant American commentator and journalist, who went from being a Democrat to a Republican once opined, "*Anyone who stops believing in religion, can believe in anything*".

the public spotlight, is when to give up the reins of power after ensuring a coterie of capable leaders are available and prepared for the country's highest office with ample time to demonstrate their leadership qualities to the public. This flaw occurs so often that it may be endemic to most leaders.[27]

I came to observe, firsthand, Prime Ministers from 1961 to 2010 during almost half a century of political activism, as political militant, elected Party official, Ministerial Assistant, Senator, and by choice, robustly engaged with all of them in person or against the other Party leaders as an activist and Senator. Now as party ties are loosened and I approach the sunset of my life, I think I can now reflect more objectively on those exciting encounters with Canadian Prime Ministers of both major parties, especially the Liberal Party where I remain a 'true' if somewhat jaded 'believer' after I retired from public life as a Senator for twenty-six years at age 75. My years, near or in politics, were crammed with years of excitement and may hold some interest or even lessons for others who believe while public service is most demanding, it can also be most enriching and rewarding time to broaden one's life experiences. There was a time when, as most politicians, I measured my life between elections.

A Leader's 'Charisma'

Modern behavioural psychologists, based on study and research models, cannot predict adequately or divine the

[27] Mike Pearson was a clear exception to the norm. He appointed Trudeau, Turner and Chrétien to his Cabinet at the same time who each in turn became Prime Minister. John Turner sent me an autographed photo of this turning point in his life and the lives of Pierre Trudeau and Jean Chrétien.

effective amalgam of leadership qualities.[28,29] Some leaders look great and fail, while other surprise us with their often-hidden talents. Sometimes leadership qualities emerge only in crisis. We are all captives of our own belief structure. The division between the mind and emotions, and senses and sensibility cannot be readily perceived, just estimated. What is clear is that leadership involves a strange alchemy. Some observers call it 'charisma'.[30] That chemical mix of elements that involves the eyes, sounds, pleasure, and pain points that generate admiration and followership – in a word – appeal. Some leaders are more appealing to the public than others. Yet, appeal is an essential ingredient of leadership. A casual exchange with a leader, of any stripe, shapes one's attitude towards that leader. Is it our human nature that triggers a sense of awakened interest and respect, from even brief exchanges, that colour one's attitude towards leadership immeasurably?

---

28 Howard Gardner, a Harvard psychologist, wrote *Frames of Mind: The Theory of Multiple Intelligences* (Basic Books, 1993). Four major indices were defined, intra-personal intelligence, inter-personal intelligence, linguistic intelligence, and logical/mathematical intelligence. This complex analysis sheds some light on leadership characteristics but are difficult to ascertain, and then, only in hindsight.

29 See also *The Presidential Difference: Leadership Styles from FDR to Obama* by Fred I. Greenstein (Simon and Schuster, 2009) who noted political skill, vision, cognitive style, organization capacity, able to communicate, but above all 'emotional intelligence' – an essential criteria – see also section – Leadership Index. Greenstein, an eminent American scholar who wrote extensively about U.S.A. Presidential leaders through the lens of behavioural science.

30 Charisma lies in the mysterious impact the leader has on his close associates and his ardent supporters who share his intense belief in the correctness of his ideas and vision. This intensity, especially after becoming Prime Minister, radiates to his larger audience directly and through the media as he imposes his will to a generally disengaged or disinterested public.

Biases and Belief Structure

Leadership qualities are highly subjective. Our own attitudes are forged by our biases and belief structure. We each build a picture in our mind of the one we choose to follow. Negative biases can be overcome by a personal brush with a leader. We invest our hopes, our dreams, and beliefs into our chosen leader. Followers live in great expectations of our chosen leader. And so, it was.

Still, the public and the leader's followers admire and respond to strength and the 'smart's when a leader's instincts rise above the din of public opposition in the media and shape public opinion in a direction he chooses especially when he goes against conventional wisdom at the time.

Each Canadian Prime Minister, different in so many ways, shares common characteristics so alike that each forms a fascinating study of the human condition. Canada is not an easy nation to govern.[31] We live in a surprising domestic political environment made even more complex by a divided governance swift moving global parts. An unexpected crisis anywhere colours the public view on how it impacts Canada.

The Prime Minister and His Caucus

One key to judging a leader is to observe him in the privacy of his weekly caucus meeting with his party team mates. I was invited to Mr. Pearson's caucus on several occasions and was a member of the Federal Liberal caucus under Prime Ministers Trudeau, Turner, Chrétien and Martin, and interim Liberal Party leaders

[31] Canada is diverse, still largely undeveloped, and holds sovereignty over the second largest landmass in the world with the second largest source of fresh water which, too much to our regret, is now polluted to a startling degree. Climate change policies do not significantly affect fresh water pollution.

Herb Gray and Bill Graham, and then Dion and Ignatieff as Party leaders. I was a member of the caucus when Justin Trudeau joined as a newly minted Liberal Member of Parliament.

I avidly sought information from insiders of the Conservative Party to divine how Conservative leaders acted in their caucus. I was also keenly interested in how the leaders of the minority parties, especially the NDP, ran their caucus.

Usually the leader sums up the consensus and action plan for the week ahead after waiting for caucus leaders and caucus committee chairs to report and after each member is allocated a slot to speak on any issue local, national, or international of interest to him or her. Watching the leader's eyes and body language after each short intervention is telling. Each speaker anticipates the leader will mention his point of view favourably in the leader's final remarks. This is a tough audience, all up-to-date on the news and the recent polls. After the leader comments, I noted that critique of the leader's performance was muted if the polls were favourable. If unfavourable, there would be a more restless reaction. Each leader listens intently to seek a good grade and hopefully a solid applause. It is the tribal leader and his tribe in real time. Some leaders become masters of this art form. As the caucus proceeded, I also wondered how I would respond. Pierre Trudeau was the most artful and convincing, always a master, developing a consensus from the disparate views and strands of argument that he heard. It was amazing to listen to his scintillating rendition on current events and weave together opposing caucus views. Pierre Trudeau was the master of painting a rich coherent tapestry of different strands of ideas after a free and open caucus debate which he relished.[32] Trudeau's powerful

[32] In caucus, Pierre Trudeau sat at the end of a long-raised dais with the caucus chair, vice chair, whip, and other caucus leaders. He never interrupted the

intellect shone through, giving his caucus members a fresh lens to consider the events of the day.

Followership

Followers are fickle, changeable, and easily replaceable. Tribalism is alive and well in politics. To be a member of a tribe, to follow a leader is natural and comforting as Canetti wrote in '*Crowds and Power*'.[33] People behave in similar ways in a crowd. Humans, needing the comfort of companionship, cannot help but follow others, whether at a political rally, a funeral, in a theatre, or a wedding. We are ultimately inherent followers and it is hard to break loose from the 'glue of the 'crowd' and separate 'fact' from 'fiction'. We want to believe what we want to believe. It's easy, comforting, fortifying, and affirming. It is our own sweet spot.

The public is anxious to overcome its skepticism of broken promises, even patent flaws, craving leadership to navigate and lead them through the turbulent often confusing waters we confront daily.

Organizing A Leader's Public Event

To organize an event for a leader and then, like a master chef, enjoy the fruits of his labour with others, cannot be easily explained when one watches the leader perform before a crowd, especially a

caucus but would rise at the very end to deliver his assessment of the issues raised and how to proceed. He was irritated if a member approached him just before, or during, caucus because he wanted to concentrate on what each member had to say, how he said it and the member's body motions.

[33] Read *Crowds and Power* by Elias Canetti (First edition, published Victor Gollancz, London, 1962). Canetti wrote his masterful work as he observed Nazi and fascist leaders fuse the loyalties of their followers that freed them to follow their own ideas without restraint. Unquestioning loyalty to the leader is the core of untrammelled autocratic behaviour.

crowd that one helped organize. It's a moment of high expectation and joy – '*un frisson*' – if the leader and the crowd behave as planned, or dismay if the leader falters and the crowd will react. The leader is visibly empowered by the energy he extracts from an adoring crowd. He can appear, for a moment, larger than life itself. Every leader loves to bask in the warmth of public affection.

Leaders As Storytellers

Political historians of late, especially in the United States, have focused on a President's storytelling ability to personalize an event by telling a story, this art form can divert public attention towards a course of action, rising above the noise and chatter of everyday news and gossip.

Lincoln, both Roosevelts and recently Obama exhibited this talent. No better storyteller in modern times to make a point was Ronald Reagan. John Diefenbaker had strong storytelling skills. Mike Pearson and Pierre Trudeau rarely used this innate talent. Brian Mulroney could also spin a yarn. Few were better than Jean Chrétien who could naturally tell a tale to make a point. Justin Trudeau in his early speeches as leader exhibited this talent.

Of course, humour is another invaluable tool in a leader's repertoire to cool a situation and exhibit self-deprecation. A joke told by a leader on himself can be a most endearing characteristic of a leader. Pearson had the ability to poke fun at himself that kept his followers in thrall of this modest multi-talented leader and his understated abilities. So could Chrétien and Martin.

First Skill: Public Communication

Without the ability to communicate, whether in small circles, private gatherings or public events in the intensity of TV or radio, a leader cannot become a leader. All leaders must possess the skill. Some are better than others at persuading, debating, and teaching the public. But communication is a necessary art form for any leader.

Transformation

When a leader takes the mantle of Prime Minister, there is almost a visible, magical transformation to his personality. Assuming the trappings of office, like being crowned, a different persona emerges. Security guards salute and surround. Doors are opened. Followers like members of a tribe ascribe special attributes and a semi-infallibility to the new Prime Minister. For a time, so does the public.

The new leader himself seems imbued with positive endorphins and feels new surges of power emerging from within that brighten up his mien. Franklin Roosevelt quickly became the 'Happy Warrior' anxious to lead. And so, it is with most newly-minted leaders. The leader feels different because he has become different. Observers ascribe this to vibes a leader feels when he wins the political contest and becomes Prime Minister and naturally concludes there is something special about himself.

The Greek concept of the god Agonis comes into play. The conceit grows that one's inherent gifts are only fully developed through contest. The motive of those who avoid contest makes the leader unconsciously distrustful of the motive of these others and their self-proclaimed altruism. Those who are defeated in a contest by the leader leaves the leader with mixed feelings. Respect for the competition, especially in a closely fought contest, along with self-satisfaction that he bested another in a national contest for public support.

Leaders and Their Opponents

A key factor in leadership is the leader's ability to size up his opponents as they vie for the Prime Ministership. Like championship boxers, they spar in Parliament, on the hustings, and in TV debates,[34] probing for strengths and weaknesses. Most Prime Ministers come to respect their opponents. Only two Prime Ministers held a visceral dislike for each other – Diefenbaker and Pearson, more so Pearson than Diefenbaker.

Leaders TV Debates

TV debates are now a fixture of election campaigns. Preparation is imperative. Speaking to their opponents and the public at the same time is an art form. Few win, many lose.

Party and Party Leadership

At the core of democracy lies the political party. Alternating parties and leaders in government give the electorate a choice and continuity in a functioning democracy. To win a free and open election is to legitimize and sanctify the democratic grant of power to a political party.

When one decides to join a political party, any individual can directly impact the nature of democratic process. One can participate in organizing, fundraising and policy development and especially the choice of leader who best represents the individual's political principles imbedded in their belief structure.

[34] Dwight Eisenhower initially had a high regard for Adlai Stevenson. This changed when Adlai Stevenson proclaimed his reluctance to run for President. "*O that this cup should pass from these lips.*" After that, Eisenhower refused to watch Adlai Stevenson on TV or listen to him again.

The leader in turn should know the Party's constitution and be acquainted with the Party's executive. Party platforms lay out the Party and the leader's principles, choices, and preferences. Each leader who fails to maintain active Party leadership does so at his peril.

Loyalty to the party and leader is a way to influence the exercise of political power. Or so goes the thesis.

Party activists share this sense of involvement with other like-minded individuals. Party life, like government, is a team effort. A party activist broadens his life experience. Party adherence opens the door to a diverse network of relationships broader than family, friends, business, professional or work circles.

The history of parties from tribes, to court circles, to political factions, to caucuses, to organized parties is the history of democratic evolution with its own norms and rules of conduct. It is the heart beat of democracy.

Of necessity, the leader, as party leader is an essence of party leadership. A leader must be able to lead by example, inspire, and collaborate with his party adherents. He cannot act alone.

Some leaders are more mindful than others of this encompassing responsibility. Some party followers are likewise more responsible although less accountable in this duality. To neglect his party and its needs, a leader does so at his peril.

Fissures in this relationship can fragment and disable political power.

Alone

Ultimately, the leader alone carries the yoke of leadership. Leaders face issues of life and death; they decide to send men and women into harm's way. Leaders face economic decisions that affect the lives and welfare of the many. When economic chaos occurs, the leaders must find the path to stronger ground. Leaders err and must seek to undo the damage of their egregious actions, the acts of commission or omission or those of their colleagues. Often times, the leader loses his confidence or the desire to make the incessant decisions he is pressed to make. Yet the leader must soldier on.

One decision, the loneliest decision of all, is when to leave public office. Some are pressed by the loss of an election, others by the loss of appetite for leadership. Some never know when to give way. The poets give guidance, "*I am the master of my fate. I am the captain of my soul*", '*Invictus*' by W.E. Henley, Nelson Mandela's favourite aphorism.

Winston Churchill's favourite poem, '*Ulysses*' by Lord Tennyson which he would repeat verbatim:

"That which we are, we are;
One equal temper of heroic hearts,
Made weak by time and fate, but strong in will
To strive, to seek, to find, and not to yield."

My favourite poem for leadership is Aeschylus:

"He who learns must suffer.
And even in our sleep
Pain that cannot forget
Falls drop by drop upon the heart,
And in our own despair, against our will,
Comes wisdom to us by the awful grace of God"

A belief structure gives a leader a moral compass and points him in the right direction when he falters, as he does and will.

Personal Encounters with Leaders

In all my personal encounters – not in the spotlight – each leader exuded a quiet, thoughtful, vulnerable, and peaceful exchange much different from their public persona.

Leadership and The Art of The Possible and The Pivot

Leadership is the art of the possible and, at times, the impossible. To go against conventional wisdom lies at the core of leadership when it's the correct course for the nation. If leader intrudes when the nation faces a crisis, large or small, and the public is disturbed or worse, the leader can become a leader when he can change public opinion from apathy to support for strong action or capture the words to make a country feel secure. Some cautious leaders wait for the right moment to pivot public opinion if the public is of a different view. Recall Franklin Roosevelt who knew of the Japanese expansionist threat in the Pacific when he enacted fuel sanctions against Japan in the 1930's well before Pearl Harbour seemed incapable, beset as he was by economic issues, and refused to invest political capital to arouse public opinion besotted with appeasement. Of course, Roosevelt's hands were tied by the Neutrality Acts passed in the '30s. He waited for the attack on Pearl Harbour to capture and galvanize public support. This was not leadership, and America paid a heavy price. The true art of leadership is leading against public opinion and against conventional wisdom. Roosevelt pivoted, blaming others for the Pearl Harbour debacle and then pulled America together. The turnabout was a feat of leadership.

So it was in England under Chamberlain in the 1930's, infected with appeasement, refused to accept the Nazi threat, scarred as he was from his World War I experiences, and was forced to reluctantly give up power, despite the continuous support of his caucus, to the disliked and distrusted Churchill. Few knew that Chamberlain suffered from cancer at the time, and he felt he could not continue to lead after the outset of World War II. Reluctantly, he turned the reins of leadership over to Churchill after war was declared (though much preferring the appeasing Lord Halifax) as Churchill's early recognition of the Nazi threat was now appreciated by the public though less so by his own party or its party leadership at the time which never fully gained Conservative Party support still infected with appeasement and the hope for peace at all costs. Churchill was mistrusted by his party and needed a united government of all parties, Conservative, Labour, and Liberal, to achieve his war aims.[35]

Bill Clinton, after his first term when both the Senate and the House fell into Republican hands pivoted to the centre to achieve many legislative goals.

Personal, Private Challenges

Each Prime Minister overcame personal challenges in their lives. Some are known, others are private. John Diefenbaker was invalided during military services in World War I. Little is known of this incident. Diefenbaker's first wife was troubled and hospitalized. Lester B. Pearson suffered a severe breakdown during his service in World War I. Pierre Trudeau suffered the loss of his father in his mid-teens and separation from his wife while

[35] When the parties dissolved their wartime union in 1945 led by the rank and file of Labour who refused to honour Clement Atlee's agreement with Churchill after the defeat of Hitler to delay the election for several years at least until Japan was defeated. Churchill lost power in that election.

in office. John Turner, born in England, lost his father as an infant. Brian Mulroney verged on becoming an alcoholic and endured periodic bouts of crippling depression. Kim Campbell came from a broken family. Jean Chrétien, the youngest sibling in a family of seventeen, a challenge in itself, suffered from a facial disfigurement and a hearing impairment in one ear and later from the travails of his adopted son while in office. Paul Martin contracted polio as a youth and overcame an early speech impediment. Justin Trudeau suffered the public breakup of his parent's marriage, the loss of his youngest brother, and the loss of his father. Each traumatic event transformed them. Each overcame.

The Chronological Order of The Book

This book is done in chronological order as I encountered, close up and personal, the last eleven Prime Ministers and contains my own idiosyncratic views. At the end of each chapter, I have appended the maiden speech, their first speech in Parliament, after each was first elected to Parliament to judge them by their own early words.

Hopefully some may gain a deeper insight from what I considered fascinating encounters. Any brush with power takes on a lustre of its own. Hereafter are only my own views which I share in the hope that others may find it a useful foray into Canadian politics that animate and excite me, still. I hope I have shed most of my narrow partisanship and render honest opinions.

Reflections on Prime Ministers

Diefenbaker led when he persuaded the Commonwealth to kick apartheid South Africa out of its membership despite fierce opposition in his Party, from U.K., and Canadian business elites.

Diefenbaker's vision of Canada's North changed the Canadian narrative from sea to sea to sea. Diefenbaker preached 'One Canada' and unhyphenated Canadians to the end of his career.

The Diefenbaker 'wheat deal' with China and Trudeau's engagement with Cuba are examples of 'engagement diplomacy' that never changed 'human rights' in those autocratic countries as promised.

Mr. Pearson demonstrated leadership qualities in his climb up the bureaucratic pole and then on the international stage in constructing post World War II international organizations like the UN and NATO as a diplomat and especially after the Suez crises as a Minister of External Affairs despite misgivings of some in St. Laurent's Cabinet and the fierce opposition from British colleagues by formulating a separation of military forces and then establishing a UN peacekeeping force with Canada leading to fill the void. Even his own government seemed hesitant and reluctant as the opposition led by Mr. Diefenbaker hammered him for his disloyal thrusts against Mother Britain.

Pearson, as Prime Minister, accomplished more lasting progressive legislative achievements during his short tenure as the Prime Minister than any other Prime Minister and all, without the luxury of a majority government. The introduction of Medicare and the Canadian flag, the national anthem '*O Canada*', policies towards bilingualism and multiculturalism, legislation on limiting election expenses, and the modernization of divorce laws, despite fierce opposition and divisions within his own party are a tribute to his muted style of leadership and were each, in their own way, transformative.

Toujour Quebec has been a recurrent theme in Canada even before Confederation, since Carter's first settlement on the St. Laurence River. Quebec, a source of political power, was always seeking more. Pearson moved to set up the Committee on

Bilingualism and Biculturalism and refreshed his caucus from Quebec with new blood. Under Trudeau, Canada faced a number of challenges like the separatist crises, political assassination of a Quebec Minister, and the kidnapping of a British diplomat in Quebec. Trudeau did not wait, he acted strongly, arguably too strongly for many at the time. Trudeau then went on to incorporate bilingualism in the public service and expand the concept of a bilingual national capital by adding Hull to the Ottawa Capital precinct. He adopted multiculturalism to reflect the changing demographics of Canada. Trudeau even adopted the metric system to modernize our internal calculation systems despite domestic opposition. The public service was opened to younger players with diverse ethnic origins. Abolition of capital punishment passed into law despite staunch public and parliamentary opposition. Canada's coastal boundaries expanded the ocean limits to 200 miles by Trudeau that saved the fishery on both coasts from extinction and gained a new extended boundary on Canada's capacious northern frontier.

Above all, Pierre Trudeau led in the repatriation of the Constitution from the U.K. and the establishment of Charter of Rights and Freedoms. The Canadian public was largely disinterested. The opposition was stiff at both the federal and provincial spheres. This singular act of leadership transformed the Canadian narrative and the discourse within Canada's civic society forever.

Trudeau refused to rewrite history when pressured to do so believing as he did that a nation should not revise the past but improve the future.[36]

[36] Like George Orwell, Trudeau believed that revising history was a mistake, a practice that in the end intensified intolerance as revealed by autocrats like Hitler and Stalin who sought to rewrite history to suit their ideologies. Trudeau refused to apologize for the wartime treatment of Japanese

As Minister of Justice, John Turner was the most progressive and innovative in Canadian history. It was Turner that Trudeau enlisted to implement the bare planks of his 'Just Society' and bilingual policies in Parliament. Turner led in Parliament on the abolishment of capital punishment. As Minister of Finance, he moved sharply to address deficits and the debt when the public, and the public served, were disinterested in the consequences. He introduced easy tax appeals as the tax system must be seen to fair and just. John Turner as Prime Minister continued as the supreme advocate of Parliament – the 'vox populae'. Almost alone, he fought the FTA believing that the detail in this free trade agreement weakened Canadian sovereignty. It was Turner who insisted on a provision in the FTA for dispute resolutions independent of U.S.A. courts. History has yet to complete this chapter on Canadian economic policy. No one was a firmer supporter of the centrality of Parliament in the lives of Canadians, nor held its arcane rules and traditions in greater regard.

Joe Clark was a fair, hard-hitting, and diligent leader of the Opposition while his short tenure as Prime Minister did not allow him ample time to implement his 'progressive' conservative ideas at home or abroad.

Brian Mulroney led on the FTA when Canada didn't even enjoy free trade across its provincial borders – and still doesn't! Turner opposed the FTA pointing out its defects knowing he would lose support from the business establishment. Their leadership was transformative in different ways.

Mulroney led on the Consumer Tax which was bitterly opposed as was the Free Trade Agreement with the U.S.A. Both

---

Canadians as rewriting history was a sham. This was the subject of my maiden speech in the Senate shortly after he appointed me to persuade Trudeau to change his mind. I did not succeed. Perhaps he was right after all. You cannot rewrite history. Only improve it in the future.

were enacted under maelstroms of opposition and dissident public opinion. The consumer tax placed Canada's finances on a broader equitable tax platform at both the federal and provincial levels. The FTA opened the constrained protectionist channels towards faster and more cost-effective economic growth.

Mulroney took up the gauntlet left by Diefenbaker and pressured the Boer South African government to free Mandela which brought a relatively peaceful end to apartheid.

Kim Campbell became the first female Prime Minister after achieving a series of female firsts from Minister of Veteran Affairs to Minister of Justice and Attorney General to Minister of Defence. She failed to serve as Prime Minister in Parliament and so never had an opportunity to transform the government as she planned.

Jean Chrétien led the opposition at home and abroad to the Iraq war and his innovative Clarity Bill muffled and stifled separationist activism. After 9/11, recognizing the danger of U.S.A. closing Canadian borders, he swiftly introduced a tough terrorist bill, tougher than the Americans at the time that eased American concerns about infiltration of terrorists across our border. Chrétien increased female participation in politics, appointing the first female deputy Prime Minister and increased the number of female senior public servants. Together with his Minister of Finance and avid rival Paul Martin Jr., he transformed the debt and deficit ridden federal government and the national economic narrative to balanced budgets that placed Canada on a sound economic platform for growth. He refused to allow Canadian banks to merge despite strong lobbying by the powerful banking community easing the bank disruption unlike the United States. Then Chrétien directed innovative investments in science, higher education, student loans, and making higher education a national priority. At all times, he was a superb shrewd, even crafty, frugal administrator of the burgeoning federal government.

Paul Martin Jr. as Minister of Finance successfully arrested the runaway burgeoning national debt and the endless deficits and balanced the budget without rupturing the 'social set' – a remarkable economic legacy. No Minister of Finance was as diligent and astute in collecting all the national accounts in one place for the first time and then setting stiff rules to keep injudicious runaway spending under principled restraint. His appointment of a public judicial inquiry into the Liberal Party's Quebec-based 'sponsorship' scandal was both brave and feckless. As Prime Minister, he initiated an expansive program of reforms on greater financial support to cities, education, and Aboriginal affairs that were clearly articulated but curtailed by his short tenure as Prime Minister. He opened the door to more private members bills in Parliament to widen the scope of federal governance beyond the Cabinet.

Harper, a politician of conviction, led by actively advocating human rights in Russia and China while the Canadian public was largely disinterested and preferred to exchange trade and jobs and sideline 'human rights' public advocacy in these foreign lands. His political opponents and predecessors, with some exceptions like John Diefenbaker, cherished 'engagement' with autocrats over harsh and open advocacy of human rights. However, Harper preferred open engagement with autocrats, though he realized that this public advocacy would not, in the short run, dilute their egregious conduct. He sought to reform the flawed relationship between Aboriginals and the Federal government. His immigration legislation clarified and modernized, muddled, episodic porous immigration policies while expediently avoiding future problems. Harper sustained a strong balanced budget approach to public finances leaving a solid legacy of fiscal integrity.

Justin Trudeau's sunny ways united the Liberal Party divided by tribalism and then the nation and introduced sweeping gender parity recognition in his entourage, the Cabinet, the Senate, and public service. His abrupt reforms on the Senate (separating the National Caucus from Liberal senators participation and the appointment of only 'independent' senators with no Liberal ties) removed the Senate as a recurring thorn in the side of public dialogue enhancing its legitimacy while diminishing the validity of its natural political structures, for now. Party groupings are inevitable in the Senate as in any other political democratic body. The legalization of cannabis is a singular act of leadership, yet too early to determine its impact on civic society. Trudeau advanced feminine parity in party structures, in the elected membership, in the Commons, and the Senate. Climate change policies continue to evolve but his leadership to raise public awareness at home and abroad is undisputed. His 'celebrity' has reached further and wider abroad than any Prime Minister before him, giving Canada a modern up-to-date gloss and an international platform to expand his views and the national interests of Canada. How this will play remains too early to predict. As problems emerge, especially on the trade front and in governance, it is too early to measure his qualities and effectiveness as a leader. Relations with major powers like Russia and China are chilly, yet evolving, and too early to judge outcomes. Increased military spending and reorganization of military research works in 2017 is a step forward, yet too early to assess, as is the large commitment to renew aging infrastructures. Reaching a 'free trade agreement' with a revised mandate with the United States and Mexico over provocations was a triumph of patience especially when dealing with the American President. Recent promises to reduce poverty are welcome. Trudeau's goal of inspiring Canadians to become leaders in artificial intelligence is laudatory. Steps towards

Aboriginal justice continue. No one can question his dedication, energy, and focus to sell his policies at home or abroad.

Leadership is viewed through the prism of coloured lens and cannot be viewed otherwise. Most times, leaders build on the successes of their predecessors while maligning their record. Leadership is highly subjective, and power can only be viewed with suspicion by students of politics or historians, through one's subjective mind's eye. It is always thus!

Leadership and Legacy

Carlyle, the noted 'liberal' English historian wrote about the 'Great Man' theory of history: "*The history of the world is but the biography of great men.*"[37]

Leadership requires a toxic cocktail of infinite egoism, invincible self-confidence and excessive competitiveness, an unshakeable belief structure, love of bathing in public acclaim while being immune from personal idolatry, and an interior vision that history can be altered by their actions better than others.

Politicians have a fetish for reshaping their contributions to history. They can't resist embellishing their own accomplishments, flawed or otherwise. Presidents in the U.S.A. are addicted to bending history to suit their version of their contributions to history. It is done in three major ways – their Libraries, their autobiographies, and books by their fervent acolytes. First and foremost is the creation of a Presidential Library where all the President's artifacts, papers, and history are archived to polish their legacy. Each Presidential Library is designed to tailor the

[37] The British philosopher, Isaiah Berlin, in a delightful essay entitled *The Hedgehog and the Fox* divided leaders as a 'fox who knows many things' or a hedgehog that knows one important thing.

President's version of his legacy within a permanent institution. The first Presidential Library was situated in the country home of Franklin D. Roosevelt in Hyde Park, NY and to archive his personal papers.

American Presidents' Obsession with Enhancing Their Legacies

Intrigued by their quirks, I have visited many of the Presidential Libraries. My two favourites are the Libraries of Harry Truman and George W. Bush. Modest enough to call them Libraries. Each Library contains an exact replica of the Oval Office. Truman's Library is a simple one-story brick building designed in a square. In the centre of Truman's quadrangle building in Independence, Missouri, is his final resting place marked by a simple granite tombstone marked *Truman* befitting his simplicity and modesty. George W. Bush's Library is likewise an unpretentious three-story brick building on a raised knoll in a corner on the campus of the Southern Methodist University in Dallas, Texas.

John F. Kennedy's Presidential Library is a monumental modern glass-walled structure located in Boston with wonderful views dedicated to magnifying his stunted legacy during his short tenure that was so full of mishaps early on and ended in a tragic assassination.

Ronald Reagan's Library in California is larger than an air terminal hangar housing his Oval Office and also a replica of Air Force One, the outsized Presidential jet that was outfitted to match his Hollywood taste. Perhaps his ranch in the foothills of California was more suited to his outdoor image of himself.

Bill Clinton's Library has an outsize modernistic building in the smallish capitol of Little Rock, Arkansas where he once served as Governor after being defeated the first time, imitating his outsized sense of self-esteem while diluting his tarnished record of impeachment and debarment from law. Clinton remains, despite his known flaws, a most popular President notable for his communication skills, his legislative expertize, his political insights, and reading political trends.

These Libraries each present a concrete benchmark to demonstrate their own 'virtual reality' of each President's role in history.

No recent President was so overt in pursuit of his own vacillating wandering legacy as Barack Obama while in office and after. To elect his Republican successor would be 'treason' to his legacy, he viscerally proclaimed on the campaign trail as his successor, perhaps not his preferred choice, and former adversary was defeated. We are told his Presidential Library will cover well over a hundred thousand square feet of building space near the pristine waterfront of Chicago and owned in part by his own foundation, a first in post presidential self-aggrandizing actions.

Of course, each President feels compelled to write his own version of history via an autobiography. In the case of Kennedy,[38] due to his premature death, his 'autobiography' was left to his gifted speech writer, Ted Sorenson, and his literary advisor, Arthur Schlesinger Jr., who each wrote paeans of praise to JFK's limited accomplishments while diluting his early major errors. A romantic version that hankered for chivalrous Camelot was carefully crafted by his wife.

[38] Kennedy, a skilled writer, wrote *While England Slept*, a history of English appeasement that led to World War II and *Prelude to Leadership: The Post-War Diary of John F. Kennedy* published in 1945 by Regnery Publishing in his '20s. Later as a Senator, he wrote *Profiles in Courage*, stories of heroes, public figures, who went against public opinion as he never did! His book on immigration (*A Nation of Immigrants*, Harper Collins, 1964) is an interesting insight of the current debate about immigration in the United States and elsewhere.

We can read history through the filter of each President's mind by examining their memoirs. Truman, like the man, was straightforward and modest. Nixon was different. After leaving public office in disgrace, he wrote a series of well-written books on government leaders, politics, and foreign policies to reinstate his place in history. Later on, his autobiography rationalized his defects while paying tribute to his undoubted accomplishments coloured by his quick resignation from his high office to avoid impeachment. Ronald Reagan, George H. Bush, Bill Clinton, and George W. Bush followed suit. All wrote autobiographies that reflected their biases and apologia for their patent errors while embellishing their considerable accomplishments. So did their wives. Obama wrote books of his early life as paeans of praise to himself and wonderment to his interesting, if skewed, early years. He even penned a children's book while in office. Really. The public anxiously awaits the publication of the memoirs of Obama who received a million in advance to tell his stories of his time in public office. His wife's autobiography entitled *Becoming* is a masterpiece of history of a black woman growing up in middle-America and reaching the ring as America's First Lady.

Maiden Speeches

A maiden speech is a new Member's first speech in Parliament; by custom, this first speech is not interrupted. The Member's maiden speech gives Parliament its first taste of the Member's interests and aptitudes. Usually a new Member waits for a period before he makes his maiden speech to acclimatize himself to the House. Usually a new Member does not intervene to ask questions until after his maiden speech. This was not always the case with respect to future Prime Ministers, especially John Diefenbaker and Pierre Trudeau who both asked prolific questions and intervened in other Member's speeches. It was appropriate for Pierre Trudeau as he was made Parliamentary Secretary to the Prime Minister 'Mike' Pearson immediately after his election to Parliament and he was required to answer questions in the Prime Minister's absence; but Pierre Trudeau went further. He immediately challenged opposition members especially from Quebec on their views of the British North America Act and their views of Quebec within Canada.

Leaders and Autobiographies

Each British Prime Minister, from Gladstone to Lloyd George, from Anthony Eden to Harold McMillan, from Harold Wilson to Margaret Thatcher, from John Major to Tony Blair, wrote their own outsized autobiographies and incorporated their version of their contributions to history.

Churchill was different. Churchill was, by profession, a journalist and a writer. His majestic accounts of the Boer War, World War I, and magnificent volumes on World War II garnered him the Nobel Prize all contained subtle and no so subtle self-praise to demonstrate his depth of intellect and undoubtable achievements. Churchill wrote an early autobiography before he became Prime Minister called *My Early Life* that laid bare his version of his early aptitudes and lack thereof as well as his early love of politics. He wrote a definitive massive biography of his early ancestor Marlborough, the first notable Churchill, to enhance his roots. A stunning biography of Lord Primrose, a short-lived Prime Minister and Liberal icon stands out in its concise swift dramatic strokes. Churchill's majestic *A History of the English-Speaking Peoples* is studded with colourful vignettes of English political leaders. His work on his paternal beacon, Lord Randolph Churchill, is both poignant and elucidating as Churchill sought to embellish his father's short-lived and somewhat tragic political career. After World War II, he wrote a multi volume saga as war time Prime Minister, each volume is a classic that stands the test of time. After retirement, he engaged his son, Randolph, also a talented writer but flawed politician, to write his father's authorized biography only to be taken over by Sir Martin Gilbert who was granted access to Churchill's voluminous papers. Churchill's life is a gift that keeps giving. Churchill once said, "*History will be kind to me for I intend to rewrite it.*"

Canadian Prime Ministers followed Canadian expectations of historical revisionism seen through their eyes from early life to Prime Ministership.

Politicians of all stripes simply cannot resist a fetish to publish their autobiographies. Two of the most commendable are the two volumes by Paul Martin Sr., Paul Martin's father, which are both well-written and insightful.[39] Another is the multi-volume autobiography in French, now out of print, of Jean-Louis Gagnon, an activist Liberal and 'liberal' who bravely fought the reactionary Duplessis Regime in Quebec during the '30s, but regrettably has yet to be translated into English. In his later years, I became well acquainted with Jean-Louis Gagnon when he was appointed by Pierre Trudeau as a Commissioner to the Canadian Radio and Television Commission regulating broadcasting in Canada. Jean-Louis regaled me with tales of how Quebec leaders, including federal politicians, and the Church hierarchy appeased Duplessis's autocratic policies, especially his own Liberal Party.

John Diefenbaker waited until Mr. Pearson's third and final memoir was published after his death, when he published his own

[39] *A Very Public Life*, 2 vols., by Paul Martin Sr. (Deneau Publishing, 1985).

third and final volume entitled *One Canada – The Turbulent Years* notable for his full-throated attack of Liberal policy shifts, most especially when Mr. Pearson switched his policy to allow Bomarc nukes to be based in Canada. A detailed defense of scrapping the Avro CF-110 fighters is rendered. Mr. Diefenbaker's rationale on the Coyne Affair when he removed him as Chair of the Bank of Canada remains of interest. In each case, Diefenbaker described how the Liberals shifted their positions on each major issue. A fascinating apologia. He details how he felt the Americans meddled in his national election campaigns in 1962 and 1963 which they did. Americans had, and still have, a fetish to meddling in other nation's elections, democratic and otherwise.[40] I cannot recall an important foreign election since the 1960's when the United States did not meddle to some degree to gain a foreign political result aligned to their hegemonic policies, especially all former Communist led European autocratic governments as they evolved into nascent democracies, and of course throughout Central and South America.

Lester B. Pearson wrote superb essays and published collections of his graceful speeches, *Four Faces of Pearson* in 1964 when Prime Minister, *Nuclear Diplomacy in the Modern World* was published earlier when he was leader of the Opposition in 1959 and finally his biography published in three volumes entitled *Mike*, all with a view to shape history with his insights and the impressions he alone made on international and domestic politics, which were noteworthy and considerable. The third volume of

---

[40] *One Canada, Memoirs of the Right Honourable John G. Diefenbaker: The Crusading Years 1895 to 1956* (Macmillan of Canada, 1975). *One Canada, Memoirs of the Right Honourable John G. Diefenbaker: The Years of Achievement 1956 to 1962* (Macmillan of Canada, 1976). *One Canada, Memoirs of the Right Honourable John G. Diefenbaker: The Tumultuous Years 1962 to 1967* (Macmillan of Canada, 1977).

Mike was published after Mr. Pearson's death on his period as Prime Minister, based on his dairies, memos and research, and was a spirited record of his tenure as Prime Minister - gracious, honest, and understated as was the man himself.[41]

Joe Clark wrote a straightforward account of his political rise and record, modest, factual and understated without artificial drama.[42] He outlines his regrets and his ambitious goals.

Pierre Trudeau collated his essays and speeches that is required reading for any Liberal. Finally, he published his memoirs which lack the verbal bite of his early polemics.[43] He shades over his youthful extremist views. Perhaps the greatest intellectual to be Canadian Prime Minister, his views are still hotly contested by critics on the left and right. The cover on Trudeau's memoirs illustrates his love of nature and the image he chose to project, dressed as he is in an Aboriginal deerskin jacket and paddling a canoe. Trudeau had a penchant for the dramatic. His portrait in Parliament displays him theatrically wrapped in a cape depicted Trudeau as he wanted to be depicted – with romantic flair.

Each Prime Minister chooses the artist to render his portrait to be exhibited in the Halls of Parliament. Each portrait tells a story in itself. Statues of Prime Ministers dot the grounds of Parliament Hall and tell a different story. My favourite is the noble statue of Sir Wilfred Laurier.

---

41 *Democracy in World Politics* (Princeton University Press, 1955). *Diplomacy in the Nuclear Age* (Cambridge, Mass: Harvard University Press, 1959). *The Four Faces of Peace and the International Outlook* (Dodd, Mead, 1964). *The Crisis of Development* (Praeger, 1970). *Mike: The Memoirs of the Right Honourable Lester B. Pearson* (Quadrangle Books, 1972).

42 *How We Lead: Canada in a Century of Change* (Random House Canada, 2013). *Nation Too Good To Lose: Renewing The Purpose Of Canada* (Key Porter Books, 1994).

43 *Memoirs* (McClelland & Stewart, 1993). *Towards A Just Society: The Trudeau Years*, with Thomas S. Axworthy (eds.) (Viking, 1990).

Turner's slender book is a collection of his speeches published before becoming Prime Minister and remains reluctant after office to write his memoirs.[44]

Brian Mulroney in his own hand wrote his massive autobiography *Brian Mulroney Memoirs*[45] notably reducing the smudges to his political record. Fair game, as he defended his solid public record with wit, insight, and relentless charm.

Kim Campbell wrote *Time and Chance*[46] that belies her frothiness and inexperience. She dove into the detail of each ministerial post prior to her successful leadership run and finally her elevation as Prime Minister. Her depth, commitment, energy, and probity were unquestioned. Perhaps her acknowledged naiveté, shallow judgement, and failure to focus on priorities and her divided entourage and divided national campaign crew was her undoing.

Jean Chrétien co-wrote a best-seller in 1985 called *Straight from the Heart*, written as he wished to be judged by history.[47] Later in 2007, Chrétien published a full account *My Years as Prime Minister* (Vintage Canada, 2008), an excellent primer on how to manage the Cabinet and bureaucracy effectively. It is a clearly written record of his formidable public service and superb administrative skills. In 2018, Chrétien published a meandering account of reminisces – warm, endearing, insightful and so Chrétien.[48]

---

[44] *Politics of Purpose: The Right Honourable John N. Turner, 17th Prime Minister of Canada* (Queen's University, 2009). I helped collect his speeches with Lloyd Axworthy and David Smith, some which I helped draft when I served as his first Executive Assistant and speech writer which was first published and released during his drive for leadership in 1968.

[45] *Brian Mulroney Memoirs* (Emblem Editions; 2008).

[46] *Time and Chance* (Doubleday Canada, 1996).

[47] *My Years as Prime Minister* (Knopf Canada, 2007) and *Straight from the Heart* (Key Porter Books, 1985).

[48] *My Stories, My Times* by Jean Chrétien (Random House of Canada, 2018).

Paul Martin Jr. wrote his version of his political contributions *Hell Or High Water: My Life In And Out of Politics*[49] in the straight forward manner that belies his leadership; free of froth and focused on his factual record – straightforward, self-depreciating, likeable, witty, and approachable, like the man himself. He displays his wide range of interests, perhaps too broad, and lacking priority, much like his tenure. Most important, he honestly set out in great detail his achievements as Minister of Finance rarely so accurately written not omitting failures, always giving credit to his associates. Of interest is his tumultuous relationship and rivalry with Jean Chrétien, giving Chrétien credit for his political judgement when they disagreed, honest and concise, and accepting of criticism which he considered fair and balanced – a feverish inside look at intra-party political rivalry at its hottest.

Stephen Harper, after leaving public life, published a concise exegesis of a modern conservative setting out the rationale for his convictions.[50]

Justin Trudeau published his early memoirs of his youthful life and early political career during his first election campaign for Prime Minister.[51] A book always adds gravitas to a budding politician while revealing the contours of his character and lessons learned from youthful experiences and early political life.

All these words written by Prime Ministers should be required reading for any wannabee politician or activist.

May I repeat as Churchill is reputed to have said, "*I will be well treated by history because I intend to write it.*" So it is.

---

49 *Hell or High Water: My Life in and out of Politics* (Emblem Edition, 2009).

50 *Right Here, Right Now: Politics and Leadership in the Age of Disruption* by Stephen Harper (Signal, 2018).

51 *Common Ground* (HarperCollins Publishers, 2014) which was written in cooperation with a skilled journalist, Jonathan Kay.

The leader's fervent acolytes, especially members of the leader's inner circle, cannot resist writing about the attributes and actions of their leader and in the process, embellish their own minor roles in the leader's desired legacies enhancing their own contribution to that legacy, faux or otherwise.

Prime Ministers and Families

One chapter in the lives of each Prime Minister that needs further exposition is the leader's family circle and the impact on each leader's political ambitions and actions. Distinct patterns emerge from a review of these Prime Ministers early lives and careers, their potent family influences and close friends on their lives and political careers and above all, their innate competitive spirit remains a vibrant chapter yet to be written. 'No man is an island' as the leader is swept by the waves of impact from father, mother, siblings and especially wives that have played such a keen part throughout their public careers.

Prime Ministers and Their Sense of History[52]

While all Prime Ministers were intensely interested in their legacies, few have a rounded sense of Canadian domestic and foreign history or parliamentary history and a Prime Minister's role in the tangled web of the undulating currents of history as it unfolded rooted is it in the past.

Winston Churchill was a lifelong student of history, who excelled in history from his days at Harrow while he struggled with other subjects. There he was first inculcated in the annals of

---

52 "*Study history, study history. In history lies all the secrets of statecraft.*" – Winston Churchill to an American student before a Royal coronation in Westminster Hall (1953).

British history from the days of the Anglo Saxons till the British imperialism which he and his teachers saw as the procreation of rights and freedoms. His memory of history, especially British history was unique, both sweeping and technical in detail. His majestic volumes on *A History of the English-Speaking Peoples* attest to the depth of his comprehension of the factors and personalities that flow grinded out the annals of Britain step-by-step advance in civilization.[53] Churchill believed that British history marked the progress of western civilization and the rule of law.

Ronald Reagan, considered by most observers to have limited intellectual depth or historic understanding, had a surprising sense of history and held deep political principles which he deployed (see *Ronald Reagan: An Intellectual Biography* by David T. Bryne (Potomac Books, 2018) for a revisionist examination of Reagan's intellectual roots. Reagan believed in the ideology of freedom based on his Christian beliefs. No modern President wrote more about his ideas than Reagan. Reagan wrote his own scripts for his early radio shows.

Diefenbaker was an early student of history. His father, a small-town teacher, ignited his interest in political history especially Laurier.[54] He was a fervent supporter of the Crown and was knowledgeable about the history of the evolution of British

[53] Churchill wrote numerous histories and historical biographies. These include a history of World War I *The World Crisis*, *The Second World War*, a multi-volume history of his ancestor John Churchill, Lord Marlborough, the storied victor over Louis XIV in Europe, a biography of his father and inspiration Lord Randolph Churchill and many others. Read J.H. Plumb's *The Making of An Historian* (University of Georgia Press, 1989) for a more nuanced assessment of Churchill as a historian which I do not share. Judge for yourself, after your reading selection of Churchill's books on Churchill's version of history.

[54] Laurier's life and times inspired all Prime Ministers.

law from the days of Magna Carta and the ways and means of Parliament. As a criminal lawyer, he sharpened his knowledge of the criminal law as his studies and legal practice led him to introduce the Charter of Rights in Parliament codifying in large part the rights and freedoms under British common law. He maintained an insatiable taste for political biographies but little beyond that is known.[55]

As a history student at Oxford and then a history professor at the University of Toronto, Pearson maintained an avid interest, reading books on history and diplomacy throughout his career. As the son of a pastor, he had an acquired familiarity with the Bible and the Church social gospel. As a public servant and diplomat in foreign service, he acquired intimate knowledge of European history.

Prime Ministers born and educated in Quebec like Pierre Trudeau, Mulroney, Chrétien, and Justin Trudeau by French Canadian priests were all indoctrinated with French Canadian nationalist ideas of the possibility of the reconquest of North America led by French speakers[56] just as Churchill believed in the influence of the English speaking people in the U.K. and the U.S.A. The voyageur spirit of travel and discovery was equally

[55] In World War I, Diefenbaker saw military service overseas. Invalided, he returned to Canada to continue his education. Diefenbaker got an M.A. in Economics and Politics from the University of Saskatchewan. Then he went on to Law School also at University of Saskatchewan.

[56] The most candid of modern leaders from Quebec of their early indoctrination by priests on French Canadian exceptionalism was Rene Levesque in his book *Memoirs* (McClelland and Stewart, 1986). He wrote on page 200, "*We formed a people who were distinct and consequently unique in the world. We, that is, we French-speaking Quebecois, are not French, or at least haven't been so for centuries. Observers of the French regime had recognized this fact well before the Conquest. A new continent had already forged a new and original type of man, and the small interest the Old Country showed in him only reinforced his spirit of independence...*"

burned into their inner thoughts and political ideology. They all had a sense of exceptionalism about the French idea in America. Mulroney, though born an Irish Catholic, shared this schooled indoctrination. This early education coloured their world view in many aspects. Pierre Trudeau could repeat large gulps of French poetry and was familiar with Latin poetry and Greek mythology.

While Turner was well schooled in British history at Oxford and owned a voracious memory, he did not retain a passionate interest after he left university. However, he was called to the Bar at the Inner Temple in London and was deeply influenced by the history and precedents of English law and the evolution of English rights. This influence manifested itself after he became Minister of Justice. This study of central place in Parliament in British society never left him.

Joe Clark was and remains an avid student of history, the biographies of great political figures and the evolution of multilateral organizations.

Brian Mulroney never claimed nor held profound views of history. Yet, having been born and schooled in Quebec, he was fascinated by the history of Quebec, the travels of the couriers du bois across America, and the relationship of Quebec with Confederation.

Jean Chrétien viewed history through the eyes of a 'rouge' from Quebec. His father's work sojourn for almost a decade in the United States broadened his outlook as did the experience of his and his wife's relatives when they settled in western Canada and lost their French language skills.

Kim Campbell was not particularly obsessed with the study of history though she was an excellent student of politics and economics, read political biographies and feminist literature and the role of the women's movements as it affected history.

Stephen Harper was a self-proclaimed student concentrating on economic theory and economic history rather than political history. Yet, he studied political history and political party history to assist him as he built the modern Conservative Party.

Justin Trudeau's interests were not by design intellectual nor is he interested in history which he shares with most millennials. Trudeau had and maintains an abiding interest in literature.

Still the study of history remains vital as a vital navigator to plot future progress and to avoid pitfalls and missteps along the way for any Prime Minister. To know history is to avoid its pitfalls.[57]

Measuring A Prime Minister

In the end, each Prime Minister is judged by both his own singular acts of leadership, some obvious, others less transparent, and the legislative and institutional footprints left by his administration. Did the nation fare better or worse under each stewardship? This remains a comparative question for historians.

One simple test remains for a liberal and a 'progressive'. Did illiteracy and poverty rise or fall during the Prime Minister's tenure?

[57] There is little written or known about each Prime Minister's personal library. If a historian can pry out these facts, we will gain insight into the Prime Minister's mind and sense of history. I visited Churchill's library at Chartwell Manor, his country home in Kent, numerous times. It was capacious and well ordered. David Ben Gurion's home in Tel Aviv, Israel, has four libraries containing over 20,000 volumes, one of which served as a meeting room. His library includes Latin, Greek, Turkish, English, German, Russian, French, and other Slavic languages. Pierre Trudeau in his last home in Montreal had a large well-arranged library on one floor.

Leadership Index

A foremost American scholar of Presidential leadership qualities, the late Fred I. Greenstein, taught at Princeton University. Greenstein's deployed behavioural science to dissect Presidential leadership, an elusive art form, at best. Greenstein's analytic Presidential index may have relevance to the exercise of Prime Ministerial leadership. He noted six criteria to measure presidential leadership performance:

- Effective public communication
- Organizational capacity
- Political skill
- Vision
- Cognitive style
- Emotional intelligence

"*In the real world, human imperfection is inevitable but some imperfections are most disabling than others...*" "*Above all*", Greenstein emphasized "thought and emotion". "*Beware*", he concluded, "*the presidential contender who lacks emotional intelligence. In the absence of all else, one may turn to ashes.*"[58]

I leave it to the reader to determine the applicability of the complex application of behavioural science to Canadian Prime Ministerial leadership.

Measuring A Prime Minister's Record

The Prime Minister of Canada, the leader of leaders in Canada, can be measured by his government's record on four fronts

---

[58] Fred I. Greenstein *The Presidential Difference: Leadership Style from FDR to George W. Bush* (Princeton University Press, 2004).

– national unity, the sauce that keeps Canada together, the domestic record of economic growth and home economics, and the economic well-being of the family. Moving towards equality in the treatment of individuals and groups with a measured record of improving literacy and decreasing poverty lies at the core of a leader who wishes to be defined by his 'progressive' policies and as a liberal. Lifting the Aboriginal community to economic independence is also a long sought-after benchmark. The renovation of the justice system for Aboriginals regretfully continues to move at a snail's pace. Finally, our external relationships beyond our borders especially with our adjacent neighbour, the United States of America and members of the Commonwealth and of course advances in multilateralism remains a linchpin of Canada's foreign policy.

Let me dwell on the last, our external affairs with other nations. Until the Justin Trudeau administration, the Department responsible for external affairs was called precisely that, the Department of External Affairs. Now it has been rebranded as the Department of Global Affairs. I must say as my work and research[59] of foreign affairs was lengthy, I prefer the older description.

[59] The only time I led my class at the University of Toronto Law School was in international law. I served in the Senate Committee of Foreign Affairs and International Trade for twenty-six years. Law School at The University of Toronto taught me three things which continue to resonate in my mind. Dean 'Caesar' who taught Torts emphasized the search for facts. Facts make a difference. Find the facts and then truth based on fairness and justice will emerge. Eugene La Brie who taught International Law opined that international law initially based on power was evolving slowly on comity, history, fairness, and justice. Bora Laskin who taught Constitutional Law insisted we read the Constitution and precedents with great care to understand how judges are tempted to place their policies above the 'rule of law' and the written Constitution. Good advice to Prime Ministers and judges.

Prime Ministers and External Affairs

Each Prime Minister has always given external affairs his personal attention especially relationships with foreign leaders and their policies. Each Prime Minister craves to leave his imprints on world politics.

Louis St. Laurent was Minister of External Affairs before assuming the office of Prime Minister as was Lester B. Pearson.[60] Pearson had only admirers from foreign leaders of all shapes. Diefenbaker loved the direct exchanges with foreign leaders. While Diefenbaker was at odds with President Kennedy, he was highly regarded by De Gaulle in France. Pierre Trudeau was a world traveller before becoming Prime Minister and considered himself knowledgeable about most aspects of foreign affairs, especially France, China, the Middle East, and Africa. His final tour to Eastern Europe was a last gasp peace mission to reduce nuclear arms and foster co-existence – lofty in aim which left little tracks. All Prime Ministers love to travel abroad and relish their goodbye tours before leaving office. Some are more skilled than others. Joe Clark's early disastrous trip abroad when luggage was lost dented his reputation as leader. Turner was comfortable travelling abroad especially in Britain and France where he had longstanding educational and political relationships. Mulroney relished foreign travel as did Kim Campbell. As for Paul Martin, he loved foreign travel, especially Africa. Stephen Harper prepared meticulously for each foreign trip and enjoyed the challenge of exchanges on issues rested in his convictions on human rights especially with China and Russia that ran against both the grain

---

[60] St. Laurent's speech on the principles of Canada's foreign policy remains a masterpiece of insight and analyses (*The Foundations of Canadian Policy in World Affairs* at the Duncan and John Gray Memorial Lecture, University of Toronto, 13 January 1947).

of both nations. Previous leaders like 'Mike' Pearson, imbued with the theory of diplomatic engagement even with autocrats. Justin Trudeau was the most confident from the very outset of his leadership when he travelled abroad. Each purchased a different outlook and legacy in external affairs yet to be fully explored and compared.

Justin Trudeau entered the world scene with poise attracting early attention and approval. His travels abroad especially India with his family shredded his judgement as a leader both within India and Canada. He was the first Canadian Prime Minister to address the French Parliament – a notable achievement where he was well received. The contours of the most important relationship with the unpredictable United States President remains a work in progress for Justin Trudeau. Trudeau will fare better as the American President gains broader experience and understands the historic relationship between Canada and the United States.

Leadership, Social Media and The 'New Politics'

When I first began my activist career in the Liberal Party in the early 1960's, the rage was the 'New Politics', the theory that politics could only be reformed by committed volunteers at the grassroots. Today the 'New Politics' via the social media allows every volunteer to participate in the direction of politics easily and cost effectively. Each volunteer can be a leader.

Tweeting

In this era of the two-hour news cycle and the speed of government decisions expected by the public, tweeting has become a powerful tool for the Prime Minister to show instant leadership in his actions and reactions to fast breaking public events. The Prime Minister leads in his tweets while his administration races to keep up. Yet, only the Prime Minister elected to lead should tweet and he alone bears the accountability and consequences of his Cabinet and leadership.

The Defense of Canada – Failure of Leadership

Starting with John Diefenbaker in early 1960's when he scrapped the prototypes and plans to build the most advanced interception fighter plane in the world, the Avro Arrow CF 105 to match the Soviet build long range bomber fleet, each successive Prime Minister since has failed to maintain an adequate defense force on land, sea or air to meet the changing strategic needs and NATO defense commitments of Canada commensurate with the nation's wealth and GDP.

At the end of World War II, Canada had the largest merchant marine fleet in the world[61] and one of the best trained military and air forces. During World War II, Canada was a training centre for allied pilots, especially pilots whose countries were members of the Commonwealth. Canada had the largest per capita pilot training program amongst all the allies. These national assets were not converted to the private sector.

Canada's love of the air started with the two national airlines in the '30s – TransCanada (later Air Canada[62]) and Canadian Pacific. Early in the '30s and '40s, Canada's pilots were the leading 'bush' pilots in the world as travel and transport to the northern frontier was expanded.

---

61 Greek merchants bought used Canadian ships at low cost and converted them to large commercial fleets.

62 Jean Chrétien as a young M.P. introduced a private member's bill to change the name of TransCanada to Air Canada.

Since Diefenbaker, Canada has failed to keep the 'True North – Strong and Free'.[63]

Our commitments to NATO have not been met since the 1950's. Each year, our budget for defense has been assiduously cut and depleted. This changed in 2017 when the Justin Trudeau government introduced a sweeping review of Canada's defense forces and its budget promising to increase the budget by 70% from 2017 to 2025, still lagging in per capita growth. The defense budget and the current related research organization in government hands has not kept up with the transfer of commercial defense technology to the private sector.

In the United States, the 'Silicon Valley' and its innovations started with the transfer of technology from the military to domestic companies. Stanford University under the leadership of its innovative President Talmadge, an engineer in a humanities-based school, decided to add Engineering expertise to its curriculum in the '30s. As a result, at the start of World War II when investment in the military was ramped up, Stanford established a research arm called the Stanford Research Institute (SRI) where teachers and students could collaborate to develop military and aeronautic innovations. This was the start of Silicon Valley where SRI was successful in transferring its cutting-edge military innovation to private sector commercialization. Now the United States is sought after as a global tech behemoth to share the fruits of these innovations. Israel followed the same path and now is a leader in technological innovation.

---

[63] Russia, our neighbour to the north with 1/10 the size of Canada's economy with a population of 147 million compared to Canada's 37 million has a larger fleet for the far north and a larger better equipped land and air force. While Russia occupies the globe's largest landmass of 17 million square kilometers, Canada occupies the second largest landmass (10 million square kilometers).

Canada never took this innovative step. Rather defense research was husbanded by crown agencies. In 1990, the various military research labs were amalgamated as the Defense Research and Development Branch. In 2017, Justin Trudeau via his Defense Minister announced a strategic review of the defense policy and a reorganization of Canada's defense research agencies while pledging to increase military spending by 70% of the next seven years. This is a good step forward. Still, publicly funded technology advances in government have fallen behind the rate of private sector innovations and commercialization. This is a failure of leadership.

Leadership and Scandals

Power incites malfeasance. Each Prime Minister has experienced imbroglios and scandals to tax his leadership. How the Prime Minister moves to quickly squelch problems that quickly arise is a test of leadership.

Most Prime Ministers have these issues. The Munsinger Scandal, The Spencer Spy, the Hal Banks prison escape, the Rivard Affair, Terminal One Inquiry at Pearson airport, the Airbus Scandal, the Shawinigate hassle and the Quebec Adcam Sponsorship Commission Enquiry and trials, the John Duffy imbroglio, the India travel fiasco, the Wilson-Boulter dispute, the SNC Lavalin matter, just to name a few. Politics is littered with scandals large and small. How each Prime Minister reacts and reacts quickly is a test of leadership, if not his longevity. The only solace to leaders is that time seems to dilute, if not dissolve, the scandals as the leader's legacies outlive the false steps and foibles taken during his tenure. History acts as a marvelous healer as the leader's virtues outweigh his vices.

The Hedgehog and The Fox

Isaiah Berlin, the astute English observer of leadership, divided the leaders into two categories – the hedgehog and the fox. "*The fox knows many* things, *the hedgehog one big thing*", he wrote.[64] There appears an inherent contradiction. Leaders must know many things to even decide on one big thing. Mr. Lincoln knew and did many things before he did one big thing. I leave it to the readers to decide.[65]

---

[64] *The Hedgehog and the Fox: An Essay on Tolstoy's View of History* by Isaiah Berlin (Weidenfeld & Nicolson, 1953).

[65] Read *On Grand Strategy* by John Lewis Gaddis (Penguin Press, New York, 2018) who explores the complex question of leadership with erudition and compelling insight as he offers his take on measuring leaders. One of the most interesting reads on leadership is Doris Kearns Goodwin's beautifully written examination of four American Presidents and how they overcame personal challenges to achieve their political goals – Abraham Lincoln, Theodore Roosevelt, Franklin D. Roosevelt, and Lyndon B. Johnson (*Leadership in Turbulent Times* by Doris Kearns Goodwin, Simon Schuster, 2018).

John Diefenbaker

John Diefenbaker and the True North

(13th)

Date Elected to Parliament: March 26, 1940
Date of Maiden Speech: June 13, 1940
Date Sworn In: June 21, 1957
Date Left Office: April 21, 1963

It was while in law school at the University of Toronto in 1956 that I began to observe John Diefenbaker more closely on TV, a tall, strangely compelling man with weird jerky mannerisms, chortling voice and stiff, upright, almost military bearing who surprised and astounded all – the experts and the polls, Liberals and Conservatives alike, when he defeated the Liberals under the amiable leadership of Louis St. Laurent, and provoked St. Laurent's quick resignation in 1957. Liberals were suddenly in disarray especially the Liberal Party activists and its elites now led by 'Mike' Pearson, newly anointed and unsure as a freshly minted political leader in 1958.

Until 1957, the Liberals were the longest governing party in Canada in any democratic country in the first part of the 20th century. Led by the likeable, modest, competent, Quebec corporate lawyer, Louis St. Laurent dressed in immaculate double-breasted suits, stiff collared white shirt and dark tie – 'Uncle Louis' – fluently bilingual, comfortable at the helm. St. Laurent went down to disastrous defeat in 1957 as Diefenbaker formed a surprising minority government. Only Quebec, the Liberal firewall, kept Diefenbaker from gaining a majority in Parliament. St. Laurent, the gentleman that he was, quickly and gracefully resigned, gave the nod to 'Mike' Pearson to pick up the reins of the leadership of the Liberal Party and asked Pearson, then Minister of External Affairs, to draft the press release of his resignation.

In a leadership convention that followed, Pearson gained an impressive majority of Liberal Party support.

After St. Laurent's bruising defeat, the Diefenbaker 'vision', delivered by the Diefenbaker rants, were hard for Liberals to swallow. Liberals considered Diefenbaker an outsider, erratic, unfit for leadership, and an aberration. Despite the advice of his inside advisors that the Liberals were not ready, Pearson followed senior elected Liberals like Jack Pickersgill and made an arrogant fumble, forcing a premature vote of confidence in Parliament only to be drowned by the Diefenbaker election sweep of 1958 who won with the largest majority in Parliament in Canadian political history. To be fair, the economy took a tumble after 1957, and the public wanted to give Diefenbaker a chance. The public was as tired of the Liberals as the Liberals were of themselves. The Liberal establishment had grown stale in office and at the grass roots.

John Diefenbaker broke every mold. He was more than a flashy populist. A leader of a different kind, in name, demeanor, and humble origins in Saskatchewan,[66] far from the mainstreams

---

[66] Diefenbaker was born of Scottish and German descent in Neustadt, a small town in Saskatchewan in 1895. His father was a teacher and taught him to love history. Diefenbaker's early admiration for Laurier ignited his dreams of political leadership. After service in World War I, he was invalided and returned to Canada. He got his BA from the University of Saskatchewan and then his MA in Economics and Politics. He decided to become a lawyer

of power, his unorthodox victory surprised friend and foe alike. Until 1957, he had been a serial loser with nine tries before he became a Member of Parliament and twice for Conservative leadership.[67]

In public, Diefenbaker relished the role of prosecuting attorney with an accusatory pointed finger, blaming the Liberals for the stumbling economy, the corruption surrounding the TransCanada pipeline and most of all, for neglecting the 'average' working Canadian.

All this I witnessed while attending law school in Toronto at the time. As an instinctive believer in the underdog with a law student's growing interest in a Charter of Rights, I was astounded when the Diefenbaker government kept its promise and in 1960 passed Charter of Rights legislation. For the first time, rights, lifted and messaged by centuries old common law precedent, were modernized and legislated into the laws of Canada. Though limited to the federal sphere, by separation of powers between provinces and federal governments under the British North American Act,[68] this modest reform measure, effecting

---

and graduated Law School at the University of Saskatchewan. Diefenbaker practiced criminal lawyer, quickly gaining a reputation as a defender of the 'downtrodden' and an opponent of capital punishment.

[67] These losses gave Diefenbaker an internal beacon that drove him to continue to believe in his destiny as leader even after he had been defeated in two national elections in the '60s. Diefenbaker, for a short time in the '30s, was a leader of the Saskatchewan Conservative Party and when defeated turned his energies back to becoming a Member of Parliament.

[68] Britain believed in dividing power between the federal governments and the regions as it did in India so that its hegemony could not be easily challenged by a strong central government. Hence the British North America Act in 1867 divided powers between the federal and provincial levels of government with a lock on allowing any amendments without provincial assent – almost impossible to allow for change. It was a delicious recipe for keeping colonial Canada in lock step with the Imperial power in

the federal sphere, set a new tone and direction of governance and established a platform that culminated in Pierre Trudeau's legacy legislation: the repartition of the Constitution to Canada, wrestling sovereignty from England decades later in 1982. In the process, Trudeau established the Canadian Charter of Rights and Freedom to apply to both federal and provincial spheres in Canada. Diefenbaker could claim legitimacy as a godfather of this stunning idea in parliamentary democracy – rights which till then were steeped and stirred in the common law's languid changing case by case precedent. The legal establishment, judges, lawyers, and academics alike, brought up in the common law tradition, were skeptical and critical. The step-by-step case-by-case common law experience was preferred, they argued. They were marinated and comfortable in the common law tradition. Rights carved in legislation was too much in the American and French traditions. The unwritten Constitution of U.K. based on case-by-case common law precedent was the softer, slower, surer Canadian legacy, the legal elites believed.

Diefenbaker, early in his tenure, had instructed his key legal advisor, his Minister of Justice, Davy Fulton to seek an amending formula as the first step to change the British North American (BNA) via the Fulton Formula that never carried. The Fulton Formula under Diefenbaker later became known as the Fulton-Favreau formula, amended by Pearson's Minister of Justice Guy Favreau. Yet, constitutional change continued to lag and flail from inertia and lack of provincial approval until Pierre Trudeau invested all his political capital and cut the 'Gordian' knot in the early '80s with his Charter of Rights and Freedoms and repatriation of the Constitution, ripped away from British oversight, to Canadian sovereignty.

---

the U.K. especially after the loss of the American colonies a century earlier in 1783.

John Diefenbaker, thin, ramrod straight, broad shouldered, over six feet tall, a raspy gulping voice of many octaves, immaculately tailored double-breasted suits, with big burning coals of dark eyes buried in dark circles, and with grey streaked, dark, curly, wiry hair in an old-fashioned middle part neatly coiffured that was both memorable and oddly disconcerting. He had a saturnine almost Hollywood look of devilish demeanor with his devil's peak, parted in the middle and arched saturnine dark eyebrows. While television was in its infancy in the late '50s, Diefenbaker was magnetic and mesmerizing. Words tumbled out in a jumble, in a torrent, but Canadians connected to his drift and his passion. St. Laurent's TV appearances were staid, low key, passionless, much like a corporate president reading an annual report!

The 1957 federal campaign had been launched hurriedly without finesse and was rushed out into the raw rough tumble politics at the grass roots. There was a mood of change. The Liberals had run out of ideas and were out of touch. The Liberals offered more of the same, mostly sound economic management. Politics remains Canada's 'blood' sport and rarely are the Marquess of Queensbury rules followed and so it was under the lashing tongue of Diefenbaker. Politics is not for gentlemen or gentlewomen I learned, and Diefenbaker was an authentic natural at this rough house game. Too often, he had been on the receiving end of scorn and ridicule in his long career. Now it was his turn to turn his 'fire and brimstone' rhetoric on his Liberal opponents.

Diefenbaker emerged as the arch disruptor of the comfortable Liberal-laced Ottawa establishment headed by the graceful soft-spoken Louis St. Laurent who governed his Cabinet and the public as if he were the Chairman of the Board of a large corporation. Diefenbaker optimized disruption – a whirlwind of change. Pointing an accusatory finger in his speeches, the image lingered in the mind of the electorate. He slavered, he roared (at times incoherently) with unfinished sentences, he whispered, re-altering every inch of the public agenda in Parliament and then on to the campaign trail. A gifted, at times witty, storyteller, he could spin yarns that ended with a whiplash bite. He was relentless, a volcano of energy and worked seven days a week without respite on the campaign trail. Of course, Diefenbaker was handed a prime target, the low hanging fruit of the TransCanada Pipeline debacle – C.D. Howe's prize attempt to quickly build a pipeline across Canada to connect the oil rich west with the oil poor provinces in the east. The corruption uncovered along the way added to the ripeness of the political target. It was Bay Street, and it was the business establishment, the all-powerful self-satisfied men who felt comfort with the Liberal centre and the Liberal right personified by the powerful C.D. Howe, the American born economic czar to whom St. Laurent ceded power, while St. Laurent acted almost as a watchful observer.

Louis St. Laurent was graceful, likeable, and steady, but grew out of touch with the changing Canadian dynamic. Canada gained an appetite for change. Howe dared to push the TransCanada Pipeline Project quickly through Parliament, convincing St. Laurent and his Cabinet to invoke closure and limit debate to a few days of cramped Parliament time. Liberals were then caught openly influencing the Liberal appointed Speaker of the Commons to do the Liberals' bidding, overnight changing the Speaker's ruling that initially favoured the Opposition in its request for extended debate. Pearson, whose reputation was steeped in diplomacy, gave a furious out of character defence in the House of the Pipeline imbroglio attempting to highlight his leadership ambitions and the qualities he and his advisors deemed necessary for the consumption in domestic arena in Parliament.

Pearson attempted to show he was ready for leadership in the rough and tumble of Parliament to convince those that his honed international diplomatic skills could be adapted to the raw bare-knuckle fights in the domestic political arena.

Diefenbaker barely spoke French and when he did, it was fractured and incomprehensible. He chortled when he spoke from a surreptitious whisper to booming thunder at a second's notice as he slayed and lacerated his political opponents on all sides with zest and delight. The media could not make up its mind, or better didn't know what to make of his populist rants while puzzled by his public performances, they welcomed the contrast to the steady as they go Liberals. The media hungered for 'new' news and Diefenbaker satisfied their craving. The House of Commons was composed of the two major parties, Liberals and Conservatives, and three minor parties, the Social Credit in the West allied with the Socreds in Quebec on the right and the CCF on the left. Diefenbaker enjoyed the cut and thrust of Parliament and even more felt less constrained on the campaign trail where he sensed the crowds were with him and reveled in public applause.[69] Meanwhile Pearson, once leader, seemed unsure of himself, failed to gain his groove or traction seemingly unable to arouse passion and acted like a reluctant unsure suitor for power. Diefenbaker regularly outshone and bested Pearson in Parliamentary debate skirmishes and both knew it.

As leader, Diefenbaker came early under the tutelage by Allister Grosart, a suave lawyer turned journalist turned ad man and who later became a Senator and then Speaker of the Senate. Grosart enlisted American pollsters to test and freshen

[69] Peter Newman, one of Canada's leading political journalists and authors and a Diefenbaker antagonist, considered Diefenbaker in his essay on Canada in the 20th century, one of Canada's greatest orators.

the Progressive Conservative message. Grosart's polling told him the Liberals vulnerabilities. The country had grown tired of the Liberals boring, almost arrogant exterior. The country was ripe and ready to give change a chance, he found. The economy was sputtering. The Liberal team looked and acted tired lacking passion without a dynamic plan for the future.

Diefenbaker's campaign propaganda team, as devised by Grosart, focused on Diefenbaker, 'the man', and his 'vision' while the Liberals, reacted indifferently, and became upset, riled, and angry without a tangible alternate offering in people, policy or messaging for the future.[70] Diefenbaker was all about the promise of the future, while the Liberals rested on their past record. The skilled criminal lawyer that he was, Diefenbaker could make any compelling case with ease, throwing darts quickly at easy soft targets to the cheers of his supporters, especially in the ignored West and the Maritimes who felt left out of the Ontario/Quebec political radar screen. Diefenbaker targeted farmers, lumbermen, fishermen, steel workers, coal miners, vets, pensioners, recent immigrants, and struggling small businessmen – the working-classes – the 'forgotten' Canadians. They all felt they had been ignored by the Liberals while elites on Bay Street and in Montreal held visible sway, ignoring their household needs. Television made a crucial difference. Diefenbaker was explosive and electric on TV.[71] His eyes flashed with 'fire and brimstone' as he lacerated the Liberals. Pearson was uncomfortable, understated, and

[70] Grosart was based in Toronto. I was introduced to 'Red' Foster, a pal of my father-in-law Harry Sniderman. 'Red' told me how first his ad group were dismissive of Diefenbaker but soon jumped on his band wagon when he began to arouse the Canadian public.

[71] McLuhan, the Canadian guru of the media, later opined that 'cool' on TV, in effect, quiet and understated was more persuasive 'hot and loud'. Diefenbaker shredded this thesis.

undramatic by comparison. Pearson had a high wavering voice with a slight lisp that rose in decibels as he lamely attempted to demonstrate passion.

In 1957, Diefenbaker won an uphill victory to the astonishment of both parties, the mainstream media and public. It was the 'outsider' against the 'establishment' – 'Main Street against Bay Street'. His publicists touted him as the 'man from Prince Albert' to emphasize his small-town origins. The intellectuals, skewed academics, and bureaucrats allied with the Bay Street businessmen who believed they knew what was best for them and so for the rest of Canada. They queried how a prairie upstart with such a weird Germanic name could dare to run and gain power over the schooled experienced eastern elite governing party. Diefenbaker who had failed repeatedly before he was elected to Parliament and never even received a senior position in his own caucus until he became a leader was a surprise. "*Inexperienced*", "*inept*", "*dangerous*", "*upstart*", and "*not fit for office*", they murmured. Diefenbaker was at best a 'rabble rouser'. His tirades against the establishment and United States was encapsulated in his theme 'Canada First' and his subtle, not so understated sub-theme 'Main Street, not Bay Street'. The business establishment with its deep financial and policy ties to the Liberal Party was exposed.

When Louis St. Laurent quickly and gracefully stepped down, Mike Pearson, the modest political leader soundly defeated Paul Martin Senior, the most well-rounded experienced politician in the St. Laurent Cabinet at the Liberal Party leadership convention. Liberals felt they had an upper hand with Pearson, the recent 1956 Nobel Prize for Peace winning diplomat and world acclaimed Foreign Minister, comfortable in the international corridors at the UN and the Commonwealth. No one was more likeable than Mike Pearson. When your first met him, he was quiet, rational, sensible, vulnerable, and warm in all his personal relationships. In 1958, Pearson, based on the advice of Jack Pickersgill and other former Ministers, called for a quick vote of confidence on Diefenbaker's minority government insisting it was time for a Liberal government to return quickly to power again before Diefenbaker ruined the Canadian economy and antagonized our staunch American ally. They fell into Diefenbaker's trap. It was an act of reckless judgement that Pearson immediately regretted. The 1958 federal Diefenbaker team drowned the Liberal Party. Experienced formidable ministers like C.D. Howe in Ontario, Jimmy Sinclair in British Columbia[72] and Robert Winters in Nova Scotia went down like ten pins. Liberals were in shock and so were the Canadian elites.

Diefenbaker, the unknown and quirky leader became Prime Minister, while Pearson who had won worldwide accolades at the UN for his international leadership leading to the Nobel Peace Prize for his work on the Suez Crisis was shut out and the Liberal Party left in the worst shape in modern history. The Liberal Party officials and the grass roots had grown old and lazy. The media was in shock. And so was I. Diefenbaker's sleazy attacks first on St. Laurent's record, a politician I admired, and then Pearson were questionable, but Diefenbaker hit the soft targets. Pearson's leadership style, hesitant, thoughtful and reasonable, was the polar opposite of John Diefenbaker in all aspects. Who could fail to admire Mike Pearson? Pearson, a graduate of University of Toronto, then Oxford, a World War I vet, a fanatic sports fan, a university sports coach, an excellent hockey, baseball, lacrosse and tennis player, a well-liked history

---

[72] James Sinclair became Pierre Trudeau's father-in-law and Justin Pierre James Trudeau's grandfather named in part after his grandfather. Had Sinclair not been defeated in 1958, he would have been a formidable Liberal leadership contender.

professor and who, later through the years, had been groomed by Mackenzie King himself first as a young public servant, then senior bureaucrat, then diplomat and then Member of Parliament then Minister of External Affairs for leadership from the outset on his career. Pearson, a son and grandson of Methodist pastors, was comfortable with Toronto-Ottawa elites, attracted to public life, experienced businessmen, lawyers, former public servants - the best of the best - like Robert Winters who easily gained well paid jobs in the private sector when he was first defeated or Walter Gordon, a top business consultant and government advisor who became Pearson's Campaign Chairman and others like them.

Pearson was not a joyful warrior in public. He was a joyful, witty, warm companion in private. Diefenbaker relished public performances. He could enthrall even those who were not his admirers. Pearson shrunk from public displays of emotion. Diefenbaker easily attracted the 'average' Canadian who felt left out of the Liberal establishment radar which had ignored them.

Even the reluctant comfortable conservative business establishment from Ontario began to rally to Diefenbaker's banner led by the Ontario Progressive Conservatives especially the astute, successful and popular Premier of Ontario, Leslie Frost, who was early convinced Diefenbaker could gain power and would then cooperate with Ontario to help fill its growing economic needs. War vets and men of business experience like George Hees joined Diefenbaker's bandwagon as did others. John Bassett Sr., another leading Tory, threw his Toronto newspaper The Telegram, behind him.[73] Later John McCutcheon, a Bay Street baron and partner of the business titans, E.P. Taylor and

[73] John Bassett Senior ran for Parliament under Diefenbaker in Toronto, perhaps as a leadership aspirant in case Diefenbaker gave up the Conservative leadership. Bassett was defeated in the Spadina Riding.

George Montaque Black Jr.,[74] was added as a Senator. Pierre Sevigny from Quebec, a bemedalled war veteran who lost a limb in World War II, joined the Diefenbaker banner.

Pearson and Diefenbaker had polar opposite leadership styles as Prime Ministers. Diefenbaker relished conflicts in his Cabinet, while Pearson was a quiet consensus builder who abhorred conflicts. Pearson believed in careful thought and reform step by step while Diefenbaker gushed, gulped and rushed at reform. He relied on his instincts as he had when he had overcome adversity throughout his long career climbing up the 'greasy' pole to power.

Diefenbaker stormed the government in 1958 when he gained the largest majority in history – with 208 seats in the Commons to the amazement and dismay of the Liberal stalwarts. The bureaucracy was in the hands of Liberal mandarins who believe it was in the 'national interest' and theirs to undermine Diefenbaker's policies and leadership directives that flooded their desks.

Diefenbaker's key political architect was Allister Grosart, a quick-witted lawyer but now amicable newsman, who had turned his skills in advertising to assist George Drew as Conservative Leader in Ottawa. When George Drew withdrew from the Conservative leadership, Grosart became Diefenbaker's first loyal senior Ontario political operative. Grosart was Diefenbaker's image maker. Allister never budged and remained loyal to Diefenbaker to the very end. Grosart felt the tired Tory Party brand had to pivot to focus on 'Diefenbaker the Man' to gain wider support beyond the narrow hardcore Tory support. The focus on 'The Man' rather than 'the Party' was a first in

---

[74] George M. Black's son is Conrad Black. Together Taylor, McCutcheon and Black built the first Canadian conglomerate, Argus Corp., composed of different businesses like insurance companies, insurance agencies, mining, broadcasting, food stores, and breweries.

modern Canadian elections, now geared by the electronic media that began to relish 'celebrity'. Pearson and the Liberal team were left behind. Diefenbaker, the unknown, became the 'celebrity'. Pearson, already a recognized widely respected international celebrity, shunned 'celebrity'.

Diefenbaker's government's first year in office in 1957 unleashed a torrent of legislation and regulatory changes: increased price supports for agricultural products (butter and turkeys); raises for federal employees; aid to veterans; grain supports; tax cuts for lower and middle-classes; increases in old age pensions; assistance to coal miners and fishermen; low cost home loans; winter work projects to stoke seasonal unemployment; hospital insurance; higher unemployment benefits – all passed with breathtaking speed - and all transformational. There were 'giveaways' to every alienated hard-working sector of the economy – the 'average' Canadian.

Diefenbaker relished diversity in his caucus and Cabinet appointing Michael Starr, a Canadian of Ukrainian descent, and Ellen Fairclough, the first female Cabinet Minister. He enlisted iconoclastic ministers like Alvin Hamilton, a bright Saskatchewan farmer in 1957 who became Minister of Northern Affairs and in turn gathered about him a brilliant group of young advisors led by Roy Faibish.[75] This talented youthful team galvanized by Roy

[75] Roy Faibish, who I first encountered in 1961 working for a CBC program *This Hour Has Seven Days*, became a lifelong mentor, friend, confidant, and gadfly. He never left off cajoling me about my Liberal loyalties. Roy Faibish became a trusted advisor to Diefenbaker, Trudeau and Mulroney, respected by all for his political judgement and profound intellectualism. Roy, a polymath, knew and had studied, it seemed to me, everything! There was no book on any subject I read that he had not already read and analyzed. Amazing! He spent his last years in London, reading every week day for a few hours in the Reading Rooms of the London Library where he joyfully served with distinction on its privileged oversight committee.

attempted to give substance to Diefenbaker's electoral promise of 'vision' that had caught the public imagination. 'Roads to Resources' and the promise of development of Canada's North, neglected by Liberals, captured the Canadian imagination. The contrast to the tired worn out Liberals was palpable.[76]

In 1960, Hamilton was shifted to Minister of Agriculture. Roy was asked to advise Diefenbaker and write speeches, policy papers, and invited Brian Mulroney, a young Conservative activist from Quebec, to join Hamilton's staff for a summer stint to replace him temporarily. Hamilton quickly introduced more decisive steps to enhance the struggling agricultural sector. His breakthrough was the large wheat sale to drought-stricken China, a first for Canada and its western allies. Roy Faibish, a China expert, led on the wheat deal.[77] This upset the Americans,

---

Not a week would go by when Roy did not send me a blistering note or long fax or later emails castigating Liberal policies and personalities except Trudeau who he respected for his intellect.

[76] Diefenbaker was mindful of Parliamentary history. He admired Churchill and avidly devoured his books and speeches. In 1958, Diefenbaker took the time to write a graceful foreword to the catalogue listing Churchill's paintings that were then touring Canada.

[77] Roy worked hard to become an 'old hand' in China and a leading expert in Chinese affairs. He travelled to China often and had a large circle of Chinese intellectuals in his network. Some I had the pleasure of meeting during my travels in China. Two were elderly Canadian communists who married Chinese women, settled in China and each raised a family. From the outset, he cajoled me to become knowledgeable about China as he predicted early that China would become a leading world economic and technological power, outstripping the west. I was too Eurocentric, he charged and sought to change my interest in China which he did. Immediately after the Tiananmen Student Massacre in 1989, Roy, upset and dismayed, travelled to China and got a firsthand look including the precise number of victims. For my 50th birthday, my wife had arranged our first long trip to China with my two young sons to follow Marco Polo's Silk Road into the heart of the Middle Kingdom that accelerated my later

especially President Kennedy, who were trying to place a frame around Communist China and Soviet Russia as enemies of American 'democratic' interests. Roy became the sparkling 'idea man' and phrase maker for both the Hamilton and Diefenbaker teams.

Another spark plug in the Diefenbaker Cabinet was Davie Fulton, an ambitious Rhodes Scholar from Kamloops, BC whose family predecessors were amongst the political elite of that province and included judges, well-respected ministers, and senior public officials. Diefenbaker quickly appointed him to the prestigious Minister of Justice.

Fulton too attracted a bright circle of young advisors with an intellectual bent, Michael Pitfield of the Montreal establishment family (later to be the senior bureaucratic advisor to Pierre Trudeau)[78] and Marc Lalonde (a talented well-schooled brilliant French Canadian who also went on to become a key advisor to Mr. Pearson, then Mr. Trudeau and then in turn became Minister of Energy and later Finance). Fulton and his team drafted the groundbreaking federal 'Bill of Rights' legislation pushed by

---

visits and studies of China, especially the deep Canadian connections that started before the turn of the 19th century by Toronto based Protestant and Catholic missionary movements originating in Toronto. This historic connection between China and Canada, especially in west and southwest China, and the influences of both countries on each other is a tale in need of historic rediscovery. How the Canadian China missionary movement in the later 19th and early 20th century influenced the first members of the External Affairs in Ottawa in the '20s is a vital piece of Canadian history necessary to understand deep principles of both our domestic and foreign policies. The 'social gospel' gained and promoted by these Canadian missionaries in China early influenced our public policies especially in external affairs and continues to this day.

78 After a successful career as a senior bureaucrat, Pitfield was appointed to the Senate where he sat as an independent and became a thoughtful colleague while I served in the Senate as a Liberal.

Diefenbaker that ultimately led to the Canadian Charter of Rights and Freedoms and the Constitutional Repatriation decades later in the early '80s under Pierre Trudeau. Fulton and his team organized federal and provincial constitutional conferences as they ceaselessly sought to gain an agreement on an amending formula necessary to gain provincial approval, a first step to patriate the Canadian Constitution. The Fulton Formula under Diefenbaker followed by the Fulton-Favreau formula under Pearson, never gained the necessary provincial traction to success.

Diefenbaker appointed a Royal Commission to renovate Canada's outmoded tax system. He rampaged and proposed radical changes on every front.

At times, Diefenbaker appeared clairvoyant. Wednesday evenings in Ottawa featured the 'Late Show' after his loss of the Prime Ministership. The Commons held an evening session after dinner. Political staff joined a skeleton press gallery to audit these late evening speeches. It was my regular habit to observe from the government gallery when I served as John Turner's Chief of Staff called, in those days, the more modest 'Executive Assistant'. Diefenbaker was always in attendance in the House.

Most members of the Commons were slightly in their 'cups' and glowing with camaraderie looked forward to fun after a nice dinner and well lubricated in the Members dining room. Most had been assigned evening house attendance. The mood was warm and friendly on all sides as each designated speaker rose first on the government side to be gently heckled or questioned by the Opposition and then when the Opposition spoke to receive equally witty interjections. It was great fun.

One evening, Bryce Mackasey, a jovial Liberal Irish Quebecer from the Riding of Verdun in Quebec City, rose unsteadily to speak, obviously under the 'influence'. Bryce was the Liberal

Minister of Labour under Mr. Pearson. Bryce, starting from humble beginnings as an electrician on the CN Railway, rose in the ranks to become a union activist and then Member of Parliament. Bryce spoke easily in street chatter in both languages, at times with earthy language propelled by an endearing lisp. Who could not fail to like Bryce? He held a number of portfolios, first as Labour with Mr. Pearson, then Manpower and Immigration under Trudeau. Mr. Turner later appointed him to become Ambassador to Portugal.

By the time Brian Mulroney, himself from Irish working-class stock from Quebec, became Leader of the Opposition, Mulroney attacked Turner for Bryce's diplomatic appointment as he ranted at another blatant example of Liberal patronage. Mulroney, phrase maker that he was, crafted these memorable words – "*There is no whore like an old whore.*" When Mulroney won the election as Prime Minister, true to form, he cancelled Bryce's appointment and then quickly and artfully appointed Lloyd Francis, a disenchanted Liberal and former Speaker to replace Bryce as Ambassador to Portugal. Ah, patronage never ceases to flow in many directions like a fountain.

In any event, back to this one memorable Wednesday evening in Parliament. Bryce was Minister of Labour and 'under the weather', as they say. He rose unsteadily on his feet to speak in the House, red-faced, standing swaying from side to side, and called for a controversial position on a current Labour issue in Quebec. Diefenbaker religiously attended these lively evening sessions surrounded with his clippings and notes piled on his desk, as he listened to the debates as he read. Suddenly Diefenbaker rose and said, "*The Honourable Member says one thing tonight in this House, but last night he was saying something quite different in Quebec*" and sat down. Bryce was flummoxed, mumbling some reply, finished his speech, visibly shaken.

Curious, I went downstairs to the Government Caucus room behind the Government side in the Commons. Bryce was slouched in a big red leather chair, stunned and more florid. "*Are you all right? What happened, Bryce?*" I asked. Bryce murmured, "*I don't believe it. Last night I had drinks with two close friends, confided to them about my own position that was different from the Government's position which I took tonight. How did Diefenbaker know that?*" I left Bryce but remained curious about Diefenbaker's clairvoyance. Much later I discovered that one of the men Bryce met in Montreal that night was Bill Wilson of the Montreal Star who Bryce would leak stories to and who he considered a friend. It seems that Bill, a respected member of the Press Gallery, also kept in regular contact with John Diefenbaker. Diefenbaker always paid attention and curried favour from his preferred sources in the media. He developed a remarkable network of information and advice from favoured journalists. Some newsmen who had come to loath the Liberals arrogance loved Diefenbaker's underdog stance. Politics is a great teacher about human nature.

Diefenbaker was a practicing Baptist, a teetotaler or so he presented himself! I was told that he and Paul Martin Senior, both not revered by their party elites, respected and liked each other. Both, when they spent private time together, would imbibe a glass or two of wine as they shared experiences and friendship.

Wives are important to the success of any leader. Olive Diefenbaker, Diefenbaker's second wife, was inseparable. She was constantly at his side, calming him and directing him. He felt lost without her as they campaigned and travelled together. Diefenbaker would glance at her to seek her approval when he spoke. It was lovely to watch the true love, admiration, and friendship these two held for each other, especially when they looked at each other.

The Israel and the Mid-East turmoil in the '60s and '70s continued as a constant almost irritating sore that wouldn't heal. Diefenbaker always felt a visceral connection to the plight of Jews starting with the episodic anti-Semitic outbreaks in Western Canada in the '30s, during World War II and later directed to the State of Israel. In 1960, Diefenbaker appointed a senior diplomat, Margaret Meagher. Until then the one diplomat headed by both Greece and Israel embassies together. Diefenbaker decided to separate these two diplomatic posts. Meagher became the Canadian Ambassador to Israel alone for the first time. In 1973, I had made my first visit to Israel. I was invited to join a small group of Torontonians led by my university school chum, David Dennis and businessman Jimmy Kay, who had arranged for John Diefenbaker to inaugurate the John Diefenbaker Forest planted on a desolate piece of the land outside Jerusalem and the John Diefenbaker Parkway leading to Jerusalem. The trip was organized by the Jewish National Fund[79] in Canada.

A brief backstory to my unexpected relations with John Diefenbaker. In 1965, when I arrived in Ottawa as the Executive Assistant to John Turner for my first stint in public service, I was anxious and green. While politically active and familiar with Mr. Pearson, most of the Liberal Cabinet and their senior appointed political staff, Parliament itself, the bureaucracy and how a government really worked was a mystery to me. I sought advice from Alistair Fraser, a knowledgeable Ottawa hand and top assistant to the irrepressible Jack Pickersgill. John Turner had been appointed to the Cabinet as an Associate Minister to Pickersgill, who dominated the Cabinet and held the powerful

[79] The Jewish National Fund, considered the first ecology organization in the world, was started by early Zionists at the turn of the century to plant trees and promote water and other ecological projects in the then mostly arid Palestine.

Minister of Transport, considered the all-knowing political guru. Alistair later became Clerk of the House of Commons, a chunky, short man from the Maritimes; he was the 'go-to guy' about the workings of everything in government. He gave me a long precise lecture with a list of 'do's' and 'don'ts' as a political assistant, especially my relations with the senior bureaucrats and their aides who looked on all political staff as inferior and irritating. Ottawa under Pearson, himself in former Mandarin, was influenced by the mandarin class of seasoned deputy ministers, their hand-picked associate deputy ministers and senior staff. Politicians and especially their politically appointed staff were seen as irritating distractions from good governance.

It was a closed elite bureaucratic circle that ran our government in the '60s rather than the elected officials to my surprise and bewilderment. "*You had better learn to go along to get along*", Alistair admonished me.

Alistair then suggested I go and seek advice from John Diefenbaker who loved Parliament and knew the workings of government better than most and would give me a contrarian perspective as well as anyone. I was surprised. Though Diefenbaker was Leader of the Opposition, he was the avowed Liberal political nemesis. The Liberals had demonized him in the last two federal elections that gave birth to Pearson's first Liberal minority in 1962. Now as Leader of the Opposition, the 'Chief' had time on his hands. "*Don't worry*", Alistair advised, "*He would surely meet with you. Make sure you speak to his right side. He is slightly deaf in the left ear and it upsets him if he can't hear you.*"

I called Diefenbaker's office on the Hill and immediately got his secretary and heard 'Dief' growl in the background demanding who was on the line. She shouted my name and I could hear him say, "*Well, tell him to come right over.*" I was astonished. Timidly I entered his quiet outer office and was immediately ushered into his large inner sanction. His large desk was a jumbled mess covered with clippings and notes. He waved me to sit down and asked what I wanted. "*Alistair Fraser had suggested that I ask you for advice*", I blurted out.

John Diefenbaker, a tall ramrod straight broad-shouldered angular man, filled the room with his piercing fiery eyes that glowed like burning coals from deep dark sockets. He wore a dark bespoke double-breasted suit, with a crisp white shirt, dark tie, and a carefully folded white starched hankie. His manner of speaking surprised me – softer, familiar, friendly, confidential, less raspy, with a flashing wit. His tone was a deep, quiet, resonant baritone. Most convivial, he quickly put me at ease. "*I know who you are. You work for John Turner and you worked for The Truth Squad led by that Judy LaMarsh that flopped*", he chortled. Indeed, Keith Davey had asked me to do some research for his idea – The Truth Squad – led by Judy LaMarsh which briefly followed Diefenbaker on the 1962 campaign trail across Canada. It was set up to correct Dief's factual errors or mistakes about Diefenbaker's record and his allegations against the Liberal governments, past and present. Keith's colourful idea had flopped quickly as 'Dief' laughed it out of business. Keith tried comic books and the 'Diefenbuck' or 'Diefendollar' when Diefenbaker had devalued the Canadian dollar to 92.5 cents, who knows to what effect. Still the Liberals won a minority government under Mr. Pearson, so maybe these stunts had some effect.

In any event, 'Dief' proceeded to give me a long list of 'do's' and 'don'ts' with quick, quirky anecdotes about most of the Pearson Cabinet Ministers except Paul Martin Senior whom he held in high esteem. Later I found out why.[80] After praising John

[80] Diefenbaker and Martin, though political antagonists, were close good friends, spent private time together sharing a glass of wine (though

Turner as a 'comer' who he respected as a politician, especially for Turner's fervent belief in the primacy of Parliament, a belief 'Dief' shared. I had held a grudging admiration for Diefenbaker as a law student when in 1957, he had introduced the first Bill of Rights Act that applied to the federal spheres of power in his first government. Turner respected him too. Later I discovered that Pierre Trudeau also admired Diefenbaker for his Bill of Rights, passed in 1957 creating Canada's first Bill of Rights, an oversight law that applied to the federal jurisdiction and for his eloquent and passionate stand on 'One Canada', a belief Trudeau shared. Diefenbaker, in his farewell address to the 1967 Conservative Leadership Convention, where he posted a poor sixth place showing, to lose to Robert Stanfield, railed against 'extremism' and the 'Two Nation' theory, then a growing analogue to the 'separatist' movement that was spiking in political popularity in Quebec to the frustration of all federal parties, as if the 'Two

---

Diefenbaker was considered a teetotalling Baptist) and held each other's talents in high esteem. Both were life long skilled, successful politicians yet, were never fully respected by their party elites. Paul Martin, Sr. had an extraordinary career in public service from the '30s to the '80s. Martin's remarkable two volume biography *A Very Public Life*, published in 1983 and 1986 by Deneau, I consider one of the best of its genre. Martin detailed his rise from humble beginnings, effected with childhood polio and maimed for life to becoming the leading 'progressive' in the Liberal Party. Martin single-handedly transformed Windsor, his political base, to a decades long Liberal stronghold despite strong union activism and CCF then NDP staunch opposition. As Minister of Health, he introduced the first stage Medicare in 1948 with grants and tax credits, then aid to hospitals in 1956, threatening to resign if the St. Laurent government did not keep its election promises. Martin went on to be Secretary of State for External Affairs under Mr. Trudeau, Leader of the Senate and High Commissioner to the U.K. government and finally a University lecturer in Windsor – all in all, an astonishing 'progressive' 20th century record of accomplishments and commitment to public service.

Nation' theory would somehow better unite a divisive Quebec with the rest of Canada.

Dief's, like Fraser's, most pessimistic yet, insightful advice related to the bureaucrats, the Liberal Mandarins, who could slow down or derail any new reforms that they didn't own. "*Make sure they feel they own any Turner reforms and they might have chance*", he advised with a mischievous gleam in his eyes. Then after more than an hour, I left 'Dief' thoughtful but invigorated.

During my time as John Turner's assistant, I would receive the odd hand-written note from Diefenbaker when I sat in the Common's Gallery listening to Turner deliver a speech that I had helped draft. Diefenbaker always sat in his front seat in the House reading his mail and papers while listening to the Debates, even during the evening Debates, when the House was almost empty. He would send me a note up to the gallery, delivered by a page boy with cryptic comments, "*Not bad, Chief of Staff*" or "*Missed the mark, Chief of Staff*", and he would smile up at me as I read his note and nodded to him as he returned to intently listening to the Debates never stopping to forage through his small heap of notes, clippings, and correspondence cluttering his Parliamentary desk.

Later in 1967 when Diefenbaker ran for Leadership at the Conservative Convention for the last time in Toronto at the Maple Leaf Gardens, I called 'Fast' Eddie Goodman, a Conservative stalwart I knew, and a key member of the 'dump' Diefenbaker movement led by Dalton Camp for two tickets. Eddy was the Chairman of that convention. He barked at me dismissively over the phone, "*No way*", and that was that. I decided to call Diefenbaker's office. I immediately received two tickets seated several rows behind 'Dief' in the Gardens. I attended with Carole. When Eddie spotted me as he raced about the packed audience, he shouted one of his creative expletives, "*What the ___ are you doing here?*" Diefenbaker, sitting a few rows below overheard Goodman's loud remarks, stood erect, turned, hands akimbo on his hips and then pointed to us, and then to himself and lip-synched, "*They are with me*" and smiled to Eddy's consternation. Nonplussed, Eddie shouted, "*Grafstein, you are impossible*", larded with another of his stream of endless expletives. And so was 'Fast Eddie', I smiled to myself.

I shared my admiration for Diefenbaker with the late and lamented Doug Fisher, a heavy-set, tall, chunky, lumbering war veteran and lifelong socialist, an astute journalist, hockey fan, and the best political historian on the Hill. Doug had toppled C.D. Howe, the most powerful minister in the St. Laurent cabinet in 1957 and became an CCF (later NDP) M.P. at the Lakehead. He lost in the Diefenbaker landslide in 1958. Later he returned to Toronto to run against a Liberal, my cousin Bobby Kaplan, and was soundly beaten and hence he harboured a lifelong grudge against anything Liberal. It was in Ottawa in 1965 that I first met Doug in Ottawa, often in the West Block Cafeteria, and we became lively sparring partners for the rest of his long storied career as one of Canada's best read insightful political journalists. He admired Diefenbaker deeply and regaled me with inside stories about him.

When David Dennis, a University chum, a Conservative, and loyal Diefenbaker supporter, wanted a bipartisan group to join the Diefenbaker visit to Israel in 1973 to dedicate a forest and a parkway near Jerusalem in Diefenbaker's name, no other Liberal agreed to go. 'Dief' suggested David call me. David knew I was an active Liberal but he didn't know of my relationship with 'Dief'. David called me with some hesitancy and was surprised and pleased that I readily agreed to join the group to travel with 'Dief' to Israel. It would be my first visit to Israel. The purpose of the trip was to inaugurate the John Diefenbaker Forest outside Jerusalem. So, we travelled across the breath and width of Israel by bus, from desert settlements to collective farms to Israeli towns to government sponsored events, watching Diefenbaker speak spontaneously to his enraptured audiences from leading politicians to military leaders to settlers ('Kibbutzniks') in tiny windswept enclaves or large agricultural communes. He had the common touch. We met the Speaker of Knesset, the pint-sized Yitzhak Shamir, the celebrated underground fighter, who became head of the Mossad, Israel's secret service and later to become a controversial Prime Minister who hit it off with 'Dief' and then privately with Golda Meir, the outgoing Prime Minister who had just resigned who also was an obvious admirer of 'Dief', known as a staunch supporter of Israel.[81]

John Diefenbaker was seen as a staunch friend of Israel who was adored by the Israeli public and the media. In one interview during that trip in 1974, he called for the Canadian recognition of Jerusalem as Israel's eternal capital. Diefenbaker reveled in meeting rabbis, students, farm workers, union leaders, politicos of all stripes, always with genuine warmth and enthusiasm as he listened to them and then responded with a quip or a story. Israelis loved him.

Back to the 1958 campaign which started with a Liberal fumble. Egged on by Jack Pickersgill, Mike Pearson, the newly minted Liberal leader, called for a vote of confidence on the

---

[81] We travelled outside Jerusalem to inaugurate the John Diefenbaker Forest and Diefenbaker Parkway. All of us were invited to plant a tree. I planted mine very close to the 'Chief's'. He looked up and asked why I had planted my tree so close to his. I told him that I would return later and water both trees when I urinate on mine and his tree at the same time to his great laughter and delight.

premise that the public would want to return the government to safe Liberals hands. Pearson knew at once that it was the wrong call. Diefenbaker had set a trap.

Diefenbaker immediately launched into the campaign and never stopped a day! Anxious to pour substance into his 'version' for developing Canada's north, Diefenbaker worked to match Sir John A. MacDonald's promise of expanding Canada across the west. Diefenbaker wanted to brand his legacy with expanding Canada to the north. He wanted his policy plans to match his 'vision'. He knew, as did his key advisors, the untapped riches across the North from minerals to energy. Diefenbaker's team called on Alvin Hamilton, young idea men, Roy Faibish and Don Johnson, to give the 'vision' substance. How? By building roads, 'Roads to Resources', improving the northern sea routes, calling for self-government for the Yukon and Northwest Territories to dilute this northern fiefdom of the federal bureaucracy.

'Canada of the North' became a campaign slogan to add flesh to the skeleton of his 'vision'. How to shift focus to the untapped North? While Diefenbaker's actual policies were, as some critics said 'feeble', starts were made in the fulfillment of 'vision'. The second TransCanada Highway was started. Still the north's promise remained unfinished.

Today, northern development remains a slow work in progress. While oil was discovered along the Arctic coast before the 'oil' bust in the '90s, the vast riches of Ontario – the 'Ring of Fire', and 'Quebec Nord' still remain untapped on the planning tables of bureaucrats waiting for roads and rails, the promise of a northern sea passage and the political will to monetize Canada's hidden treasures. The 'True North, strong and free', remains on the drawing tables waiting for new political will to exploit Canada's hidden riches. Still, it was

Diefenbaker's vision of the north that opened new, exciting, hopeful vistas and lifted the scope and reach of Canada's future for the first time.

Diefenbaker was the first Prime Minister to constantly use the telephone to network and keep apprised of politics at the grass roots levels. He sought out reactions and ideas from more than his inner circle. He wanted to keep in touch. He reached out regularly across country to young comers like Brian Mulroney, Joe Clark, Ted Rogers, and local newspaper editors, to gossip, which he loved. He would entertain them, confide in them, seek their advice about what was going on across the country, build bonds of loyalty but mostly to demonstrate he knew more than his peers, and even more than his staff. The phone was Diefenbaker's focus group.

Brian Mulroney also loved the phone to reach out and keep in touch first as a political activist, then lawyer, then businessman, and finally as a politician. Mulroney was the best telephone network operator of any modern Prime Minister. He used the network to keep in touch, to gossip, to offer assistance and gain information. Most politicians like Paul Martin Sr. had a regular list of contacts that he phoned. I was on that list. Martin would call every two weeks or so and ask to be brought up to speed on local politics. The conversation was always a one-way street with Martin. You talked briefly, then he took over for the rest of the conversation and then signed off. To be in touch with power was enough to attract supporters. Mulroney succeeded because he deployed his telephone network as a two-way street. He bonded, got information, ideas, but also helped out members of his network and members of their family if needed. Mulroney was reputed to be a good listener. Pearson and Trudeau were reluctant telephone users. They preferred one-to-one contact. Diefenbaker, however, remains the pioneer of regular telephone contact by Canadian political leaders.[82]

Rarely in the usual quarrelsome debates between party leaders has there been so much vitriol and mutual demonization observed and practiced between Diefenbaker and Pearson. It was a sterile embrace. Pearson, who loathed to hate anyone, hated Diefenbaker. It was this public discourse spewing vitriol between two very different leaders that I observed when I first joined politics as an ardent fan of Mr. Pearson. Peter Newman, the chronicler of this venomous period, placed the responsibility on Diefenbaker in the 'Renegade in Power'. At the time I thought Peter's book, a best seller, hit the target. Later on, when I became better acquainted with Mr. Diefenbaker, my first Liberal tribal impressions changed. Diefenbaker was by instincts a 'progressive'. So, I dug back into the history of the party starting with Mr. King and came to perceive a different set of circumstances. John Diefenbaker was an unusual politician a different breed who started with a weird Germanic name as a self-made crusading criminal lawyer who saved men from the gallows and who lost nine elections before he gained a seat in Parliament.

My astute mentor and friend Roy Faibish who had travelled across the political spectrum from communist or at least an early sympathizer to avid Conservative felt that Diefenbaker with all his patent flaws was an honest contrarian who took on unpopular causes including defending Roy's father who was attacked by some rowdy anti-Semitic rednecks after they sought to hang him in a large hemp wheat bag upside down, sought them out and beat them, was defended by Mr. Diefenbaker successfully or so Roy told me. Or the fact that Diefenbaker defended murderers and became a

[82] Mike Pearson was an avid letter writer sending his concise reports to other foreign leaders who valued his insights. John Turner sent short notes of congratulations and condolences to friends and foes alike.

life-long capital abolitionist, an action that endeared him to me and 'abolitionists' like Arthur Maloney (a friend and one of the leading criminal lawyers in Canada and one time Member of Parliament), and more so when he passed the first federal Bill of Rights as Prime Minister. In the late '50s, his courageous wheat deal sale to China was again a first. The deal helped western farmers as it opened up China to trade with Canada that Roy helped engineer as the erstwhile assistant to Alvin Hamilton, the Minister of Agriculture. Or in the 'Northern Vision' speeches and the 'Roads to Resources' speeches that Roy helped craft based on phrases he helped coin that became part of the Canadian political lexicon.

It was Mr. Diefenbaker's northern development speeches and policies that reoriented the Canadian public to think of Canada from coast-to-coast to northern coast. These visionary speeches lifted Canadian eyes to our northern landmass that stretched longer north and south than east to west.

Diefenbaker, an early vocal opponent to South Africa's apartheid practices, was not popular with the Canadian bureaucracy or business elites. His fierce opposition to communism, when the bureaucracy in external affairs was still rife with communist sympathizers and the media were soft on communist supporters due to the overreach of McCarthyism, did not gain him deep support amongst the left leaning senior civil servants. Or Diefenbaker's innate distrust of Americans who sought to actively undermine his leadership.[83] Or his articulate and lonely support for dissidents in Communist Russia.[84] Or his

[83] Diefenbaker in his last volume of his memoir *One Canada* detailed how President Kennedy and the Americans had undermined his election and his administration and meddled in his national campaign elections in 1962 and 1963.

[84] Rabbi Monson of Toronto, a friend of my wife's family, was a strong supporter of Diefenbaker. On learning of Diefenbaker's visit to Russia, he

equally lonely and vigourous support of Israel. All these things Roy drummed into my noggin' taken as I was and am taken with the Liberal Party. But all this came after Mr. Diefenbaker was no longer Prime Minister and I came to spend time with him after being carefully briefed by Roy.

One of my first acts on the national political scene in support of the Liberal cause was to provide research and support for Keith Davey's imaginative idea the 'Truth Squad', spearheaded by Judy LaMarsh, a tough rowdy opinionated federal politician who would travel on the campaign trail in 1963 following Mr. Diefenbaker and give a press conference after Mr. Diefenbaker's campaign speeches and to 'tell the truth' to correct the Diefenbaker record. Great idea. The execution less than satisfactory; but perceptions of Mr. Diefenbaker as a fabricator and exaggerator were established. His devout supporters defended him against these attacks, but it provided fodder for his Bay Street cabinet appointees who thought they could wrest power from him. Keith's other idea to illustrate the devaluation of the dollar and Diefenbaker which he called the 'Diefenbucks' or the 'Diefendollar'. The public understood this easily – Keith would argue. Diefenbaker had been forced to peg the dollar at 92.2 cents to gain World Bank support when Canadian reserves were under attack.

Tories did what the Tories did best – divide and attack their own. How much more superior a political party were we, I believed. Liberals believed in 'unity' and 'loyalty to the leader'. I believed all the Davey crafted messages about the 'goodness' of Mr. Pearson and the propaganda about the 'blackheart' of Mr. Diefenbaker.

---

turned up in Ottawa and asked him to deliver several heavy suitcases of Hebrew prayer books to the large Moscow synagogue. To the surprise of the local Jewish Moscovites, Diefenbaker dropped off the suitcases, filled with prayer books, to the startled Moscow rabbi.

I also learned early that the most effective political tactic in the Liberal toolkit was to frame and demonize the Tory leader. Of course, the Tories helped as they sometimes ignited the demonization of their unpredictable leader Mr. Diefenbaker themselves.

When I started to read history more carefully, my ingrained attitudes changed about both. Mr. Pearson's strengths were more grandiose than I thought, and Mr. Diefenbaker's flaws were not as deep as I had believed. But these changes and attitude came later as I reread history and my mind gained a different perspective of both. I learned to admire both Diefenbaker and Pearson for their acts of undisputed leadership and dedication to principles, their personal probity, and felt less animated by their apparent weaknesses. This became my first self-imposed political lesson. Facts first. Condemnation later in light of the facts. The closer to other political leaders I came, the more I came to respect their character, dedication, and accomplishments. Both Pearson and Diefenbaker left politics and public life economically diminished, without personal gain from public service or seeking gain from their former office when they left public office.

Diefenbaker like the lonely northern star, blazed a trail that others followed. He was an original!

Diefenbaker left a lasting legacy of accomplishments. He woke up the Conservative Party and broadened its tent to include the working-classes, the 'blue' collar workers and moved it in a progressive direction, modernizing the Progressive Conservative Party. He introduced the first Bill of Rights. He commenced concrete steps towards repatriation of the Constitution by the Fulton Formula and a Royal Commission. He opened trade with China by its first wheat sale. He was a staunch supporter of Israel.[85]

[85] Diefenbaker was without religious bias. No doubt he was a man of deep faith. He was a practicing Baptist though he occasionally had a glass of

He was a strong supporter of the Russian dissident movement. He started the early steps to Medicare. He opened the Cabinet to its first ethnic ministers, and his caucus to diverse Members of Parliament (Asian and eastern European). He intensified close relations with Aboriginal leaders. He stood against American hegemony over Canada or elsewhere. He and his Cabinet sought out and enlisted bright young talented men to politics like Ray Faibish, Michael Pitfield, Marc Lalonde, Joe Clark, and Brian Mulroney and other ambitious talented young men.

In the start of the 1958 campaign, Diefenbaker was anxious to pour substance into his 'vision' for Canada's north. Diefenbaker wanted to broaden Sir John A. McDonald's vision of the west to include the north in his campaign messages. His campaign team turned to the likes of Roy Faibish and Don Johnson to carve out distinct new policy ideas and plans to match his own instincts to unleash the untapped natural resources of oil and minerals hidden beneath the tundra and along the arctic coastline. Diefenbaker, because of the disdain J.F. Kennedy had for him, fanned the flames of anti-Americanism and the still sputtering the Canadian psyche. Diefenbaker decried of American interference in the 1962 election surreptitiously supporting Pearson because of the Bomarc missile testing issue that Diefenbaker refused. Diefenbaker openly challenged American hegemony and, in the process, became a kindred spirit with Charles de Gaulle.[86]

---

wine. He developed deep loyal roots in Jewish circles, first in the west and later across Canada. He was a staunch defender of Israel and a vocal supporter of the Russian dissident movement and especially the Jewish leaders in Russia who led in that remarkable movement.

[86] Charles de Gaulle and John Diefenbaker had a little-known excellent relationship. Both challenged American hegemony in foreign affairs. Read De Gaulle's second volume of his memoirs, *Charles de Gaulle Memoirs of Hope: Renewal and Endeavor* (Simon and Schuster, 1971, pages 238-242)

While Sir John A. MacDonald spoke of Canada from East to West, Diefenbaker added the North. How? By building roads to these resources, improving the northern sea routes and adding self-government to the Yukon and the Northwest Territories, fiefdoms of the Federal government.

'Canada and the North', Diefenbaker repeated, sketching in his 'vision' to little known expansive outer boundaries of Canada. Canadians trained to look east and west now lifted their eyes to the unknown north. While investment increased and feeble starts were made and the vision faltered, the vision remains intact today, if undeveloped.

The northern promise remains unfulfilled. This we know. Billions of oil reserves and minerals lie untapped in the north, especially along the northern arctic coastline in Ontario (the Ring of Fire) and Quebec (Quebec Nord) where massive mineral resources have been detected but lie buried, waiting for a new political will to excavate and monetarize Canada's vast hidden storehouses of richness.

While Diefenbaker left his Party divided, he left a strong cohort of followers to continue his work more than two decades later. Joe Clark took down Pierre Trudeau and led the Progressive Conservatives back to victory. Mulroney picked up the Progressive Conservative Party mantle. Harper, also influenced to some degree by Diefenbaker's western takeover of the federal government, brick-by-brick, rebuilt a new Conservative Party in his mold, restoring pride in Canada by increasing respect for the military, veterans, and patriotism. Harper recognized the sorry relationship with Aboriginals and attempted to recognize their leadership and broader rights, a task still in progress. Diefenbaker

---

to gain a clear insight into DeGaulle's and Diefenbaker's shared thoughts about this issue usually overlooked by most historians.

relished being named honourary 'Indian Chief' and wore his Aboriginal feathered headdress with obvious joy. Diefenbaker's travails were never far from the minds of his successors and unity of party became an architectonic of Conservative success by party leaders who inherited his mantle.

For one fleeting moment, "*O Canada*" became the cry of Canadians from coast to coast-to-coast – the 'True North' that still lies hidden, beating in the hearts of all Canadians, waiting for discovery.

John Diefenbaker - Maiden Speech

748 COMMONS

Defence of Canada Regulations

Mr. J. G. DIEFENBAKER (Lake Centre): As a new member, rising to speak here for the first time in debate, I cannot but admit how impressed I was by the concluding words of the Minister of Justice (Mr. Lapointe). He pointed out that in this house, as throughout the country, forbearance should be shown, that we should recognize the fact that each of us is individually trying to contribute something irrespective of any divisions that there may be among us. I think that was a proper stand to take and with it I entirely agree, as do all other members of this house. Each of us is trying to contribute something; and from this side of the house, in what we have to say or in the criticisms we have to make, I ask the government to recognize the fact that we too are trying to do what we can to further and not, as was suggested this afternoon, to sabotage the war effort. Our attitude in this time of national danger is the attitude that was exemplified this afternoon when all the members of this house stood up in one of the most inspiring scenes that I have ever witnessed, showing the solidarity of this country.

I would not have risen on this occasion were it not for the fact that I have been placed upon the committee of the house which is charged with the consideration of the defence of Canada regulations. Since the outbreak of war various orders in council have been passed dealing with such matters as the treatment of aliens, the safeguarding of information and the prevention of sabotage. As I understand it, the committee will be charged with two duties. It will consider whether or not the regulations require to be amended, and what alterations must be made by reason of changing conditions; and with that will be coupled a consideration of the question whether or not those regulations which are to-day in effect have been properly enforced.

I realize that, as the Prime Minister (Mr. Mackenzie King) said the other day, there has been a considerable change in public opinion since the outbreak of war, particularly in relation to the defence of Canada regulations. At the beginning there were some, and there are some to-day, who challenge these regulations on the ground that they abrogate the rights of free men. In particular there is the criticism that they take away the almost inalienable rights of British subjects, the rights of habeas corpus and certiorari, and are thus the negation of democracy. My answer to that is that national safety is of paramount importance over private rights. These rights have not been lost; they are held in abeyance until victory is attained.

[Mr. E. Lapointe.]

Their abrogation is required in the interest of the safety of the state. These rights will return to the people of this dominion when victory is won. To those who criticize the defence of Canada regulations as taking away the liberty of the subject, I say, better have the rights remain in abeyance than lose them altogether if Hitler should win.

To-day public opinion is aroused, and as the Minister of Justice has said, reasons are urged why certain people should be proceeded against. We can understand why public opinion is aroused. In recent days Canada has been invaded, as directly as though the enemy were on our own shores, by the capture of that portion of France upon which rests the Vimy memorial, soil which was deeded to the Dominion of Canada. We know what defeat would mean. In the ledger of nazism there is no credit side; there is nothing but debits, pagan brutality, the destruction of those things that are nearest and dearest to us, our liberties entirely taken from us. For that reason people are aroused.

The experience of other countries has shown the result of the subversive activities of nazi sympathizers; in Austria, Norway, in Holland and Belgium, the same course is pursued—conquest following a ghastly programme of the honeycombing of the national fabric by treasonable propaganda from within. To-day the general feeling is that subversive activities in this dominion, whether they be nazi or communist or fascist, must be curbed if not altogether extirpated. The people of Canada feel that the trade of treachery and of traitors, the undermining of the country from within, must be made dangerous for those who engage in it. Yesterday afternoon the hon. member for Parry Sound (Mr. Slaght) made the suggestion that in certain cases the death penalty should be enforced, in particular in the matter of subversive activities leading to sabotage. In Great Britain they have had to adopt such a penalty. For certain classes of people it becomes necessary in order to deter them from acts of sabotage. To-day we realize that eternal vigilance is the price of public safety. The administration of such an act as the defence of Canada regulations, as was so eloquently pointed out by the Minister of Justice, must be characterized by sound judgment and understanding. There must be prosecution; there shall not be persecution, the minister said. To-day in the shadow of the passing of a great Canadian, the late Hon. Norman Rogers, the message that his sealed lips never delivered is one which in my opinion epitomizes in true measure the principle for the enforcement of war-time measures. These words are from the report of the speech he was to have delivered:

"It has been suggested the present emergency requires the internment of all naturalized Canadians of enemy alien origin." "We shall never, I believe, subscribe to that policy of total proscription.". . .

He said action had already been taken against certain Canadians, fortunately few in number, who would set themselves up as leaders of fascist or communist groups and would cast aside forever all the essentials of democratic freedom.

"So far as it lies within us they (who come to these shores) should receive what they expected to secure. But they must not cross the line that divides loyalty from treason in this country. If they do they forfeit the rights they have acquired and will be dealt with accordingly."

Some reference was made the other day to the fact that the 1931 census showed that there were in Canada 473,544 people of German origin. In that connection it is interesting to note that according to the census of sixty years ago there were 202,000. But the census does not tell the whole story. The manner in which the census in Canada is taken prevents the creation of an unhyphenated Canadian nation. There is no question of the loyalty of those of German stock who were United Empire Loyalists, of those who came over in the forties, fifties, sixties. There is no question as to the loyalty of others, except the few who are to-day disturbing our unity and whose activities must be curbed. Other than those, the people recorded in the census as German are loyal to this country and intend to contribute to it of their best. My criticism of the census is that, regardless of the number of generations that have elapsed or the admixtures of nationality that have taken place during forty, fifty, seventy-five or one hundred and twenty-five years, so long as persons must register under the nationality of their paternal ancestor, there will never be that Canadianism which we wish to establish.

Who was not inspired the other day by the address of Mayor LaGuardia of New York? When he spoke he did not speak as an Italo-American, he spoke as a great American. One of the greatest proponents to-day of the allied cause in North America is the former commander of the United States troops in the last war, General Pershing, who is of German origin; but is no German-American, he is an American. It is said that the census regulations are based on ethnological grounds. Let us register our Canadians as Canadians, and have another paragraph dealing with racial origin, and let us build up in this country an unhyphenated Canadianism that is dominant, proud and strong. There are those who are disloyal; and in the interests of the majority of loyal citizens, of various national strains, those who are treasonable must be shown their place, so that those who are loyal and patriotic shall not be denied the fruits of their loyalty.

Some say: "What are you going to do with the naturalized? Are they to be proceeded against?" They are in a position different from that of those who were born here as Canadians. Sir, naturalization was never intended to be a badge of immunity from treason. A naturalization certificate is an admission that the state recognizes that the person who has been accepted for membership in that proud heritage of British citizenship is a citizen whose loyalty is unquestionable. Naturalization is predicated upon the assumption and the acceptance, at face value, of the loyalty of the person affected, as pledged in his oath of allegiance. If those who are naturalized prove recreant to the loyalty to which they swore, then naturalization or a certificate of that kind should be no badge of immunity. Naturalization is a privilege, not a protection against sedition.

What about the provinces of Saskatchewan and Manitoba? The Minister of Justice has said that there has been considerable criticism. While I am not going to place them on *Hansard*, I have before me a number of press clippings from Saskatchewan and Manitoba calling upon the government to do something in respect of the peculiar circumstances there prevailing. As a matter of fact, so difficult has the situation become in some parts of Saskatchewan that recently representatives of the veterans met with the provincial government and decided to form what is known as the Saskatchewan veterans civil security corps. It is to be composed of from 8,000 to 10,000 veterans, as security against anti-British and subversive activities in Saskatchewan.

The Minister of Justice has said that at no time has there been political interference in respect of orders which allow release from internment. I believe him when he makes that statement, because I cannot conceive of any occupant of the position he at present holds, permitting in any way in a time of national need political considerations to take precedence over national safety. But I shall set out one or two reasons why in Saskatchewan the suggestion has arisen that there has been political influence.

First, fifty per cent of those released from internment camps in Saskatchewan were released between January 25 and March 26, 1940. Second, there can be no suggestion, and there is no suggestion, that the Royal Canadian Mounted Police would in any way brook political interference. The Minister of Justice has stated that they investigate with care, that they compile the information so obtained, and that in the last few days as a result of the acquisition of information over a long period of time they have been able to move forward with dispatch and place in custody various persons of Italian birth or ancestry. He has pointed out that they have the information and that they work; they do not talk.

That being so the Royal Canadian Mounted Police must have had some reason when it acted as it did in September last in taking into custody throughout western Canada numbers of men who were known to be nazi sympathizers or workers. There was no oppression in their attitude, because only three hundred out of sixteen thousand alien enemies in Canada were taken into custody. The minister has pointed out that Schneider, who was released some time ago, has been reinterned. That is all to the good.

The suggestion I humbly offer to the minister is that so long as section 26, subsection 7, permits the Minister of Justice to order the release of any enemy alien from arrest, detention or internment, there will always be statements to the effect that there has been political interference, if the political allegiance of the man released is known, regardless of the fact that the suggestions are foundationless.

The suggestion has been made that instead of the minister accepting this power, or having it placed upon his shoulders, a tribunal should be set up in the constituency or judicial district where an internment takes place, and that such tribunal should be responsible. Such tribunal might consist of a district or county court judge, as the case may be. In such circumstances judicial wisdom would be brought to bear upon the decision as to whether or not a person or persons should be released, and the evidence taken be complemented by the knowledge of local conditions of the judge resident within the local judicial district.

The Minister of Justice has said that the cases he mentioned were the only ones regarding which there has been criticism. I am not going to refer to other cases this afternoon. I would point out, however, that we have gained much benefit from the information given by the minister this afternoon. The public want to know. They want to know why those men are released. The minister has given the assurance that they were released under circumstances which could not be considered political.

There is always the suggestion of partisanship. However that may all be removed by the means I have suggested, or by the appointment of a superior court judge, as the case may be. In this way we would bring to the people a feeling of security which until recently they have not possessed. There are those who may say that at a time like this, representing as I do a constituency in Saskatchewan, the stand I take is an unpopular one. As a representative from that province I feel at this time that party political expediency must pale into insignificance before public safety.

This speech I have to make in order to point out that in Saskatchewan there is an ever rising body of opinion to the effect that there are men who would undermine our institutions but who are free. It is felt the result will be that unless authorization is given for the creation of a home defence corps—and some suggestion was made to-day by the Minister of National Defence for Air (Mr. Power) that such a corps was being formed—there will arise in various parts of Saskatchewan and throughout western Canada generally committees or, if you will, vigilantes who will take the law into their own hands.

I have a few suggestions to make in addition to the one that the minister should be relieved of his responsibility under section 26 of the regulations. I believe there should be a national registration. This would give the government an opportunity of finding those who are willing to serve at this time. The women gave the lead last September and October when they had a national registration, but so far their services have not been utilized. There are men all over the dominion who want to serve. All they need is the opportunity, but that opportunity can come only from leadership. Leadership can be given only when the government is fully aware of those who are prepared to serve. Moreover, such a registration, if properly carried out, would bring to light the names of many who are to-day in Canada without having complied with the immigration regulations and who are in position to carry on subversive activities.

The necessity for establishing local defence corps throughout the dominion has been pointed out already. In this connection I should like to refer to an editorial which appeared in the Winnipeg *Free Press* of June 6. That paper deals with this problem in these words:

> Why is Ottawa showing such reluctance in authorizing the formation of the volunteer defence unit here? The public wants it.

And further down:

> Presumably the dominion government believes that the potential internal dangers to the state are being adequately looked after by the presence in Canada of our active armed forces, by the militia regiments, by the newly formed home guard and by the Royal Canadian Mounted Police. It may be recalled to Mr. King and

[Mr. Diefenbaker.]

his colleagues, however, that they have just been found guilty by public opinion of having been up to now far too complacent about their war plans. The scope of their effort, in the light of present emergencies, has been inadequate. They are therefore hardly in a position to announce that they are right, and the public wrong, about the formation of this additional auxiliary force. The public quite properly can reply: "You were wrong in the other matter. How do we know you are right about this?"

The editorial then goes on to point out the necessity of the government authorizing the formation of such corps. The acting Minister of National Defence (Mr. Power) said to-day that it was impossible to allow these corps to be organized outside government supervision. He stated that in any event it would not be possible to supply them with arms and ammunition. To-day in Saskatchewan General Ross is organizing such a corps. Although such an organization is not authorized by the government, the need therefor is felt in Saskatchewan because there is in some sections a strong current of anti-British feeling.

How can we expect not to have anti-British feeling when we permit periodicals to enter Canada which attempt to destroy the morale of our people? Why should such anti-British publications as the *Saturday Evening Post* and the Chicago *Tribune* be allowed to enter the country? What is the use of having a department of information to furnish dependable information to the people if such information is neutralized, if not completely destroyed, by malicious articles appearing in these particular papers? If I understand the defence of Canada regulations, the only provision for prosecution in such a case is that provided by section 15. Under this section prosecution can be carried out only when a newspaper or periodical is published in Canada.

Parliament to-day realizes as never before that we have but one duty—to provide the maximum war effort to win this war. This war is being waged on two fronts—the battle front and the home front. The defence of Canada regulations were designed to ensure the solidarity of the Canadian people and to prevent malicious disaffection from destroying the continuity of our war effort or interfering with the production and transportation of munitions, materials, and food for our armies here and overseas. The safeguarding of our interests overseas as a nation, of our homes, of our right to live, is in the hands of our gallant boys. They will not fail us. The safeguarding of our nation from destructive and subversive influences that would nullify their sacrifices is in the hands of this parliament. We must not fail them.

Mr. T. C. DOUGLAS (Weyburn): Mr. Speaker, it was not my intention to take part in this debate. However, some remarks that have been made during the course of the debate prompt me to rise for just a few moments in order to make one or two observations. The hon. member for Rosetown-Biggar (Mr. Coldwell) outlined quite adequately the stand of this group with reference to this motion of the Prime Minister (Mr. Mackenzie King). I should like to touch upon four points and emphasize them quite briefly. First, we realize that under present circumstances there is a need to give the government extraordinary powers. We are engaged in a war carried on by a new technique. This is not only a war of nations; it is a war of ideologies. The people who believe in these ideologies have no particular mark upon their foreheads. They have carried on a programme of peaceful penetration in many nations of the world. They have undermined the states that they sought to conquer. In order to meet this threat the democracies have had to speed up and alter their method of dealing with it. With that in mind, we realize, as must all people who believe in democracy, the need of giving to the executive extraordinary powers.

The Minister of Justice (Mr. Lapointe) has claimed that there are two points of view in connection with these regulations. The one is that the regulations were too severe; the other, that they were not severe enough. I doubt if that is a fair appraisal of the situation. I think the real position is that there is one group of people who feel that the regulations are not lacking in severity so much as that they have not been enforced with sufficient aggression. I cannot say whether that is well founded, but the fact remains that there is that feeling. It is quite understandable. For instance, in western Canada we have had for a number of years an organization known as the deutscher bund. Many of the men who joined this organization did so out of bravado, while others were attracted by the cultural association. Many had no knowledge of the unscrupulous intent of the organization and they left when they became aware of its real purpose. The fact remains that in western Canada this organization was in existence in many German-Canadian communities and has aroused considerable concern. As the hon. member for Lake Centre (Mr. Diefenbaker) has suggested, this is quite understandable.

The people are perturbed. They feel, not that these regulations should be made more severe, but that they should be enforced and that proper precautions should be taken. We

Lester B. Pearson

Lester Bowles Pearson – The Most Underrated Leader

(14th)

Date Elected to Parliament:	October 25, 1948
Date of Maiden Speech:	February 4, 1949
Date Sworn In:	April 22, 1963
Date Left Office:	April 19, 1968

Lester Bowles Pearson had an unlikely name and was an unlikely leader. His was more like a friendly, avuncular professor or football coach which he was at University of Toronto when he lectured in History there early in his career. He had interrupted his studies at the University of Toronto to join the service overseas in World War I.[87] His nickname 'Mike' was much preferred by him. He always remained Mr. Pearson to his closest advisers.

Physically compact, the size of a middle-weight boxer, with a wisp of hair from a receding hairline, he owned a broad toothy smile, and a discernable lisp. An aura of likeability surrounded him. Still, there was an elusive sense that his mind was always

[87] Pearson was an officer in the Medical Service in England and then switched to become a pilot officer in the Air Force. Hard luck pursued him. His first plane solo crashed, and he was injured. Then in a fluke, he was hit by a bus in London. As an invalid, he was discharged from active service and returned to Canada to resume his university studies.

somewhere else, distracted. As a former athlete, with a sturdy frame, he was a handsome man who carried himself along in a slight rolling gait. Early in his career, he became a skilled, nimble baseball player reaching semi-pro status.[88] He loved baseball and followed the game throughout his life and especially during his political career which gave him the opportunity to change gears and enjoy his favourite past time. In addition, he was an excellent hockey player who played hockey at Oxford as a student. Lacrosse was also one of his skilled team sports.

While Pearson didn't particularly brief well orally, he had a capacious memory for printed material like the experienced bureaucrat he was. He was adept at reading through his voluminous briefing papers and quickly grasping and analyzing the key points. An insatiable worker at every stage of his public service career from lowly public servant, to senior mandarin, to diplomat, to Minister of External Affairs to Prime Minister, he preferred to prepare his own speeches even after he became Prime Minister. His memoirs were models of clarity laced with heavy doses of subtle wit and hubris. Ambitious, he moved up the ladder of success, one job at a time, working hard and effectively at every step. He had no early political goal or plan like Diefenbaker who once told Pearson he wanted to be Prime Minister from the time he was a youth. Mr. Pearson was imbued with the Protestant work ethic. Unlike most leaders, Pearson had not a hint of narcissism about him. Always self-depreciating, he was witty about his gaffes, flubs, and flaws. He never intentionally hurt another person's feelings. Mr. Pearson just wanted to excel at each job he chose or was called on to do and to enjoy each moment of contribution to public service, his chosen career.

[88] Pearson played semi-professional baseball for a time with the Guelph Maple Leafs of the Intercounty Baseball League in Ontario.

With a limitless reservoir of personal charm and outward vulnerability and modesty, Pearson quickly gained friends and admirers at every stage of his illustrious career fueled by his infectious humour and twinkle in his eyes. A pleasant man who had a deep reservoir of genuine warmth and curiosity. His apparent vulnerability made his friends and followers protective. Both in private and public settings, Pearson was always self-depreciating. Slow to anger, he could privately erupt when misled or when a foolish mistake was made. He didn't suffer fools lightly. Nonetheless, his staff worshipped him. Mary McDonald, his vivacious diminutive executive assistant, was enthralled by him and served as his tenacious chief protector and gatekeeper. Mary with short cut blonde hair had a ready dazzling smile that belied her tough actions to protect, defend, and promote Mr. Pearson at every step.

Seeming to shun power, Pearson owned an insatiable but disguised ambition under his easy, gay amiability. Though an astute judge of character, he was often misled. He could turn to steel when necessary, but always reluctantly. Modest in demeanor, he came across as a hesitant, if reluctant leader. Beneath that benign surface lurked a shrewd ambitious politician. Mr. Pearson always preferred to think of himself as a public servant, a public steward of the common good in the Protestant tradition. Pearson was a brilliant and graceful diplomat, his first love, in the understated British manner. A perfect gentleman, easy going, well-mannered, humourous in private and public, he didn't change persona. He seemed false and uncomfortable when he feigned passion on the public stage. It was just not in his make-up. Pearson recognized acting on the public stage may be necessary but he did so reluctantly. His brilliant diplomacy could connect the dots into patterns not seen by others as he moved to accomplish his goals and ultimately, political legacy – some of which remains unnoticed by history.[89,90]

---

89 As a diplomat, he was a key architect of the UN. Then, disappointed with UN gridlock, he turned his attention and reliance on the construction of NATO – an alliance of democracies. He added section 5 of the NATO Charter to insert 'economic cooperation'. He believed that a coalition of democracies was more effective for world peace than the UN, which he never gave up trying to improve. He was a key architect of the Colombo Plan to organize aid to the underdeveloped nations. Both initiatives were undertaken despite reluctance by King and St. Laurent. This initiative laid the foundation of Canada's outreach to the 'Third World' and was part of Pearson's belief in spreading a secular social 'gospel' as a moral imperative underlying Canada's foreign policy.

90 Little known, or remembered, is Mr. Pearson's personal involvement and leadership in the creation of the State of Israel and later, its survival when Israel was almost annihilated by the Arab armies of Egypt, Syria, Iraq, and Jordan. There were seven well-equipped armies in all that invaded and outnumbered Israel on all sides in military forces and armaments on the land and in the air. In 1947, Mr. Pearson had chaired, despite Prime Minister King's reluctance, the UN Committee (UNCOP) subcommittee that recommended the creation of the State of Israel. Mr. Pearson felt a deep connection to the Jews in Holy Land based on his Sunday school training; some suggest. He was a key advocate and architect of the UN Palestine Partition. In 1948, Israel was about to be eliminated by Egypt whose forces were on the march reached just seven miles south of Tel Aviv, while the Jordanians with their British trained and equipped Legion had swarmed across the Jordan and occupied most of Jerusalem and the West Bank, while the well-equipped Syrians and the Iraqi forces raced across and occupied strategic territory on Israel's northern border. Israel's defence forces, much smaller and less equipped than the opposing Arab forces, had their tiny arsenal depleted. Again Mr. Pearson came to Israel's rescue and engineered with a Canadian resolution adopted at the UN in 1948 a truce armistice allowing Israel to catch its breath, and build quickly an air force which it smuggled in from Czechoslovakia and surplus fighters and bombers from U.S.A. despite the U.S.A. embargo which allowed the tiny state to replenish its forces with arms and armaments which were depleted. U.S.A. via General Marshall's dire advice, never a friend of Israel, as Secretary of State convinced President Truman to place an embargo on

His personal brand of diplomacy as Minister of External Affairs, his first elected position, was evident in his groundbreaking leadership during the Suez Crisis in 1956. Before that, his leadership in 1950 on the Korea War over the opposition of King gave birth to the phrase '*Pearsonean Diplomacy*'. His creative ideas and actions during the Suez Crisis led to the Nobel Prize for Peace, a first for a Canadian. Pearson originated the idea of UN peacekeepers that still lies at the core of Canada's self-image. This idea continues to reverberate and embellish Canada's international reputation.

Pearson's life-long colleagues in the public service respected, envied, and trusted him. He maintained a large network of old friends and colleagues outside his political circle by contact

---

military arms to the Middle East that especially effected Israel. It was Mr. Pearson's ideas, action, and leadership at the UN that made it possible for Israel to survive and fight another day. After the Suez Affair in 1956, again it was Mr. Pearson who rebuffed Dag Hammarskjöld's plan to return to the status quo ante after the Suez Affair and insisted on the expansion of UN peacekeepers to enforce the truce and keep the peace. In 1956 when Israel finally convinced Dulles to send modern jets to modernize its air force, Dulles's hands were tied by the Eisenhower administration. Dulles agreed with Mr. Pearson that the UN should take a new direction. Dulles told Pearson to send Sky Hawk jets to Israel that were part of U.S. allotment to Canada which Mr. Pearson did as asked and this undertaking was essential to Israel's military survival, to gain air supremacy. When Chaim Weizmann, a founder of Zionism and Israel's first President died, Pearson convened a special session of UN Assembly despite Arab objections and led with his own tribute. It was Abba Eban who extolled Mr. Pearson's role in the affairs of Israel. In his biography *Personal Witness*, Abba Eban, Israel's first ambassador to the UN who came to rely on Mr. Pearson, wrote this about Mr. Pearson – "*His temperament and skills enabled him to maintain aa sense of proportion in all things and to avoid being swept away by the wonder of his own accession to political power.*"

Pearson, in words and action, demonstrated his innate sense of fairness and justice towards Israel and his sense of history as a reverent student of the Bible.

and hand-written letters. His political bosses like King and St. Laurent both shrewd judges of character in politics geared him for leadership. Pearson admitted he was most comfortable with his work with the Conservative Prime Minister Mr. Bennett, and of course, Mr. St. Laurent who he deeply admired and respected. Not so with Mr. King who puzzled him. Pearson's policies of engagement at the UN, NATO and especially with Israel irritated King who believed Canada should not be committed to solving international problems or international organizations as King was with the League of Nations in the '30s when he instructed the Canadian representative not to support action against Italy when Mussolini had invaded Ethiopia or become embroiled in overseas disputes or even mediate violent outbreaks. King's action helped weaken the League of Nations and Pearson saw this as a perilous course of action. King was a keen supporter of appeasement and disengagement from European conflicts which Pearson was not though he had suffered serving in World War I.[91]

At the outset of his public service from the late '20s to the mid '30s, Pearson undertook what seemed like a stream of endless thankless jobs. Each work experience was an invisible step up the ladder of power. He served as Secretary to a Royal Commission on Price Spreads in the '30s. The Commission had run out of time and he was asked by Prime Minister Bennett to complete the report quickly. As Secretary, he collated the evidence from scattered threads and disparate testimony from all entrenched interests and all regions and wove them all together into a remarkable report. To read that report and its recommendations

---

[91] Mr. Pearson was the second Prime Minister in the modern era to serve on active military duty. Mr. Diefenbaker volunteered in World War I, saw active service, was invalided, and returned to Canada. Pierre Trudeau was conscripted in the military in World War II but never saw active duty overseas.

today, almost 80 years later, attests to the remarkable relevance of his work then and now – a memorable feat for its time. He recommended consumer protection mechanisms that took 30 years to be legislated as Prime Minister when his government established the first Department of Consumer and Corporate Affairs in 1966 despite the stiff opposition within the bureaucracy.

Pearson had, on reflection, one of the most remarkable record of personal accomplishments and understated career achievements of any Prime Minister of Canada in history. From semipro baseball to war veteran to University lecturer in history to college football and hockey coach to entry level bureaucrat to senior mandarin to junior then senior diplomat as High Commissioner in England to Minister of External Affairs to Leader of the Opposition to Prime Minister to respected world leader. Yet, Mr. Pearson never gained a majority government in Parliament and served just five short years as Prime Minister. He always laboured under the knife of a minority government. When he lost the confidence of the House on a mishap while he was on vacation, Pearson returned, and resigned to make way for a new leader, he continued to work assiduously to repair the damage and gained a new vote to erase the 'confidence' measure. Mr. Pearson respected the unwritten laws of Parliament.

His personal accomplishments and legislative legacy burn brighter compared to any other modern Prime Ministers. There was no need in his case for excessive narcissist embellishment – an ingrained habit of some modern leaders. Pearson would have been appalled at the present self-aggrandizement amongst leading politicians. He would have found it distasteful and so unCanadian.[92]

---

[92] His own autobiography (two volumes and a third completed with his notes after his death) was understated, factual, and gave excess credit to his Cabinet, his advisors and leading bureaucrats. He gained easy comfortable

Pearson hid a gourmet's taste for fine wine and good food. He relished oysters and champagne for lunch in his Parliamentary office before Question Period. Yet, he could gobble down hotdogs at a ballgame with the gusto of a true baseball fan. His suits were tailored in Saville Row. Reluctantly gave up his preferred jaunty bow ties from pleas by his wannabee images makers. As a devout hockey and baseball follower, he had a capacious knowledge of players and statistics in both sports.

Pearson's wife Maryon was his partner – an elegant and urban well-travelled acerbic critic. She enjoyed a stiff martini or two. He valued her judgement, her acid wit, and quick mind. She too shared his career ambition and galvanized him to rise from an entry level civil servant to political leadership. She was with him every watchful step of the way. She disliked politics and was happy as a wife of a senior bureaucrat and an accomplished hostess in diplomatic circles. But she went along with his political ambition and he trusted her judgement.

'Mike' Pearson, outwardly a modest man, hid his fierce competitive spirit and ambition under a genial cover of good manners and conviviality much like his father and grandfather, both admired Methodist ministers engaged in the lives of their Ontario small town parishes like Aurora and later Hamilton. Pearson's book, *The Four Faces of Peace and The International Outlook*, published in 1964 after he became Prime Minister is a telling exposition of his belief structure, and his vision that

---

rapport with other foreign leaders. Only Lyndon Johnson was viscerally upset when Pearson spoke out boldly against the Vietnam War. Pearson was a gifted writer, essayist, and speech writer. He wrote two books before his memoirs written after his retirement one in 1959 and 1964 – one as a leader of the opposition and the other as Prime Minister. In 1959, *Diplomacy in the Nuclear Age* influenced John F. Kennedy. *Four Faces of Peace* published in 1964 is a model of sustained erudition and insight.

emanated from his deep religious Protestant background and roots in Ontario. Pearson had a deep knowledge of the Bible and although not a churchgoer, could quote freely from it.

Fiercely competitive as an athlete in football, lacrosse, hockey, and baseball – these interests continued as lifelong passions. He was a fierce, attentive sports fan. As Prime Minister, he would interrupt his most important meetings to watch baseball and tune in the radio for a play-by-play.[93] An energetic competitive tennis player, he played vigorously well past middle age. His pal, frequent tennis partner and friendly adversary was the elegant Roland Michener, a Conservative and Commons Speaker who he met at Oxford. Studied in the scriptures, he wore his religiosity lightly, but was proud of his pastoral roots.[94] Educated in Ontario public schools, then University of Toronto, he volunteered in World War I first for the medical corps, finally the air corps – a most dangerous service area, when he suffered an emotional set back. Obviously scarred by the horrors of that war, his experience marked him for life and left a dark space that he never disclosed.

After University of Toronto, he went to study history at Oxford on a Massey Scholarship after his service in World War I and returned to teach as a lecturer in history at University of

---

[93] When he visited with John Kennedy, who was briefed on Pearson's interest in baseball, Kennedy invited Dave Powers, Kennedy's Irish political pal from Boston, to test Pearson's knowledge of baseball statistics. "*What pitcher pitched a no-hitter but didn't win the game?*" asked Powers. Pearson astounded both Kennedy and Powers when he mentioned the game, the pitcher and the name of the relief pitcher who finished the game! Later, Pearson modestly admitted he remembered the relief pitcher's name, Mackenzie, because the pitcher was Canadian.

[94] My old friend, David Smith, former Cabinet Minister and Senator repeatedly regaled me with his conversations with Mr. Pearson who never failed to mention that David and he shared similar roots as sons and grandsons of Protestant ministers.

Toronto. He always considered himself a historian and read widely. An opportunity to enter the federal public service beckoned in the mid '20s where some sons of the manse like him had landed jobs. He joined the nascent External Affairs Department created under the watchful eye of King who tapped O.D. Skelton, a professor from Queens, to head this new unit under King's direct control in the East Block. Many of the young men Skelton enlisted, like Pearson, came from pastors' roots, mostly Protestant. All Methodist ministers in Ontario (including Pearson's grandfather and father) were enthralled by the China missionary movement which practiced the 'social gospel' as an organizing engine to inculcate the young in China, especially in western China.

All his life, Pearson practiced the Protestant work ethic. Pearson was hard working, studious, and fiercely competitive especially in tennis. He could still pitch a baseball or throw a football or play a robust round of tennis well into middle age. Following the English style of public servant who disguised their ambitions, he had his sights clearly set to reach the top of his peers in diplomacy who were equally competitive, ambitious highly educated and well-travelled. Pearson owned a gifted practiced pen, who could easily define his objectives and his world view in a wide range of speeches and essays that he himself had written and delivered. He kept a well-written diary to record his public and private meetings with public figures and that helped him sort out his thoughts. Published excerpts of his diary in his memoirs are examples of clarity and modesty. He was adept at witty concise memos as a bureaucrat and later as a diplomat.[95] Everybody who encountered him, liked 'Mike'!

[95] Pearson was a gifted letter writer. His lengthy letters to President Johnson during the Vietnam War were models of clarity, sensitivity, and modesty.

Most Liberals loved him. While he could be tough minded, he was polished, down to earth and thoughtful in the English languid manner. He learned from his diplomatic stints in Britain. When he lost his bid to be senior bureaucrat in External Affairs to a friend and rival Norman Robertson, he dismissed rumours of his disappointment, which was real by announcing, graciously, at a dinner that he would be privileged to serve under Robertson, a younger man, which he did with vigor and without complaint.

Vulnerable and approachable, he was like a man whose true face was hidden in an outward mask of conviviality as he purposely disguised his true feelings to modify and mollify his listeners. He could build consensus in his diverse all talented Cabinet – perhaps the best in modern history. He was a great, patient listener in meetings. By all accounts, he was a superb Chairman of the Cabinet and at international meetings.[96] One could hear him think as he listened patiently. While a self-professed progressive, he was careful to ensure a consensus in Cabinet on issues when ideology and differences ran deep. He was cautious about economics as, admittedly, economics was not his strong suite and welcomed diverse prudent views

As a student of history and public servant, he was interested in government and political processes. When he became Leader of Opposition in 1957, he immersed himself in political memoirs and biographies. Most telling was his interest in Cabinets and

He kept careful diaries, especially his encounters with leaders like Kennedy, Johnson, McMillan, and DeGaulle. Leaders welcomed his views of other leaders.

96 By accounts, and especially as shown on film, Mr. Pearson was equally a superb Chairman in international forums alike the UN, its Committees, or the Commonwealth, who prepared carefully and always sought a consensus while having thought out in advance a clear-cut action plan and adjusting tactics to others' views.

Cabinet making that he studied from memoirs of English Prime Ministers. He was preparing himself for the office he knew might soon be within his reach.

Always ready to lavish credit to others, he always kept his eye on his strategic goals. One example is when I worked as John Turner's Chief of Staff in 1965-1966, each morning I assiduously read all the Cabinet documents delivered to Turner prior to a Cabinet meeting to alert Turner to issues of interest. It was an enlightening experience to read the complex and variety of issues facing the government all set out in concise and elegant memos with alternative actions concisely defined. Every government decision went through this rigorous process.

Pearson, experienced bureaucrat that he was, could easily plow through reams of documents. Yet, as Prime Minister, he did not brief well orally. If it was in writing, he could remember with precision.[97]

When Mr. Pearson chose to speak in Winnipeg to a Canadian Legion meeting, not exactly a friendly audience, and unveiled the new Canadian flag, I was surprised. The new Flag design that Pearson chose had not been run through Cabinet. Curious, I called up Don Peacock, an assistant to Mr. Pearson, and asked what happened. Peacock explained that Mr. Pearson was tired of endless wrangling about the flag and decided to choose the design and lead by ignoring further comments and delays. If he led, the Cabinet and caucus would fall in line and end the bickering which upset him when they did. Pearson did not enjoy confrontations. He went on to choose '*O Canada*' as the new Canadian national anthem.

---

97 Churchill suffered from the same problem. Clementine, his wife, advised an angry advisor, "*Put what you have to say in writing! He does not listen or does not hear as he is thinking of something else. But he will always consider a paper carefully and take in all its implications. He never forgets what he sees in writing.*"

When Turner was appointed as Registrar General of Canada to the Cabinet that included in the Ministry responsibility for Patents and Private Corporations, it was with Mr. Pearson's directive that Turner transform that small department into a modern Ministry of consumer affairs. Ralph Nader's consumerism was the rage at the time, and I was an acute student of this movement in the United States as was Turner. This, I felt, was Turner's opportunity to showcase his abilities. As Turner's Executive Assistant, Turner directed me to prepare the dossier and oversee the legislation. The first impediment was the Deputy Minister. We plotted and succeeded in sending him to an extended international conference in Europe with his wife who love all things European. Now we were clear to get the work done without senior departmental or bureaucratic interference. We had not counted on the stiff opposition from the Privy Council Office especially, the Clerk to the Cabinet who felt that since the federal government that had no power to deal with consumer prices or consumer issues except by the blunt instrument of the criminal code, and the federal criminal power and that consumer legislation would raise false expectations. Turner was rebuffed at Cabinet committee meetings. The senior bureaucrats preferred the Department title as Corporate Affairs.

I did my homework and discovered that when Mr. Pearson was Secretary to the Price Spreads Commission in the '30s, he had drafted a report that called for consumer protection and a consumer affairs ministry. I got a copy of the report and marked the passages where the consumer issues and recommendations were made and handed it to Turner before a crucial Cabinet committee meeting chaired by Mr. Pearson to decide the department's mandate and what its title would be – Corporate Affairs, Corporate and Consumer Affairs or Consumer and Corporate Affairs. Before the meeting, Turner handed Mr.

Pearson a marked copy of the old report. Pearson ruffled through the report as he chaired the meeting. When the time came to decide the name of the department, Pearson chose Consumer and Corporate Affairs. Mr. Pearson never forgot a written document.

Pearson attracted and managed the most talented diverse Cabinet in modern history. They represented the right and left of the Liberal Party. Gordon, MacEachen, Winters, Sauvé, Sharpe, Hellyer, Pelletier, Marchand, Trudeau, Turner, Chrétien, Green, Mackasey, Donnell, Pickersgill, Pepin, Hays, Favreau, Laing, McIlrath, Chevrier, Drury, LaMarsh[98] – just to name a few. There is a picture I was given by Turner of Pearson, Trudeau, Turner, and Chrétien which he signed to me as '*one tiger to another*' when all three were all appointed to Cabinet posts on the same day and all became Prime Ministers. Remarkable!

I observed firsthand one example of Maryon Pearson's fierce protectiveness of her husband. I was an advance man in the 1965 campaign. Keith Davey always flowing with campaign ideas decided to hold a rally in the Yorkdale Mall. We organizers did better than expected. When Pearson spoke on a small raised dais in a crowded open space in the middle of the mall, the overflowing crowd was jammed into the corridors pressed against the glass shop windows. The glass heaved visibly, and disaster was close at hand. The rally was quickly dispersed to the dismay of both Pearson and his wife who were alerted to the danger. The lead

[98] Judy LaMarsh was a blustering, opinionated lawyer and former military officer. She was tough, obstinate and difficult. However, Pearson would laugh at her outspoken views and charmed her, and she became an avid loyalist. I witnessed the Pearson charm offensive with Judy several times and he never failed to impress me with his talent for developing a consensus amongst his cohorts with such diverse ideologies and outsized egos.

organizers led by Gordon Edict – Keith Davey's buddy – was sternly advised never to come in the presence of Maryon again who would have chewed him out and scalped him alive. Luckily, I escaped the focus of her wrath.

Another example of Maryon's wrath was the wind-up rally to the 1965 national election campaign! Again, I served as an advance man for the final rally held in a movie theatre to be televised on national television in the heart of Hamilton opposite the Royal Connaught Hotel, the finest hostelry in Hamilton where Pearson was staying. My job was to ensure that Pearson would enter the stage door at the side and rear of the theatre when his limo drew up less than a block away from the hotel on an adjacent side street. By mistake, the limo stopped at the fire exit doors leading into the middle of the crowded theatre. There had been a bomb scare the day before. All entrances were heavily guarded by the RCMP. Pearson absent-mindedly got out of the limo and headed to the side exit of the theatre when the police let him enter rather than the rear exit leading to the stage where I frantically was waving and shouting to no avail. Jim Coutts, Pearson's assistant, got out the wrong side of the limo and was prevented from following Mr. Pearson into the theatre by the security guards. Coutts was furious. Pearson, once he entered the side entrance of the theatre alone – found himself mobbed by the cheering partisan crowd. Pearson could barely make his way to the stage to the waiting M.C., Vic Copps (father of Sheila Copps), the colourful Hamilton Mayor. It was disastrous. Pearson was visibly shaken. I watched this all, helpless from the stage wings. Finally, Mr. Pearson mounted the stage from the audience side followed by his Scottish Pipe Band with kilts flying. Pearson began to speak, weakened and exhausted by the shoving crowd. He could barely stand. Maryon was furious with me and the rest of the advance team. It was a lame finish to the national campaign – all to be seen on tape delayed television coast-to-coast later that evening. A disaster waiting to be viewed by an interested Canadian public.

After the rally, we headed back in a motor cavalcade to stay at the Constellation Hotel at the Toronto airport to view the television version anchored by Don Jamieson, a Liberal and radio star from Newfoundland. I could feel the heat in the crowded limo and was told by Coutts to stay out of sight. Then came the delayed TV coverage. Under the smooth skillful baritone words of Don Jamieson, the disastrous event was turned into a triumph for Mr. Pearson, noting how vibrant and excited the crowd was. "*The crowd is wild, wild*", he said breathlessly, "*with excitement.*" "*Look, look*", Jameson said breathlessly, "*They can't keep their hands off Mr. Pearson*", he intoned. "*What a finale to a grand campaign.*" After the TV news coverage and Jameson's adulation of Pearson, I was summoned by both Mr. and Mrs. Pearson to their hotel suite who congratulated me on what a marvelous job I had done. Whew!

Some background of my involvement in Liberal politics began with my romance with the Liberal Machine which started in Toronto in 1961.

My wife Carole has lived to regret it. I had just been called to the Bar of Ontario a year before and was starting my criminal law practice. She was bored with my single-minded obsession with the law. All my free time was taken with law, lawyers, and legal friends. After 70-hour weeks of office and court work, the weekends were taken by reading the law reports, the Dominion and England Reports, and Law Journals. Saturday nights were usually dinner with members of my law school study group or other young lawyers. Sundays were reserved for workouts, the Sunday New York Times, and reading law reports and files brought home to prepare for the following week. And then came Liberal politics, like an addictive drug habit, that became a blinding passion and has preoccupied me ever since. One Wednesday evening, from our small apartment in North Toronto, my wife urged me to go to a local Liberal riding organizational meeting held that evening in York Centre. I had just received an organization flyer in the mail. "*Get out and meet some new people*", she admonished me. That changed my life, and hers!

My familial connection to the Liberal Party was my immigrant father. He served as a Liberal poll captain and scrutineer in Federal and Provincials Elections in my home town of London, Ontario. He also was an enthusiastic grassroots worker in London's municipal elections. As a learning lesson, my father took me to Liberal meetings and polling stations and introduced me to Roberts Rules of Order. Participation in local politics, he believed, was a civic duty. He loved Canada and his knowledge of both Canadian history and European politics intensified his affection.

Walking home from the Federal election in 1945 where he served as a polling station scrutineer for the Liberal Party as a ten-year-old, I asked my father, "*Daddy, why are we Liberals?*" "*We are Liberals*", he said slowly and thoughtfully, "*because Liberals help people that cannot help themselves.*"

Anyway, back to my wife's chagrin with my obsessive preoccupation with the law. The fall of 1961 was on the cusp of a Federal election between the great antagonists Mr. Pearson and Mr. Diefenbaker. The Liberals in Toronto under the active eye of Keith Davey, the master organizer, were in the throes of a grassroots revolution in party organization. A small group in Toronto composed of Keith Davey, an advertising executive, and now located in Ottawa as Chief Political Organizer for Mr. Pearson, the ebullient Dick Stanbury, later President of the Liberal Party and Senator, and Jim Service and Vernon Singer, the taciturn Reeve of North York, all lawyers in North York, Royce Frith, an urbane sophisticated, always immaculate in his Savile Row cut suits[99] communications lawyer (later to become Deputy Leader of the Senate Liberals), David Anderson, also a lawyer, born in PEI but a large, droll, avuncular hulk of a man who walked in a shambling gait, Gordon Dryden, a short querulous former farmer from south-west Ontario, now lawyer in Toronto and a lifelong student of Canadian history and the Liberal Party, Dan Lang, an elegant Bay Street lawyer (also appointed later by Mr. Pearson to the Senate), and a few others called 'Cell 13' were the core to the Liberal organizing machine in Toronto. The undisputed leader was Walter Gordon, conservatively attired with military style tie. Mr. Pearson's close friend and key organizer.

"*Work out or get out*" was Keith Davey's war cry to remove the old party stalwarts who refused to reach out into the community or work. The same call echoed in ridings across Canada, most especially in Toronto as the city that came alive with new ambitious young people, with an equally strong ethnic mix, new to the Liberal Party.

That night I became President of Young Liberals in York Centre at my very first Liberal meeting. Six months later, I was elected President of Toronto and District Young Liberals. My mandate was to organize young Liberal groups in each riding across Toronto. Three months later, I was elected English speaking Vice President of the National Young Liberals of Canada and appointed a youth member of the National Campaign Committee headed by Walter Gordon and ran by Keith Davey, and found myself sitting next to Mr. Pearson at a national campaign committee meeting in Ottawa, all in nine months.[100]

---

[99] When Royce left the Senate to become the High Commissioner in London, it was said that he was the first who never had to change tailors.

[100] When I sat beside Mr. Pearson and chatted about my involvement in politics, he told me three things I never forgot, "*Aim high, work hard and be*

On that fatal Wednesday evening back in the fall of 1961, my wife repeated her mantra that I had to get out into the community and meet new people. I had to shake off my bookish time with other young lawyers. "*What do you suggest?*" I meekly offered. "*Here, here is a flyer for an organizational meeting right here in North York a few blocks from our apartment.*" I got mail from the Liberal Party as I had been a member of University Liberals at Western where I had joined and participated in mock Parliaments, but was lukewarm to politics except for Mr. Pearson who I admired. Now the attractiveness of politics was John Kennedy, a fresh youthful figure with an eloquent turn of the phrase who inspired me. I loved reading Kennedy's speeches and his book about *Profiles in Courage* had started my deeper interest in politics. The first U.S. presidential TV debates in 1960 between Kennedy and Nixon were mesmerizing. The handbook of the era was Theodore White's *The Making of the President*. For any wannabee interested in politics, it was a must read.

That fateful Fall Wednesday night, an organizational meeting for the North York riding, called York Centre, was held in the pine paneled basement of Jimmie Mizzoni, a local real estate salesman who had a warm, endearing and up-beat personality. He had been pushed hard for the job as President of the York Centre Liberal Association by Keith Davey. That night, as I said, I met Keith Davey, Dick Stanbury then Toronto District Liberal President, Jim Service, Vern Singer, Walter Gordon, and others. The federation of all Toronto ridings was under the umbrella of the Toronto and District Liberal Association (T&D) headed by Dick Stanbury. The guest speaker that evening was Walter

---

fair". I have tried. Sometimes I succeeded. Many times, I failed. However, I have been motivated by these three pieces of advice that Mr. Pearson gave me when I first entered politics and I sat beside him. Three things: Aim high, work hard, and be fair, I repeated to myself all my years in politics.

Gordon, the mastermind behind Mr. Pearson and the Liberal Party revival. Later, I discovered that Keith and Walter had a tight relationship with 'Bea' Honderich of the powerful Toronto Star. Keith's father, 'Scotty' Davey, was a long-time employee of the Star and Walter Gordon had helped 'Bea' to acquire control of the Star. The Star would prove invaluable when Walter ran in the Davenport riding, in the heart of Toronto and as a staunch advocate of Liberals under Mr. Pearson. That night, I was elected as York Centre Young Liberal President and invited by Dick Stanbury to attend a meeting of Toronto District and Liberal Association meeting to be held a few weeks hence. Dick was T&D President.

Within six months of whirlwind political activity, I was elected President of the Toronto and District Young Liberal Association and made a member of Dirk Stanbury's Toronto and District Liberal Executive. Within nine months, I attended a meeting of Young Liberals in Montreal and became a friend and organizer for Michel Robert who became National Young Liberal President while I was elected as English-speaking Vice-President of the National Young Liberals of Canada.[101] Then, I was selected by Walter Gordon and Keith Davey to serve on the Federal Liberal National Campaign Committee. Suddenly I found myself sitting next to Mr. Pearson when I attended my first national campaign meeting in Ottawa. I could not believe it. Mr. Pearson was friendly and curious about where I was born and where I went to school. I discovered, to my amazement, that he knew my father-

[101] It was in Montreal in 1962 in a bar on Crescent Street that I was introduced by Jean David, the twenty-five year old precocious, youthful editor of *LaPresse*, who became a good friend, to a political gadfly and gifted polemicist called Pierre Trudeau, then a CCF fellow traveler and Trudeau's pal, Pierre Vallières, author of the *White Niggers of America: The Precocious Autobiography of a Quebec 'terrorist'*

in-law, a lifelong Conservative, Harry Sniderman, an all-round star athlete who played on U of T's basketball team during Mr. Pearson's time there. Harry went on to become one of Canada's greatest sandlot baseball pitchers and hitters. He became known as '*What a Man, Sniderman*' in sports circles. Mr. Pearson knew all about Harry and we developed a quick bond. "*Give my regards to Harry*", Pearson said when the campaign meeting ended. It was an exciting whirlwind experience, rubbing shoulders with Mr. Pearson, Walter Gordon, and other Liberal political honchos from across Canada.

I was proposed by Keith who became my mentor, life-long friend, and supporter to do one job. As President of Young Liberals in Toronto, I was mandated to organize Young Liberal Clubs in each of the twenty-nine ridings in Toronto's District. Within six months from a standing start, I had organized eighteen of twenty-nine ridings and working feverishly to get the rest organized for the looming Federal election.

My daily routine was set. I worked from 8 A.M. to 6 P.M. in law and then each weekday evening except for Friday, I went to a different riding, met with the Riding President and members of that executive, drew up a list of bright young volunteers and encouraged one or two to organize a Young Liberal Group in his or her riding. I attended a blizzard of organizational meetings and held regular policy meetings for the new Young Liberal Presidents. At Toronto and District, I served on the policy committee and the outreach committees for labour and ethnic groups as part of the Liberal outreach agenda. Davy had devised large college-style weekends called 'Campaign College' to teach election organization skills. I helped him in that effort speaking and enlisting key organizers to teach grass-root techniques – how to organize, how to raise money, how to develop policies groups, and how to outreach to ethnic communities – all basic ideas that needed to be implemented, refined, and activated. Keith, first and foremost, taught us that it was essential to have fun being a volunteer. Each volunteer could make a difference – he preached – but you had to have fun doing it. It was a crash course in grass roots politics from the bottom up. The enthusiasm was infectious. The key was to find and work with people who were committed, honest, and loyal to the leader and held Liberal views.

The 1962 campaign was my first introduction to a national political election. There the Liberals who were the 'white hats' led by the amicable Lester B. Pearson. The 'black hats' were led by the so-called 'Renegade in Power' John Diefenbaker as painted by Peter Newman, the leading author on politics,[102] in his best-selling book. I was a riding organizer, advance man, contributed policy, and filtered speech ideas through Keith to the national campaign. On much later reflection, I felt Diefenbaker had been unfairly demonized, but that's politics. At the time, I didn't regret my role in the demonization.

Keith taught that our first job was to dive into the organizations of each riding, animate the executive, organize Young Liberals, search out a good candidate, discover young energetic volunteers, and work to make sure all the machinery was in place and working in unison like an engine with many cylinders for Election Day. Another key organizer I met during this period was Dorothy Petrie (later to marry Keith), one of the most astute organizers in her calm unruffled way, who owned great skills and greater political judgment. We became instant allies. Jim Brown, a local volunteer in the North York riding of York Centre, also became a good trusted friend as did Jim

---

[102] During this period, I came to know Peter and his then wife Christina Newman who later wrote a history of the Trudeau era entitled *Grits: An Intimate Portrait of the Liberal Party* (MacMillan Of Canada, 1982) where she included a chapter on my Liberal activities.

Mizzoni, the federal President of the Riding, who never failed to have a broad, toothy smile plastered on his face. Our candidate in York Centre we agreed on was a former community volunteer and a local insurance man called James Walker, 'Jimmy' to his friends. Jimmy was a short, brisk, likeable man with a wide smile and comfortable pleasant face who came from the West and settled in North York to begin a small business career in real estate sales and insurance. While likeability and amiability were the keys to Jimmy's sunny disposition, organization, policy or public speaking were not his areas of expertise.[103] So, one of my jobs as a key organizer was to simply divide the riding into regional teams and find enthusiastic volunteers like Monte Kwinter.[104] The team could espouse the Liberal Platform at every door and hand out our literature. In the end, I became Jimmy's policy and speech writer as I had admired John F. Kennedy and Winston Churchill and had poured over their political speeches for pleasure.

I was also selected by Dan Lang, the tough minded, astute Ontario Campaign Chair to do advance work with outside speakers like Paul Martin Senior and for Mr. Pearson around Toronto.

Two incidents came from that campaign. The York Centre campaign in North Toronto was tough and close. We organized teams, including me, to increase the lawn signs to show momentum. We deployed lawn signs in waves; they were

---

[103] Jimmy Walker became trusted by Pierre Trudeau and respected by his Parliamentary colleagues, later was elected Whip of the Liberal caucus and was excellent in the job.

[104] Monte Kwinter was a friend I enlisted to work for the Jimmy Walker campaign, and he went on to become the longest serving Member of the Ontario legislature and effective Minister. Monte's provincial riding overlapped York Centre.

everywhere and it worked. The race was between Jim Stinson, a well-liked Conservative local lawyer, and Val Scott, a good-looking, verbose, tall, lean NDP. Both were good on their feet. Jimmy survived by his likeability and modesty. Because York Centre was a must-win riding, Keith called me and said that Mr. Pearson was going to make a quick helicopter stop one afternoon in North York. "*Where should he hold the event?*" he asked. I immediately thought of the Jewish Home of the Aged called Baycrest on north Bathurst Street in the Jewish district. There was field nearby where the helicopter carrying Mr. Pearson could land. The photo op with old people would be great. We needed the seniors vote. Diefenbaker had made pensions an issue and so did we! Winning the Jewish elderly element would be a plus because many of the old Jews living there were still smarting from the refusal of King in 1945 to appoint the only elected Liberal member in Toronto who was Jewish, David Croll (a former Mayor of Windsor, provincial Minister and now a decorated war veteran), into the Cabinet. Croll was told he would not be a 'congenial colleague' and was offered a seat in the Senate, the first Jew to be appointed to the Senate, which he accepted and still sat as a sitting Senate member.[105] Keith quietly agreed because there was a field beside the main building which was convenient for a helicopter landing and only steps away from the auditorium. Then I said to Keith, "*We have one problem.*" "*What's that?*" Keith asked. "*The audience mostly speaks mostly Yiddish so we need someone to translate.*" It occurred to me that my distant

[105] I had articled for Senator Croll in his Toronto law office and much later joined him while he still sat in the Senate. Ever active in the Senate, Croll led a benchmark study and report on poverty in Canada – *Report of the Special Senate Committee on Poverty*'(1971). This report led to increased family allowances in 1973 and the Child Tax Credit in 1978 under the Pierre Trudeau government.

cousin, Phil Givens, a city councilor, a Liberal and friend of Keith who spoke a sparkling Yiddish, was a great strong speaker and translator. "*Great*", said Keith, "*let's go and get it organized. Call Phil and tell him I asked him to help.*"

I was well acquainted with a large number of the old aged male residents at Baycrest. My own grandfather now lived there, and he had introduced me to all his cronies. Several were from my home town of London, Ontario. I knew each of them as I visited the home every Sunday afternoon to spend time with my aging, blind grandfather.

The mid-week afternoon date for the rally was fixed. Givens agreed to translate. My key resident organizer at Baycrest was Rubenstein and his pals who were enlisted as in-house organizers. This would ensure a grand and welcoming turn-out.

Mr. Pearson and his entourage, including Keith Davey, Jimmy Walker, Walter Gordon, Dan Lang (Ontario Campaign Chairman), and Jim Coutts (Pearson's assistant) who all showed up promptly on time, Mr. Pearson and Coutts by helicopter and the rest by car. Mr. Pearson, looking ruffled from the whirly helicopter props, emerged ducking down from the helicopter blades, walked across the nearby fields to walk through the main entrance of Baycrest now crowded with cheering staff. The nursing staff carrying hand painted cardboard signs and emblazed with Liberal slogans that I and my crew had painted. Mr. Pearson began to relax and smile at the warmth of the welcome as he walked down the corridor to the main auditorium now packed with happy old male and female residents, many in wheelchairs, with the walls festooned with the Union Jack, the Red Ensign, mixed with the Israel's Blue-white Star of David flag. Mr. Pearson seemed less frazzled as he approached the podium, buoyed by the welcome. It was show time!

Handmade signs were waved by elderly volunteers to enliven the event. The news media was there in great numbers at the front. Cameras were placed to catch all angles as Phil dressed in a snappy double-breasted dark suit beamed from the podium when he introduced himself in Yiddish as MC to translate Mr. Pearson's speech. Mr. Pearson sat on the small podium smiling but wary. Jimmy Walker, sitting beside him, was beaming.

First in a rousing introduction, Phil introduced Jimmy Walker and Phil concluded by calling Mr. Pearson Canada's staunchest supporter of Israel and the next Prime Minister of the Canada in the government in Ottawa in splendid, booming Yiddish to great rising enthusiastic waves of applause.

As Mr. Pearson ambled up to the podium speakers dias, he spoke dryly about jobs, pensions, and foreign policy. Phil translated in Yiddish with his own wild interpretation after each policy idea noting how great it will be for Jews in Canada and how great it will be for Israel. He concluded by saying that Mr. Pearson wants peace in the world but most of all, he wants to support and protect the State of Israel. Mr. Pearson was surprised by the enthusiasm for his pedestrian speech as he knew he was not a great stirring speaker on the hustings. His high nasal voice and lisp, though endearing to his acolytes, was not universally admired and didn't play well in a public forum. Only to our loyal ears could Mr. Pearson be considered a spellbinder.

Leaving the building, Mr. Pearson turned and thanked me warmly as he had heard from Keith that I was a key organizer for the event. "*They really like my speech*", he offered. "*They loved it, Sir*", I said. Jimmy Walker was also in dreamland as he got to, for the first time in the campaign, sit on the platform besides Mr. Pearson. Walter Gordon, the National Campaign Chairman, thanked me as well. I was flying high. We waved Mr. Pearson off as the helicopter swept him away. Keith, with his arm around me, couldn't be more pleased. To please Keith and get a compliment meant the world to me in my new found political life as a volunteer and Liberal activist.

This earned me another job as a researcher for the 'Truth Squad' headed by Judy LaMarsh, a heavy-set former army officer and lawyer from Niagara Falls and strong friend of Keith's who was running for Parliament. She was asked to head up a small tactical group to give press conference after each of Mr. Diefenbaker's campaign stops to separate fact from fiction. I was asked by Keith to feed Judy and her travelling team ideas and talking points. I kept track of all of Mr. Diefenbaker's campaign speeches. I found them informative, well-crafted. and fascinating.[106] At times, Diefenbaker would exaggerate and these exaggerations I pounced on.

Each national campaign starting in 1958, 1962, 1963, and 1965 that pitted Mr. Pearson and John Diefenbaker was vitriolic. Mr. Diefenbaker was the expert in vituperation. He bested Mr. Pearson in Parliament regularly from Mr. Pearson's first days as Leader of the Opposition. Diefenbaker sizzled on the campaign trail. From the Pipeline debate in 1957 to the litany of scandals during the Pearson Prime Ministership – the Rivard affair, the Hal Banks affairs, the Norman affair, the Spencer affair, and especially the scandals around a Pearson Cabinet Minister Yvon Dupuis and political aides. Diefenbaker could cut deeply and effectively. In my view, these waves of scandals kept Mr. Pearson from achieving the majority in Parliament I thought he richly deserved.

Mr. Pearson admitted he hated Mr. Diefenbaker.[107] Mr. Diefenbaker felt Mr. Pearson was weak and ineffective, and

[106] Later I discovered that Roy Faibish, now my friend, told me he had drafted many of them. Diefenbaker would go off script, but the script was coherent and well-written.

[107] Pearson gleaned from his Methodist roots a respect for the written and spoken word. He was careful with both. No doubt, his visceral dislike for Diefenbaker was in Diefenbaker's penchant for the spoken word coated in

worse, a pawn of the Americans and so it was easy to rip him and his government apart whether in Parliamentary debate or on campaign trail. Mr. Pearson recognized his deficiencies. Mr. Pearson was loath to hate anyone. One other exception. Mr. Pearson wrote in the final volume of his memoirs called *Mike* that he 'detested' American Senator McCarthy for the public servants and others whose reputations McCarthy had unfairly destroyed. Mr. Pearson was not a man given to 'hating' others, but these were the two exceptions.

Right after the election when I was in Ottawa and Jimmy Walker was safely elected, Jim Coutts, Mr. Pearson's assistant,[108] called and said Mr. Pearson asked to see me. Mr. Pearson wondered how we had done in the polls at Baycrest. In fact, that poll went overwhelmingly for the Tory candidate. When the results came out election night, I raced to Baycrest the following day to visit with Rubenstein, my key organizer, for an explanation. "*Rubenstein*", I said, "*I brought you the Prime Minister, and we lost the poll. What happened?*" Rubenstein saw I was upset as I knew Keith and Mr. Pearson would want to know what happened. It turned out that Stinson, the Tory, just before the election had sent his key Jewish organizer to the Saturday afternoon meal at Baycrest traditionally held before the final Sabbath service. He had arrived with two bottles of Canadian Club and one bottle

exaggeration and embellishment which Pearson saw was far from the facts and the truth. Diefenbaker's attacks during the 'Norman Affair' especially upset Pearson as Norman was an old friend from the Public Service. Pearson felt Diefenbaker destroyed Norman and his reputation and led to dire consequences.

[108] Jim Coutts had run for the House of Commons in a riding in Alberta and lost but gained Mr. Pearson's attention. Jim became an agile and bright assistant. He fell out of favour once when a TV documentary including shots of Mr. Pearson at work in his office and gave the impression that Jim rather than Mr. Pearson was in charge.

of Crown Royal, the preferred whiskies of the male residents, all provided with great fanfare by Stinson's key Jewish organizer.

When Mr. Pearson asked me the question "*How did we do at the old age home you organized?*" I was prepared. "*Swept, Sir, we swept the poll.*" Mr. Pearson offered, "*I knew it!*" – with a broad smile of satisfaction on his face. That too is politics.

One other incident in that hard-fought National campaign. The neighbouring riding from York Centre was York South. The socialist CCF candidate was none other than the great David Lewis, arguably the best political debater and speaker in Canada. A former Rhodes Scholar and first Canadian to win the coveted the Head of the Oxford Union,[109] Lewis in a strange but wonderful mix of Welsh, English, and Yiddish accent was a daunting stump speaker. Keith convinced Jimmy to represent the Liberals at a meeting held in a Legion Hall in the building in Youth South bordering on York Centre. Others had refused, daunted by Lewis's reputation. Jimmy was nervous. I was given the task by Keith to help Jimmy with his speech and give him confidence. We prepared carefully, and strategically. Jimmy gained confidence as he accepted the plan. He was comfortable and still nervous, but he was prepared.

We were herded together into a small smoke-filled Legion Hall in York Street crammed with war vets, unionists, and local notables. The Conservative went first and made a lackluster speech with occasional boos from the audience. Lewis went second and made a brilliant articulate persuasive case for the CCF cause in his finest Oxford University style to thunderous applause. Jimmy went last. He rose from his seat on the stage slowly, approached the mike clapping his hands with the rest

[109] My older son, Laurence, also a Rhodes Scholar, was the second Canadian to head the Oxford Union.

of the audience joining in the applause vigorously with a wide friendly smile on his face. Jimmy had a friendly welcoming face.

Jimmy started slowly waving for his audience to sit down and quiet down. He spoke slowly and quietly. "*That*", he said still clapping slowly, "*was one of the best political speeches I have ever heard in my life. David Lewis is one of the greatest speakers in Canada, if not the world, educated as he was in England at Oxford University*", he said slowing and continued lavishing Lewis with praise and superlatives.

Then he came to his message. "*I am privileged as you all are to be in the presence of such a brilliant speaker and brilliant leader. I can't dream or hope of reaching his excellent political skills, debating and trained as he was at the Oxford Union in England, the greatest debating place in the world, so I* (slowing down for emphasis and modesty) *can only speak about the few things I care about, that the Liberal Party under Mr. Pearson cares about, and that is good pensions, health care, jobs and fair treatment for veterans, their families and if I am elected to join Mr. Lewis in Parliament that I would hope to work for the workers of South and North York to accomplish those things.*"

"*Thank you for the privilege of sharing the platform with Mr. Lewis and your kind invitation to have me here in this Legion Hall and again thank Mr. Lewis to allow me to hear one of the greatest political speeches I have ever had the privilege to hear in my life.*"

There was a moment of silence. It was an awful long moment. Then the crowd rose, clapped, and roared their approval of Jimmy's modest speech. Jimmy won the day in my humble opinion. But that is politics too.

Later, I found that Mr. Pearson was curious about David Lewis after the event and asked me to carefully debrief him, especially about the content and reception of Lewis's speech. Mr.

Pearson held a grudging admiration for Mr. Lewis, less so for Tommy Douglas.

Once Prime Minister, Mr. Pearson's political objective to have 'at long last' a made-in-Canada Flag free of British emblems that attracted vociferous opposition from all sides of the spectrum, especially Quebec. Mr. Pearson made '*O Canada*' Canada's national anthem and removed the royal emblem on Canada's postboxes and elsewhere. Today, the Flag, '*O Canada*', and Trudeau's Charter of Rights and Freedoms are considered in polls the three most important and respected institutions in all parts of Canada. The Flag and Charter, in Quebec so vigorously opposed by all the political classes there, are now the most approved Canadian symbols and institutions across Canada. '*O Canada*' is now proudly sung in French and English in Quebec and across Canada. Watch any hockey game televised in Montreal. In practice, Canadians have become a 'rights' obsessed society. Great leaps of cultural change are almost never supported at the outset, until well after their appearance.

Mr. Pearson, on the campaign trail, could be disappointing. The Liberal Party and the Campaign Committee had come up with a small policy booklet called the Red Book crammed with progressive policy ideas from Medicare to pensions to job creation to effective foreign policy to correct the excesses of Diefenbaker's administration. I, and others interested in policy work, had a hand in the Red Book. In 1963, it was hard to attract large crowds. We came up with the idea to rent the O'Keefe Centre that held 3,400 seats that we could easily fill with Liberals and volunteers. Keith asked me to organize the event. The Liberal crowd was primed to explode. Mr. Pearson took the stage alone. I stood in the balcony overlooking the event, ensuring all key organizers were placed throughout the auditorium primed to cheer. Mr. Pearson made a lack-lustre speech. He was exhausted from campaigning. In his conclusion, Mr. Pearson said slowly, "*People want to know what Liberals stand for.*" he intoned. The crowd on cue exploded, "*Yes! Yes!*" "*People want to know what we Liberals intend to do.*" Again, the crowd exploded, "*Yes! Yes!*" "*Well, if you asked me, it's all here, it's here in this book*" as he waved and pointed the pamphlet. He then waved to the deflated crowd and left the stage. It was anti-climactic to say the least. Pearson was not just a spellbinder. Yet, in a private room in a Chinese restaurant afterwards, he could mesmerize a small group joining him for dinner. He was exasperating in public but energizing in private – that was Mr. Pearson.

On reflection, I was amazed how different Pearson was on the world stage and how comfortable he was. When he spoke, he rose to the heights of elegance in international forums. With wit and understatement, he could mesmerize his audience. He rarely rose to that same degree in Parliament or on the campaign trail. It was as if he had two different personalities and each voice had a different timbre.

Mr. Pearson once invested in party politics was appalled at campaign financing. It begged for reform. He carefully selected Gordon Dryden, a diligent farmer and Toronto lawyer with encyclopedic knowledge of party politics and especially the Liberal Party. Gordon was asked to recommend campaign financing reform. He regularly met directly to Mr. Pearson about his progress and the obstacles. Gordon would report on his meetings with Mr. Pearson at the regular meetings in my law office of a small group of Liberal activists that met weekly. In the end, his recommendations approved by Mr. Pearson upset the Liberal Party financial establishment, but the reforms won the day. It was the start of election campaign reforms in Canada that put a cap on riding and campaign expenses.

In 1963, with Mr. Pearson and Keith's support, I founded the *Journal of Liberal Thought*, a self-proclaimed Liberal Party thinkers' magazine. At Mr. Pearson's suggestion, I enlisted Barbara Ward and Kenneth Galbraith to write articles. I kept it going for several years. Mr. Pearson read each edition carefully and was quick with credit and ideas.

The most important Party meeting (other than the Kingston Conference in 1961) during the Pearson era was the Policy Convention held at Maple Gardens in 1966 and the key issue was 'Medicare'. The Party and Cabinet were deeply divided. Medicare had been a Liberal promise since 1919. It was not Medicare; it was the public financing that some felt would beggar the national budget. Mr. Pearson wanted to implement Medicare as soon as possible. Pearson wanted a form of publicly subsidized health insurance to ward off disastrous medical bills for the working Canadian. The Cabinet was divided. On one side were the restless liberals like Walter Gordon, Allan MacEachen, and Jim Munro, and on the other side were the more cautious conservatives like Robert Winters, Paul Hellyer and Mitchell Sharpe including the Sharpe's Parliamentary associate at the time, Jean Chrétien.

Mr. Pearson overcame waves of scandals like the Hal Bank Affair, the Norman Affair, Spencer Affair, the Rivard Affair, and political ineptitude by one of his ministers and others that weakened his leadership, but his towering legislative achievements remain unimpaired. Mr. Pearson was unwavering in seeking to legislate and implement his progressive reforms, especially Medicare, as soon as possible despite opposition in the Commons and at times, within his own Cabinet. His Cabinet opposition argued now is not a good time because of the uncertain economic conditions. Mr. Pearson felt it was now or never! There was never a good time.

MacEachen, Munro, and Keith had designated David Smith, Lloyd Axworthy, and me to be floor managers at the convention to whip the pro-vote. It was a robust debate and a raucous vote. We were well organized. It was Mr. Pearson's wish to have the Party finally approve the Medicare implementation with a good Party majority as soon as possible. Mr. Pearson felt that he needed broad party support for any divisive issue. The vote carried for postponement with regrets.[110] Mr. Pearson was clearly upset, so he proceeded to implement Medicare by 1968 before he left public office. For that Medicare legislation alone, Mr. Pearson earned a sterling page in Canadian history. His leadership on a National Pension Plan, a Canadian Assistance Plan, and the 'Autopact' with U.S. remain as irreversible benchmarks to his sterling legacy.

Mr. Pearson was a modernizer and futurist. Under his tenure and the forceful leadership of Paul Hellyer, the Armed Forces were unified. The Department of Industry was created to help with training for the chronically unemployed and job training for youth. Canada won the international competition to host Expo 67 and with Mr. Pearson's astute selection of managers for the gigantic project, put Canada on the world map for creativity and innovation. Expo 67 came in on time and on budget. It was the spirit of Expo 67 that resonated across Canada and the world that remains a Pearson legacy.

Another personal backstory from the Pearson years as Prime Minister and the 1965 campaign. In that campaign, Pearson and company were seeking an elusive majority government. While attending high school in the late 1940's, my father in our early

[110] Conservative leaning ministers on the Cabinet, Hellyer, Winters, Sharpe, his Parliamentary assistant Jean Chrétien, and others who felt the economy could not carry the costs of this new social initiative. Pearson felt that 'there was never a good time' for a new social policy so it was now or never.

morning daily education sessions, was reading the London Free Press or a Toronto or a New York Yiddish newspaper, I can't remember which, when he became very animated and visibly upset. This was rare for him because he followed Hasidic training to be moderate in all things and seek resolutions, not become mired in anger. He read that the Ontario Supreme Court of Appeal had approved a lower-case decision upholding a restrictive clause in a property case on a vacation cottage area north of London. The leading Jewish merchant in London, Bernard Wolf, and a friend of my father had sought to buy a cottage property in a small enclave on a lake north of London. His purchase was stopped because an adjoining owner sought to enforce a restrictive covenant in this small vacation community that said: 'No Jews allowed'. Wolf and the vendor Noble took the case to a single judge of the Supreme Court of Ontario where the restrictive covenant was upheld. On appeal to the Ontario Court of Appeal, it was upheld again led by Justice Schroeder. Wolf, a principled man, appealed to the Supreme Court of Canada, where the restrictive clause was finally set aside allowing the sale to proceed. My father turned to me solemnly and said, "*In Canada, these attitudes can be changed. If you ever have a chance*", as he knew law was one of my career goals as an early teenager, "*You should try to change that court in Toronto that discriminates against Jews. It is not right.*"

Years later, in 1965 to be precise, an opportunity to fulfill my father's early advice appeared suddenly. By this time, I was a Liberal activist and had acted as an advance man and as a youth representative on the Liberal National Campaign Committee and on both the National and Ontario Campaign Committees. My main mentor and key promoter was Keith Davey, then the National Director of the Liberal Party. Pearson's minority government was struggling to obtain a majority government.

Mr. Pearson and Keith had high hopes but with little forward traction in the polls. Both were keenly aware that every vote counted. Except for the Toronto Star, the press, the Globe and Mail, and the Telegram, led by big John Bassett was not supportive in Toronto. Toronto contained a small number of key seats that were tightly divided.

Suddenly in the run-up to the federal campaign, there was a vacancy on that reactionary Ontario Court of Appeal. I immediately went up to University of Toronto Law School to seek advice from Dean 'Caesar' Wright, another of my mentors, who I continued to see regularly weekly for an hour or so on Friday afternoons after my graduation and call to the Ontario Bar. 'Caesar' saw me at once as I indicated I needed his advice on a pressing political matter. Wright's close friend, Sidney Smith, a former President of University of Toronto, had an abortive political career as Conservative Member of Parliament and Minister of External Affairs in Diefenbaker's time. Smith died suddenly of a stroke in 1959. So 'Caesar' was a close student of politics. Deep down, 'Caesar' was a Liberal and a friend and admirer of Mr. Pearson. I told him of my idea to get a liberal appointed to the reactionary Ontario Appeals court and felt it could be a great game changer in Ontario. My first choice was Bora Laskin, with liberal instincts who had friendly social ties with Tories like Charley Dubin and Eddie Goodman. 'Caesar' immediately responded that Bora should be my candidate. 'Caesar' admitted that he had antagonized too many establishment lawyers and judges and politicians with his reformist ideas. This was my idea in the first place. But I owed it to 'Caesar' to have the opportunity to say no which I anticipated he would. Bora was Jewish and there was not a Jew on any of the High Courts of Ontario. There had been Jews on County Court and Magistrates, but no Jews on the Ontario High Courts despite the high quality of many Jewish legal practitioners. Bora, a constitutional and labour expert, was well respected, Caesar pointed out especially by both labour, management and constitutional academia, well known and held in high regard by the Toronto Star, the Liberal paper and the Tory Toronto Telegram run by John Bassett, a former Conservative candidate, who was great friends of both Goodman and Dubin who acted for Bassett and who were Bassett's minor partners in CFTO TV. The Globe and Mail had strong conservative leanings. Bora in his role as labour mediator had acted to resolve disputes between the newspaper unions and the press ownership so he was in every key newspaper player's good graces. The fact that he was Jewish and would be the first Jew on the Court and a liberal, I agreed, was a great idea and viable. 'Caesar' said that Bora was in his office down the hall, but he cautioned me that Bora was above partisan politics and would not do a thing to advance his own cause. So, he counselled that I ask him only one question, "*If the appointment was offered, would he accept?*"

I immediately went down the hall at the law school building to interrupt Bora who was deep at work editing the Dominion Law Reports and didn't like to be disturbed when he worked. By happenstance, he knew and admired my father-in-law, Harry Sniderman, who was a great all-round athlete. Bora was a great athlete himself at University of Toronto and as a result, Bora had been invited to my wedding as were all my other law professors at my father-in-law's insistence. I took all his courses and faired reasonably. So, when I popped my head in his door, the usual impatient scowl turned to a smile and he asked what he could do for me. I asked for a minute of his time. He paused and invited me into his book lined office and desk piled high with cases he was reviewing to include in the Dominion Law Reports. "*Bora*", I asked timidly, "*If you were asked to fill the vacancy on the Ontario Court of Appeal, would you accept?*" Bora had taught me Property

Law, Labour Law, and Constitutional Law and I remember he had eviscerated the Courts for their decisions, especially the Ontario Court of Appeal, upholding that invidious privative restrictive clause. In that moment as 'Caesar' had acutely predicted, he rose, came around his heavily crowded desk and glared at me. "*I won't do anything. It's not proper.*" I told him I wasn't asking him to put his hand in cold water or do anything. But if he was called by the federal government to appoint him, would he accept. The government no doubt would want assurances so as not waste time or face. "*Yes, of course, under those conditions*" he agreed, he would accept, but repeated he would do nothing, nothing, to advance his candidacy. I told him that I would work on it immediately. I returned to 'Caesar's' office congratulating him on his astute analyses of Bora's attitude. Then we reviewed the Ministers from Ontario that would be called by the Prime Minister to make recommendations. Again, 'Caesar' showed his political smarts as we went through the ministers from Ontario who were lawyers like Joe Green, Judy LaMarsh, and especially Paul Martin Senior who would always have a preferred local candidate from Windsor to propose. So, I should hurry up before other candidates loomed up, especially one proposed by Paul Martin Sr.

The following day, I flew up to Ottawa to see Keith Davey then deep in election mode planning for the next federal campaign. There was a crisis in Ottawa that day. A national railway strike was on the brink. Certain ministers were involved in seeking to avoid a massive nation-wide rail strike that would be devastating to the Pearson government's flagging political fortunes. I caught Keith's attention by asking what he would do if I could get a lead editorial in all three Toronto daily newspapers praising Mr. Pearson and the Liberal government. Keith said with a big grin, "*I would kill for that. What's your idea?*" "*What would you say, Keith, if the Pearson government appointed Bora Laskin to the Ontario Court of Appeal? Bora is a great liberal and non-partisan and highly regarded by labour, management, the press and all parties, Liberals, Conservatives, and CCF. Bora had good ties especially with David Lewis and Tommy Douglas for his enlightened views on labour.*" Keith's eyes gleamed. "*Great idea. Let's get working on it right away. The guy who is handling this file is the Solicitor General, Larry Pennell. Larry is an outstanding criminal lawyer who was a true liberal and opponent of the death penalty. But he is tied up today as he is the Cabinet point man trying to bring unions and management together on the rail strike.*" I told him I was only here for the day and time was of the essence before other candidates got a head of steam. Keith quickly agreed. So, Keith characteristically picked up the phone and called Pennell's office to set up an immediate appointment for me. Keith told me to hightail it to Parliament Hill that morning before Pennell and other ministers would be preparing for an explosive Question Period. While I was an activist and knew many ministers by this time, I did not know Pennell except by reputation. Pennell was an outstanding criminal lawyer and an avid advocate for the abolishment of capital punishment. He was a Liberal in every sense of the word.

When I arrived at his office, it was crowded with rail union reps and management waiting to see Pennell. I approached his secretary and she phoned in to Pennell that a Jerry Grafstein from Toronto, sent by Keith Davey on an urgent matter, was here to see him. Pennell appeared at his door, apologized to his waiting guests and quickly ushered me into his spacious ministerial digs. Pennell looked frazzled and was upset. "*What is so important that it couldn't wait? Do you see I have a national emergency on my hands? What could be more important? And by the way, who are you?*" I quickly introduced myself and told him

I was brought up in London not far from his riding in Brantford. "*Well, what is it?*" he impatiently asked, "*And be quick about it.*" I said it was about the Ontario Court of Appeal vacancy. As Solicitor General and from Ontario, Pennell was Chair of the Cabinet Committee to vet and choose these appointments. The Chief Justices of the Provincial High Courts and Supreme Court of Canada appointments by tradition were left to the Prime Minister's discretion. But Provincial Supreme Courts were vetted by Ministers who were lawyers from those appropriate provinces. Quickly Pennell's mood changed. He was interested. "*Who do you have in mind*?" "*Bora Laskin*", I responded. He paused, smiled, and after a moment of thought said, "*That's a great suggestion. Come around to my desk and let's review the other candidates and who could canvas the Ontario lawyers who were Ministers and who were on the Cabinet Selection Committee.*" We quickly reviewed each minister and he asked me who Keith could handle and who I could and leave the others to him. The big problem would be Paul Martin Sr. who always had a candidate from the Windsor region. I knew and liked Joe Green and Judy LaMarsh, and Keith would also help with those and others and Pennell would deal with the rest and advise Mr. Pearson who he felt would be supportive when I mentioned he knew and liked Bora. I told him about my commitment to get lead editorials from all three Toronto dailies. He was impressed but said he would support Bora's candidacy in any event. So, I returned to Keith's office to thank him for the meeting and the successful outcome. Keith said he would follow-up as I should, and he would coordinate with Pennell. That was in the winter of 1965.

I heard little after I reported to Pennell that while Joe Greene who had been taught by Bora at Osgoode Hall was on side, Judy was less forthcoming. "*Don't worry about her. I know just how to deal with her. Forget about Martin, it is a waste of time.*" I heard nothing from Ottawa till late June of that year. On Friday mid-morning, I received a call from Pennell in Ottawa who advised me that the matter we discussed a few months ago would be dealt with at the last cabinet meeting before summer adjournment later today, but it wouldn't happen as the candidate cannot be reached for his consent to the appointment. I said, "*Minister, you are the Solicitor General and the head of the RCMP. What do you mean you can't reach him?*" Pennell explained that the candidate is apparently overseas and cannot be reached. "*Leave it to me. I will get back to you in a couple hours.*" I immediately got on the subway from my office downtown to College Street station raced across Queens Park to the Law School on Queen's Park Crescent. The Law School was almost empty as I raced from office to office. Finally, I found Horace Krever,[111] a friend and law professor working in his office. I told him it was a matter of life and death. "*Where is Bora?*" "*Oh, Bora is in England for lectures at Oxford.*" "*How do I get hold of him?*" Horace said, "*Well perhaps John, his son might know. As a matter of fact, John was just here a few minutes ago. He was headed across campus.*" I tore out of the building and ran towards the Convocation Hall on the open square and there was John Laskin leisurely walking across the wide expanse of grass.[112] I shouted to him and he turned and waited for me. "*Where's your dad? How do I get hold of him? It's a matter of life or death.*" "*I don't know*", said John. "*He is travelling with Charlie Dubin and your classmate Marty Friedland.*[113] "*Wait*

---

[111] Horace later became an outstanding Ontario Court of Appeal judge himself.

[112] John Laskin later also served on the Ontario Court of Appeal with distinction.

[113] Marty, a classmate and lifelong friend, a Professor of Criminal Law, and later Dean of the University of Toronto Law School, and then as Scholar at University of Toronto wrote a remarkable one volume history of the

a second, what's today? Every Friday, he comes to London for dinner with an old friend. "*How do I get this friend?*" John pulled out his small telephone book and gave me Bora's friend's address and telephone number in London. I thanked him and hurried back to my downtown office on Richmond Street. There I called the number but there was no answer, so I sent Laskin an urgent cable saying, "*Expect a call from the Solicitor General and make sure you are available for the call.*" I immediately called Pennell and gave him the address and the telephone number. Amazed, Pennell asked how I got it so fast. "*Minister, you might be the Solicitor General and head of the RCMP, but I am a Toronto Liberal*", to which he burst out laughing and said, "*Keith Davey told me you were incorrigible*", and hung up.

I heard nothing until the following Tuesday afternoon when I received a call from Charles Dubin who had travelled to the U.K. with Bora to attend law lectures. Dubin said, "*I am sworn to secrecy, but I can tell you that the call was received and accepted.*" Knowing the announcement was imminent, I immediately arranged to see 'Bea' Honderich of the Toronto Star, told him in confidence about the possible imminent appointment and asked him to help fulfill my pledge to get a lead editorial in the Star praising the Pearson government for this creative appointment. 'Bea' smiled and immediately agreed. He liked and admired Bora. The next stop was 'Big' John Bassett Senior, a leading Toronto Conservative and owner of the Toronto Telegram. He was a social acquaintance of Bora's and admired his work as a labor mediator for the newspapers. 'Big' John loved the idea. He

University of Toronto that was a good read. To be candid, he included in his chapter on the history of the Law School a reference to our study group that included Harry Arthurs (who went on to be Dean at Osgoode Hall and then President of York University), Harvey Bliss (an outstanding barrister) and me, who all helped me pull through law school.

said he would write the editorial himself and it would be on the front page of the Toronto Telegram and so it was. The last visit I felt would be the most difficult with the publisher of the Globe and Mail, also an avid Tory. But, he too, was delighted especially when I told him of Bassett's promise to write a lead editorial himself. Actually, he seemed more bemused by my audacity and undertook to have the Globe and Mail issue a lead editorial. The appointment when announced was well received across the country and the Pearson government got lead editorials in all three Toronto dallies which I clipped and delivered to Keith and to Mr. Pearson.

Three postscripts. In the fall of that year, the Law Society of Upper Canada hosted a lunch to celebrate Bora Laskin's appointment where he had once taught before joining 'Caesar' Wright to teach at University of Toronto Law School. Paul Martin Sr. was invited to speak on behalf of the government. It was a crowded lovely lunch in the great hall at Osgoode with leading lawyers and judges and academics in attendance, the elite of the profession. Paul Martin Sr. when asked to speak said that Bora had been his candidate and how thrilled he was to attend such a historic event.[114] Two weeks later, McLean's magazine wrote a strange article stating Bora's appointment was due to the influence of his friend and Tory activist, Eddie Goodman. All of this would not have been possible without the enthusiastic support of Mr. Pearson who knew and respected Bora and Larry Pennell and of course, Keith Davey.

Finally, history was made again when later Pierre Trudeau as Prime Minister appointed Bora, the first Jew, to the Supreme Court of Canada and then as Chief Justice. I never heard from

[114] Paul Martin Sr. – ever the political realist – I was later told, joined the unanimous vote of the Cabinet Committee and Cabinet to support Laskin's appointment.

Bora except at a communal dinner in his honour when he became Chief Justice of Canada. I was at a table at the rear. Bora made a beautiful speech using the Hebrew expression from an ancient Hebrew prayer to recount his climb to history as the first Jew on the Supreme Court of Ontario and then as a member of the Supreme Court and then as the Chief Justice of Canada. He said, "*If I had just been a Professor of Law at the University of Toronto, 'Diyenu', it would have been sufficient. To become a member of the Supreme Court of Ontario, 'Diyenu'. Then to become a member of the Supreme Court of Canada, 'Diyenu'. And finally, to appointed Chief Justice of the Supreme Court of Canada, 'Diyenu'. And as I think about this*", Bora concluded, "*it would not have happened but for a former student of mine who wishes to remain anonymous, 'Diyen*u'". And I say 'Diyenu'.

Mr. Pearson had a Methodist's concern for the poor and the unemployed. When the coal mines with deep shafts under the sea were closed on Bell Island, a small island just off St. John's, Newfoundland, Pearson asked John Turner to visit and make a private report on what could be done to alleviate the dire situation. Turner took me with him. Miners and their families had lived there for generations and the major activity was mining. A few made a sparse living as fishermen. Many had never been off the island. Turner and I attended this beautiful but now depressing tiny island. We made a brief inspection tour and visited the local pub where the out-of-work miners gathered and were in a deep state of depression. I visited a nearby small modern clinic and chatted with a doctor, a young immigrant from Europe. Later, I rejoined Turner in the pub and told him how impressed I was with the clinic and the doctor. The miners who overheard our conversation were not impressed. Several confided that the doctor had assaulted their wives and daughters. That's horrible, we agreed. We intended to call the RCMP on our return to

Ottawa. The miners urged us not to do that because if the doctor was charged and left the island, they could not easily get another doctor to replace him.

Before we took our leave after our short visit to Bell Island, a union leader gave Turner and me each a large old darkened 1850's Newfoundland penny to demonstrate their thanks for our visit and interest in their problem. I learned then why Newfoundlanders were amongst the most gracious and generous of all Canadians.

Turner and I decided we needed a plan that would put dollars in the miners' pockets quickly so that they could leave the island and start a new life if they chose. The only thing of limited value was the small miners' houses that dotted the island built by the mining company and mortgaged to the hilt by CMHC (Central Mortgage and Housing Corporation). Turner and I agreed to recommend in our report to Mr. Pearson that CMHC would buy the small properties and give a modest cash payment to each miner. On our return to Ottawa, Turner and I, at Turner's insistence, went to brief Mr. Pearson. Pearson, dismayed by the Report but pleased with our suggested solution, quickly agreed. CMHC was ordered to buy the houses for a reasonable sum so the miners' that chose would have the means to move to St. John's or away across Canada which many did. Mr. Pearson understood poverty and acted quickly to solve a problem that had proved insoluble by bureaucrats.

Mr. Pearson always considered 'national unity' of highest priority especially for any Canadian Prime Minister besieged as he was by the 'Quiet Revolution' and the rising tide of separatism in Quebec. He established the Commission of Bilingualism and Biculturalism. His comprehension of French was good, but his spoken French left much to be desired. Still, he insisted that any French speaking Cabinet minister speak in French in Cabinet. Sympathetic to Quebec's concerns, his closest advisor in Quebec was the urbane Maurice Lamontage and then Marc Lalonde. He made his business to hold lengthy private meetings with Jean Lesage and Rene Levesque, both Liberals provincial leaders and Daniel Johnson, leader of the Union Nationale. Pearson had met Levesque earlier when Levesque was a journalist covering Europe and came to admire and respect him. While he liked Jean Lesage, the Liberal Provincial Premier, who he felt while brilliant, was very temperamental. He also enjoyed a close working relationship with Daniel Johnson. In this process of these close collaborations, Pearson developed policies like 'Co-operative Federalism' to allow Quebec to opt out of Medicare and his Pension Plan. He helped Quebec when Lesage sought a constitutional amendment to get rid of the upper chamber in the Quebec assembly. He sought out and convinced Jean Marchand and Jean Pelletier to run in 1965. They, in turn, insisted that Pierre Trudeau, a critic of Mr. Pearson and some of his politics, join them and so Pearson opened a seat for Trudeau in Mount Royal-Westmont. Pearson's work on repatriation of the Constitution with Trudeau as Minister of Justice at Victoria laid the groundwork for Trudeau's later constitutional triumph.

Pearson had to deal with Charles de Gaulle who on a state visit to Quebec, fanned the flames of separation with his 'Vive Le Quebec Libre" speech in Quebec City. De Gaulle had refused to visit Ottawa. Mr. Pearson felt betrayed as on an earlier visit to Paris, de Gaulle picked his brain on issues from China to Russia. Pearson thought he and de Gaulle had developed a good rapport. Mr. Pearson had the last word when he reminded de Gaulle of his previous laudatory statements about Canada at de Gaulle's farewell luncheon in Quebec City. Pearson could be tenacious, tough, and upfront about criticism or interference from foreign leaders.

Pearson's pleas to Lyndon Johnson to halt bombing in Vietnam was also a tough tact to take with the leader of Canada's largest trading partner.

Mr. Pearson had warm relations with the Queen who is said to have valued his advice. Pearson was the mostly highly regarded leader in the Commonwealth and sought to energize this weakening international institution.

Pearson started discussions to expand the Capital precinct from Ottawa to include Hull while intensifying bilingualism in the public service. He named Lionel Chevrier as Ambassador to France and then Jules Léger as High Commissioner to the U.K., both Quebecers who represented Canada abroad in Europe in Canada's two most important postings at the same time. He was sending Canada and the world a message about the intrinsic nature of Canada's bilingual diversity.

Perhaps the least recognized major cultural shift was the passage of the new Canadian Broadcasting Act. An independent regulatory agency was created – later the Canadian Radio and Television Commission during the Trudeau era that quickly moved to repatriate Canadian ownership and increase Canadian content on TV and especially radio.

The Company of Young Canadians – the Canadians version of President Kennedy's Peace Corp opened a unique opportunity for young people to render volunteer public service in far off lands. This creation was consistent with Pearson's philosophy like the Canada's Peacekeeping missions to provide a unique brand of Canadianism to exemplify Pearson diplomacy. These ideas came from Mr. Pearson's deep belief in the social gospel dedicated to helping others.

Pearson opened a path to Trudeau's leadership by appointing him as his Parliamentary Secretary as soon as he was elected[115] and then as Minister of Justice giving him a national platform

[115] Becoming Parliamentary Secretary to the Prime Minister allowed Trudeau instant experience in Parliament as he was called to answer questions on various hot topics when Pearson was not present in Question Period.

at constitutional meetings. Mr. Pearson planned for the future of the Party and appointed three Prime Ministers in waiting to his Cabinet the same day - Trudeau, Chrétien, and Turner - a remarkable insight to Mr. Pearson's foresight. Pearson felt as a steward of the Liberal Party, a duty to plan carefully for his succession as leader.

Pearson created a Commission to examine the status of women. This commission was composed of a distinguished group of Canadians. This was the start of the public debate to gain feminine parity in the federal service and beyond into the private sector.

Personal probity in public life was a high bar set by Mr. Pearson's example. As a long-term public servant, he was meticulous about his public expenses. When he became Prime Minister and occupied 24 Sussex, the Prime Minister's official residence, he instructed his household staff to do likewise. One example of this were his three bars stocked for entertainment. One bar for private family use was paid by Mr. Pearson personally. A second bar used for Party purposes was paid by the Liberal Party. The third bar used for public or government events was paid for by the government. Mr. Pearson was meticulous in his public expenditures from the public purse.

When he resigned as Prime Minister, he moved to a modest home in Ottawa and spent time in a small suite at Park Plaza while in Toronto where he ended his days, modest and self-effacing to the end after retirement. He was appointed as a senior UN advisor and became known as one of the three 'Wise Men' of international affairs advising on the issues confronting the world. Pearson became a Professor and Chancellor of Carleton University sharing his expertise and knowledge with students and academics alike. These aspects of Pearson's final acts as a teacher and statesman needs much further exploration and recognition. He was an example of continuing public service after retiring from public life.

Rarely can leaders differentiate or tap into what's best for themselves from what is best, in themselves. Mr. Pearson could and did.

Mr. Pearson on Leadership (Except from '*Mike - The Memoirs of the Rt. Hon. Lester B. Pearson, Volume Three 1957-1968*', University of Toronto Press, 1975, pp. 109-110)

"I have never believed that the political arena is primarily a place for blood sports, nor do I believe that political greatness is to be measured by a capacity to create debating confusion. I do not think that results, and those are what we are seeking to achieve, flow from rhetoric, but from facing up to facts and acting according to requirements those facts impose upon us. This does not mean that you should see things only as they are, not as they can be.

I have no illusions about my infallibility or my indispensability. I have not the divine certitude that I am always right or that I am one who has been called on by God to save the country. I even admit that I can see both sides of a question when, as is usually the case, there are two sides, unless there are four or five. That, I admit, is a great handicap for a political leader. John Kennedy once pointed out that it is the politician who sees more than one side of a question who has a depressing and a worrying time. On the other hand, a politician who can see only one side of every question, and who stubbornly digs himself in on that side, can, if it is wrong, lead his party and his country to disaster.

Remaining firm and immovable in a bucket of hardening concrete is nothing to boast about.

Political leadership is to be steady, not stuck. In politics, as in any group activity, leadership is persuading people to work hard and loyally with you, and for you, in a good cause. It is getting the right things done, even at the price of conflict or controversy.

So, I hope you will pardon me for saying that I hope my leadership will not be judged by the excitement generated by partisan conflict and controversy, but by a record of achievement; by what I have helped to do to increase the unity and well-being of the people of this country.

I have learned – I supposed it goes back to my parsonage origins – that the triumphs and the failures of political life, the hottest partisan debates that command the top headlines, are seldom of enduring importance. The real trends and the big changes that determine human events flow too slowly, too far below the surface, to be readily marked by day-to-day reporting or to be affected by day-to-day political in-fighting. It is a man's relation, and it is a party's relation, to these enduring trends and changes which advance or retard the progress of a nation, that really count. And it is by this that we should all be content to be judged."

Lester B. Pearson - Maiden Speech

FEBRUARY 4, 1949 — 235

The Address—Mr. Pearson

is the minister in a position to say whether the government intends to proclaim this legislation in 1949?

Mr. G. J. McIlraith (Parliamentary Assistant to the Minister of Trade and Commerce): This question involves a pronouncement of government policy, and I am afraid I shall have to leave it for the minister.

SPEECH FROM THE THRONE

CONTINUATION OF DEBATE ON ADDRESS IN REPLY

The house resumed from Thursday, February 3, consideration of the motion of Mr. D. F. Brown for an address to His Excellency the Governor General in reply to his speech at the opening of the session, and the amendment thereto of Mr. Drew, and the amendment to the amendment of Mr. Coldwell.

Hon. L. B. Pearson (Secretary of State for External Affairs): Mr. Speaker, my first words in this debate, indeed my first words in any debate in this house, must be those of appreciation for the privilege of representing the riding of Algoma East. In this riding live friendly and industrious people. It is a riding of great undeveloped resources, of beauty of lake and stream and mountain, which makes it a tourist's paradise. I have been given a very difficult task in succeeding, as member for Algoma East, a man who has now been translated to another place and who held for so long the confidence of his constituents. I shall do my best, Mr. Speaker, to follow his example, both in service to his constituents and in his ability to sit here for so long a time. I already realize there is a connection between those two things.

I should also like to add my very warm congratulations to those that have gone before, to the mover and seconder of the address in reply to the speech from the throne. I assume there will be a debate on external policy later in this session and possibly a debate devoted more particularly to the ratification of the North Atlantic pact. Much, therefore, of what I should like to say in regard to external affairs generally will have to be reserved for those occasions. Today, I should like to attempt to do two things. In the first place, I should like to deal with some of the points that have been raised in this debate concerning international matters. Secondly, I should like to make a few general observations on the international picture with particular reference to communism and the proposed Atlantic pact, both of which are mentioned in the speech from the throne.

The hon. member for Peace River (Mr. Low) in his speech suggested, if I correctly understood him, that it was a mistake for Canada to become a member of the United Nations, and that the reference in the speech from the throne to the Atlantic pact constituted an admission by the government of this error in judgment. If I interpret him correctly, he seems to think that the weakness of the United Nations is due to some fault in its structure, and that the members of his group discerned the inadequacy of the United Nations when the charter was signed. No one claims or has ever claimed, Mr. Speaker, that the United Nations charter is a perfect document.

On many occasions this government has expressed the hope that the United Nations will be improved in many respects. The basic difficulty, however, which the United Nations encounters at the moment is not constitutional but political. The unsolved problems which divide the soviet union from the rest of the world today make it impossible, under the present circumstances, for the organization to fulfil all the purposes, or indeed most of the purposes, for which it was designed. It is precisely for this reason that the government is now giving its support to the discussions which are taking place in regard to the North Atlantic pact. By that fact we do not, however, admit that we were wrong in signing the United Nations charter in 1945 or that we are wrong in supporting the United Nations in 1949.

The hon. member for Peace River raised certain other points to which I may just refer, though I am afraid I cannot deal with them in detail. He stated that the unfortunate situation in Berlin, at the present time blockaded, with no corridor leading to the west, could not have been the result of stupidity some years ago, but he suggested it might have been, in part at least, due to the influence of perfidious civil servants. I think those were the words he used. These civil servants, he implied, may have been responsible at that time for keeping Great Britain and the United States out of Berlin and permitting the Russians to enter ahead of them before the end of the war. It has been pointed out on numerous occasions, Mr. Speaker, that that particular decision which resulted in the occupation of Berlin by the soviet union was made not by civil servants, perfidious or otherwise, but by the supreme commander himself, General Eisenhower.

The hon. member also referred somewhat critically to his experience in Germany when he witnessed the dismantling of a steel plant which was going to Yugoslavia. The house will recognize of course that, since Canada is not an occupying power in Germany, we are not directly concerned with these matters which fall within the province of Great Britain, France and the United States. I believe the hon. member said this was a matter about which I should be informing

29087—16½

myself and, therefore, I should like merely to tell him that, in my opinion, this might well have been a legitimate procedure because reparations from Germany were worked out at an international conference at which an overriding agency was set up on reparations to be levied on Germany. These reparations were to be divided by percentages among the eighteen active belligerents. These belligerents were entitled to take their share, and no doubt this was part of Yugoslavia's share, Yugoslavia having been a devastated country.

The hon. member then referred to the question of steel scrap in the Ruhr valley and the many millions of tons which were lying there idle. He believed that steps should be taken to get it out of Germany. Such steps are being taken. I believe the day before he arrived in Germany, early in October, an agreement had been reached between the United Kingdom and the United States by which 500,000 tons of this scrap was to be sent to each of those countries, and 225,000 tons to the other countries. It is hoped that within the present year more than two million tons of this scrap will have left Germany. Indeed, it is hoped some of it will come to Canada.

The hon. member for Vancouver South (Mr. Green) asked if we could state the views of the government on the situation in the Pacific. He believed the House of Commons was entitled to have those views at a time when we were talking so much about the Atlantic. I would remind the house that last year in the discussion on external affairs there was a very complete statement by the then Secretary of State for External Affairs (Mr. St. Laurent). At that time, he dealt with the Pacific, and I hope there will be an opportunity at this session for me to go into greater detail on this subject than at present. I should like to quote one sentence from a statement made last year by our present Prime Minister when he said:

> It is also the view of the Canadian government that the immediate menace of communism in the far east should not be met by the restoration of Japan to a position of such power she could once again become a threat to peace.

That remains the policy of the Canadian government.

The hon. member for Vancouver South, not unnaturally, was somewhat perturbed lest the preoccupation of the government with the Atlantic pact might indicate we were not alive to our responsibilities in the Pacific. I can assure him, however, there is no better way of ensuring the security of the Pacific ocean at this particular moment than by working out, between the great democratic powers, a security arrangement the effects of which will be felt all over the world, including the Pacific area. Our preoccupation at the moment with the North Atlantic alliance does not suggest that the government need do nothing in regard to the Pacific. We are, in fact, actively participating in the far eastern commission. We maintain a diplomatic mission in Tokyo. We took part in the commonwealth discussions in 1947 in Canberra. In various other ways, we are participating in Pacific affairs.

In his remarks the hon. member for Vancouver South referred to newspaper reports which stated that some Pacific bloc was being formed. He wondered why the government had not made any announcement in regard to that situation. I can tell him and the house that, so far as we are concerned, no proposals of that kind have been made to us by any government. We have no knowledge whatever of proposals for a Pacific alliance, nor have we been asked to give our blessing to any such proposals. The statement which he read, and which I have also seen, was a purely speculative one and, so far as we know, had no foundation at all.

To deal with more general subjects now, Mr. Speaker, I should like for a short time to give the house a review—and it can be only a cursory review at this time—of the international position as I see it. Naturally that position still gives cause for much anxiety. However, the situation should be considered, I suggest, without panic but without illusions. There is no doubt that fear has gripped the world again, fear arising primarily out of the extension of the brutal domination of revolutionary communism, based on the massive and expanding militarism of totalitarian Russia.

As yet, though there is still no ground for undue optimism, there has been, I think it is safe to say, an easing of the tension in recent months. Hon. members, and in fact the people throughout this country, will be asking themselves the question, why is that? I suggest, Mr. Speaker, that it is certainly not due to the so-called peace overtures which have recently been made in Moscow, in Rome and in Paris, by communist leaders. To my mind it would, of course, be folly and even worse to reject or discourage any genuine move toward a peaceful solution of the problems that divide the world today between the democratic west and the totalitarian east. In this connection the house, and I am sure the country, will have read with much interest the answers given recently by the head of the soviet government to certain questions asked him by a United States newspaper correspondent. I suggest that we should be careful, in our reaction to these answers, not to

[Mr. Pearson.]

confuse words with deeds or to be lured by them into wishful thinking. There is no doubt that much of the icy dread and fear in the world today would tend to melt away under the warm radiance of Mr. Stalin's smile if he could only hold it, and if it were the smile of genuine friendship. But Mr. Stalin himself has said that "there is no logic stronger than the logic of facts." That is true, and I think it can be applied to statements which come from Moscow or indeed from any other capital. The leader of the soviet government also once said to a journalist:

> The export of revolution?—that is nonsense.

But to his own people he has said in the soviet bible, which is called Problems of Leninism:

> The goal is to consolidate the dictatorship of the proletariat in one country, using it as a base for the overthrow of imperialism—

—that is noncommunism—

> —in all countries.

The people of Czechoslovakia know which of these statements is true. The leader of Russia and his followers in the various countries may now be willing to issue conciliatory statements. Of course, we should not go out of our way to rebuff them but at the same time we should not forget, in our anxiety to go far beyond half way to meet peace, that those leaders have affirmed and reaffirmed that it is inconceivable that communism and the soviet republic should continue to exist indefinitely side by side with capitalistic states. "Ultimately", Mr. Stalin has said, "one or the other must conquer." By peaceful means? There is nothing of this in the communist dogma. Let me quote again from Stalin. He said:

> Transition from capitalism to socialism can be accomplished not by means of slow change, not by means of reform, but by means of revolution.

In bringing about this revolution, tactics of course may change and misleading answers may be given to questions asked by American journalists, and which the soviet people are not allowed to see; but the strategy outlined above remains fixed and consistent. Again to quote Stalin, and I think this is the last time that I shall have to draw on his speeches or books in this speech of mine, he said:

> . . . Tactics change dozens of times, whereas the strategical plans remain unchanged. Tactics deal with the forms of struggle and the forms of organization of the proletariat, with their changes and combinations . . . The object of this strategy is to gain time, to demoralize the enemy, and to accumulate forces in order later to assume the offensive.

Is it any wonder, therefore, that the western world looks to the future with anxiety?

Men of good will continually and rightly hope for a basic change in the relations of soviet Russia with the noncommunist world. But easy optimism and self-delusion are disastrous substitutes for cool analysis and consistent policies. The door to real co-operation should always be open but not to admit Trojan horses.

If then, Mr. Speaker, the tension has recently decreased—and I think it has—it is not because of words which have come out of Moscow or because of any fundamental alteration in communist doctrine. It is because of the policy of steady but unprovocative resistance to communist aggression; of progress toward an Atlantic security league; of the steps taken to restore the military and economic strength of western Europe. These policies are working and they may have provoked one of those recurring changes in communist tactics of which we have had examples in the past.

We may welcome any such change, but we should not permit it to divert us from the course that may well have brought about the change. We should keep on the road which the democracies have recently been following and which is the best road to peace.

We must continue the policy of deepening and broadening the basis of economic and social co-operation between free democratic states; of pressing forward toward economic and social justice within our own states. By showing that democracy can contribute more to the dignity and well-being of the citizen than communism can ever hope to do, we are making our best ultimate contribution to the defence, the "home defence", against communism. This, however, will not be effective if we rely exclusively on the building up of armed forces or if we allow ourselves to be frightened into reaction and repression. In every country the communists have two great allies, social and economic injustice on the one hand, and political reaction on the other. If we can destroy these allies and build up a strong, healthy, and progressive society on a democratic foundation, we can destroy communism. That should be, I suggest, our purpose and our objective.

But, while we are attempting to reach this objective, immediate protection is necessary against aggressive forces outside our country allied to subversive forces within it. If these aggressive forces should lead the world once again into war in a struggle between totalitarian communism and our Christian democratic way of life, Canada, in my view, could not and should not remain aloof. If we attempted to do so and the other free democracies, including our two mother countries and our neighbour, were involved, as they would be, what would happen then?

Leaving aside for the moment the diplomatic and strategic strain that this would put on relationship with our mother countries and our neighbour, isolation would split our own country wide open in a way which we have avoided happily, but not too easily, in two world wars. It would be the end of Canadian unity, and therefore it would be the end of the Canadian nation. For this reason alone, Mr. Speaker, and quite apart from the fact that the next war, if we permit it to occur, would make the last one like a militia skirmish, the foreign policy of this government must be directed to one single end, the avoidance by every means within its power of this atomic catastrophe.

How can we do this? By burying our heads in the snow and allowing others to make the decisions, without our participation, which would bind us in spite of ourselves? There is no safety there. Or relying wholly on the United Nations? That to my mind would be clearly unrealistic, because that body, though it must remain the basis of our policy on international co-operation, and we should spare no effort to improve and strengthen it, remains, under present circumstances, quite unable to provide the means by which any country can ensure its security; nor does it, in present circumstances, provide an effective instrument for use in removing the causes of war.

What is the remedy, then? Surely, Mr. Speaker, the best way to minimize the possibility of war is for the free nations to stand together on a regional basis, and, by doing so, to make it clear that no aggressor has any possible chance of winning any war which he may be tempted to start. It is necessary to accumulate enough force now to preserve freedom in order that ultimately freedom can be preserved without force. This force must be organized in such a way as to ensure that it will guarantee that the free nations cannot be defeated one by one. This is the policy, sir, which I think would have prevented war in 1914 and in 1939. It is our best hope of preventing war in the years ahead. It is a policy of peace.

In the pursuit of this policy, the government has been for some months now negotiating with other north Atlantic countries who share our democratic ideals a treaty for collective defence, which would strengthen the national security of each of the participants. I hope that these discussions, which have been taking place in Washington on an ambassadorial level, will soon be concluded, and that the representatives who have been participating in them will be able to submit to their governments a complete draft of a north Atlantic treaty, which in its essentials at least can, I hope, be made public at the same time that it is submitted to governments. The next stage will be a careful study by each government, and careful examination by the public opinion of each country, of the principles embodied in this draft. Amendments can be submitted, and then a conference will be held at which I hope the treaty can be signed. It would then be for each government to submit the treaty to its legislature, in the democratic way, for approval or rejection.

What has been said about this proposed Atlantic pact in the present debate, Mr. Speaker? The leader of the C.C.F. party (Mr. Coldwell) has declared that his party agrees that Canada should support and join such a north Atlantic pact. Similarly the hon. member for Peace River (Mr. Low) said the other night:

> We of the Social Credit organization favour the Atlantic pact and support it.

There is, however, Mr. Speaker, a serious omission in the unanimity with which this matter is otherwise regarded in the house in that no single Progressive Conservative member has so much as mentioned the pact. I think I am not strictly accurate in that statement, because the hon. member for Vancouver South (Mr. Green) did mention it. He said that he thought we were busy on it. The hon. member for Carleton (Mr. Drew), the leader of the official opposition, went back two thousand years and talked about the Achaean league, which he seemed to think was a federal state, but he had not a word to say about the Atlantic league of 1949. In his opening speech, all that the leader of the Conservative party had to say about international affairs was:

> No one will disagree with the fact that the first concern of this and every other government and every other parliamentary body is to do everything humanly possible to preserve the peace and to protect the people in the country which it serves.

That of course is quite true and very well said; but why this omission? Why no reference of any kind to this very important measure which is forecast in the speech from the throne? Is this parliament not united in the objectives that we are seeking through this pact? Or are any of us playing politics with peace at this time?

Mr. Smith (Calgary West): Would the hon. member permit one question?

Mr. Graydon: The first speech and he plays politics.

Mr. Smith (Calgary West): Will the minister permit one question? In view of the fact that foreign policy has been a matter of co-operation of all parties, does the minister think he is doing any good now by making this a political issue?

Mr. Graydon: We expected more of him than this.

Mr. Abbott: Suppose you listen to the answer.

Mr. Pearson: It is because I think and hope that the foreign policy of this country can be the foreign policy of all parties in this house and of all sections of opinion in this country that I am so disappointed that no reference to this important aspect of foreign policy was mentioned in any speech from the other side of the house. I agree that foreign policy should be as nonpartisan as is consistent with responsible government and I hope it will continue that way.

Mr. Graydon: That is a poor way to start.

Mr. Fleming: Why did the government cut off the debate?

Mr. Speaker: Order. May I remind hon. members that the hon. member who has the floor should not be interrupted without his permission.

Mr. Graydon: That is bargain-counter politics; that is all.

Mr. Sinclair: The big foreign affairs expert.

Mr. Smith (Calgary West): Cheap playing with the nation's future.

Mr. Pearson: The reason I mentioned this particular matter, and this important omission, is that it seemed to me that I have been reading about and hearing about speeches on foreign policy made in other parts of this country which are far removed indeed from some of the statements that have been made in this house. That is why I express the hope once again that we will not play politics with peace in this house.

Mr. Graydon: Hear, hear; give us an example of that. The minister had better set the example on that.

Mr. Pearson: I have known the hon. member for Peel for a long time, and I do not think he believes for a minute that he is going to be able to intimidate me or throw me off my balance.

Mr. Graydon: He won't show you how to play politics.

Mr. Pearson: He used to be so effective, Mr. Speaker, in our college debating society. May I return to the main stream of my remarks. May I mention to the house certain principles which have guided the Washington discussions about which I have just spoken, and which will be embodied in the resulting treaty. In the first place, this pact will be a regional agreement, if it is concluded, under the united nations charter. It should be subject to the provisions of the charter and it should be registered with the United Nations, which it is designed not to replace but to supplement. Indeed, if by some chance the security council of the United Nations should become an effective body for the preservation of peace, then our Atlantic pact would be unnecessary and it could be allowed to disappear.

We should also make sure that the Atlantic pact does not become merely a screen for narrow nationalist suspicions and fears; an instrument of unimaginative militarism or an agency of power politics or imperialistic ambitions of any of its members. In this respect I agree entirely with what was said the other evening by the hon. member for Rosetown-Biggar (Mr. Coldwell). I feel strongly, as he does and as I am sure all hon. members do, that this regional association must be far more than a military alliance. It must make a collective contribution to the social and economic betterment of the peoples of its member states.

In the past, alliances and leagues have always been formed to meet emergencies and have dissolved as the emergencies vanished. It must not be so this time. Our Atlantic union must have a deeper meaning and deeper roots. It must create the conditions for a kind of co-operation which goes beyond the immediate emergency. Threats to peace may bring our Atlantic pact into existence. Its contribution to welfare and progress may determine how long it is to survive. The Canadian government, therefore, attaches great importance to the part which the pact may play in the encouragement of peacetime co-operation between the signatories in the economic, social and cultural fields.

There is another point and it is for us an important one. The parliament of Canada, when the time comes, must be in a position to take its decision, in regard to this proposed security pact, deliberately and in full knowledge of what it means. The nature of the obligations which we undertake must be clear. Further, our own constitutional processes by which we call these obligations into action must be preserved. There must be mutual confidence and mutual trust in the will and ability of each member of the league to discharge its responsibilities. This mutual confidence is something which we do not now find in the United Nations, and it is a fatal defect in that organization at the present time. In our Atlantic league we can hope that the situation will be different.

Canada's obligation under this pact, however, must be within the measure of our resources and as part of the plans agreed to by all and by which each member of the group does the job for which it is best qualified. If I were asked now what precisely those obligations will be, what they will involve, I would have to reply that I am not at the moment in a position to answer. But I can say this: The pact will be a group insurance policy and group insurance is cheaper and more effective than any individual policy.

Finally, every member of the group must share in all the decisions of the group even though we may recognize that the greater responsibility of some in carrying out these decisions must give their views special weight in reaching them. The treaty must therefore establish a constitutional basis by which that which concerns all is decided by all. Canada is no satellite of any country and would not be one in this association. If Canada is to be asked to share the obligations of the group, it must also share in the responsibility for determining how those obligations shall be met. On no other basis could Canada, or indeed any self-respecting state, sign such a pact.

On the other hand, it is by full partnership in a group of this kind that we can best hope to exert any influence which we possess to ensure that peaceful policies are followed by all its members.

This Atlantic pact, if we can bring it to a successful conclusion, does not give us the certainty of peace. No pact, no human achievement can do that. But it may give us a chance to establish peace in the future; and it is essential to our security in the present. It is certainly our best hope now for the prevention of aggression. It is our best hope for the establishment of relations between the two worlds on a basis, if not of friendship, at least of mutual toleration. That would give us time for men's minds to change and their souls to be freed so that toleration may turn to something better. That is all that we can ask for at this time from an Atlantic pact, but that is much and I think it is within our grasp.

In this breathing space which we may now secure, there will be time to resolve the eternal struggle that goes on between conflict and co-operation; the paradox of good in the midst of evil, of life in the midst of death. That paradox, and the utter futility of war as a method of resolving it, was never more dramatically illustrated than by the fact that the same bombers and bomber pilots who smashed Berlin and its people in 1945 are keeping those people alive in 1949.

There is nothing inevitable about war; there is nothing unchangeable about evil. If we of the free world can pursue the firm and constructive policies of resistance to communism that are now in train, refusing to be dazzled by the delusions of appeasement or stampeded by the rash counsels of panicky men, we may emerge from this wasteland of our post-war world into greener fields.

I feel certain that the people of Canada will support this Atlantic pact because it can lead us just in that direction. They will support it, not primarily because under it they can successfully wage war but because it will help them successfully to wage peace.

We Canadians know that, no matter how great the effort we make, how large the armed force we may try to build up, how peacefully we may behave, we cannot preserve our security and maintain our freedom by our own unaided efforts. To do this we must join our fortunes with those of the other north Atlantic democracies.

This is for us a new venture. But it is also a new adventure. It is an adventure in the building of a new community—the north Atlantic community. This year 1949 is an historic one for Canada. By union with Newfoundland we shall complete the work of confederation begun long ago. By helping to create a north Atlantic pact we shall have begun the work of uniting the north Atlantic community.

Mr. George C. Nowlan (Digby-Annapolis-Kings): Mr. Speaker, my first words must be of appreciation for the kindly greetings which have been extended to me by all members of the house regardless of the side upon which they sit. In that connection I should like particularly to express my personal appreciation of the greetings tendered me by the right hon. Prime Minister (Mr. St. Laurent). These are things that shall never be forgotten. I realize that some of these expressions may be tinged with regret, but I realize also that they are nonetheless sincere and they certainly are most welcome.

If it were not for the ordeal confronting me I would think that this was a most pleasant place in which to find one's self. I am sure that I have the sympathy of all those who have preceded me in this rather trying experience.

I appreciate that on an occasion such as this one does not engage in partisan political discussion. I trust I will have the indulgence and forbearance of the house. I should also like to express my best wishes and congratulations to those other fellow sufferers of the other afternoon who were introduced to the house prior to myself. I am sure that like myself they found the walk from the door to the clerk's table one of the longest walks upon which they ever entered in their lifetime.

I think most of them have already participated in the debates of the House of Commons despite the fact that only a little over one week has elapsed. I wish to congratulate all of them and express my good wishes to them,

Pierre Trudeau

The Pierre Trudeau Comet – A Leader Must Be A Leader

(15th)

Date Elected to Parliament:	November 18, 1965
Date of Maiden Speech:	December 4, 1967
Date Sworn In (1st term):	April 20, 1968
Date Left Office:	June 3, 1979
Date Sworn In (2nd term):	March 3, 1980
Date Left Office:	June 29, 1984

Comets travel millions of miles through outer space until they are seen by keen eyes flashing across the dark universe leaving a trail, dazzling streams of light. Comets are shaped and reshaped from the moment they break off from a far-off planet and make their own way through endless space across Earth's sphere.

Pierre Trudeau[116] personified a sudden burst of political energy, lighting the Canadian political landscape as no other that came before him. When he first campaigned as leader in 1968, it was called 'Trudeaumania' – unlike anything we have witnessed before or since.[117]

---

[116] Pierre Trudeau's full name was Joseph Phillipe Pierre Yves Elliot Trudeau. He preferred to be Pierre Elliot Trudeau and used the acronym PET. Elliot was his mother's name born of Scottish and French-Canadian descent.

[117] It was the spirit of Expo 67 and the era of the Beatles and the memories of movie-like political 'celebrity' of John F. Kennedy that still resonated across in Canada. Pierre Trudeau offered Canadians their first political taste of political 'celebrity' marked by raging 'teenyboppers' who ranted

A careful parsing from his life, one finds an overly energetic, then suddenly passive youth, quixotic, quick-silver mind, raised in a comfortable wealthy upper-class family in Montreal who had fallen for extremist motifs as a youth. As a teenager, he had written a play with anti-Semitic stereotypes. He took up fascist causes and public protests railing against conscription during World War II typical of his Quebec milieu. Then he began to invent and reinvent himself with little parental guidance. He had lost his father while in his teens. No doubt his mother was a strong woman and a steady influence, but she was not a disciplinarian. He came from a bilingual family. Trudeau could choose early on how to spend his own time, free from monetary concerns or parental restraints. At an early point as a teenager, he decided that he could be a leader, but how?[118] He was trained by Jesuits at Brebeuf College, the best school of its kind in Quebec.

Travelling widely after World War II to far-off places like Africa and China, he was always carefully observing and noting local customs and practices. A study in contrasts, he travelled frugally, but could enjoy a life style of comforts with fine clothes and expenses spent carefree. At all times, he had the comfort of his wealthy background. He rode a big motorcycle in a German helmet and drove a sleek foreign sports car as he raced around Montreal. He was a pilot as well.[119] My late cousin, Bob Kaplan[120],

---

and screamed at him as if he was a 'rock' star. He personified a distinct break in politics away from the vitriolic exchanges between Pearson and Diefenbaker and the sedate politics of the St. Laurent era.

[118] In retrospect, this seemed a strange early ambition in Pierre Trudeau himself a loner. Perhaps the two tropes intersected as he also considered to be a man destined for action.

[119] Later as Prime Minister, he flew a jet fighter with a RCAF pilot and broke the sound barrier – the only Prime Minister to dare to do so.

[120] Robert (Bob) Kaplan was a second cousin. His mother Pearl, my first cousin, was born a Grafstein. Bob was a brilliant multi-linguist and close

travelled with Trudeau in Africa before they entered politics and regaled me with Trudeau's curiosities and interests which led him away from the group to venture off on his own, to satisfy his incessant curiosity that ranged from native languages, to tribal food, to artifacts, to clothing, to customs. Reveling in going 'native', Trudeau fancied dressing in local headgear. He loved to pose in photographs taken in his travels. An adept linguist,[121] he was a lover of languages with a quick ear to pick up foreign tongues and local dialects. He travelled to China with his closest friend Jacques Hébert and they wrote a book on their travels there.[122] Nudged by Hébert, Trudeau became a passionate capital punishment abolitionist. His early visit to Russia where he caught public attention by throwing snowballs at iconic statues was a harbinger of his iconoclastic public style.

That he chose to prepare for politics and leadership early can be seen by the schools he attended, the books he read, the courses he took, and the travels he chose. Never far from his religious beliefs, as a practicing Roman Catholic trained by Jesuits, he demonstrated a deep devotion to the Church as he attended Catholic retreats by Dominicans and Benedictines regularly well into middle life. Without fanfare, he would regularly attend mass

---

friend of Trudeau before politics, ran for Parliament in 1968 and became Solicitor General in Trudeau's cabinet in 1980.

[121] Trudeau by far was the most multilingual of all Prime Ministers. Trudeau had an ease with languages. He could order Chinese food in impeccable Mandarin. Of course, he was fluently bilingual in both speech and writing. He easily acquired a good speaking ease in Latin, Spanish, Italian, and passing knowledge of German and some Arabic. He could order a Chinese dinner for eight or so in impeccable Mandarin with ease and then frugally divide the tab between each diner based on what they asked him to order for them.

[122] *Two Innocents in Red China*' with Jacques Hébert (Douglas & McIntyre, 2007).

at home and at times abroad. Apart from his Catholic beliefs, he held a deep curiosity for other faiths – from Islam to Buddhism. He was a student of ideologies from fascism to communism to socialism, always searching for the political path to an elusive utopia. He trained himself in the rigorous arts of self-defense to gain confidence and poise. Early on, after being enamored by fascism, not unlike some other Catholic thinkers and activists of his genre, he quickly became disenchanted with fascism and nationalism, maintaining to the end, a softness towards Communism. Socialism continued to hold for him its utopian goals, like many of his French-Canadian intellectual milieu. At times, he equated socialism with 'progressivism', but later muted this topic as his experience began to beckon otherwise.

His early colleagues like Jacques Hébert, Gérard Pelletier, Pierre Juneau, Fernand Cadieux, and Claude Ryan, each with a socialist bent, served in the Catholic Youth Movement as organizers dedicated to practicing and proselytizing the Catholic social gospel. Meanwhile Trudeau was never active in the Catholic Youth Movement but remained a passive if interested observer. He attended University of Montreal, Harvard[123] and

[123] At Harvard, he worked towards a Masters Degree in Political Economy where his Harvard dissertation was on Communism and Christianity and then went on to study in Paris in 1947 at the Institut d'Études Politiques de Paris where he intensified his interest in Emmanuel Mounier, the French philosopher and founder of the 'Personalist' school premised in the individual's choice of political action. Paris was then in a political, philosophic, and cultural ferment, divided between the Gaullists on the right and the Communists on the left that affected every part of civic society and culture. Trudeau considered himself a 'personalist' influenced deeply by. He was also attracted to the writings of Nicolai Berdyaev and his book *Slavery and Freedom*. Politicians, academics, journalists, writers, and artists were deeply divided. This attempt to build a third political force ended a few years with little or no impact to break the stalemate was led by established writers like Albert Camus, Jean Paul Sartre, Simone

finally London School of Economics where he fell under the sway of Harold Laski, the leading intellectual labour socialist whose influence continued throughout his long career.[124] One belief he gained and held throughout his career was intense anti-nationalism. Nationalism, he felt, narrowed the mind and encourage intolerance and stunted liberal progress. In this sense, he disagreed with Walter Gordon, an anti-American economic nationalist. By instinct and desire, he remained a lifelong globalist. His interest in socialism ebbed and flowed agreeing with some of socialist nostrums yet critical of their means and party structures that were enthralled with extremist solutions.

Bud Estey – a friend and mentor of mine, lawyer with wide skills, and later as Supreme Court Justice – who attended Harvard at the same time as Trudeau confided that Trudeau was an indifferent student at Harvard and failed to make an impression on his co-students, known more for his absences than attendance or participation in class. Trudeau, Bud was convinced, left no

de Beauvoir, Andre Malraux considered a leftist and became a major supporter of DeGaulle and his first Minister of Culture. It was called the 'Middle Way'. Budding American writers like Richard Wright, Irving Shaw, James Baldwin, Norman Mailer, Saul Bellow followed in the footsteps of Ernest Hemingway. Journalists like Theodore White and Mary McCarthy were sharpening their writing skills. The line between politics and culture was impossible to discern. No doubt Trudeau was a keen observer. Artists like Picasso, Soutine, Calder of U.S.A., and Jean Paul Riopelle of Canada were there. Paris was the world's centre of intellectual debates and artistic ferment.

[124] After Trudeau obtained his law degree at University of Montreal in 1943, he was conscripted into the Canadian army and was not sent overseas. While he said he was prepared to serve overseas, he felt betrayed by the Federal Government's Conscription Act and became an outspoken opponent of conscription. He became politically active for the first time in the 1942 Outremont riding federal campaign for Jean Drapeau, an anti-conscription candidate and later Mayor of Montreal.

academic trail at Harvard. This was not fully accurate. Trudeau, by nature, was a loner, especially when he went to Harvard alone for the first time in an English-speaking environment. At Harvard,[125] he came away with A's in his chosen subjects which included tough courses – economics and political philosophy. He studied Keynes and Hayek – the leading economic thinkers of the time. He was diligently preparing his ideas for leadership even then. Then onto the London School of Economics where he deepened his thinking on ideas of governance and social policy directly influenced by the socialist gadfly Laski.[126] By nature, Trudeau was, and remained, a contrarian. Trudeau relished going 'against the grain' and questioned politics by consensus. His studies in Paris followed as he broadened his philosophical outlook and began to appreciate the difference between political theory and practice.

Trudeau wrote a stunning prescient essay on *Political Violence* which he prepared at Harvard that has a strong resonance in today's political world (*Citizen Trudeau: An Intellectual Biography 1944-1965* by Allen Mills, Oxford University Press, 2016).

On returning to Canada, Trudeau sought, and obtained, in 1949 a position as researcher at the Privy Council in Ottawa in the King era where he enlarged his circle of intellectual colleagues and intensified his studies in federalism and the British North American Act (BNA), the Canadian Constitution – the central tenet of his research. He learned how the federal government and the Cabinet worked. He was not impressed. The King Cabinet processes, he felt, were chaotic and failed to set out clear options

[125] Trudeau kept detailed notes of his studies and he critiqued his teachers. He established a lifelong skepticism and analyses of established political ideas and theories early on. He considered himself a 'contrarian' by instinct and preference.

[126] Trudeau wrote an obituary when Laski passed away in the *Cite Libre*.

for action. He wrote concise memos for Cabinet deliberations. No doubt, he had decided that to reach for politics and for leadership, he needed experience and grounding in government operations.

He developed distinct ideas of the interplay of government and business. Later he wrote that he envisaged governments as a counterweight to business. This thesis he polished and attempted to practice in government. Others in the Liberal party believed government should be held in check by the Blackstonian premise of 'checks and balances' at every stage government exercises power.

The only question that haunted Trudeau early in his career was where and how to make his political entry point. He opened a law office in his mother's home. Then as he taught law at McGill, he became interested in the travails of the Quebec worker during the long Athabaskan miners strikes. He began with a flourish as a gadfly using his gifted pen to write biting polemics, essays, and articles on behalf of workers and against what he termed 'Quebec feudalism'. He railed against the conservative leaning Church and Duplessis and his Quebec government and federal government describing how each impeded social progress. Trudeau set out to create intellectual ferment and disruption and reveled in it – poking holes in other contemporary polemists, especially their articles and books. He was not enamored by separatist thinkers. He ridiculed and exposed the flaws in the 'compact theory', then a premise of separatist ideology. Separatists limited Quebec's growth and opportunities, he argued. Better for French Canadians to capture the federal government than one province.[127] He began to delve deeply into political organizations

[127] In arguments with Rene Levesque and other separatists, he would say, "*Why limit France to three million in Quebec when by bilingualism, one can spread the French language to all of Canada?*"

and federalist philosophy presenting as it did for him the most efficient way to govern countries like Canada divided as it was along ideological, linguistic, geographical, and provincial lines. A Hegelian, he sought to uncover the contours of the 'perfect' government.

In the early '50s, he even attempted to cofound a new political party mimicking perhaps similar attempts in France by Sartre, Camus and others called the 'Middle Way' in the latter '40s he must have observed while in France. His efforts, like theirs, gained no political traction and were soon abandoned.

Short-tempered, even arrogant, with those he disagreed with especially his nemesis in Quebec, Rene Levesque who, unlike Trudeau, came from a working-class family, and earned his way as a working journalist during World War II[128] and afterwards as a TV Commentator who gained a wide loyal audience. Levesque and Trudeau were instinctive competitors and grew to dislike each other intensely. Levesque thought Trudeau was arrogant and Trudeau thought Levesque's ideas were shallow and undeveloped. They clashed bitterly even before Trudeau entered politics.[129]

Gerard Pelletier, editor of *LaPresse*, founded with others the *Cité Libre*, a scintillating intellectual magazine that acted as a forum for intellectual ideas opposing the autocratic Duplessis government in Quebec and at times the Liberal government in

[128] As a World War II correspondent, Rene Levesque visibly observed a 'death camp' in Europe that was liberated and later wrote that his experience shaped his interest in politics and political ideas.

[129] According to Rene Levesque in his *Memoirs* (McClelland and Stewart, 1986), they first met in 1954 or 1955 in the Radio Canada cafeteria arranged by Gerrard Pelletier to convince Levesque to contribute an occasional article to *Cité Libre*. "*Very good*", Trudeau said in the drawling tone he affected. "*But allow me one simple question – Can you write? You will have guessed by now that we did not actually hit it off.*", wrote Levesque.

Ottawa. Pelletier persuaded *Cité Libre's* reluctant board to make Trudeau a member where he immediately and actively engaged in its political direction and contributed crackling acid editorials, essays, and even eloquent eulogies. Trudeau wrote acidic essays that deplored and exonerated his intellectual opponents on the left, and the right. His articles in other intellectual magazines like the Journal of Political Science and attendances at the Couchiching Conference in northern Ontario brought him to the attention of intellectuals in English Canada, like Ramsay Cook, Ian McDonald and others, where he was better received than in Quebec. He polished his stinging polemics as he rigorously attacked the autocratic rule of Maurice Duplessis. Unable to obtain University tenure due to his censorious activities against the Union National government, he refused to shrink his articulate biting polemic criticisms.

Trudeau found comfort amongst the gilded middle-class socialist circles of the CCF in Montreal, especially Charles Taylor, a life-long socialist and ideologue. Taylor became a close friend. In the early '60s, Trudeau attacked all Liberals, mainly Pearson, for reversing his position on the placement of nukes and Bomarc missiles in Canada under NORAD and, who like Diefenbaker, was against such U.S. missiles being placed or tested anywhere in Canada. While he was combative and vitriolic, he joined the left in its blanket condemnation of Pearson on the Bomarc issue in the 1963 federal election. Later, Trudeau recanted becoming a Liberal M.P. in 1965. Trudeau quickly learned to revere Pearson who quickly set him on his path to leadership first as his Parliamentary Assistant and then as Minister of Justice.

In the early '60s, Liberals were one of Trudeau's prime target accusing Pearson and Liberals for being tardy in introducing promised reforms. This was unfair as Pearson was energetic on social and Quebec issues. Pearson established the Royal

Commission of Bilingualism and Biculturalism. Pearson recognized he needed to shore up Liberal support in Quebec. He enlisted energetic and well-schooled intellectual Quebecers like Maurice Lamontage, Maurice Sauvé, Marc Lalonde and others. Still, Pearson wanted more fresh electoral blood from Quebec. Pearson convinced Jean Marchand, the leading Quebec Union leader, and Gérard Pelletier, the editor of *La Presse*, to run for Parliament in 1965. They insisted that they would not join the Liberals banner without their colleague Pierre Trudeau who was their intellectual gadfly. Trudeau could not find a French-Canadian seat in Quebec that would have him. Mount Royal in Westmount, the seat traditionally held by Jews and Anglos, opened. And so, Trudeau took his first step in his lifelong quest for political leadership. His CCF socialist opponent in the Riding was his good friend, Charles Taylor. This campaign, and especially their sharp exchanges, cooled their relationship forever.

Trudeau rigorously practiced the art of politics. He worked hard at his technique before and throughout his political career. In the late '50s, he had tried out as a CBC TV public affairs host, only to lose out to avuncular Larry Zolf, a humourous journalist, author, and astute political observer. Trudeau's style was too studied, too laid back, too haughty, perhaps too arrogant. His first steps into television were unimpressive. But Trudeau always learned from his mistakes and worked hard to improve his style. He never gave up working on his technique.

In 1980, the historic Chateau Laurier ballroom, the scene of so many historic dinners including Churchill, the Royals, and US Presidents, was jammed by Trudeau fans, Liberal supporters and the usual fellow travellers, lobbyists, and a cluster of senior public plutocrats attempting to pass unnoticed but trying to catch the eye of Trudeau and his senior Hill staff. The crowded room, now bright with TV lights, awaited the magic moment.

Behind heavy red velvet floor-length curtains and guarded heavy wooden doors, a small group of us involved in the campaign observed an exuberant Pierre Trudeau flush with his miraculous comeback electoral victory as he graciously thanked each of us. Pierre Trudeau, like a phoenix, had risen from his defeat only months earlier in the 1979 disastrous campaign that saw a surprised Joe Clark beat Trudeau in the TV debates and exceed even his own modest expectations. Joe Clark had won that last campaign fair and square and a beaten Trudeau who had quickly resigned and ridden off into the sunshine in his classic winged door Mercedes red convertible assuming the end of his political career. He grew a scruffy beard. But fate and Allan MacEachen, Jim Coutts, Keith Davey, and others including myself had urged Trudeau to withdraw his resignation and seek another shot at the leadership.

The leader in waiting, John Turner, leading in all the polls was not taken in. He chose not to throw his hat in the leadership ring. Donald Macdonald, a trusted and well-liked minister in the Trudeau cabinet, who had decided to run when Trudeau resigned, withdrew with Trudeau's return, who now chose to quickly regain the confidence of the calculating Liberal caucus craving for an early return to power, position, and vindication. Allan MacEachen, the master strategist of the Liberal caucus, played a key role in orchestrating support for Trudeau on the caucus. The intrinsic power of the caucus at key moments such as this requires deeper analyses. Power is the magnet of attraction. Though split in factions, the majority of caucus concluded Trudeau was the best bet to return the Liberals to power though many disliked him for various reasons – less on principle than for personal reasons of pique or preferment for positions large and small.

It was a miraculous twist of political chicanery. The lust for power, the most compelling elixir in politics was on naked display. The rules for a leadership contest were quickly adjusted by a malleable national Liberal Party executive and Trudeau was back in the cat's bird seat and wildly received especially by Liberals lusting for government.

At the victory celebration, Trudeau, surrounded by close advisors, was radiant and ebullient. Messages were sent in notes from powerful supporters like Paul Demairais, the most powerful man outside politics in Canada. I know that for a fact as I was asked just before I entered the sealed room off-stage at the Chateau if I could hand a small elegant envelope to Trudeau with the Demairais name on it marked confidential. I watched as Trudeau opened the envelope, read it slowly and smiled with obvious satisfaction. Trudeau was back.

As the crowd impatiently began to chant, "*Trudeau, Trudeau, Trudeau*", his personal assistants, led by the bright and always calm, sanguine, lean and understated Bob Murdoch, pointed him to the break in the curtain leading to the ballroom, nodded as the heavy curtain was divided and Trudeau walked through alone followed several paces behind by his small respectful entourage and the waiting crowd exploded like a bomb-blast. Trudeau, also flushed with excitement, modestly weaved his way through the adoring crowd led by his security guards to the podium emblazoned with the Liberal election banners that we at Red Leaf had created and the roar of the crowd was deafening. He stood in a modest pose with eyes down and then basking in the bright lights, he raised his head and slowly surveyed the crowd slowly with glistening happy penetrating eyes said in a jubilant voice, "*Welcome to the '80s*". Jim Coutts, emotional at these moments as always, standing on the floor at the side next to the raised stage beside me, was choked with emotion and his eyes were drenched in tears. I admit my eyes were moist too. The Liberal Party was back.

Let me take a step back and relate my personal experience. After Trudeau's 1972 election debacle, I helped found Red Leaf – the Liberal media consortium – at Trudeau and Keith Davey's urging and help enlist the 'mad men' of advertising for the Liberal Party. It is a curious tale that lies forgotten in the entrails of the Liberal Party. Red Leaf started as an imitation of the 'Big Blue Machine', the Conservative advertising consortium headquartered in Toronto, and allowed the Liberal Party to enter into new wild world of media in a coherent organized way. Red Leaf's origins started right after the lack lustre Liberal electoral showing in 1972 that led to a minority government after Trudeau's smashing electoral victory in 1968.

The 1972 'The Land Is Strong' was the national Liberal election campaign slogan which Trudeau proclaimed as he went across the country 'to listen and learn' was laughable and a disaster. Even Liberal candidates giggled and gossiped about it. John Turner gagged when he campaigned on it. It had been dreamed up by Trudeau, his somewhat inexperienced campaign advisors, and George Elliot, the brilliant intellectual soft-spoken red-head who was a creative director from McLaren Advertising, the largest agency of record that had served as the major repository of Liberal advertising since Walter Gordon modernized the Liberal Party apparatus for Mr. Pearson in the late fifties and early sixties. Trudeau and Elliot who became mutual admirers, had developed a close working relationship. It was not clear who was the 'horse' and who was the 'jockey' – a great race horse needs a great jockey, as they say in politics. Trudeau had a direct hand in every aspect of that campaign.

Trudeau in a way, after his extraordinary 1968 campaign coined by the media 'Trudeaumania' campaign highly organized by his 'newbie' team swept him into office on the waves of his astounding public persona that captured the spirit of a new and exciting and youthful post-Expo era. Trudeau had inherited McLaren's advertising organization who in that campaign sustained its Liberal advertising monopoly, and in the 1968 campaign, could do no wrong. The campaign slogan was 'Towards A Just Society'.

Everything worked for Trudeau back in 1968. The crowds were lavish, excited and excitable. Trudeau, captivating like a rock star, mesmerized the media. He did stunts like diving acrobatics during the campaign. Women loved him and shrieked like groupies. The copycat phenomenon of Jack Kennedy was hard at work with Trudeau. Canadian politics had never experienced anything like it. It was the personification of the 'new politics'. "*It was like a wave*", moaned Eddy Goodman, a top Tory organizer. Robert Stanfield, Diefenbaker's successor, the former Premier of Nova Scotia, was a decent, low key and boring leader. It was a break from the dour drab past. Trudeau had worked diligently on his campaign technique, thinking of so-called spontaneous acts that captured public attention, all of which were carefully thought out.[130] Trudeau had an instinct of how to grab media attention.[131] It's as if the old party structure and players were not only unnecessary but counterproductive. The Liberal Party had been captured by the new Trudeauites who had run his successful leadership against all the establishment candidates both left and right and won after a harrowing five ballot victory.

With a flourish after his late Saturday evening leadership close victory in the spring of '68, he called on the Governor General (GG) the following Monday morning and tabled the election writs in the Commons as the first order of business. The

[130] Trudeau had privately visited the U.S.A. to observe Robert Kennedy on the campaign trail and how he handled crowds during his run for the U.S.A. Presidency.

[131] Trudeau did flips off a swimming pool board. Meanwhile, Stanfield fumbled a football.

speedy action that did not afford Parliament an opportunity to provide Mr. Pearson a final public tribute in Parliament for his decades-long career would later reverberate and come back to haunt Trudeau in 1972, especially with the Liberal establishment in Toronto who were Pearsonian loyalists. Pessimists to the core, many activist Liberals felt, as I did, that Trudeau was insensitive to Mr. Pearson who had quickly promoted his career to date. But in the 1968 campaign, Trudeau and company and McLaren's George Elliot could do no wrong.

Then the 1972 campaign with the new Trudeau's inexperienced national campaign clique in charge left the established and experienced party stalwarts sitting on their hands, neither invited nor wanted. But by this time in 1972, the glow of Trudeaumania had worn off. The first Trudeau cabinet composed of many of his adversaries had failed to gain broad spread public support. His newly renovated public service had not matched the experienced expertise of those mandarins he had shifted out. The Quebec crises and his fearless actions, ducking missiles at a separatist parade seen on television, that had garnered him accolades in English Canada and launched him into the Prime Ministership in 1968 faded from memory. Trudeau himself seemed to have lost his way in his inept policies to transform the public process by an unending stream of policy papers. There seemed no priorities but rather a limitless range of meandering public policy discussions. He had launched a review of foreign policy that was dull and unimaginative. His 'new look' Aboriginal policy wobbled. Nothing seemed to work. His reforms of Cabinet processes were ineffective and seemed to snarl up the process and the public was, as ever, indifferent to bureaucratic reforms. The exacting theme of the 'Just Society' of 1968 became an irritating memory. Just as the aspirations of 'New Frontier' of Kennedy faded, so did those of the 'Just Society'.

That moved the Liberals under the leadership of Trudeau from Trudeaumania in 1968 to the brink of disaster in 1972. The Liberal machinery under Walter Gordon and Keith Davey that engineered the new wave of Party reform (the 'new politics') since the disastrous defeat of the Liberals under Mr. Pearson in 1957 was not renovated or updated but left out to pasture unattended. The established Liberal Party was not needed, the 'newbie' Trudeau entourage proclaimed. The 'old guard' was discarded and so they sat on their hands.

After the disastrous 'The Land Is Strong' campaign in 1972, the 'new' politics led to the creation of Red Leaf. A consortium of hip Liberal bent advertising agencies was modelled on the Big Blue Machine that originated in Toronto in the '60s, started by Allister Grosart, Mr. Diefenbaker's top communication advisor.

A short history of political advertising in the two major parties might be illuminating. Starting with a memo from Grosart as campaign director of the 1956 and landslide Diefenbaker Conservative campaign of 1957, the agency that housed these talented ad men from J. Walter Thompson and other older standbys like 'Red' Foster were brought under one roof in a creative and executive consortium. There congenial Grosart and later a brusque Dalton Camp and his brother-in-law, the shrewd and avuncular Norman Atkins, evolved and spawned a new advertising consortia way of engaging media experts across agencies when the media environment was about to explode into the cable world of multi TV channels and electronic news cycles. For his dynamic efforts, Grosart was appointed to the Senate by Diefenbaker and later, while he continued as a loyal insider to Diefenbaker to the end of his career, became a most courteous and graceful Speaker of the Senate.

No idea in politics or art is original. New ideas are adapted or stolen from other successful ideas. Red Leaf was adapted from the successful model called the Big Blue Machine that brought together talent from a number of also politically sympathetic agencies all craving federal or provincial business contracts. This Tory consortia worked for Bill Davis in Ontario. Coming from New Brunswick, the experience of Dalton Camp combined with the earlier Grosart provided zippy commercials for the Diefenbaker winning campaigns, then the Bill Davis campaigns in Ontario and Stanfield into Nova Scotia and then the unsuccessful Stanfield federal campaigns onto the Clark and continued with successful Mulroney campaigns. The concept of a consortium of talents from a number of sympathetic agencies adapted from the Big Blue Machine model was inculcated into Red Leaf. Keith was the godfather and I was his faithful executor. Polling had been learned from Americans like Harris and at Keith Davey's suggestions was now taken over by Martin Goldfarb, another Davey recruit. Robert 'Bobby' Squires, a leading Democratic strategist in Washington, became my good friend after I headed Red Leaf when Keith insisted, I befriend him. Keith advised I could learn from him which I did. Bobby taught me the art of 'advocacy' adverts sometimes wrongly named 'negative' advertising. If they were humourous, factual, accurate, and memorable, they worked. Blend the positive that were bland with 'advocacy' adverts that had traction was the appropriate mix, Squires advised!

Keith and I had shared our concerns with one agency, MacLaren's, running the show. A monopoly approach that left out other talented ad men, anxious to help. Trudeau and Keith Davey asked me to head this new approach because I was a communications lawyer involved in media enterprises, a grass roots organizer, but most important, while knowledgeable about the media and advertising, had no interest or desire for government advertising contracts. More important, the competing heads of sympathetic agencies would work together under an outsider they respected but would not take direction from anyone connected to a competing agency. So, with Keith's advice and help, and outside advice from Bobby Squires, how to structure this 'new agency', we gathered an outstanding group of ad executives and built a 'virtual' agency. From McLaren came Tony Miller, an account executive, and David Harrison, tall and handsome, English-born a wry and witty media 'buy' expert, from Vickers and Benson, a Harvard graduate and addicted runner Terry O'Malley considered the most talented creative writer and award-winning ad man in Canada (cars and hamburgers), and the Bremner Brothers especially Ron also an adept media buyer and the handsome low-key Michael Koskie, a suave account executive and a former son-in-law of a broadcast pioneer Ken Soble, the pioneer head of CHML radio and CHCH TV in Hamilton, to handle and coordinate the myriad details and accounting. Michael looked like a movie star, soft-spoken, smooth, effortless, and a joy to work with especially under the time pressures of a campaign. Gabor Apor, a talented independent commercial director, was chosen to act as a semi freelance producer to execute the TV commercials, Henry 'Hank' Karpus, the witty warm-spirited former child radio actor and comedic writer for CBC Wayne and Shuster show, senior partner and creative director of Ronald Reynolds, and of course, the irrepressible Gerry Goodis – more than a handful at the best of times.

With the avuncular elder executives like Bill Bremner and Brian Vaughn at Vickers, and George Sinclair at McLaren's who provided experienced sounding boards, Morgan Earle, Canada's top radio commercial producer and independent TV directors like Ted Kotcheff who went on to fame and fortune as a successful director in Hollywood, provided gems of free time for longer pieces on TV that allowed for a narrative and commentary more suited to films than TV. Later Norman Glowinsky, a bright young advertising partner in his own small firm, was added to the roster of talent at my insistence. To this mega talented pool, we invited Jim Coutts to coordinate with Mr. Trudeau and quick-witted genial Tom Axworthy, Trudeau's favoured speech writer and policy advisor. We added Gordon Ashworth, a bright young Liberal activist from British Columbia to negotiate the detail of the leaders' debates that have become a mainstay of political campaigns but then were in their pioneering state. Red Leaf quickly became a smooth, effective, vertically organized, 'virtual' advertising machine.

Polling was the platform to measure effectiveness and focus groups to test each commercial before airing. Keith had enlisted Marty Goldfarb, who I befriended years ago when he was working as a kitchen helper at a summer camp I attended as a counsellor. Marty had provided research and strategic advice to Ford Motor Company and other large international organizations. He did all the polling for the Liberal Party and Red Leaf as an executive group. Marty, an anthropologist by training, was a key player and sounding board and brilliant common-sense strategist. He did more. He could divine the public's shifting tastes and interests and characterize them for our advertising campaign in TV, print, and radio.

To demonstrate to the Liberal Party during this lead up to the 1974 election, it was vital to enforce change and modern techniques of canvassing and organization in each riding. Keith Davey set up Campaign Colleges across Canada to teach volunteers at the grass roots level to canvas, talking points and poll organization leading up to Election Day to get out the vote. The most graphic change was to illustrate the unity of the Liberal Party from the streets up. So, we at Red Leaf devised a new uniform graphic look for lawn signs, t-shirts, and political paraphernalia to be deployed in each riding. Easier said than done, but this was accomplished. The graphics were carefully designed with a bold modern font in white and passionate red. The first launch was York University in Toronto. Pictures and posters of Pierre Trudeau were on display as Pierre Trudeau and Margaret showed up to display the new logos and to ignite the volunteer base. I came up with an idea to give Trudeau red coloured running shoes and have him try them on. Dorothy Petrie, the astute unflappable Ontario Chair, was there to help. There was a great 'foto op'. It worked. To launch the campaign, we arranged for Trudeau to board a large train engine to show power and movement. That worked too.

So, in the run up and during each campaign, I lived in various advertising office board rooms and editing suites for 80 hours a week in the weeks leading up to and into the campaigns themselves while constantly on the phone to Keith or Jim. It was the era of the 'mad men' of advertising. They were all 'mad men'. Their sleek, elegant offices and equally elegant attractive staff were a joy to behold. Liquor or beer, to which I was not accustomed to imbibing, especially during the work week, was readily available before the magical hour of noon. I divided the work and supervised and collaborated on every aspect of creation, production, and execution. Most invaluable was Marty Goldfarb to this process – vetting the copy or testing lines for the ads, both for TV, radio and print, the polling, and focus groups to test the commercials and revise them to suit and persuade the public. Gabor Apor was the brilliant director of the thirty-second and one-minute adverts written by Terry. Each word and image was important. Gabor and I slaved in the edit room to cut each commercial. Then I had the daunting task to preview the finished ads before exhibition on radio or TV to the entire National Campaign Committee and the Prime Minister himself in Ottawa. I would cull those ads that failed to meet a consensus. It was exhilarating, at time hilarious and exhausting. Seeking perfection and consensus is an acquired taste and many talented minds clashed. Everyone pictured themselves in politics as advertising experts. It was hard to corral the cats but with Keith's help, I did.

Keith Davey had a hands-off approach on the creative side but played a pivotal role to settle disputes on the utilization of limited funds, who to ignore and where to heavy up and keep the provincial campaign committees at bay and in line. The most sensitive collaboration was with the Liberal Montreal advertising consortium that were responsible for French language TV, radio and print, and 'free' time in Quebec. We in Toronto prepared the materials and it was my job to convince them to allow the same line, if not the same execution. Pierre Trudeau insisted on the same messaging in Quebec as we broadcast across Canada. Keith would send me off on a tour across Canada to visit Provincial Campaign Teams to get their read on our media plans especially TV spot commercials. Keith was the master at reading this rigorous art form allowing me to concentrate on the production of the TV commercials themselves, radio, and free time television and print adverts. Mr. Trudeau was both an engaged and detached participant, as our 'star' and leader. Nothing was exhibited without his prior approval and he had a good gut sense of what would be effective.

In 1974 with rising inflation across the country, Stanfield and team decided to run on wages and price controls. With Goldfarb's guidance, we dissected the issues of wages and price control; and decided to centre and frame the Tory campaign with a clever ad. "*Mr. Stanfield wants to freeze your wages and it just won't work*". Or "*Mr. Stanfield wants to zap your wages.*" The advertising campaign gained traction. Terry favoured full page newspaper adverts stuffed with details of the Liberal platform promises as an analogue to our more emotional TV and radio campaign.

Four vignettes from the 1980 campaign. To provoke humour and interest in the campaign committees, Terry O'Malley and I designed a TV commercial of a rooster that morphed from the image of Joe Clark for 1980 campaign with the slick creative production work of Gabor Apor. It was a wicked but humorous thirty-second advert that we produced only for internal consumption. When we presented all the ads to the National Campaign Committee, including Trudeau, in Ottawa, all were aghast at this one ad. I was closely cross-examined. What were the results of the focus groups? What could be the negative consequences? I had only intended the controversial ad for fun and internal consumption and create respect for our creative endeavours because every political hand became an instant expert and critic of commercials – the 'narcissism of small things'. In any event, I responded that this 'ad', the 'turkey ad', was the most powerful ad we had ever produced. It had strong after images, I argued. It was persuasive. It was tough but witty. Everyone didn't know whether to laugh or criticize. But I got the go-ahead except from Trudeau, who was silent throughout the presentation. After the meeting, Trudeau asked Keith to invite me to have a private conversation in his office in the Langevin Building near the boardroom where we had exhibited all the commercials. Keith stood leaning at the closed door in his bespoke Harry Rosen dark blue pin-stripe suit and matching vest with his arms crossed, head down. Trudeau came around his large neat desk and beckoned me to sit down.

He wanted me to review again the focus groups data about the 'turkey ad'. Trudeau was clearly uncomfortable. I then gave him an exaggerated version of the focus group results as there was none! "*This was the best ad we have ever done. It tested better than any other ad. It moved people to laughter and affection affirming the negative feelings they had about Clark…*" and so on and on. All this I did quietly, with a firm, passionate conviction as Trudeau listened intently. Then Trudeau glanced over at Keith leaning against the closed office door with his arms tightly folded across his chest. Keith was looking down at the floor smiling. When Trudeau glanced at him again, Keith couldn't control his mirth. He broke out laughing at my preposterous claims about the impact of this thirty-second commercial. Trudeau knew he had been had. "*Get out of here! Both of you!*" he said barely able to contain his own laughter as he waved us out. Keith was roaring outside the office and I finally broke my control and laughed with him. Keith taught me the joy of politics.

Trudeau worked assiduously on his technique and became a quick study and even a more gifted communicator. He continued alone to practice with a private coach, a former CBC musical producer, a pixie-like Irishman, who would regularly critique, improve, and fine tune his public persona and public performance.

All Trudeau needed was a line or so for a precise take of a thirty-second or sixty-second commercial. In the 1980 campaign, a television session for political commercial spots was arranged in Toronto in the Sheraton Centre. The breathtaking backdrop was the Toronto city skyline. Trudeau was dressed in a bespoke dark blue pinstriped three-piece suit with a fresh rose in his lapel.[132] The strategy in this campaign was to 'low

[132] In the 1980 campaign, Trudeau first dressed in a crumpled, comfortable, tan-coloured corduroy suit. I talked to Keith to see how to fix or improve his wardrobe. Keith called Jim Coutts and was warned off. Trudeau, he confided to Keith, did not fancy advice about his clothing. So, Gabor Apor and I conspired without Jim and Keith to see if we could fix it. Gabor and I decided when he was next in Toronto to take him after his TV shoot to

bridge' Trudeau. The public liked Liberal policies, but were still disenchanted with Trudeau, especially in the West. I thought the rose in the lapel was out of place. Just before I asked him to do a thirty-second close-up shot on energy policy, a hot issue in the campaign, I took the rose from his lapel holder. Trudeau paused, called me over and whispered, "*Put the rose back in my lapel.*" I quickly did so and then whispered to Gabor to do only a head shot so the rose would not show.

Weeks later as we reviewed all commercials for approval with the campaign committee and Trudeau in Ottawa, I placed the Trudeau head shot at the end of the spots, No.19 to be exact. Trudeau said nothing as they were all approved. At the end of the meeting, Trudeau beckoned me to join him alone in his office. He said pleasantly, "*Don't run No.19.*" Trudeau had a sense of himself and he was true to his own deliberately crafted public image.

Trudeau was a gifted polemicist. His early essays are unrivalled, before he entered politics focusing on his 'ideas fixe' about federalism and his staunch opposition to separation. Trudeau, who was always very conscious of his image and his brand, chose a photograph of him in his Indian beaded jacket, paddling a canoe into the wilderness – like a voyageur of old as the cover for his autobiography *Memoirs*. Later he had his speeches carefully collected and published, again modestly seeking to embellish his role in history.

But back in 1972, Pierre Trudeau was not very happy with me. While for years in the '60s, we had been members of a

---

Studio 467, a fine men's clothing shop, on Richmond Street and Yonge after hours. There we had earlier selected suits, shirts, ties, overcoats, and hats and laid them out for his inspection. Trudeau, quizzical, tried on a jacket or two, and asked why we had done this. I said, "*You, Sir, are our star and we want you to look like one.*"

small circle who regularly exchanged intellectual fusillades and at Chinese dinners or small dinners at the Club Universitaire in Ottawa and we shared a devotion to Fernand Cadieux, the brilliant thinker and provocateur, Trudeau had brought Fern to work in Ottawa in the entrails of the Privy Cabinet office in 1968. I had played a leading role in John Turner's leadership campaign in 1968. When Turner stayed on until the second last ballot, Trudeau was not amused or pleased. We fell out.

As for me, I shared Pearson Liberals' unease about Mr. Trudeau, because of his earlier broadsides at Mr. Pearson before he ran as a Liberal in 1965, and especially since his decision to drop the Election Writ in 1968 before Parliament could pay tribute to Mr. Pearson. Mrs. Pearson was miffed, to say the least – less about Trudeau's earlier criticisms and more about his treatment of Mr. Pearson after becoming Prime Minister, especially since Mr. Pearson and his aides had quietly given Trudeau special scope and opportunities and opened his path toward his leadership aspirations.

Then, after the outburst of 'Trudeaumania' in 1968, Trudeau's 1972 national campaign, heralded as an 'Encounter with Canadians', and bearing the campaign slogan 'The Land Is Strong', had begun to flounder and fall flat. Public adoration of Mr. Trudeau's charisma and charm had changed to public chagrin. Liberals were sinking in the polls. The Toronto Liberals, whom Trudeau had failed to cultivate after his sweeping 1968 victory, sat back. A Progressive Conservative government was looming. Stanfield was leading in the polls.

Several weeks after the launch of that disastrous 1972 campaign, I received a call from the PMO, inviting me to meet with the Prime Minister on his next campaign swing through Toronto. The Conservatives, under the brilliant direction of the 'Big Blue Machine' in Toronto, were steadily gaining momentum.

I had barely spoken to Trudeau for several years and his campaign team remained leery of Toronto Liberals. We met at the Prince Hotel in north Toronto, the Japanese-style hostelry that Trudeau favoured.

Pierre Trudeau had one uncanny knack. Dispassionately, he could separate himself from his persona and performance, and analyze his own strengths and weaknesses as if reading his own X-rays.

After the usual family pleasantries, he asked, "*How are we doing?*"

"*I am doing fine*", I answered. "*You, Prime Minister, are losing Toronto*", I rejoined.

"*Why so?*" he asked softly.

"*Because, you, Sir, have failed to engage Liberals. Besides, Liberals in Toronto are unhappy with your treatment of Mr. Pearson, and now he is dying.*" By then, Mr. Pearson was suffering from cancer. Liberals knew this. Trudeau fell silent and pondered, chin in hand, looking down.

Then he slowly raised his head, captured me with his penetrating look, and asked quietly and firmly, "*Is there anything that can be done to change the situation?*"

I knew that was why he had invited me. I immediately responded, "*Yes, there is something that can be done.*"

"*What would that be?*"

"*We would have to transfer the love and affection the Toronto Liberals have for Mr. Pearson to you.*"

His eyes narrowed and then lit up. "*Is that possible now?*" he asked, given that we were in the midst of the election campaign.

"*Yes, I believe it is possible*", I said.

"*How?*"

"*You, Sir, could throw an intimate surprise birthday party for Mr. Pearson. Toronto Liberals know that Mr. Pearson was dying.*

Toronto Liberals are sitting on their hands. All that we would need would be Mr. Pearson to attract them back."

"*Would it work?*" he asked.

"*It can only help, and it cannot hurt.*"

"*Where would you propose to hold such an intimate surprise birthday party?*"

"*At the Maple Leaf Gardens of course.*"

Trudeau broke up. "*Where?*" he laughed.

"*At the Maple Leaf Gardens.*"

"*Why do you think you could fill Maple Leaf Gardens when our campaign crowds have been so sparse? I can't get 500 people to an event.*"

"*Because, Sir, every Liberal in Toronto would want to come and have a last chance to pay their respect to Mr. Pearson. I think we could fill the Gardens, at least 18,000.*"

"*Would you help organize it?*"

"*Yes, on three conditions.*"

"*What are they?*"

"*First, your campaign team agrees not to interfere. Second, we must convince Mr. and Mrs. Pearson to attend, which I believe is possible with the help of Keith Davey, Jim Coutts, and others. Finally, you have to agree yourself to work that whole day in Toronto until midnight.*"

Pierre Trudeau was most curious about the third condition. "*Why is that important?*"

"*Because, Sir, Liberals work hard in Toronto. Meanwhile, your campaign has been working half-time and you have been meandering.*"

Trudeau agreed and immediately called to instruct his national campaign chairman, Bob Andras, from the Lakehead, to support the event. Trudeau handed the phone to me and Bob agreed to help in any way. We quickly set out to put the restless Toronto Liberal machine not only in motion but in high gear.

Keith Davey, Jim Coutts, Royce Frith, Dick O'Hagan, and I attended on Mr. and Mrs. Pearson's corner suite at the Park Plaza Hotel, which Mr. Pearson always preferred. Despite Mrs. Pearson's initial reluctance, Mr. Pearson overcame her irate vocal objections and agreed to be the 'surprise' guest at 'a surprise birthday party in his honour'. He was bemused by the idea and anxious to help the Party.

Dorothy Petrie (later married to Keith Davey), a superb Liberal organizer, agreed to be Co-Chair. One call to Harold Ballard, who revered Mr. Pearson, gave us the Maple Leaf Gardens. Dorothy and I set out to call every Liberal candidate and every riding president in the greater Toronto area to get their commitment to bring four hundred or more from their riding to the rally, or if not would not be allowed entry into the arena.

Angelo and Elvio Del Zotto (then in the baking business) agreed to provide a six-foot-tall birthday cake, billed as 'the biggest birthday cake in Canadian history'. Popular Canadian musicians were enlisted to volunteer their talents. A snappy downtown Toronto media blitz was quickly deployed. Liberals came alive in Toronto. We decided to calibrate the seating capacity of the Gardens to eighteen thousand, confident of an overflow crowd. We prepared a wagon top outside on College Street, from which Pierre Trudeau could address the disappointed throngs unable to enter the Gardens.

The City buzzed with excitement. Mr. Pearson's appearance was not announced to the media. The event was billed as a Liberal Rally to rejuvenate the Liberal team. The local media woke up. Liberal organizers were quietly informed about the 'surprise guest' and outdid themselves to bring as many Liberals supporters from their ridings as possible by bus, car, and transit.

Liberals knew Mr. Pearson, their adored leader, was dying of cancer. A curious public appeared in droves.

At the rally, over twenty-eight thousand people showed up, effortlessly filling the Gardens and overflowing onto all the streets around. Trudeau spoke to those jostling outside just before the event. Loudspeakers were made available so outsiders could listen to the program and speakers inside.

Royce Frith, then a seasoned broadcaster,[133] was MC for the event. All the Toronto Liberal candidates were on the stage to bask in the glow of their two inspired leaders. Mr. Pearson was introduced as 'the surprise guest'. The giant six-foot birthday cake was wheeled in, candles ablaze, and Prime Minister Trudeau, Mr. Pearson, and all the Toronto candidates clustered around the cake and joined in to blow out the candles, followed by a rousing chorus of 'Happy Birthday'. That was the image that would be pictured in the papers and TV.

Mr. Pearson spoke briefly and beautifully. There was not a dry eye in the jammed arena. Then Mr. Trudeau spoke. A stirring rendition of the national anthem of '*O Canada*' followed as the audience roared with one voice and the evening came to a tearful and emotional end. The volunteers streamed out of the building, energized with the new sense of purpose.

It was only 9 P.M. Mr. Trudeau came backstage to thank me and the other organizers and take his leave. I asked him where he was going. He seemed surprised. He thought his job was done. I reminded him of his promise to work until midnight. He laughed and asked, "*What is left to do?*" I motioned him into a small room backstage, where there were a thousand or more

---

[133] Trudeau appointed Royce to the Senate where he became Deputy Leader. Later, he was appointed High Commissioner to London. I told him at the time it was easy for him to make the transition for Royce always wore finely tailored bespoke suits.

small white cardboard cake boxes lining the walls. I then invited him to autograph, with a black marker pen, every single white box.

Eyeing the huge stacks of cardboard boxes warily, he asked, "*Why?*" I told him when he finished his final task, I would tell him. I smiled and said, "*For Toronto Liberals, our work is never done*" or – as Keith Davey would put it with apologies to Yogi Berra – "*it's never over 'til it's over*".

Trudeau began to autograph each box with his scrawled signature – Best Regards, Pierre, Best Wishes, Pierre, Thank You, Pierre, All the Best, PET. Shortly before midnight Mr. Trudeau completed his task. I then told an exasperated Trudeau that each small cake box would now be hand-delivered to each newsman, radio reporter and commentator, TV anchor, TV reporter, and (for that matter) disk jockey in Toronto, and to each member of the national media covering the campaign. The national TV news coverage was upbeat that night, with sympathetic shots of the audience.

The next morning on CFRB radio, an ever-caustic Trudeau critic Gordon Sinclair but an admirer of Mike Pearson, with the largest listenership in Ontario reported on the rally at length. The lines went something like this: "*Even that arrogant Trudeau cannot be that bad. Look how he treated Mr. Pearson. Good for you, Mr. Trudeau.*" That refrain was repeated endlessly in television, radio, and print. The echo chamber was alive and well. The Toronto media warmed to Mr. Trudeau, as did the Toronto public. The Tory momentum slowed. The Liberal polls in Toronto started moving up. Don MacDonald held his seat in Rosedale. The Liberal government held on as a minority government.

Throughout the many political challenges ahead, Toronto formed the bedrock of Trudeau's support that enabled him and Liberals to achieve such historic milestones as the Charter of

Rights. Two years later, in 1974, Trudeau, now fully supported and engaged with Pearson Liberals, won a surprising victory and recaptured a strong majority government.

Trudeau never forgot the lesson. The 'Land Was Strong'. So was Pierre Trudeau. So were Liberals.

Trudeau sought out Jim Coutts as his Chief of Staff, he turned to Keith as his chief political organizer and enlisted Tim Axworthy as his policy and speech advisor. Keith, in turn, built an outer circle of advisors that included me and Marty Goldfarb. We all liked and trusted each other.

The first Party to recognize the need to gather the top talent from a number of agencies were the Conservatives led Allister Grosart, an adviser to John Diefenbaker and Red Foster, followed by Dalton Camp and his brother-in-law, the rotund jowly Norman Atkins, built like a butcher, had a curiously high pitched tenor-like voice asked to join his brother-in-law Dalton Camp to form the nucleus of the Big Blue Machine, a consortium of conservative advertising agencies like the Foster Agency that from early 1950's ran the advertising, polling, and communications for the provincially and federal elections culminating in the 1984 and 1988 federal triumphs of Brian Mulroney. Dalton Camp was a suave politico who as President had led the revolt against John Diefenbaker and split the conservative party from 1966 till 1984 when the party finally united under the shrewd political hands of Brian Mulroney. A key to those successes was Dalton and Norman whose acolytes now swarmed around Parliament Hill in the offices of the Mulroney cabinet and in conservative party headquarters. This skillful team that learned from the Nixon team (i.e. Roger Ailes and Bob Haldeman), and later the Reagan ad techniques and political organizational know how and American pollsters were a formidable election machine. The charisma of Pierre Trudeau allowed him and his amateur but enthusiastic leadership campaign group of neophytes to sweep away the remnants of the Diefenbaker era now under Stanfield and gain a large nationwide victory without the help or indeed the need for the Liberal Party apparatchiks.

This all changed as Trudeau's inexperienced, almost amateur-like leadership clique stumbled and frittered away his electoral popularity that was exemplified by his 1972 campaign led by two key players, the quietly brilliant George Elliot of McLaren's Advertising, the leading liberal ad agency and since Pearson, when Walter Gordon, the agency of record for the liberal party themes and paid media, Bob Andras, his avuncular and likeable campaign chair, a former automobile dealer in North Bay. Together Trudeau and Elliot had agreed on a campaign theme. It was to be a low-key conversation with Canadians, an unconventional soft sell approach with the mystifying almost comical slogan – 'The Land Is Strong'.

Pierre Trudeau used the polls to calculate how they might be deployed to achieve his political objectives. He refused to be a slave to polls, but he learned to use polls to accomplish his political objectives. In 1979, in the short run, the polls indicated that the public was disinterested in repatriating the constitution from the British Parliament. There was little public support for the Charter of Rights and Freedoms. On the contrary, the public opposition for both those goals was fierce. The status quo had its robust and fervent followers.

The paramount preoccupation by polls inhibits progress especially when economic interests stultify change and the media, increasingly in the hands of corporate interests, does little more than fellow travelers in reform or change obsessed by sensationalism in violent crimes or disasters. Now the social media is transforming the players and political agendas, but then the polls ruled. Yet, the polls were just snapshots in time. This Trudeau understood.

The secret of the national caucus lies hidden behind opaque curtains. The heart of power in our political system is 'confidence'. Maintaining a vote of confidence is the key to gaining and retaining political power in Canada. Yet, less is known about the traditions and practices of party caucus than any other aspect of political governance. The nature and custom of caucus other than sporadic and distorted leaks, is not studied in courses in schools, little discussed by experts, rarely considered in law schools where the focus is on dissecting legal process from law to its enforcement. Nor does the public understand the fragility of our system of governance that all hinges on confidence in caucus behind closed doors and open votes of confidence in legislatures.

To explore how different leaders mastered the art of caucuses is a necessary prequel to a clearer understanding of political power as obtained and held in Canada. Trudeau, unlike other leaders, sat at the raised lead table facing the caucus, but did not sit in the middle as did his successors. Instead he sat at the end listening and scribbling the odd note. The Cabinet ministers sat in the front row with the assembled caucus facing the Prime Minister, the Whip, the Chairman of Caucus, and the Senate leader. Trudeau never intervened except to ask Ministers to respond to a member's query or criticism of a report.

In an early Liberal caucus under Pierre Trudeau that I attended as Senator, a stunning lesson was learned. Trudeau, in the winter of discontent in 1984, was languishing in public opinion for him historic lows, in the lower twenties. Trudeau's constitutional reforms, more pleasing to the elites than the public, had failed to gain wide public approbations. Trudeau, unlike his successors, never took steps to manipulate the disorganized and disparate views of his caucus. He never preempted caucus discussion and waited until the very end of each caucus to knit together a stirring consensus. One Toronto M.P., when the open discussion took place in caucus, reported in guarded terms the negative reaction he had received about Trudeau when he had returned to his Toronto riding to mend fences over the holidays. I now attended caucus as a newly minted Liberal Senator. My eyes turned to Trudeau sitting at the end of the raised table in front of caucus who listened as he did very intently to everything that was reported by the various regional and special committees after reports by the house leader and whip. Cabinet ministers would sit at the front facing the raised table and were asked by Trudeau to respond if Trudeau felt an M.P. or Senator had made a telling critique.

At the end of caucus, Trudeau rose and knitted together a brilliant summary of the rambling and, at times, conflicting views of the caucus members and at the end, gathered his notes and papers together and this time, standing after a long pause, said in slow measured terms directly to the one lone mildly critical member, after carefully gazing around the crowded room which leaned forward to catch every word – that "*this was the last time*" Trudeau said quietly and firmly that he would sit "*and listen to criticism in the caucus of his leadership*". Then he swiftly left the capacious Railway room to the stunned silence and then, the sotto voce whispers of amazement. A day later, he took his celebrated winter walk alone in the woods and to the surprise of all, including many of his closest friends and advisors, announced his decision to give up the leadership of the party and turn the reins of power over to a successor.

Aghast, I immediately asked to see him privately to urge him to reconsider. A day later, we met privately in his office on Parliament Hill. I urged him not to resign. There was unfinished public business for him to complete. The caucus, I argued, was overwhelming supportive. One lone dissenter didn't speak for the party or the public. Trudeau said that I had not yet learned the basic principle of governance which rested on the principle of confidence of the caucus. I disagreed and said that the caucus was solidly supported. He then said, "*From your vantage point, standing at the back of caucus, you could not read the caucus as I can. I watched carefully the eyes of the members when the M.P. criticized me. The caucus was losing confidence in me and my leadership. I have no other choice but to resign.*"

Astounded I left his office speechless. For the very first time, I learned and never forgot the lesson of what 'confidence' means in our political system, taught by a master practitioner of parliament – the unknown power of the national caucus.

Other stories will be told of the limitless power of the national caucus, unknown to historians and even the weekly media voyeurs, but few understand its central position or our form of responsible government. This event defined the word 'responsible' for me.

One first-hand story from Trudeau's last turn in office. Before he chose to announce his retirement, Trudeau decided to film his version of his legacy. A brilliant documentary filmmaker was retained to film and supervise the editing under Trudeau's watchful eye. Keith Davey and I were invited by Mr. Trudeau to join him in a filmed three-way conversation as part of the film. The film made use of sixteen-mm rather than tape for a better cinematography result.

We were invited to sit at a small round table, Trudeau, Keith and me. The Producer would name the topic and we entered to an easy, unrehearsed conversation to illuminate and elucidate Mr. Trudeau's take on his accomplishments. Every eight minutes, we would pause while a fresh film cartridge was loaded with the Producer giving us the next topic to consider. We all had a great and relaxing time.

For one segment, the Producer raised the question of the infamous swimming pool installed at Trudeau's behest at 24 Sussex. Private donors had been enlisted to pay the cost. This created some negative public controversy as the donor names were not made public while the media suggesting conflicts of interest and worse.

When the Producer suggested this topic, I turned to Mr. Trudeau and asked not to be part of this segment. He and Keith could do this alone. Trudeau was curious. He wanted to know why I balked at my participation. I asked him if he had control of the content and editing of his film. Trudeau affirmed that yes, he had the final say. Then why, I asked him, would he want to include this controversial episode in his version of his own record. Trudeau paused and told the Producer to skip this subject. So we continued. Leaders want to sanitize their version of their history.

All this happened because of my willingness back in the early '60s to volunteer to work hard at party grass roots organization with energy and enthusiasm and some skill at rousing my peers like Monte Kwinter[134] to join and become active in the Liberal Party at the precise time when Keith's motto of work or get out opened the party from the bottom up to new resourceful hard working volunteers. It was fun. You felt you could make a difference. It was the post-Kennedy period of politics that so influenced Canadian politics – "*Ask not what the country can do for you but what you can do for the country*" was the organizing metaphor.

My first opportunity as the Young Liberal President of Toronto was to organize policy came in late 1962 at a small

[134] Monte Kwinter went on to be elected to the Ontario Legislature and retired as the longest serving member in Ontario history.

conference in Toronto billed '*What Does Quebec Want?*' Keynote speakers were the exuberant Maurice Sauvé, a leading reformer for Quebec, and Donald McDonald, a downtown lawyer then seeking election in St. Paul's, a downtown Toronto riding. It was an eye-opening success. This was followed by a like policy conference in Montreal that I helped organize with Jean David,[135] the youthful editor-in-chief of La Press under Gerard Pelletier, Michel Robert, a young militant 'reform' Liberal, and others, all of whom became great friends.

After that meeting in downtown Montreal in 1962, Jean took me and the other organizers to a bar on Crescent Street to continue our excited discussions. While drinking beer, Jean suggested I meet with a friend and political activist, then a fellow traveller of the CCF. Leaning beside the bar was this nonchalant man dressed in a thick, white turtleneck sweater and a dark leather jacket and beside him was a shorter balding man wearing tiny round owlish spectacles. "*Pierre, I want you to meet Jerry Grafstein, a Liberal militant from Toronto.*" Pierre Trudeau nodded nonchalantly, still leaning against the bar. "*I know all about Trudeau*", I said to Jean to the surprise of Trudeau. "*I read a lot of your pieces, especially your recent piece 'Towards Economic Rights' – not very well developed*", I lamented. Trudeau suddenly became alert. "*What did you think wasn't well developed?*" We started into a heated exchange to the bemusement of Jean and Trudeau's drinking buddy. "*You can do much better than that*", I exclaimed, as our argument continued. The discussion ended with my suggestion that it be continued at a later time. Trudeau's companion, a short, stocky smiling man with wire-frame glasses, smiled and Jean introduced me to Pierre Vallières, the author of

[135] Jean David was by far the most insightful Quebecer I met especially about Quebec. He died prematurely in a car accident. Had he lived, no doubt he would have become a major political actor in Canada.

the *White Niggers of America: The Precocious Autobiography of a Quebec 'terrorist'* that had recently been published and became a leading separatist tract.

Our first meeting was memorable for me and remembered later by Trudeau when he came a Member of the Parliament from Montreal from an Anglo-Jewish riding of Mount Royal-Westmont as he could not, by his own admission, be elected in a Francophone riding. When he came to Ottawa as a freshly minted M.P., I was serving as John Turner's Executive Assistant. We renewed our relationship and met regularly for dinner with a small circle of politicos and public servants.

When Pierre Trudeau became Minister of Justice in 1965, I was working as an executive assistant and speech writer for John Turner. The afternoon of his appointment, Trudeau came racing down the hall ripping off his tie. I was in the hallway as he was passing near my office. I accosted him and congratulated him. Then I said, reminiscent of Trudeau's criticism of Pearson, "*You have been Minister of Justice since this morning, what have you done for the country today?*" Trudeau stopped in his tracks, paused and in his thoughtful way, looked me in the eyes with a smile and offered, "*What do you think I should be doing?*" I immediately went into my office, came out and handed him a series of speeches Turner had given on law reform. Turner was as disappointed as I was when he wasn't appointed Minister of Justice. "*Here are some ideas in John Turner's speeches. Wait*", I said, "*I will get you the French translations in case you don't understand.*" Trudeau laughed and took away the bundle of speeches. The next morning, he called me at nine o'clock. "*I've read Turner's speeches. They are very interesting. Let's keep in touch.*" which we did.

One other anecdote. In 1973, I was asked to write an article for the 50th anniversary edition of the Canadian Bar Review

(The Canadian Bar Review was founded in 1923). I chose the topic *Law and Technology: Towards An Economic Bill of Rights.* I sent the article to Trudeau who was then Prime Minister. He wrote me a letter detailing my faulty analyses. I responded with a detailed reply to his criticism. He responded with a brief note. This went on for several months. Finally, I wrote him that while I appreciated our exchange, he had better things to do like running the country. His last note said, "*You are right... but you are still wrong.*" These notes should be found in the Trudeau files in the National archives. Trudeau, from his early years, was assiduous in keeping files on his writings and correspondence.

But now in 1979, Trudeau was stuck. The polls had tanked. The 1979 campaign was faltering before it got started. Trudeau had waited too long to call the election. Loyal troops were leaving. Pierre Trudeau was pre-occupied with his private life and was listless and unenergetic. The country's economic performance was anemic. The team around Trudeau, including me, searched for a theme. The polls were dismal in all categories and indices except for leadership. Desperately combing past campaigns for ideas and policies based on jobs, hope, vision, action, future – all to build a clothes line to hang rewoven policies on it. Nothing felt right. In the end, the theme must connect and resonate with reality and with disinterested, unhappy or distracted voters. Each member of the inside team had ideas. Marty Goldfarb had a batch. Jim Coutts and Tom Axworthy had other takes. I had a hamper full of ideas. Keith, as always, waited to review other ideas immersed as he was in the myriad details of staffing, stroking candidates' ruffled egos, leaders tour, cabinet concerns, and each provincial campaign team demands for funding ridings, leader's time and allocation of slender resources.

I convened a meeting of the Red Leaf team anxious to weigh in, to review theme ideas after a presentation of some of the less contentious results. The full story was too grim, so Marty was asked to polish the positive highlights with polls which clustered around the leadership index. We were optimistic that Trudeau compared Joe Clark would pull us out of the mud. Trudeau's leadership index was the only winning poker card in the hand. On most other issues, the Conservatives were well ahead. Finally, Terry suggested a private session with just the two of us. Terry O'Malley was the cerebral Harvard trained creative director at his agency, Vickers & Benson. Terry was not good at large unstructured meetings. He rarely spoke out, could not focus, and he was restless if he could not get 'the message' in the material. His right knee increased its jerking movements when the meeting was a waste of time as we circled around looking for a theme that resonated as his sharpened pencil tapped on the table beside his open notepad.

So, we met alone in his sleek modernist boardroom. Terry, quiet, thoughtful, and terse as always, asked what I had gathered that we could work on the quickest – a theme for the TV commercials and print ads. Radio would be an echo chamber for the TV while the print adverts would be long and factual, crammed with policies, a technique Terry preferred.

"*What have you got?*" We went through the list and nothing seemed to move him or me. Until I concluded that the only positive in the polling was 'Leadership'. Trudeau was much higher in public opinion on 'leadership' than Joe Clark for obvious reasons. "*Leadership' is all we got, all we have right now!*"

Terry, with his long lined legal pad in front of him and several sharp pencils at his side ready to write, asked, "*What do you mean by 'leadership'?*" "*I really don't know.*" – a little exasperated with myself for the thin gruel of warmed-over ideas, I had put before him. "*You know Trudeau's a leader. He's a leader. A leader does what a leader does.*"

Terry wasn't satisfied. "*What do you mean? Be more specific.*" "*Well*", I said, "*A leader leads. A leader is, you know, a leader.*"

Terry started to write. "*Keep talking*", he said. '*A leader is a leader*', he wrote. "*Yes, a leader can only lead*", I said. Then Terry wrote and said, "*A leader must be a leader.*" "*Right*", I exclaimed, "*that's it. A leader must be a leader.*" It was circuitous but it resonated.

And that became our underlying theme of the 1979 campaign. We lost. But Martin Goldfarb, who reading the tea leaves had gone to China before the end of the losing campaign and when he returned called to tell me that he will help in the next election that he predicted will become Trudeau's best. Marty was right. A 'leader must be a leader' stuck in the minds of the Canadian public. Trudeau had branded 'leadership'. Trudeau won the 1980 election by allowing the public to give Trudeau's leadership a second chance.[136]

Since that 1979 election, each successive Liberal leader and national leaders of all parties have sought to imitate and mimic Trudeau's leadership characteristics as Goldfarb predicted. Trudeau's baseline for political leadership became the goal of each successive Canadian leader – how to be a leader and how to out-do the Trudeau legacy. So it was for Turner, Chrétien, Mulroney,

[136] The 1980 campaign was not without its humourous moments. A key line of attack was against Joe Clark's two cents a litre gas price increase. So, the Red Leaf team had the idea of doing some TV adverts with Trudeau at a gas station pumping gas. Trudeau, usually adept, seemed awkward looking as if he didn't know how to pump gas into a car. This followed by another idea, Trudeau in a small restaurant crowded in a booth with workers in their working gear. One guy ordered chips and poutine while Trudeau was asking questions. It just didn't work out. We scrapped the outtakes. Not before we showed Trudeau the proposed commercials in rough cut. The best was a shot of Trudeau disdainfully watching as a heavy-set worker munched on his chips and poutine and we all had an uproarious laugh.

Martin, even Harper. The Trudeau leadership haunted them all – they each in their own way sought to emulate him in their own tailored style and in substance.

After the 1980 campaign, Trudeau hosted a small victory dinner for the core federal campaign team at 24 Sussex Drive. Keith Davey, Jim Coutts, Marty Goldfarb, me and half a dozen others. It was a joyous self-congratulating event. The 'low bridging' of Trudeau devised by Keith that had been worked through with Trudeau worked. We worked to project the mystique of leadership. The Liberal Party was popular, but Trudeau was not. Trudeau was given a short speech for two to three events each day and he began to balk at it. He was getting bored with the same repeated economic-tinged message. Jim Coutts kept him in harness. We all agreed it was working. The advertising and limited facetime was working. Yet Trudeau, in harness began to buckle. He wanted to talk about the repatriation of the Constitution. We all agreed that would be counter-productive. One day, when I joined him on the campaign trail, he complained. He was bored by the same talking points. Jim Coutts had prepped me. I was ready. "*We don't care how you repeat the message. You can use your own words. But stick to the message. Use your imagination*", and he did.

At the victory dinner at Sussex Drive, we joked about this and other incidents. Finally, Trudeau who became reflective, asked around the table what we should focus on for his next turn as Prime Minister. When it came to my turn, I said, "*Repatriate the Constitution and a Bill of Rights*". Trudeau turned to glance at Jim. They had obviously discussed this. Jim had involuntarily nodded agreement. It was a night worth remembering! Later Mart Goldfarb would remind me of what I had said that evening.

Once Mr. Trudeau told me at a meeting, "*Jerry, you have great ideas, but you have not overcome one problem that you have.*"

"*What is that?*" I said. "*I do not have any problems.*"

"*Yes, you do,*" he said. "*Each time you advocate a great idea, automatically and spontaneously, a coalition of 'antis' spring up to fight any good idea. Your job as a politician is to navigate around that coalition and get to the other side.*"

In early January 1982 on a Friday afternoon, I received a call from Trudeau. Episodic calls were not unusual. I had developed a pattern of regularly sending lengthy confidential memos to Trudeau after 1972 seen by only Jim Coutts, Tom Axworthy, and Trudeau himself. To my surprise, he would comment on each of them in writing or make a brief call. Once he asked why my memos never blamed him for his gaffs but blamed the Liberal Party or the government. I replied, "*Because it's all our fault if the government makes a mistake*".

In any event, Trudeau after exchanging quick pleasantries about my wife and sons, startled me by saying, "*We need you in the Senate. Are you interested?*" I immediately responded, "*Of course, I would be honoured to serve.*" "*Do you want some time to think about it?*" "*No*", I said, "*I would be honoured to serve but I have one question.*" "*What's that?*" he asked. "*Why did you say, 'we need you in the Senate'?*" I heard the phone fall and heard laughter from the phone. "*What's going on?*" I asked. Trudeau apologized. He was surprised by my question and it provoked laughter. He told me he has made hundreds of appointments as Prime Minister. I was the first one to ask why! "*Well, you said we need you in the Senate and I wanted to know why.*" Trudeau paused and then he said slowly, "*You have given your ideas to me and to the Party and now I want you to use the Senate as a platform for your ideas.*" With that, I thanked him again and left to ponder my fate.

Trudeau may have rued that decision. Some months after my appointment, I was due to make my maiden speech in the

Senate. At the time, the issue of apologizing and compensation to Japanese Canadians interned during World War II became a point of heated public discussion, and in Parliament. Trudeau was reluctant to do this. He felt you couldn't revise history but needed to move on. Politicians can change many things in their time. Revising history is what totalitarian governments do. You can't change history, you can only improve it, he admonished. I had embraced this issue from high school when one of my friends was Ray Suzuki (whose cousin was David Suzuki) told me how their fathers, both brothers, had been interned in camps out west during World War II and then left the west to settle in my home town of London, Ontario. I decided to do careful research into this question and went through each case Trudeau had rendered in his speeches to support his refusal to acquiesce.

His argument, facts, and history were flawed, I concluded. So I made my lengthy maiden speech in the Senate against Trudeau's refusal to apologize or compensate Canadians of Japanese descent who had been interred during the war. When I handed him a copy before I delivered it, he apparently read it and in the following week in caucus, he told me that I was wrong then and I am wrong now. "*You cannot rewrite history.*" Years later when Mulroney as Prime Minister did apologize and set up a compensation fund of sorts, I called Trudeau, then in retirement, and told him. He laughed and said again, "*You were wrong then and you are wrong now*" and we ended that exchange pleasantly as always.

Once Trudeau decided he was right, he never altered his convictions.

Back in 1967, when Trudeau was considering a run for the Liberal leadership in the fall of that year after Mr. Pearson resigned, he made an electrifying speech to the Quebec Liberals at the Bonaventure Hotel in Montreal. Other Quebec hopefuls like Maurice Sauvé and Jean Marchand spoke, but Trudeau bested them all. Trudeau had the practiced gift of arguing a complex case with originality, careful logic, and quiet passion. Trudeau mesmerized me and the audiences. Included were speeches by Jean Marchand, Maurice Lamontagne, and Marc Lalonde. Trudeau spotted me in the crowd, beckoned to me, and asked me to see him for a few minutes in his hotel suite. I headed towards his suite only to discover there was a big line up ahead of me. Mitchell Sharpe and Mike McCabe, his assistant, were waiting at the head of the queue. I bided my time. As I leaned against the hallway wall around the corner, I overheard two muffled voices, I recognized one as Norman DePoe, CBC news anchor. The other was Blair Fraser, a leading Canadian journalist. Both were in their cups. "*We're not going to let them do to Pierre what they did to Mike*", they mumbled to each other. They were referring to 'Mike' Pearson who they both admired and who they had befriended during his long career as diplomat, Minister of External Affairs and Prime Minister. They felt that politics had weakened the authentic 'Mike' Pearson. Fraser said words to the effect of, "*Norman, we both have had too much to drink. Let's talk tomorrow when our heads are clear.*"

I was committed to John Turner in his leadership run, but I knew then the media would be with Trudeau. Trudeau strode by a few minutes later and asked me to follow him to his suite past the long lineup waiting to see him. When he reached the door to his suite, he asked Mitchell Sharpe, then Minister of Finance, and his assistant, Mike McCabe, to wait for a minute or two while he spoke to me. When we got into the suite, I told Trudeau that was not a good idea to have Sharpe wait. Trudeau waved it off. I predicted Sharpe's leadership campaign would cave before the convention as he did, and that Sharpe would support him if he had a good chance of winning, so he shouldn't keep him waiting.

Trudeau was flushed and yet relaxed after his barn burning speech. He had electrified his 'Liberal' audience. "*Well*", he said, "*what do you think?*" "*What do I think about what?*" I responded. "*What's the question?*" I asked. "*What is the question?*" he responded. Thus, was Trudeau at his Jesuital best, always asking questions and rarely showing his cards.

I understood this exchange, but I felt that I didn't want to antagonize Sharpe waiting outside. So I cut to the chase. "*The question you are asking yourself is if you ran, could you even win.*" Trudeau laughed and said, "*Yes, that is a good question. What's the answer?*" I was ready for this. "*Blood is thicker than tomato juice*", I said with a straight face. "*What do you mean by that?*" he asked quizzically. "*You are worried about support here in Quebec.*" Quebec, where Trudeau was still unpopular, had, as some said, a 'divisive' personality. Three years before, he could not get a nomination in a riding in Quebec with a French majority and so ran on Montreal-Royal Westmont, where Anglo-Jewish enclave riding in the elections elected either an Anglo or Jewish candidate. Trudeau nodded slowly in agreement, waiting for my further comments. "*Well, Quebec craves power so they want to back a winner. Prove to Quebec that you have support in English Canada and Quebec will run to support you.*" "*Will you help in my campaign if I decide to run?*" he asked. I told him I could not as I had already agreed to help Turner run his campaign and Turner had agreed to stay in the race till he loses. He will not quit. But I said, "*If Winters or the others on the right are ahead, then we should agree whoever is ahead, you or Turner, will join the other.*" Trudeau was thoughtful and quiet, and on that note, we took our leave, with Trudeau saying to keep in touch.

There is a background to this meeting. When Trudeau was elected in 1965 to Parliament as I was John Turner's assistant, I gave Trudeau, on the day he was appointed Minister of Justice,

Turner's earlier speeches on law reform. We shared a common circle of friends, especially Fernand Cadieux and Roy Faibish. Fern would hold forth every Wednesday evening for a small group in the small bar at Chateau as would we. We would have dinner every two or three weeks, usually at a Chinese restaurant in Ottawa. Trudeau, ever parsimonious, would divide the bill, asking, "*Jerry, you had an egg roll, what else did you have?*" I was on a tight budget, so every penny counted.

In any event, we kept in touch regularly exchanging comments on the turbulent issues confronting the Pearson administration. Trudeau was having trouble getting law reform ideas past his conservative bureaucracy and we shared our common frustration. When my agreed year was up as Turner's assistant. Trudeau invited me for lunch. I told him I can't afford it. "*No, no*", he laughed, "*I will pay.*" So, we had lunch at the tax subsidized Members' dining rooms in Parliament. After a pleasant meal, Trudeau got to the point. Would I be interested in being his Chief of Staff at the Department of Justice. "*No*", I said, "*I promised my wife I would spend only one year in Ottawa and my year was up.*" Then he surprised me. "*Would you be prepared to become an Associate Minister of Justice, Law Reform…?*" I immediately said that was the nicest compliment I had ever received. But no, it was not doable. "*Why?*" he asked. "*Because I will never be appointed an Associate Deputy Minister from the outside.*" "*It's Mr. Pearson who appoints senior bureaucrats with the advice of the Clerk of the Privy Council.*" "*But Mr. Pearson likes you.*" "*I know, but Mr. Pearson is a mandarin, he will not appoint someone from the outside. Besides I will report to your Deputy Minister who is your problem. But I will help from the outside with speeches or policy memos.*" With that, we parted promising to keep in touch.

After leadership convention, where Turner stayed on tie the fourth ballot, that did not please Trudeau and our relationship faded until 1972 when Trudeau was in trouble in 'The Land Is Strong' campaign. I helped and we became close after that. I began to write a stream of confidential policy and strategic memos, each of which he would respond to with a call or a note until he appointed me to the Senate in 1983. These should be in the Trudeau archives.

I would be remiss if I didn't mention four other staffers Trudeau appointed to his office as Prime Minister. Colin Kenny, who later became a Senator, made the trains run on time for Trudeau. Most notable was Dennis Mills, formerly of Chairman Mills, a company founded by his grandfather that provides rentals for public and private events in Toronto. Dennis was the superb event idea man with a deep and natural feel for politicians and politics. He had a 'golden gut' for politics. Nothing was too small or too big for Dennis to handle. He went on to become a Member of Parliament for Danforth seeking a seat to run for John Turner. We became and remain best friends. When in the '80s, he sought my advice for a Toronto seat to match his interests. He had decided to run in Danforth against my advice. Liberals had not won that seat in decades. There were safer seats for him to run. I implored him. Dennis was Dennis. Dennis wanted to run to show he could make the impossible possible, which he did. Last but not least, on the staff was Tom Axworthy, who became Trudeau's talented speech writer and trusted policy advisor. Tom was the younger brother of Lloyd Axworthy, a friend and also an assistant to John Turner who I enlisted to work for Turner who went on to win a seat in the Commons and became a distinguished Minister of External Affairs.

Heading the Trudeau team, of course, was Jim Coutts, the brightest, quickest Liberal I ever met, embedded with the history and mores of the Liberal Party who started as a young Liberal candidate in Alberta where he was born and raised and caught the attention of Mr. Pearson and became Mr. Pearson's youthful appointments assistant and built an extensive network, political and business network that became a framework for his later successful business career. Likeable and always pleasant, Patrick Gossage was the shrewd press advisor. Joyce Fairbairn, a former journalist and later a Senator, added journalistic experience and a nuanced touch to the media. Bob Murdoch, a lean, quiet writing aide was also an important if understated player in the inner Trudeau team. The spark plug that kept us all together were the regular calls from Keith Davey, sometimes several visits a day, always starting with "*Well, Counsel, what do you think?*" He became emotionally attached to Trudeau and the Liberal Party and was the indispensable linchpin to his advisors under Mr. Pearson and later for Mr. Trudeau.

As for me, I enjoyed the frequent intellectual exchanges with Pierre Trudeau in person or in writing. I learned early never to take up an issue and debate with him unless I was prepared with facts and principles to back up my views. Otherwise Trudeau became impatient and lost interest.

When an objective observer reviews Trudeau's multiple accomplishments, they are long, memorable, and cast in stone:

- The Repatriation of Canada's Constitution from the U.K. and the Charter of Rights and Freedoms, and Responsibilities, Trudeau believed there could be no rights without concurrent responsibilities
- The expansion of the National Capital precinct from Ottawa in Ontario to include Hull in Quebec top make it a truly bilingual capital
- Opening the senior federal bureaucracy to wider diversity
- The institution of bilingualism in the federal service
- The creation of the Department of Multiculturalism
- The recognition of China, the day before the Americans, which miffed Richard Nixon

- The introduction of increased Family Allowances and the First Child Tax Credit to alleviate poverty
- The modernization of measurements by introduction of centigrade
- The reform of the criminal justice system affecting youth – the Young Offender's Act
- The expansion of the ocean limit to 200 miles offshore
- The judicial appointments that included Bora Laskin as first a Supreme Court member, then Chief Justice, the first Jew to head that court
- The War Measures Act introduction to lance the boil of separatism.
- The modernization of intelligence services called the Canadian Security Intelligence Service (CSIS)
- Tour of European capitals and Washington to persuade leaders, especially Ronald Reagan, to lead the world in nuclear disarmament. Rebuffed at the time and scoffed at by the media, Reagan later went on to agree with Gorbachev to a mutual Reduction Declaration.

For all these, he became an exemplar of leadership.

One final, unnoticed, aspect of the Trudeau legacy was his interest and imprint in the construction of new and exciting cultural structures open to the public. Early in his administration, he had envisaged Parliament Hill surrounded by new and graceful constructions of cultural institutions to be enjoyed by the hundreds of thousands of tourists visiting Ottawa each year. He insisted that expansion of the national capital to Hull, Quebec, building on Mr. Pearson's move to make Ottawa a bilingual capital in both Ontario and Quebec to include new buildings to house federal departments and cultural venues like the Museum of Civilization. Trudeau entrusted Moshe Safdie, as the architect of the National Gallery of Canada and worked with him on the detail of this architectural jewel. He intervened to select architect Arthur Erickson of Vancouver to build one of the most beautiful embassies in Washington DC on Pennsylvania Avenue with a spectacular view of Capitol Hill and approved much of the key details. Pierre Trudeau brought an esthetic sense to the landmarks of Canada, and beyond, unlike any Prime Minister before or after him.

Just as Pierre Trudeau repatriated to Constitution to enhance Canadian political culture and Canadian sovereignty, so he did with Canadian cultural sovereignty. Under Mr. Pearson, Parliament had passed the Broadcasting Act to usher in the age of television and cable. Pierre Trudeau by his extraordinary appointments[137] to the Canadian Radio and Television Commission under the Broadcasting Act began to Canadianize the ownership, increase Canadian content of the airwaves and invest in Canadian films and television. No Prime Minister was more active in transforming the political and cultural life of the Canadian nation both in English and French. In this, Pierre Trudeau was a Canadian nativist and nationalist.

After retirement from public life, Pierre Trudeau returned to public spotlight only a few times. Though he kept abreast of current affairs and travelled widely, he kept his opinions to

[137] Pierre Trudeau, due no doubt in part to the influence of Fernand Cadieux, appointed Pierre Juneau Chairman and independent outstanding Commissioners to oversee Canadian radio, television, and cable including Harry Boyle, a writer by profession, Northrup Fry, one of Canada's avid literary critics and essayists, Jean-Louis Gagnon who stood almost alone against the autocracy of Maurice Duplessis in the '30s and Roy Faibish, an outsider polymath – one of the most talented diverse group of appointees in recent history.

himself – grace after power. He returned once to public attention to help defeat Meech Lake when he spoke to a Committee of the Whole in the Senate how Meech Lake would alter the political landscape and weaken the central government while strengthening provincial power which was already too excessive. He spoke for three hours only checking his notes for a correct quote. When he opposed Meech Lake, Mulroney's grand constitutional gambit fell apart.[138]

Pierre Trudeau kept a close eye on the courts, especially the Supreme Court of Canada, after his retirement. When the Charter of Rights and Freedoms was introduced, politicians, lawyers, and judges with opposing views argued like John Turner that the supremacy of Parliament would be overtaken by the courts. Judges would substitute their political opinions for Parliament. Trudeau felt that the court would exercise judicial restraint. Democracy, he felt, was not about the exercise of power, but restraint in the exercise. That applied to Parliament and the Courts. It appears that often the Courts have overreached their mandate as envisioned by Trudeau. John Turner and other thoughtful critics were right. It would have pained Trudeau, especially when senior judges feel the need to enter into political discourse, to give their political views in public, or worse to consider themselves 'legislators'. This aspect of Trudeau's legacy should rightfully be reviewed. It is too much to hope that self-restraint will return to our Courts and respect for Parliament as the ultimate arbitrator of the public will. The cat is out of the bag. Social media intensifies this runaway problem.

Though pressed to make public addresses, Trudeau only attended three forums after retirement, all at universities.

[138] After Trudeau's masterful presentation on Meech Lake in the Senate that followed with questions from Senators, Trudeau asked me to review the Senate Hansard for grammatical errors, if any. There were none. No editing was needed. It was perfect.

The one I attended with delight was the opening of the Bora Laskin Library at University of Toronto Law School in 1991. Pierre Trudeau couldn't resist the opportunity to set the record straight – his version of the mistake the Supreme Court of Canada made in the majority decision written by Mr. Justice Dixon on the Constitution, holding that the amending powers of the Constitution required by convention, provinces approval. Trudeau had decided to break the Constitutional log jam after a careful reading of the law and precedents concluded the Federal government could so do unilaterally. Joe Clark disagreed. Clark argued that the Constitution demanded all the provinces agree. Trudeau disagreed. In the end, the matter went to the Supreme Court of Canada. Trudeau felt the Supreme Court decision was wrong.[139] Conventions are not legally binding, Trudeau argued. The change to Constitution was ready if the law took precedence. There was no binding convention. Trudeau wanted the last word.

The period when Pierre Trudeau was at his full power and totally engaged was during the period of his battle to repatriate the Constitution from the U.K. and pass the Charter of Rights and Freedoms. I never saw him so engaged, so energetic, so deeply involved in the strategy and each word of change in the Charter. Each word. He had a special zest for this detailed work like an artist ensuring every brush stroke was carefully painted on his canvas. Never has a Prime Minister been so deeply involved in every step of the strategy and every word of the legislation. As Isaac Berlin once wrote, "*A great man either knows many things, or one thing.*" Trudeau knew he had created one 'big thing' that changed Canada forever.

Trudeau believed that powers of provinces to intervene was limited in constitutional amendments. Trudeau gave an

---

[139] Supreme Court Justices Laskin and Estey dissented from this decision.

eloquent defense of his position supporting the dissenting decision by three Supreme Court judges including Bora Laskin, then the Chief Justice, and Bud Estey at the Bora Laskin Library inauguration at the University of Toronto. I sat in the front row reserved seats away from Mr. Justice Dixon, then the Chief Justice of the Supreme Court in audience sitting in front of Trudeau on the podium. It was delicious. I turned to observe Mr. Justice Dixon whose face grew florid, seething. After the address, Mr. Justice Dixon stormed out. I turned to glance at Trudeau on the stage who was quietly smiling. He nodded to me with a sparkle in his eyes with a toothy smile and slightly raised eyebrows as he feigned surprise. Trudeau always sought and got the last word.

A final recollection. Trudeau had a razor-sharp wit and, at times, subtle humour. Trudeau's subtle humour was evident in an incident that occurred during a G7 Summit meeting held in Ottawa during his administration. A cabinet Minister was designated by Trudeau to meet each foreign leader at the Ottawa airport and transport him to lunch held at Kingsmere, a Prime Ministerial country retreat near Ottawa, acquired by Mackenzie King, and then donated to the nation. Trudeau sent my friend Lloyd Axworthy, a left-leaning Cabinet Minister to pick up President Reagan at the Ottawa airport and accompany him by helicopter to the lawn of Kingsmere. The expansive lawn was well tended and set up for lunch for invited guests. Each leader landed behind a row of trees and his national anthem was played as he was escorted by the designated Cabinet Minister and did a walk about on the lawn to greet the guests and then was taken into Kingsmere for a luncheon for only foreign leaders hosted by Trudeau himself. When President Reagan appeared accompanied by Lloyd, I could see that Lloyd was discomforted. Lloyd was relieved when he spotted me and my older son Laurence, then a first-year student at Harvard who had joined me. Lloyd introduced me as an active Liberal from Toronto with the emphasis on Liberal and my son Laurence who Lloyd knew, as a student at Harvard. Reagan, as a small group assembled, reacted gently. "*No, no*", he said. "*I can't be seen talking to this young man from Harvard. My Vice President George Bush is a Yale man and he may not let me back into the United States*", Reagan said smiling to the outburst of laughter from the small group that had encircled us. Trudeau had a sense of humour and so did Ronald Reagan.

Trudeau could make one laugh, cry, and be in awe of his luminous intellect. All in all, he was an unforgettable leader who left an indelible legacy.

- *Towards A Just Society: The Trudeau Years* edited by Thomas S. Axworthy and Pierre Elliot Trudeau (Penguin Books, 1992)
- *Young Trudeau, Son of Quebec, Father of Canada, 1919-1944* by Max and Monique Nemni, translated by William Johnson (McClelland & Stewart, 2006)
- *Citizen of the World: The Life of Pierre Elliot Trudeau, Volume One 1919-1968* by John English (Alfred A. Knoff Canada, 2006)
- *Just Watch Me: The Life of Pierre Elliot Trudeau, 1968-2000* by John English (Alfred A. Knoff Canada, 2009)
- *Trudeau Transformed: The Shaping of a Statesman 1944-1965* by Max and Monique Nemni, translated by George Tombs (McClelland & Stewart, 2011)

Pierre Trudeau - Maiden Speech

that the members of this party are not prepared to give fair examination to the proposals in the bill when we see it, because this we always seek to do. When we express reservations, as did the hon. member for Greenwood, about the advisability of there being an appeal division, we do not necessarily mean we oppose the idea of a second vice chairman.

Anyone who has been in this house for a little while and has observed what has been happening understands perfectly well the situation we are in. Apparently the practical suggestion of the Minister of Labour caught certain of his colleagues a little off base. It seems to me that the house leader became somewhat confused by the haze created by the smoke from the fiery speech made by the Minister of Manpower and Immigration and really did not keep in perspective what has been happening on this side of the house.

I was about to say that I hope the house leader will sober up but I will say "sober down" because this conveys the sense of my meaning a little more accurately. I hope he will not seek to circumvent the statement that we clearly understood the Minister of Labour to make as to his intention. I also hope he will realize that if he does seek to do so at this stage of the proceedings it will only result in needless misunderstanding when we deal with very important questions in the whole field of labour relations and collective bargaining in this country, some of which are perhaps dealt with in the minister's bill but many of which, from the context of the resolution, obviously are not.

My own feeling for what it is worth is that the minister's proposal would enable the labour and employment committee to do something it has not had the opportunity to do for quite a long time, namely, to explore the many important questions surrounding collective bargaining relationships between management and employee as they affect the I.R.D. Act in a broader way than would be the case if we were to confine ourselves to a cursory consideration of the bill after second reading.

I think that the original attitude of the Minister of Labour when he made this suggestion is much more likely to bring positive results than the course he is being pressed to pursue, if I am not mistaken, by his colleague the Minister of National Health and Welfare. I hope that during the dinner recess the government house leader, the Minister of National Health and Welfare, will sort this thing out in a spirit of parliamentary co-operation, somewhat in the vein suggested in an earlier speech by the new leader of the official opposition. As a result the committee would be able to approach examination of what is contained in the minister's bill not without differences of view but in a proper parliamentary spirit, at the same time enabling the members of the committee and perhaps some of the representatives who may appear before it to put forward their views in a broader context than might otherwise be the case if we dealt with the matter as the house leader seems to desire, purely within the narrow context of what will appear in the bill after second reading.

Resolution reported and concurred in.

Mr. Nicholson thereupon moved for leave to introduce Bill No. C-186, to amend the Industrial Relations and Disputes Investigation Act.

Motion agreed to and bill read the first time.

PROCEEDINGS ON ADJOURNMENT MOTION

SUBJECT MATTER OF QUESTIONS TO BE DEBATED

Mr. Deputy Speaker: Order. It is my duty, pursuant to provisional standing order 39A, to inform the house that the questions to be raised at the time of adjournment tonight are as follows: The hon. member for Skeena (Mr. Howard), Immigration, British Columbia—non-participation in refugee settlement plan; the hon. member for Gaspé (Mr. Keays), Canadian National Railways—transportation of live chicks—lower St. Lawrence; the hon. member for Vancouver Quadra (Mr. Deachman), Post Office Department, Vancouver—employment of postal truck drivers.

Pursuant to provisional standing order 6(1) it being six o'clock I do now leave the chair.

At six o'clock the house took recess.

AFTER RECESS

The house resumed at 8 p.m.

DIVORCE

MEASURE RESPECTING GROUNDS, JURISDICTION, JUDGES, ETC.

Hon. P.-E. Trudeau (Minister of Justice) moved that the house go into committee to consider the following resolution:

That it is expedient to introduce a measure respecting divorce, the grounds thereof, the jurisdiction of the courts, and for the appointment of certain persons qualified to sit and act as judges and for their remuneration while so acting and for certain other provisions in connection with the administration of the act.

Motion agreed to and the house went into committee thereon, Mr. Batten in the chair.

[*Translation*]

Mr. Trudeau: Mr. Chairman, for a long time divorce has rightly been a matter for concern to the Canadian people.

We felt duty bound, as a government, to reform divorce laws, to try and bring them more in line with the present social climate, without, for all that, runnng against the demands which are normal and worthy of respect of those who have reticences on that subject.

In trying to draft the present bill we met with two types of difficulties. The first, Mr. Chairman, is related to the field of federal-provincial relations and the second were mainly connected with the matter of conscience troubling a number of Canadians who expressed their views either through the various Churches or outside of them. Those Canadians are anxious, just as I am, to modernize the divorce laws of our society, while complying, at the same time, with that basic requirement that the present government considers essential, namely the necessity of surrounding the family with maximum protection.

With regard to the problems of the first group we proceeded as follows. Starting from the fact that under the Canadian constitution, divorce and marriage fall clearly and squarely within the jurisdiction of the central government we decided against shirking our responsibilities and we drew up an act dealing with the divorce problem, attaching to the solution of that problem measures of a corollary nature, that is which cannot be separated from the effects of a broken marriage as such.

We did so, Mr. Chairman, respecting as much as possible the current traditions and laws in the various provinces. The province of Quebec is known to have, in the field of marriage, a certain number of laws contained mainly in the Civil Code and forming part of the traditions in that province; it was essential that they should be respected.

But it should be remembered that other provinces too have had for a very long time their practices and their courts which, in the field of divorce had adopted certain procedures to which we wanted to bring some

[Mr. Trudeau.]

degree of uniformity while bringing them up to date.

In regard to the second roup of problems, dealing with those I have included under the heading of problems of conscience and problems often referred to by religious organizations and by the churches, we have done two things. We have introduced in our legislation which Parliament will have the opportunity to see in a moment, special sections requiring the Court and the lawyers themselves to seek to reconcile the parties.

And we have also introduced in our legislation the concept of "the marriage breakdown" which is a concept that the churches themselves, in their joint briefs, have recommended.

This means, Mr. Chairman, that in this bill, we are taking into account, not only of the social problems which had to be solved but of the spiritual and moral problems and of the constitutional and legal problems.

[*English*]

This bill, Mr. Chairman, represents an attempt to codify and extend the present laws of divorce applied in Canada along the lines recommended in the final report of the special joint committee on divorce dated June 27 last. That report contains some 21 recommendations respecting the subject of divorce and related matters. The bill adopts many of these recommendations, some of them in a modified form. In certain instances, the recommendations of the joint committee have not been adopted and with regard to other matters a somewhat different approach has been followed. We shall, of course, be considering these matters in more detail at later stages.

Speaking in more specific terms, I should say something about the grounds for divorce as contained in the bill. Hon. members will be aware that there has been a good deal of debate in recent times respecting the desirability of one comprehensive ground for divorce, namely marriage breakdown. My colleagues and I are aware that views to this effect are widely held by well-meaning people in this country, and indeed many of the Christian churches have advocated this approach.

While recognizing that this viewpoint has much to commend it, the bill has not been prepared on this basis, but retains the traditional marital offences as grounds for divorce, and includes as well a modified concept of marriage breakdown as a new ground for divorce. In so far as we are concerned

Divorce Law Reform

with grounds for divorce, the bill can be fairly described as a composite one, recognising both marital offences and marriage breakdown. In this respect, the conclusions of the joint committee that breakdown could not constitute the sole and comprehensive ground for divorce, have been adopted.

• (8:10 p.m.)

The new marriage breakdown principle contained in this bill, since it is to be administered by the existing courts in accordance with our well established judicial traditions, shies away from the vesting of any broad, undefined and uncontrolled discretion in the courts, in favour of a definition of legal rights by parliament. The result is that, the so-called inquest approach to divorce is rejected in favour of the customary judicial approach by which marriage breakdown will be established by evidence or proof of the existence of specified matrimonial situations.

For these reasons the government considers it desirable to maintain the administration of the divorce laws in the established courts of this country, to be administered pursuant to the rules or principles of law laid down by parliament, rather than invest a broad and uncontrolled administrative discretion in some new courts or tribunals.

Notwithstanding that hon. members will find that the grounds for divorce are being substantially extended by the bill, they will find that the bill is not simply or merely a divorce bill in the traditional sense. It is also a reconciliation bill, in that it imposes stated duties on both the legal profession and the courts in relation to the matter of reconciliation, and these provisions have been included in the hope that as many as possible of the broken marriages that come before the legal profession and the courts can be saved.

The government is fully conscious of the important public interest that exists in our society in relation to the maintenance and continuation of marriage and the family unit, where this is possible. The salvaging of marriages is at least as important as the burying of dead marriages that cannot be salvaged. However, a bill directed to the subject of divorce is not necessarily the most appropriate or only vehicle that can be employed to strengthen and give substance to the marriage estate. The government recognizes that financial assistance and encouragement may well be necessary to develop adequate counselling and other agencies that are necessary to deal with faltering or broken marriages, and it is the intention of the government to keep this most important matter under continuous review.

The bill also contains provisions dealing with the law of domicile in so far as the existing law on this subject affects the position of married women in our society. An attempt has been made to place the married woman in a position equivalent to that of her husband for the purpose of obtaining a valid decree of divorce both within Canada and abroad.

No comprehensive bill on the subject of divorce would be complete without provisions for alimony, or pension alimentaire as the civil code of Quebec puts it, and for maintenance and the custody, care and upbringing of children. The bill therefore contains provisions dealing with these matters as corollary relief to petitions for divorce. Alimony, maintenance and custody orders made under the provisions of the statute will be enforceable by law throughout the whole of Canada upon being registered in the superior courts of this country.

The bill also contains provisions that will have the effect of abolishing parliamentary divorce, as we now understand it. In this regard we have departed a little bit from the report of the joint committee, but I think it is a step that this parliament is prepared to take. Therefore the Dissolution and Annulment of Marriages Act is to be repealed and divorce jurisdiction in respect of the provinces of Quebec and Newfoundland will be vested, at least temporarily, in a new divorce division of the Exchequer Court of Canada.

I mention that this jurisdiction might be temporary because the bill also contains a provision which will enable the jurisdiction to be transferred from the Exchequer Court to the Superior Court of Quebec and to the Supreme Court of Newfoundland by a proclamation issued by the governor in council on the respective recommendations of the lieutenant governors in council of those provinces. The idea is not to force upon any province a mode of procedure in the courts that it is not prepared to attain, but to suggest that, when these provinces are ready, we are ready, and that in the meantime we take out of parliament this outmoded way of proceeding, whereby divorces for two provinces had to be dealt with by one of the houses of parliament.

Consequential amendments are therefore proposed to the Exchequer Court Act. These amendments will establish a divorce division of that court, with special provision being

27053—317

made so that any person who holds, or who has held office as a judge of a superior or county court, may by special request sit and act as a judge of the divorce division. A special provision for the remuneration of such persons has been included to assure the judicial independence of such persons at all times. I am sure hon. members will realize that this is the reason we are proceeding now by way of resolution rather than by introducing a bill right away.

The bill will also contain detailed appeal provisions and a number of other matters that do not need to be discussed at this stage. However, it should be mentioned that there is a clause in the bill which will prevent it from coming into force for at least three months after it has been assented to. This provision has been inserted to permit the holding of such discussions or conferences as may be necessary to facilitate implementation of the new laws throughout the country.

[*Translation*]

I should like to mention here, Mr. Chairman, that such period of consultation should also allow the federal government and the provinces to discuss an extremely important other problem, that of judicial separation.

Hon. members will see that in this bill, we have dealt with divorce only; the problem of judicial separation has been, for the time being, I hope, temporarily set aside. Hon. members will readily realize the reason why we have chosen to proceed in this way. If we had included the matter of judicial separation in this bill, as it would have been easy to do when drafting this legislation, this bill would have raised very complicated problems of implementation in a number of provinces.

I do not refer here, Mr. Chairman, to constitutional problems because, although the matter is debatable, we feel that the judicial separation comes under federal jurisdiction, since it falls readily—

[*English*]

Mr. Baldwin: Would the minister permit a question at this stage? Would he be prepared to say at this time whether or not the government has adopted as being valid the opinion given by E. A. Driedger who, in response to a request from the committee, furnished a legal opinion dealing with matters which are ancillary or related to the problem of marriage and divorce? The minister's answer might be helpful in discussing this matter at other stages.

[Mr. Trudeau.]

Mr. Trudeau: As the hon. member knows, this question of judicial separation is one which draws different opinions from different constitutional authorities. For my part, I am on the side of the opinion which was alluded to by the hon. member; but as the hon. member knows, there are courts in this country which have decided otherwise—not the Supreme Court, but there are provincial courts which have decided otherwise.

Although I do not think that is binding on the government, the argument I was explaining in French, in order to justify not including that part of the provisions in this bill now are arguments of a pragmatic nature.

The provinces have procedures now for judicial separation—that is, most of them do. Even the province of Ontario, which has no law in that regard, has the possibility of solving by contract the problems arising from separation. To implement a bill which would include judicial separation at this time could have meant a very long and justifiable series of consultations with the various provinces. In my estimation that would have meant that such a bill could not be adopted as quickly as I hope this parliament is ready to adopt this present bill. It was my hope that, by dealing strictly with the matter of divorce in the bill, we would be able to get it through the house fairly soon with the co-operation of hon. members, that we would have this law on our statutes, and that we would then, as we negotiate with the provinces the applicability of the law and the change in the court set-up which it will entail in some provinces, tackle the problem of judicial separation, which is a much more difficult problem in pragmatic terms.

• (8:20 p.m.)

I am not talking of the constitutional argument now, but rather in terms of the different kinds of laws or practices which apply in different provinces. It has always been recognized that divorce is strictly a federal matter but, as the hon. member realizes, the question of judicial separation is one which is debated. I have made up my own mind, but the Supreme Court of this Country has never declared what the law in this regard is, in the final analysis. It is normal in an area like this that there would be provincial legislation in some cases, because they had the law prior to the B.N.A. Act, and these laws continued after confederation. For this reason we thought it more proper to approach the second problem, that of judicial separation, by consultation. The civil code of Quebec now deals with the matter of judicial separation. However, as hon. members will remember, the civil code of Quebec dates back to 1866, one year before confederation. Had we adopted anything without going through this type of consultation in respect of judicial separation, we would have been changing part of the civil code of the province of Quebec.

As I say, we could do this constitutionally, but this is not the kind of thing we should like to do without a great deal of prior consultation, especially due to the fact that the province of Quebec now is in the process of redrafting its civil code and the chapters on marriage. This type of argument is also true in respect of some of the other provinces which have varying provincial laws on matters of maintenance, the consequences of a judicial separation, and so on.

[*Translation*]

Mr. Chairman, that is why we have thought it simpler, in this bill, to deal only with divorce proper and its immediate aftermath. This three month period, following the enactment of the bill, shall be used not only to consult with the provinces, but also to discuss the extremely important matter of legal separation.

[*English*]

Mr. Stanfield: Mr. Chairman, in just a few words I should like to indicate that we on this side of the chamber approve of reforming the divorce law, and consequently look forward to receiving the bill and examining it in detail. I do not propose to make any comment upon what the minister has indicated will be contained in the bill because, since the bill is already drafted, obviously anything I said would not in any event affect the measure as introduced. So, I should like to say simply that we will approve of the resolution and look forward to seeing the bill.

Mr. Brewin: Mr. Chairman, I should like my first words on this matter to be those of relief and pleasure at being in this house when, at long last, a measure of reform of our divorce law is to be brought before the house. I should like to congratulate the minister on having the honour to be the one who is introducing this legislation.

The archaic divorce laws we have had have caused untold misery to many thousands of Canadians. This measure of reform is long overdue. As the minister pointed out, parliament has had jurisdiction over this matter for over 100 years and yet has never

27053—317½

boldly exercised it in any way. It has legislated in a piecemeal way, usually merely by introducing the existing laws of England at particular stages of our history.

Mr. Chairman, not having seen the bill, I do not think at this stage it would be appropriate for me to enlarge on this matter at any length or comment at any length on what the minister has said. I think perhaps it is a truism, although one which I think ought to be said, that, notwithstanding the pessimists, marriage is thriving in Canada, fortunately very many Canadians find in the marriages and families a very great source of happiness. All of us must be concerned that we do not do anything to undermine or defeat the institution of marriage.

I believe we also must recognize that, despite any individual views of our own, none of us has any right to impose on others views which no longer are socially acceptable. One thing on which most, if not all, of us will agree is that the present law is entirely unsatisfactory. The single ground of adultery is a superficial and inadequate ground. It leads not only to the commission of the offence but also to fabrication and perjury which are a disgrace to the courts. There is also the problem of those persons who, finding marriage unacceptable or impossible, form common law unions, stable unions which can never be normal unions so long as divorce is what it is at the present time. There is the problem of children of such unions.

The minister has said that by and large the report of the joint committee, on which I happened to be a member, will be largely accepted. I cannot refrain, however, from expressing a measure of regret that the legislation is not accepting the clearcut choice which exists between the two basic theories in respect of the dissolution of marriage. One is that the grounds of matrimonial misconduct upon which divorce can be based should be enlarged. The other is that the dissolution of marriage should be based upon the declaration that the marriage is dead; that is, that the marriage has broken down, and that there exists no longer any hope of reconciliation.

This is not divorce by consent; it is divorce by judicial decision. The mind of the judge would be directed to the question of whether there is hope of reconciliation, and not to the hopeless and futile exercise of deciding whose misconduct was responsible for the breakdown of the marriage. We would have much preferred to see the government accept the recommendation made initially by the

Joe Clark

Joe Clark – Undaunted

(16th)

Date Elected to Parliament:	October 30, 1973
Date of Maiden Speech:	February 26, 1973
Date Sworn In:	June 4, 1979
Date Left Office:	March 2, 1980

No leader was more transparent, more driven, and more focused from youth to become Prime Minister of Canada. Born in a small town in Alberta, to the owner of a struggling local newspaper, Joe Clark decided to reach for the highest office in the land as a high school student. Methodical and energetic, he tried from youth to look the part and sound the part with his three-piece suits, carefully coiffed hair and his sonorous, exacting words of a Prime Minister. He took himself and his goal seriously. A voracious reader of politics and political history, he devoured political biographies and political history, teaching himself as he climbed, rung-by-rung, up the political ladder. A prolific and skilled political worker with each and every job he took on that Joe Clark considered training ground for political leadership. He sought out leading political figures, as he organized and undertook thankless tasks, all to advance in the realm of power politics.

While he never had as wide a circle of friends compared to Brian Mulroney, he slowly gathered about him, a loyal coterie of supporters across the Progressive Conservative countryside. Clark taught himself assiduously to become functionally bilingual, the first English-speaking Canadian Prime Minister to do so.[140] All that he did, he did tirelessly with a relentless ambition, for power and yes, fame. He felt he could make a difference on the national stage, coming as he did from the West.

Tall, thin, awkward, and gangly, he seemed to walk in several directions at the same time. He trained his voice to slow down and catch the deeper sonorous tones of John Diefenbaker. The slow studied pause between each phrase demonstrated his thoughtfulness. Clark studied and practiced public speaking without notes gaining an unerring confidence. An early supporter of Diefenbaker, he took on jobs of speech writing for Conservative politicians, immersing himself in policy research and policy papers for the Progressive Conservative Party, and accomplished them all with rigour and dispatch. He was a Progressive Conservative in its fullest sense of the meaning.

[140] John Diefenbaker spoke a few words in fractured French in his speeches in Quebec. Mike Pearson could read and write French and could only speak with difficulty, but he insisted that Cabinet meetings allowed his Quebec ministers to speak French if they chose to. Trudeau was fluent in both official languages and had the gift of other languages like Spanish and Italian. He could speak and understand Latin and Greek to a lesser degree. Trudeau could order a dinner for eight in a Chinese restaurant in impressive Mandarin. He could speak in impeccable French especially to academic audiences. Turner was fluently bilingual with a great sense of street jargon. He maintained two secretaries, one for French dictation and the other for English. Mulroney, being born in Quebec and attended lower school and Law School in French, had ease in both official languages as did Chrétien, Martin and Harper. Chrétien regularly practiced with tutors to improve his English. Harper, as an assistant to a Member of Parliament, began to work on his French and continued when he was elected to Parliament and throughout the time, he was leader of the opposition and Prime Minister. Kim Campbell spoke both official languages well having studied and sought out French speaking mileaux. Justin Trudeau was bilingual from birth. His speech to the French Assembly in Paris, a first for a Canadian Prime Minister, was pitch perfect.

He and Mulroney were both early colleagues and instant competitors while not friendly or close confidantes. Mulroney was a master at networking within the Party, the media and business circles while Clark earned his spurs and respect, if not warmth, amongst Conservatives, young and old, for his diligent organizational and policy work and his patent care with the facts. Clark became an indispensable policy organizer. Both he and Mulroney went to Dalhousie Law School. Both failed! Mulroney never gave up his legal ambition and went to Laval in Quebec City and finally got called to the Quebec Bar after three tries. Clark never made it.

But Clark decided that there was another path to power. He went back to University of Alberta to study political science while he maintained his hyper political activism. Policy, he felt, was the platform he would build for himself to gain respect of his peers and he worked assiduously at this task of self-education and self-promotion. He was a Progressive Conservative unlike Mulroney who was much more the pragmatist than the ideologue. Both were early loyalists to Mr. Diefenbaker. Both broke away gingerly from Diefenbaker and reluctantly supported Stanfield. Both were put on Diefenbaker's growing list of the disloyal. Joe was open-minded about feminism. His wife, Maureen McTeer, kept her maiden name after their marriage. Some saw this was a sign of weakness, but Joe, genuinely open-minded, never seemed to care. Feminism was not a barrier to his political choices or engagement.[141]

[141] Joe Clark appointed Flora MacDonald to his Cabinet. Flora was a longtime party executive under Joe's tutelage. Flora became a respected Minister of External Affairs. Due to her efforts supported by Prime Minister Clark with the advice and counsel of Ken Taylor (the Canadian Ambassador to Iran), Canadian diplomats hid American diplomats sought after by the Ayatollah's Iranian regime took over in Tehran and then arranged for their

Joe made his first leap for leadership by running for Parliament and was elected in Alberta. Joe became a M.P. in 1972 while Mulroney decided his time wasn't right. Then Mulroney belatedly entered the Conservative leadership race when Stanfield resigned after 1974. Joe, with limited resources, decided to run early while Mulroney hesitated, and finally got into that race late. Joe was everyone's second choice. Wagner led early. Mulroney took over the lead in the pre-Convention polls. Wagner and Mulroney had parted badly and disliked each other. Claude Wagner, a right-leaning judge, had been introduced to Conservative politics in Quebec and assisted by Mulroney, but they had a falling out. Mulroney's weakness was that he was not an elected member when he entered the leadership race and was charged with 'inexperience' by Wagner. Joe kept his cool and shrewdly stayed away from the fierce political battles between Mulroney and Wagner.

Wagner aimed his formidable political Quebec arsenal at Mulroney. Mulroney desperately needed strong Quebec support which had been snapped up early by Wagner's entry into the race. Diefenbaker felt both Clark and Mulroney had deserted him. Diefenbaker, now retired but still in Parliament, turned his guns on Mulroney in his rousing farewell speech at the Leadership Convention who he saw as a front runner. Meanwhile, Joe came up the middle and won the leadership. Joe's skill at substantial policies won him the Party's respect and support in the countless meetings created to get to know the leadership candidates from coast to coast. Flora MacDonald, a party official and activist, and Ellen Fairclough, the first woman Federal Cabinet Minister who served in John Diefenbaker's Cabinet supported Clark for

stealthy escape under Canadian passports and fabricated Canadian jobs. An amazing feat of leadership, courage, and statecraft.

leader. Along the way, Clark gathered a larger national network of loyal supporters. As for the public and the media surprised by the Clark victory labelled Clark '*Joe Who?*' Not fair and not true!

I first met both Joe Clark and Brian Mulroney at the 1968 Liberal Leadership Convention when I was part of the leadership team for John Turner. I had prepared a new bilingual poster and a policy position showing a different picture of John Turner for every day of the Convention. The colours we chose were yellow and black. Brian and Joe were interested in all the minute details of our organization which I shared with them. We had lengthy discussions as they had attended the Convention for four days as acute Conservative observers. Both were diligent and searching in their questions about organization and graphics. You could tell that they were serious students of politics and I respected them for that.

Like Mulroney, Clark chose to use his second name. Mulroney's first name was Martin and Joe's was Charles. One can only speculate why.

Joe gained the leadership of the Progressive Conservative Party breaking Mulroney's early lead and became leader of the Opposition – the youngest in Canadian history. He was thorough and well prepared in the Parliament. Trudeau considered him a worthy opponent as he relentlessly and cogently attacked Trudeau's domestic and foreign policies. Joe was tough, fair, and relentless. Trudeau especially admired Clark's spirited opposition in Parliament and beyond to Trudeau's bespoke Constitutional efforts. While Trudeau was critical of the Supreme Court of Canada that held with three notable dissents that provincial approval was a 'convention' and a necessary precondition to Constitutional amendment, he was never critical of Joe Clark as Leader of the Opposition. Others made light of Clark's 'community of communities' slogan but not Trudeau. While

Trudeau respected Joe Clark, he did not hold Brian Mulroney in high regard. Joe was considered by many during his career as one of the best Leaders of the Opposition in Parliamentary history. He was well prepared for debates in Parliament and beyond. Joe gained his spurs.

In 1979 after a tough election campaign waged by Joe against a lack lustre Pierre Trudeau, Joe Clark became at 39, the day before his 40th birthday, the youngest Prime Minister of Canada in history. His tenure was short-lived. His foreign focus was criticized by the media for issues large and small like the loss of baggage on an early foreign trip. During his five months as Prime Minister, he named women to key posts, and he introduced the Access to Information Act that died in the order paper after lengthy hearings only to be revived and passed by the Trudeau government in 1982. Joe was the godfather of transparency in government. Joe was also the first English-speaking Prime Minister to become fluently bilingual. Mr. Pearson could read, write, and speak French, but he never achieved French-speaking fluency. Clark was honourable and painstaking in his conviction about the need for substantial party approval of his leadership. He personified the Parliament principle – the need for 'confidence'. After his defeat in 1980, though only 33.5% Party members voted against him at Party Convention, he stoutly insisted on a leadership review in a Party Convention where he lost to Brian Mulroney. Was Joe, right? Perhaps not. But Joe understood the history of divisions within Conservative politics and the principles of party cohesion necessary to back a leader. He wanted strong party unity before he faced the country as national leader. Mulroney won the Convention leadership. Mulroney appointed Joe to his first Cabinet and became an outstanding Minister of External Affairs leading in the battle to free Mandela from prison and against apartheid. He coordinated policies towards Africa,

NAFTA and outreach to Central America, and restraining the excesses of U.S. foreign policy. Clark was progressive in his activist approach to multilateral organizations. It is said there wasn't an international organization or NGO that Joe didn't love to join and show common cause. He was and remained a committed multilateral and globalist at heart.

Joe penned two books after he left public life focused on his love of policy options. Well written and clear, perhaps as he admitted, he was a 'Pollyanna', too many options, not enough focus on a few priorities – vintage Joe Clark.

Joe left public life after the merger of the Reform and Conservative parties which he did not support. He remained a Progressive Conservative. He refused to endorse Stephen Harper as he felt Harper tilted too far to the right. He turned his hand to teaching, refusing to profit from his stint as Prime Minister. As Brian Mulroney said, Joe was respected but never hated by the Canadian public – a tribute to his character and probity in and after public life. He remains a wise and durable Canadian figure quietly making his contribution on domestic and foreign fronts.

Nothing was more generous of spirit, or witty understatement than Joe Clark's introduction to Jean Chrétien's recent reminiscences published called *My Stories, My Times* in 2018.[142]

Joe wrote several books and numerous articles on public policy that were broad, encyclopedic, and detailed, especially his work with multilateral organizations. Joe had a capacious appetite to fix things large and small. His interests broadened as Prime Minister and as Minister of Constitutional Affairs, then External Affairs under Mulroney. During the heated Constitutional debates in the Commons, Clark advocated the idea that Canada was 'a community of communities'. Trudeau considered Clark

---

142 Jean Chrétien's *My Stories, My Times* (Random House of Canada, 2018).

a worthy and honourable opponent in Clark's strenuous opposition to Trudeau's Constitutional agenda. Perhaps Clark's reach was greater than Canada's ability to keep up. Little has been done to renovate the egregious practices of these international organizations. Each, from the UN to NATO to the WTO, remain in desperate need of reform. Yet, Joe Clark remains a true believer in international engagement and multilateral institutions and an exemplary former Prime Minister.

- *How We Lead: Canada in a Century of Change* by Joe Clark (Random House Canada, 2013)
- *Nation Too Good To Lose: Renewing The Purpose Of Canada* by Joe Clark (Key Porter Books, 1994)

Joe Clark - Maiden Speech

1662 COMMONS DEBATES February 26, 1973

The Budget—Mr. Joe Clark

I have only a minute or two left, but I wanted also to speak about small businesses and ways of financing them. I have discussed this several times in the past, both in the House and in committee. It is a complex subject, but a solution must be found as soon as possible. The following is a direct quotation from the Speech from the Throne:

—aid to small businesses through new initiatives to strengthen management and consulting services and to improve access to financing facilities.

I believe this is what small and medium-sized businesses mainly need, although I do not mean to minimize the importance of new measures to improve management and consulting services, which would be new sources of working and investment capital which these businesses badly need in order to broaden their operations.

• (1710)

[*English*]

Mr. Joe Clark (Rocky Mountain): Mr. Speaker, it is a great privilege for me to rise in this House. This is virtually my first chance to speak in the House of Commons, although I have had the opportunity to ask one or two questions even though I am not a parliamentary secretary. I have also had the opportunity once to speak briefly in the late show at a time when the House was slightly less full than it is now, if that could be imagined.

When one takes his place in this chamber it is with some feeling of trepidation. One cannot help but be aware of the traditions of this chamber, and one cannot help either but be aware that this is one of the few institutions in the country that is capable of drawing together citizens from across a wide and varied land. I just wanted to note in passing how appropriate it seemed to me the other day to hear the hon. member for York South (Mr. Lewis) talking about dinosaurs. That is obviously a subject of natural interest to his party. Indeed, it is difficult to think of any other group in this House which has a greater philosophic affinity to that era, or a better prospect of becoming extinct.

It is a remarkable coincidence that whenever the leadership of the NDP encounters a crisis of conscience at home, they suddenly perceive some greater evil at another hand. Faced with the challenge of principle embodied in the Waffle, their leadership conjured up the corporate bum, whom they have now embraced. And now, caught in an alliance which they consider a lesser treachery than electoral defeat, their leadership has decided that we are dinosaurs. They remind me of the itinerant evangelists we used to get, from time to time, in the towns on the Prairies. They would come in the night, usually having just created their own theology, and proceed to bilk the wealthy widows of the town with promises either of a new cathedral or a new Jerusalem, and when suspicion grew about their purposes, they would suddenly be seized of the great dangers of fluoridation, or Argentina, or some other scare. They usually lasted about five months, these prophets of phony fear, and then were never heard of again. So, in every particular, they remind one of the NDP.

On February 15, I asked the Prime Minister what plans his government had to find jobs for young Canadians. He replied with characteristic boldness and foresight and said his plan was to wait for the budget. Now, we have the budget and presumably the government's answer—which is that it intends to do nothing at all to break the pattern which has made Canadians under 24 the chief victims of unemployment in Canada throughout the life of the Trudeau government.

[Mr. Clermont.]

The most recent figures for January this year, indicate that a total of 688,000 Canadians were unemployed. Fully 300,000 of those were under the age of 24—almost half of the total number of unemployed in the country and one in nine of the people in that age group who wanted to work. That figure is appalling enough on its own. What is worse is that it is part of a clear and evident pattern that even the government has recognized. The proportion of unemployed in that age group has been rising gradually for several years. But in recent years it has been nearly 45 per cent of the total, despite the fact that many people of that age who might have been looking for work have been drained off into technical schools or CEGEPS, or colleges and universities. There is some indication now that this safety valve is closing, because young people who go into training for better jobs are finding too often that they graduate into unemployment. The result of their diversion is just that they have better skills to waste.

That pattern has been clear throughout the life of this ministry. They were warned by the Economic Council of Canada. They were warned by the Canadian Council on Social Development, by the Committee on Youth of their own Secretary of State (Mr. Faulkner), and frequently by editorialists and by spokesmen of this party. Their only answer has been to fake a response. They claim that Opportunities for Youth was created to meet this problem. But Opportunities for Youth last year employed about 3,000 non-students for the summer. If applied today to the January figures, that would amount to the stirring figure of one per cent—a one per cent response—except that OFY does not work in the winter. That is about the only thing that program has in common with the young people it is supposed to help.

The government's only other response to unemployment in Canada, the LIP program, works less well among the young than among other age groups of the unemployed. In 1971-72, 41 per cent of LIP workers were under age 24 but 46 per cent to 47 per cent of the unemployed were under that age. In hard figures, LIP that year created only 37,000 temporary jobs for Canadians under 24 and there are 300,000 out of work today.

The more serious fault of the LIP and OFY programs in relation to youth employment is that they provide the government with an excuse for doing nothing effective about the problem. LIP and OFY embody a potential for innovation and involvement which is as important now as it was when that principle was introduced into Canadian legislation in the ARDA program. They are important programs. But they are not youth employment programs. Yet every time the statistics are cited in this House which prove that this government's economic programs are victimizing the young, the government answers by pointing to LIP and OFY. The most innovative aspect of these programs is the use the government makes of them to avoid meeting their responsibility to young Canadians who want to work. In so far as youth employment is concerned, LIP and OFY have been used principally not to innovate action but to avoid it. It is very easy when discussing unemployment statistics to lose sight of the human consequence involved, and forget that each one of these 300,000 young Canadians is a single case of need.

One way to gain perspective on the youth employment problem is to realize there are about twice as many young Canadians out of work today as there were in the great depression. Now, if you treat people as statistics, you can say that is not significant, because the work force has grown but if you regard people as people, you might remember the record of personal hardship and bitterness spawned in that period when so many people started what should have been their working lives without work to do. What is particularly cruel about unemployment among the young is that so many young people have no other resources to fall back on and no real preparation for being unwanted as workers. And what is particularly dangerous about unemployment among the young is that the experience and attitudes which young Canadians develop now will last their lifetime. If they are herded into welfare or if they are taught that their energies are unwanted, that will shape their lives and could deprive our nation and themselves of their creative participation.

There is another aspect of this question. It is a myth that has grown up, the myth that kids in Canada are lazy. I think that the existence of that myth protects the government against its clear responsibility to take action to end the high and unacceptable rates of unemployment among the young. One of the tragic aspects of this is that the Prime Minister himself has contributed, perhaps not deliberately, to the view that kids in Canada do not want to work when he made his offhand remarks that anyone who wanted work in Canada should go to Thompson, Manitoba or some other distant spot. The people who suffer most from this misleading suggestion are the young people in the country.

Prior to those comments, there was some substantial sympathy for the problems of the unemployed young, but that sympathy evaporated when the Prime Minister casually entered the fray. In fact, Mr. Speaker, while the work ethic may not recommend itself to a barefoot boy from Outremont, a study by the Canadian Council on Social Development of young Canadians who applied for social assistance in November, 1971 indicated:

> The young social assistance applicants who were interviewed have by no means rejected the concept of work and its central importance to their development and self-fulfillment.

They do not reject work, they just cannot find any. So long as the government caters or contributes to the opinion that they do not want work, their problems will continue to be ignored.

We are dealing here with a budget which will do much less than it pretends. It is the budget of a parlour magician, relying on illusion, trying to trick the people who are watching. The minister held out the illusion of using tax cuts to put more purchasing power into the economy, yet in reality the total revenues of the government will be $1.7 billion higher this year than last. He talks buoyantly of creating 300,000 new jobs as he has talked before and failed, yet in reality is accepting unnecessarily high levels of unemployment. He talks about expansion, yet understimulates. He worries about inflation, yet has no

25769—33

response except a so-called contingency plan which he proposes to produce like a rabbit from a hat.

What is wrong with this budget is its purpose. At a time when the government should be preoccupied with providing jobs and growth and some stability, it is instead preoccupied with its own political survival. So, instead of introducing measures which are bold enough to work, the government relies instead on measures which seem safe enough to serve. Other speakers in this debate have indicated how far short the minister will fall of his stated goals. My particular concern today is to underline the urgency of a goal he did not state, the goal of helping young Canadians put their energies to work and to review some of the steps which the government's own advisers have urged as a means to break the shackling pattern of high unemployment among the young.

• (1720)

The Hunter Committee on Youth published its report 19 months ago, and it was heralded with that special enthusiasm this government reserves for reports it proposes to ignore. One simple, but highly valuable, recommendation of that report was that the government at least recognize that youth unemployment constitutes a special problem in Canada. At the moment, we have virtually no hard information about the special causes of high youth unemployment, about its relation to the education system, about the effectiveness of counselling or manpower, about the need and scope for new kinds and definitions of work. The Hunter Committee recommended establishing a Canadian youth employment directorate, and generally we in this party approve of that initiative, at least as an interim measure. The government has done nothing about the directorate.

The report of the Canadian Council on Social Development, entitled "A Right to Opportunity" reveals a chaos in the counselling and social assistance services available to young Canadians out of work. They recommend an early federal-provincial conference, to bring some order and equity to that field. The government has done nothing. This party has suggested that LIP and OFY be given statutory authority, so that their purposes can be debated and understood in parliament and so that they can assume some permanent place in the program structure of various government and voluntary agencies, instead of being expensive itinerants whose present status prohibits integrated national programming. The government declines that commitment as, indeed, it declines any commitment to do anything at all about the continuing crisis of youth unemployment. The government has been running away from the problem and the running has to stop. We cannot afford the enormous human cost of training hundreds of thousands of young people to be out of work and on welfare. We are wasting lives and wasting potential.

The problem of youth employment would be less acute in an economy performing nearer its potential. So, the approach of this party, outlined Thursday by the hon. member for Don Valley (Mr. Gillies), will help the young to find jobs and will help other Canadians. Even so, it will be necessary to take special measures to arrest or reverse the trends towards higher and higher levels of unemployment among Canadians age 24.

John Turner

John Turner and The Politics of Purpose

(17th)

Date Elected to Parliament:	June 18, 1962
Date of Maiden Speech:	October 18, 1962
Date Sworn In:	June 30, 1984
Date Left Office:	September 16, 1984

I first encountered John Turner[143] in 1963 at a Liberal Convention in Montreal when he was a newly elected M.P. for St. Lawrence-St. George, a working-class riding in the heart of Montreal composed of diverse voters with English, French, and ethnic origins. Turner was fluently bilingual and could banter in Italian and other languages, like Greek, with flippancy and ease. A natural politician, he had deployed modern Kennedy-esque techniques to win over his chosen working-class riding. He was a superb riding organizer inspiring a mass of youthful new volunteers to help in his campaign and run his riding. He developed new election techniques to barnstorm every home of his riding. Where there were high rise apartments, a small advance team would cajole residents to meet Turner in an open area after getting the caretaker on side. He followed the John F.

[143] John Napier Turner was born in Richmond, England in 1929, the son of Leonard Hugh Turner, a journalist and Phyllis Gregory. He had a brother, Michael who died shortly after birth in 1930. His father died in 1932 after which his sister, Brenda, and he moved to Canada in 1932.

Kennedy practice of wooing matrons at tea parties hosted by his attractive sister, Brenda, bright, energetic and vivacious.[144] He could cover more voters quickly this way. He canvassed his entire riding, unheard of at the time. Teas, beer fests, ritzy cocktail parties, and ethnic restaurants were deployed with zest and verve. Turner himself was tireless and led his excited volunteers inspired by his tactics, energy, and enthusiasm.

Handsome, dark well-coiffed hair, tall, broad-shouldered in an athletic frame and elegantly dressed with a dazzling smile, he bubbled with energy. His bright blue eyes were like lasers – he never lost eye contact when he engaged a voter. His memory for names and faces was formidable. Quickly he was considered a rising political star. The media had amped up on his publicized dates with Princess Margaret. He had danced with Margaret that gave him early 'celebrity'. A deep interest in policy – Turner, a Rhodes Scholar with degrees from University of British Columbia[145] and Oxford (he was admitted to the Bar in the U.K. and later in Quebec), gave him intellectual cachet and so was a young invitee to the Kingston Conference – a select thinker conference organized by Mitchell Sharpe and Tom Kent on behalf of Mr. Pearson who wanted to reshape and modernize the Liberal Party platform. Turner's participation at the Conference was favourably rated. For me, the most enjoyable part of politics was policy, so I followed this conference, read the published papers, and noted the attendees. When we first met in 1963, I

---

[144] Brenda Norris, had she chosen, would have been a talented politician in her own right.

[145] Turner was an outstanding athlete specializing in the 100 metre and 200 metre dashes. While at UBC, he was a student reporter specializing in sports where he gained a campus-wide reputation to the envy of others also at UBC at the time like Allan Fotheringham who went on to become a national political reporter with a unique West Coast writing style.

asked Turner if he was 'as good' as he looked. He was taken aback, and he laughed in a deep booming voice. "*What do you mean?*" "*Your speeches could be better*", I retorted. "*How so?*" he asked. Thus, led to a lengthy exchange and we agreed to keep in touch. "*Send me some ideas*", he concluded, and I did. I knew Turner was a young star in the legal firmament in Quebec, knowledgeable in the arcane fields of navigation and insurance law. He had joined a top law firm called Stikeman Elliott where he quickly became partner. He became head of the junior Bar of Quebec. Gathered about him was an entourage of young ambitious lawyers, diverse businessmen, and elder avuncular Liberal veterans.

In 1965, I was an advance man in the Ontario Federal electoral machine led by Dan Lang, the Ontario Campaign Chair. Paul Martin Sr. had refused a speaking engagement in the small town of Orillia north of Toronto. Dan called Turner who agreed to come if I would fly up with him from Toronto. When Dan called, I agreed. We met at a small airport in Toronto to fly to Orillia in a small plane. Dan was there to see us off, intense, puffing on a cigarette with his fedora hat tilted on the side of his head. Dan briefed us on the message. The weather was uncertain. We climbed into a small four-seater aircraft, Turner and I crammed in the back seat, buckled up and took off into uncertain weather. The plane shook. I am a white-knuckle flyer. I turned to Turner who was chatting away as he glanced at his speech cards to test a phrase or two. He was calm and oblivious to the plane's jerky, bumpy movements. Turner was calm as a cucumber, relaxed, and focused, I noticed. I was in a deep sweat. When we landed, late for the political meeting, we were encountered by Dan Casey, an old time Liberal organizer. Dan met us in the darkened street near the meeting hall. "*You're late*", he exploded. The crowd had just dispersed. We raced up and down the nearby streets to bring everyone back to the meeting hall. Turner took the stage after a great intro as a future Prime Minister made by the local Riding President and made a barn burning stump speech, right on message. Afterwards, Turner chatted with each attendee until we finally left for Toronto. I was exhausted and wilted, Turner was bright and energetic. He assessed the crowd and their collective and individual responses. I was impressed.

We kept in touch and I sent him the odd speech idea and he sent me copies of his speeches. When re-elected in 1965, he was made junior Cabinet Minister, attached to Jack Pickersgill, the all-powerful Minister of Transport, longtime advisor to Mr. King, and a braintrust of the Liberal Party. A week or so after his appointment, Turner called and asked if he could see me for lunch in Toronto. I agreed. I was anxious to find out what was going on in Ottawa. We had a great lunch – steak medium rare, sliced tomatoes, and a good Bordeaux Médoc. Over strong, dark coffee, he came to the point. Would I be interested in becoming his Executive Assistant? I would have no responsibility for his riding activities. My job would be to focus on policy, speeches, and his cabinet responsibilities. It was intriguing. I had previously been approached by Keith Davey, Paul Martin Sr., and Walter Gordon to work in their offices in Ottawa. I had turned them all down. By this time, Carole was fed up with my political activities. I had a young son, lived in a tiny, rented apartment and was about to be made partner in my small law firm, I hoped. I had no outside resources. I depended on my legal income to maintain my small family. Turner understood. I asked why I should join him. He looked me squarely in the eye and said, "*We will work together on everything and – with me, you will have fun. Go home and talk to Carole and let me know!*"

That evening, I returned home reluctant to even raising the subject of Ottawa with Carole because of her visceral dislike for politics. She was not surprised. Turner had invited her to tea that afternoon and he surmised that I would never be happy unless I had a stint in government. So, they had worked out a deal that I would work for only one year, one year only, commuting to Toronto on the weekends and with an additional trip on the odd Wednesday back home from time-to-time especially for the Jewish holidays.

John Turner came well-prepared for public life, armed with an encyclopedic knowledge of Canadian history, and an especially retentive memory for people and striking anecdotes as well as a deep love for the expanses of Canadian geography. He loved the great outdoors. Born in England where his mother, with humble Maritime roots, had gained a post-graduate education and married an English journalist who died prematurely. Returning to Canada with two young children, his mother Phyllis Turner (later Ross),[146] tall and striking, served during World War II as the leading female bureaucrat in Ottawa where Turner received his primary education, and encountered leading civil servants and politicians of that era as a youth, including Mackenzie King. Then it was on to the University of British Columbia where he excelled in academics, sports and sports writing, becoming a star athlete and then a Rhodes Scholar at Oxford. He was a championship sprinter in the Commonwealth Games and had he not been injured, he would have made it to the Olympics. Then he studied at the University of Paris where he polished his French language skills. He was called to the Bar in the U.K. but

---

[146] Mrs. Ross's grandfather was a coal miner from Nova Scotia. She worked her own way through school and university gaining impressive degrees along the way. After leaving the public service, she remarried, settled in Vancouver where her husband was a colourful entrepreneur and became Chancellor of the University of British Columbia. She deeply influenced Turner on his duty to serve in the public service.

returned to start his practice of law in Montreal where he rose rapidly in the Quebec Bar to be elected head of the Junior Bar.

In Montreal, he cut a dashing larger-than-life figure as a handsome, ebullient bachelor clad in fine dark, English tailored suits, bespoke British shirts and dark brown suede shoes,[147] exuded robust restless energy and a booming staccato-like voice that could reverberate in a small auditorium. A 'bon vivant', he relished theatre, good music and food, fine wines and spirits, Cuban cigars, attractive company, and scintillating conversation. It was John Turner who attracted Zubin Mehta,[148] then an unknown conductor to serve as Conductor of the Montreal Symphony and who went on to worldwide fame. He was an avid reader with a capacious memory. He had an interesting publicized turn with Princess Margaret.[149] As a rising political star, he radiated an electric energy and a certain attractive charisma. His fiery blazing blue eyes riveted and captivated everyone who encountered him. He married an attractive, bright, equally energetic, Harvard educated woman, Geills Kilgour,[150] from an established Winnipeg family. Geills was an accomplished photographer. Turner was sought out, then fought for and obtained the Liberal nomination in 1963 and gained a seat in the polyglot riding of St. Lawrence, St. George in the heart

---

[147] Later, when Turner ran for leadership, I stole his brown suede shoes that he favoured as I thought were unsuitable for a leader. Angry when he discovered what I had done, he insisted I return them. He continued to wear them, albeit, with less frequency.

[148] Zubin never forgot how Turner had lifted his musical career and continued their long friendship. When Zubin Mehta returned for a short tour in Toronto in 2018, he insisted after the concert at Thomson Hall personally to assist Turner to my car as he left the crowded concert hall.

[149] Princess Margaret later related that 'she almost married him'.

[150] Geills was bright and independent minded who raised a large family during Turner's political career.

of downtown Montreal in a hotly competitive tough campaign against an equally energetic young Conservative.

During his swift rise in politics, John Turner became a witty, often mesmerizing, 'stumpspeaker' who had an excellent eye for the organizational detail of riding politics. He loved campaigning and was both a creative and inspiring 'grass roots' team leader. He loved 'pressing the flesh' and his piercing blue eyes became riveted on each voter he met. He gave each his undivided attention. His urban riding introduced cutting-edge political innovations at the time, for gathering lists, telephone numbers, and especially a keen talent for 'blitz' canvassing in high-rise apartments and for soliciting votes among new 'ethnic' voters.

John Napier Turner's story is a gripping, sometimes soaring and too often painful account of his life and times and the Liberal Party in the '60s, '70s, and '80s.

Deftly stripping away the varnish from John Turner's star-crossed life, we uncover a searing passion play, a potent concoction of strong competitive personalities, the magnet of power, venal Party politics, raw ambition, self-interest and high public purpose. We illuminate the dark, even reprehensible, actions of so-called party players, and their willing wingmen, and the origins of the onslaught of the internecine, tribal wars that bedeviled the Liberal Party during those three turbulent decades, but broke out with a vengeance during Turner's return to politics in the '80s.

Once Turner easily won the Liberal leadership, clandestine and not-so-clandestine conspiracies became a miserable reality of Liberal Party life. Loyalty to the Leader, the attraction of translating liberal principles into activity, the paramount duty to promote national unity and to advance Canada's domestic and foreign interests, all the hallmarks that traditionally fused the disparate factions of the Liberal Party, were ripped asunder, motivated by personal pique, triggered by imagined slights and ruthless petty egoism that vaulted personal ambition above Party and, at times, country. The Freudian principle of the 'narcissism of small differences' was in play. The old Liberal saw – "*How can you hope to unite the country if you cannot unite the Party?*" – was shredded by even its most ardent advocates. Anonymous wounding gossip coloured the darker shades of the underside of politics. This divisive factionalism, once the characteristic of the Conservative Party, which had kept it from power for decades, now, like a virus, infected the uppermost echelons of the Liberal Party, once noted as the Party of unity and loyalty to the Leader, as its dual operational coda. The self-defined 'natural governing party' was seen to be ripping itself apart, and from the inside. Lyndon Johnson once opined "*You know the only difference between liberals and cannibals...cannibals eat their enemies.*" This, too often, became the miserable new norm in the Liberal Party.

In retrospect, what still amazes me is the absence of either shame or remorse by the instigating party players. As if internal Party politics, played by amoral, rancorous rules, is doomed to travel a different route in public life rather than personal character or intellectual probity. Narcissism seemed to rule. Is power, at all costs, the goal? Was this to be the 'new norm' of Party politics or the 'norm'? Is hypocrisy the name of feigned virtue?

Unnoticed by public observers is the loss of 'character' in public opinion and public opinion polls as an element or aspect of measurement of leadership qualities. When did 'character' lose its importance, let alone relevance in defining modern leaderships? Did its descent start in the Kennedy era when, as an adored darling of the media, John Kennedy's tainted 'character' and inappropriate private conduct was kept from public view by a willing coalition of advisors and a cohort of 'liberal' media who conspired to keep the darker side of Kennedy's character hidden from public view until well after his assassination? Kennedy's conservative inclinations were glossed over by his liberal advisors as were his flawed errors of judgement. Certainly, since the Kennedy era, and more notably since Clinton, 'character' no longer plays a central role defining the modern political leader in Canada or our southern neighbour. Perhaps Turner was a throwback to an earlier era, steeped as he was, in high purpose principles and public service. Turner saw politics and public service as a 'calling', as a public stewardship as his mother did before him.

The pathology of Party politics and the deeper nature of public affairs in recent Canadian history still awaits to be written with the objectivity for a later vantage point. There are, and have been, various different narratives illuminating politics as a high calling culled from Canadian history. Perhaps the availability of the more revealing sources, the absence of personal restraint, the seeming need for each minor player to shamelessly illuminate his miniscule role, the advent of 24/7 news cycle, now brings a different deeper insight, and throws a brighter light on the history of Party politics, and the primacy of Party politics, a topic not fully explored and rarely understood by academics.

'Mike' Pearson in his public persona did not exude charisma. Yet, in close quarters, he displayed a remarkable lively intellect and witty self-deprecation that endeared him to his Party followers and charmed them. He wore this patent vulnerability coupled with a unique ability to bind diverse grouplets and factions on principles rather than personalities. He was an expert in smoothing the ruffled feathers of Party peacocks. The so-called 'left' wing led by Walter Gordon and Allan MacEachen, supported by Tom Kent, held strong policy views; yet these views did not destroy the unity of the Party. The so-called 'right' wing led by Robert Winters, Paul Hellyer, and Mitchell Sharp, to whom Jean Chrétien was an early acolyte, almost split over funding for 'Medicare' in the 1966 policy convention. Yet, loyalty to the Leader, to Mr. Pearson, his soothing, down-to-earth personality, his honesty and fairness was the glue that preserved Party unity. Pearson gave more than he got from politics, leaving public service, as he had entered, only a modest, comfortable home to call his own. Not unlike his predecessor, Louis St. Laurent, who for many years lived with his wife in one small room in the Elgin Hotel in Ottawa, and then left politics to return to his family home in Quebec City. Pearson retired to his modest home in Ottawa and while in Toronto, lived from time-to-time in a small plain suite in the Park Plaza Hotel. Those days were from an earlier era when public service was deemed a 'calling', not a grasping occupation.

One 'mea culpa'. My close Party experience spanned the Pearson, Trudeau, Turner, Chrétien, Martin, and other interim leaders like Herb Gray, Bill Graham, party leaders like Dion and Ignatieff. I was invited to Mr. Pearson's caucus from time-to-time, as a young Liberal activist, and participated in all the others as a full member. I served as John Turner's first Executive Assistant, policy advisor, and speech writer when, in 1965, he became a Minister without Portfolio attached to the estimable Jack Pickersgill then Minister of Transportation[151] in Mr. Pearson's

[151] Jack Pickersgill was the legendary man of ideas at the heart of King, St. Laurent, and Pearson's Liberal administrations. He rose from Private Secretary to Mr. King's close advisor to St. Ms. Laurent's and then he was elected to Parliament to represent a small riding in Newfoundland called Bonavista Twillingate. He became an influential advisor to Mr. Pearson. He was the authorized editor of the *King Diaries*, a must read for those interested in politics. A close confidant of Joe Smallwood, I had my first opportunity to travel to Newfoundland with him and John Turner as he met with Smallwood, his Cabinet in the Parliamentary Buildings on St. Johns, Newfoundland. Pickersgill's subtle brilliance was at play as he respectfully sparred with Joe Smallwood, an equally skilled politician and

cabinet, and later served as a Campaign Head in his 1968 bid for leadership, after urging him to run.[152] *The Politics of Purpose*, a collection of John Turner's speeches delivered during that period from 1965 to 1968, many of which I helped draft, was published to coincide with the leadership contest in that early era and has been recently republished. It might be read as a companion guide for that period. Having acted first as an advisor during his period as Minister of Consumer and Corporate Affairs and then as an advisor when he was Minister of Justice, and episodically thereafter, I joined the throngs of fervent admirers who urged Turner to return to politics in the early '80s after he had resigned abruptly from the Trudeau Cabinet in 1975, having loyally participated in the disastrous 'Land is Strong' Campaign of 1972 and the 1974 'Wages and Price Controls - Zap You're Frozen' election that saw the Liberals return to majority government, and most notably as Minister of Justice during the War Measures Act declared by Trudeau after the murder of a Quebec Cabinet Minister, Pierre LaPorte, and the kidnapping of a British diplomat by radical separatists. Walter Gordon, though they did not share policy outlooks, noted that Turner was an assiduous and loyal minister in the Pearson Cabinet.

---

die hard Liberal. All in all, a memorable education for a neophyte political assistant. My first learning curve as a newly arrived political appointee to John Turner in Ottawa was when I asked my secretary to call Pickersgill's Deputy Minister of Transportation to introduce myself. He refused to come to the phone. Turner advised me to attend at his office which I did, and I apologized for my lack of respect. Lesson learned.

152 I left Turner's office in 1966 to return to my law practice in Toronto, but we kept in regular contact. When Mr. Pearson resigned, I urged Turner to run. "*There were no downsides*", I advised him. He agreed if I would return to Ottawa for a few months to help run his campaign. I reluctantly went home to seek Carole's assent. She was not pleased but agreed with Turner if I convinced him to run that then I would have to sacrifice a few more months away from home and my budding law practice.

From the loss of leadership in 1968 and during his time as Minister of Justice and Finance Minister in the Trudeau Cabinet to Pierre Trudeau and his abrupt resignation in September 1975 until his return to public life as Prime Minister in 1984, John Turner maintained contact with a loyal network of Liberal activists across the country based on the so-called '195 Club', a loose seemingly constantly expanding circle who claimed to have voted for him on the last ballot at the 1968 Leadership Convention, until he was eliminated in the final rounds of voting. It was David Smith who had joined me in Turner's office as an assistant who coined the phrase '195 Club' in 1960. Lloyd Axworthy, who I enlisted to Turner's office, also was a founding member like me.

I continued as a volunteer party policy and communications advisor running Red Leaf, the Liberal advertising consortium I co-founded with Keith Davey during the Trudeau era and continued during John Turner's period as candidate for Leader, Prime Minister and then as Leader of the Opposition.

What emerges, from the undulating sometimes blurred pictures encased in the morass of raw politics, is the riveting character of John Turner, who believed devoutly in public service as almost a sacred calling coupled with a Churchillian reverence for Parliament as the 'vox populi' – the ultimate 'voice of the people'.

Uniquely, John Turner had lived, worked and vacationed, with vital family roots and relationships, in all regions of Canada, especially the Maritimes (where his maternal grandfather was a coal miner), Quebec (especially Montreal where he practiced law), Nova Scotia (where his family owned a vacation property), Ontario (where he lived and practiced law after his return to private life after leaving to politics the first time and later when he retired from politics), Manitoba (where his wife's family came from and his wife's family maintained a summer home), and British Columbia (where his mother, Phyllis Ross, the leading female bureaucrat in Ottawa during the world war, became Chancellor of University of British Columbia and where he ran for Parliament when he returned to public life). Travelling with him across Canada was an exhilarating experience for he shared his exuberant love for the capacious Canadian landscape from East to West, his zest for the farthest reaches of the North, and the limitless Canadian wildernesses which he knew intimately from endless canoe trips, and where he relaxed, felt comfortable and at home. From childhood, he gained an early passion for conservation, and especially protection of our fresh water sources that he was to advocate throughout his long public career.

John Turner was caught between two shifting political templates and periods: the first, during the hierarchal establishment mores of the Liberal Party under Louis St. Laurent and C.D. Howe in the late '50s, and the second which first enmeshed Mr. Pearson and his successors in the new explosive vitriolic political scatter-gun environment that transformed politics in Canada, especially after the Kennedy/Nixon TV debates in 1960 in the U.S.A.

The early '60s marked the great shift in the relationship between politics and the media. The first American presidential media debates, especially TV, had a profound impact on politics in Canada and the way we conducted our day-to-day political discourse. Canadians were, and remain, deeply influenced by American political techniques as American media reaches all comers of Canada. There is always a time lag as Canadians begin to mimic American politics. The intrusive role of television replaced print as the primary source of 'news' for the public. Electronic media extended and accelerated its pervasive presence into the '70s and '80s when Canada moved from the oligarchic new print agenda-making and combined with the then narrow prism of the national television network environment. Quickly, political news mixed with entertainment, flowed into the wider and wilder disparate world of cable television, and the even more capacious range of choices of the specialty channels universe to the current relentless 24/7 news cycle – all before the advent and even greater expansive and disparate reach of the 'web'. The line between 'news', 'politics', and 'entertainment', began to overlap and dissolve. The tipping point between the 'old' and the 'new' politics had been reached. Canadians were confronted with a new political confusing concoction where 'news' and 'entertainment' overlapped and merged at times.

The velocity and diversity of electronic news gutted the old system of hierarchal patrician pundit columnists and print editorial influence that shaped and held sway over public opinion by its daily agenda setting. Now the public got their 'news' from television and were more influenced by the political images and opinions fulminated by the electronic media. Now young, untutored media voices, that knew or cared little for historic context and read less, focused all their competitive energy on the race for instant news clips without context – the thirty-second 'gotcha' soundbite of the moment.

Gifted in so many ways with a deep classical liberal education both in Canada and in England at Oxford as a Rhodes scholar and in France at the University of Paris, well read, well-travelled in Europe and fluently bilingual, star athlete with his 'hip' jargon in early professional life, John Turner, as Leader, never seemed quite able to make the shift, the transformation from the old, more personal, structured media hierarchy to the fractured factionalized horizontal electronic environment, until almost the end of his public career. The larger complex issues, he espoused, especially those that were process driven and those of fiscal responsibility, were submerged in the waves of the new disjointed news, ripped from their historic frame and swept away in the flotsam and jetsam of disparate news from everywhere. Larger political issues of substance were diluted or drowned in the noise of meaningless disjointed 24/7 chatter. The public was distractible and distracted.

Where once the morning news first radio then nightly television news followed print front pages and editorials, thread to the public through the same information needle, now 'news' from everywhere and everything clouded, confused, and fragmented in the public mind.

The line between 'politics' and 'culture' and 'identity' blurred. The 'cultural' wars had overtaken traditional politics, especially in the United States with direct reverberations in Canada. The age of McLuhan had arrived: 'perception' became 'reality', and the 'medium' became the 'message'. Feminism was on the rise.

McLuhan held a deeper insight into the interplay between politics and imagery. He wrote: "*The Politician will only be too happy to abdicate in favour of his image, because the image will be so much more powerful than he will ever be.*" Once etched in public opinion the public image becomes indelible, almost impossible to adjust or erase. To refurbish the glistening aspects of Turner's early longer part of his public career that has been forgotten, blemished by his surprisingly awkward, ungainly return to public life in 1984.

John Turner's earliest successful battles as a newly minted junior Minister in the Pearson Cabinet skillfully overcame the reactionary bureaucracy to establish a 'liberal' Department of Consumer and Corporate Affairs, the first of its kind in the Western World, surfing the Ralph Nader consumer wave, and other issues which John Turner brilliantly steered a liberal path forward through the Cabinet, Parliament, and painted onto the public canvas. John Turner, as Minister of Justice, drafted and piloted the wide-ranging legally contentious reforms of the 'Just Society' through Parliament for which Trudeau has been given sole credit. It was John Turner, not Pierre Trudeau, who crafted, drafted, and legislated the 'criminal code' measures espoused and titled the 'Just Society' by Trudeau who handed Turner the divisive dossier on bilingualism when others in the Cabinet faltered, and failed, who rescued the renewed call for capital punishment and presided over the 'abolish' debate and smoothly navigated and traversed 'abortion' debates in Parliament that was encapsulated in legislation – all of which are now seen, in retrospect, as conventional wisdom. Yet, a clearer story of the battle for bilingualism, or the 'October crisis', or other divisive issues like the introduction of the War Measures Act and Turner's role in these crucial issues will not emerge until future writers and scholars probe the Cabinet minutes of this era now opened to public scrutiny.[153]

It is fair to ascribe to John Turner the accolade as Canada's greatest Minister of Justice and Attorney General to occupy that prestigious portfolio. As a Member of the Quebec Bar, he was an early advocate of legal aid, based on his passionate belief to rebalance state power in favour of the citizen. Invited to the Kingston Conference in 1961, he persuaded the Liberal party to adapt legal aid as a Liberal policy. In addition to legislating the contentious reforms of the 'Just Society' through Parliament, the Bilingualism Bill and liberal amendments to the Criminal Code,

[153] During the Pearson era, Turner and Rene Levesque had a good, effective working relationship when Levesque was a Quebec Liberal Minister under Jean Lesage. This relationship soured when Turner, as Minister of Justice, responsible for steering the War Measures Act through Parliament and other contentious legislations like bilingualism and advancing across Canada. Then Levesque sarcastically labelled Turner as Trudeau's 'travelling salesman'.

he faced one of the greatest existential legal threats to Canada's existence during the FLQ crisis and, despite the visceral temper of those times, relied on the 'rule of law'. Despite resistance in the Cabinet, he insisted on amending the antiquated War Measures Act which he laid before Parliament to reduce its anti-civil liberties overreach in the future. I am confident that once the archives on this era are scrutinized by historians, Turner's role as an avid liberal, in the classic sense, will come into sharper focus.

His early experience as Counsel in the Quebec Bar persuaded him that the justice system had wrongfully put the onus for bail on the alleged criminal. He reversed this by amending the Criminal Code to place the onus on the Crown to prove why bail was necessary in the public's interest.

He renovated the partisan judicial appointment process and was careful, fastidious, and fair in all the court appointments during his tenure, ranking merit over patronage, purging and transforming the Partisan judicial appointment process. For him, legal merit rather than ideology was the key. Revamping the musty and reactionary Department of Justice, he gathered an outside circle of superb lawyers and academics to advise him on law reform. He asked me to organize some of these meetings.[154] One concrete example was the establishment of the first federal Law Reform Commission as a template and replicated by some provinces to bring both the antiquated federal, provincial, and common law laws up to date. This was a radical departure from previous episodic law reform efforts, navigating past bureaucratic inertia, Cabinet objections, and Parliamentary indifference.

[154] One mea culpa. I invited my two law school classmates and law school study group members to attend - Martin Friedland, a Professor at the University of Toronto Law School and later Dean, and Harry Arthurs, a Professor of Law at York University Osgoode Hall and later Dean and then President of York University.

He followed my great law teacher and mentor, Cecil Augustus Wright's edict "*not what the law is but what the law should be*".

He agreed to convene a Conference on the Law that I suggested to him and made me a key organizer inviting leading social thinkers 'outside the box', notably Ivan Illich, a radical Catholic theologian and author of such texts as *Deschooling Society*, to influence the Department, the Caucus, the Cabinet, and Parliament, and public opinion to make law reform a comprehensive public priority. I recall when the Conference was convened in Ottawa, Pierre Trudeau was to make the introductory comments. Trudeau was interested in meeting Illich, a defrocked Jesuit priest, who had set up a seminar centre in Mexico after he left the church as a priest. I arranged for Trudeau to meet Illich at the Chateau Laurier for breakfast before the conference start for a half hour. I was anxious as the Conference commencement was awaiting Prime Minister Trudeau to open the event. Illich and Trudeau were deep in discussions oblivious to the time, spending almost an hour together. Finally, I persuaded them to continue their discussion and head for the Conference. Trudeau's curiosity in Illich and his ideas was not surprising. Later, Turner spent several longer hours with Illich, equally mesmerized by this innovative Catholic thinker whose thesis could be summarized up in one phrase from one of his books, *Deschooling Society*.[155] Illich believed that society's institutions need renovation from the bottom up as they hinder the objectives they were originally set up to achieve.

---

[155] Later, Illich invited me and a small circle of lawyers, politicians, and academics from South America and Europe interested in radical law reform to present papers in a lengthy seminar held in Cuernavaca, Mexico, his organization's headquarters. Illich, a gifted translator and linguist, would have each participant read his paper in their given language, then translate in English and Spanish and continue when others dissected it. It was a memorable experience.

What is the central importance of the Ministry of Justice? The federal Department of Justice is the unsung Ministry of Government underlying all legislative initiatives. Law, lawmaking, and the administration of justice knit together the fabric of Canada's character. The criminal law power, which exclusively rested with the federal government, was never challenged by any of the Provinces including Quebec. Equality before the law was and is an architectonic of Canadian history and part of Canada's DNA. To Turner, this was more than just a slogan.

In the 1908, Rudyard Kipling, on a visit to Canada, wrote to his family his impressions of Canada and Canadians:

> "*The law in Canada exists and is administered, not as a surprise, a joke, a favour or a bribe...but as an integral part of the national character – no more to be forgotten or talked about than trousers.*"

Earlier, in 1861, John Anderson, a fugitive slave being discharged for murder by the Court of the Common Pleas in Upper Canada, said:

> "*I have never known that there was so much law in the world as I find in Canada.*"

The late novelist, Robertson Davies, in his 1954 masterpiece, Leaven of Malice, wrote:

> "*Never go to the law for simple vengeance, that is not what the law is for. Redress, yes; vengeance, no.*"

In 1960, Mr. Pearson, then Leader of the Opposition, spoke in the House of Commons Debate:

"Incorruptible and respected Courts, enforcing laws made by free men in parliament assembled and dealing with specific matters and, with specific sanctions to enforce their observance; these are the best guarantees of our rights and liberties. This is the tried and tested British way and is the better course to follow than the mere pious affirmation of general principles to which some political societies are addicted.

The paramount purpose of our working Parliament is no more and no less than to make laws. That is what Parliament does. Parliament transforms experience into principles, and these principles into explicit laws. We make laws and administer the execution of those laws, especially criminal laws. Parliament has exclusive oversight of the criminal law power, and this power is tied to the question of freedom, liberty and security, which are the organizing principles at the heart of federal governance. Criminal laws are Parliament's definition of our civilization's standards of conduct and care. To fall below these standards of care by unwanted conduct is to invite penalties, prompting state action and, more important, to provide a clear warning against unwanted conduct. Ultimately, criminal law seeks to prevent and ostracize egregious conduct and, hopefully, in the process, to transform the attitude and intentions of those who practice such conduct. It is to transform public opinion, public conduct and private conduct."

Both Turner and Trudeau understood these truisms, but it was Turner, as Minister of Justice, Attorney General and Chief Law Officer of the Crown who turned preferred principles into the legislative sinews of our civic society, just as Trudeau did later with the Charter of Rights and Freedoms.

It was the advent of 'culture' or 'value' social warlike issues that John Turner was directed by Trudeau and his Cabinet to diffuse and he did. At the time when these explosive issues burst upon the public agenda, they were tempered, cooled, and honed by John Turner's skills as an advocate, mediator, and legislator morphing these emotive ideas into the comfort zone and quieter waters of conventional public wisdom.

Turner had great political abilities, much like the Lyndon Johnson gift (the so-called 'Johnston treatment'), to persuade key decision-makers by personal contact to accept his viewpoint. This gift was on display by Turner with Provincial Premiers who opposed bilingualism when the Turner treatment persuaded them, one-by-one, to accept the advent of bilingualism, a triumph of the Trudeau era.

When John Turner accepted Pierre Trudeau's calculated offer of the Finance Ministry, it represented a risk to Turner's future leadership ambitions, for no previous Minister of Finance had ever acceded to the Prime Ministership. At that time, he was the youngest Member of Parliament to ever hold the prestigious Finance portfolio. It was a difficult economic period. Inflation was on the rise and old notions weren't working.

As Minister of Finance, John Turner early grasped that, to sustain the spiraling of public debts and deficits fed by inflation, irresponsible runaway spending, especially Medicare, would put unrelenting downward pressure on the entire social net. Unless redressed and rebalanced, the ballooning public cost would place an economic squeeze and undermine the entire social net. He predicted that spiraling health costs, unless contained, would beggar other pressing economic needs especially aging infrastructure. This realistic view unfairly labeled him 'Conservative' by the at times profligate so called 'progressive' spenders in the Trudeau Cabinet who argued the national debt and deficits never were problems.

Rarely do academics choose to fully explore the roots of the deep philosophic similarities and differences between Trudeau and Turner on economic policy. Trudeau had studied economic theory at Harvard and the London School of Economics under the left leaning Harold Laski. Turner, while at Oxford, explored the ideas of Keynes then in vogue. When at the University of Paris, he explored European economic ideas. Keynes was a lifelong liberal and eschewed socialist prescriptions. Both had considered the thinking of Schumpeter and Hayek. Both agreed that 'Keynesian' principles could not be blindly applied in Canada at times of inflationary prices and slow growth. Yet, they had come to different economic nostrums. It was Trudeau who aggravated Turner when he assembled a group of economic advisors in the PMO/PCO, which Trudeau quickly disbanded when Turner properly argued that the Minister of Finance's duties to Cabinet as senior economic advisor could not be fragmented in this way. When, as Minister of Finance, he turned his attention to transparent fairness in the incomprehensible tax code, he gave taxpayers a simple cost-effective appeal process to address grievances with the prolix tax system. It was Trudeau's economic advisors he appointed to parallel to the Ministry of Finance primary role as economic advisor to the government that triggered Turner's resignation.

The current debate in North America and Europe about relentless inflationary governance costs and unproductive entitlements continues to strip away and slow the growth of the GDP. Turner spotted this endemic problem early and highlighted as a source of present and future malaise thus going against the grain of conventional thinking at the time when debt and deficit were spurting ahead of growth. The, then current, view in Ottawa was that deficits and debts were not even genuine problems. They were imaginary dangers imagined by some 'right wing' nuts. Many in Ottawa held rigid and distorted 'views' of 'Keynesian' economics and failed to take account of the relative size of the government and the private sector when Keynes wrote his landmark texts. Many, not having carefully culled Keynes' theories which restricted public expenditures to public infrastructures not otherwise undertaken by the private sector and carelessly expanded and misapplied Keynes' limited strictures. Many simply forgot how Keynes had railed against socialist dogma.

Two titanic issues found John Turner opposed to Pierre Trudeau's vision of Quebec within Canada and Brian Mulroney's continental views of Canada in North America. These two visceral issues framed first by the Meech Lake Accords, cleverly instigated by Mulroney to upstage and trump Trudeau's brilliant constitutional victories of repatriation and the 'Charter'. Mulroney skillfully detected the fault lines running through the Liberal Party which, to a large measure, had accepted Trudeau's version of 'One Canada' with a strong central government and ambitious provinces different but not 'distinct', keeping the federal/provincial powers comfortably and constitutionally balanced against Quebec's incessant demand for more and more Quebec-only powers. This disruptive and incessant call by Quebec, breaking from the cocoon of 'Duplessisism' into the 'Quiet Revolution', demanding 'more' powers, emerged again and again as the paramount cause of Federal-Provincial friction, then echoed by Alberta flexing its political muscles, feeling its new found-power in rich energy resources. The rapid rise of separatism created a mood in the rest of Canada to mollify noisy Quebec, which Trudeau diagnosed as weakening the central governance while John Turner believed were historic cyclical ebbs and flows in power sharing between the provinces and the federal government.

During the great existential threat to Canada's unity, even biting into the core of federalism, the FLQ crisis – John Turner as Minister of Justice modulated Trudeau 's more expansive reactions and worked in close harmony with Trudeau, carefully consistent with the 'rule of law' to pull Canada through.

John Turner's beliefs about the nature of Quebec within Confederation clashed with Trudeau's long-held and carefully evolved ideas which now resonated within the bosom of the Liberal party. Both held deeply considered views about the relationship of Quebec in Confederation. Trudeau rejected the 'compact theory' which led inevitably to the 'two nations' theory that espoused the view that Canada was a 'pact' between two founding nations, English Canada and French Quebec.

Trudeau agreed with St. Laurent that Quebec was a "*province like the others*". John Turner, unlike other more extravagant advocates of the 'two nations' theory, took a different but less extreme, more moderate view than that held by academics in Quebec, taken by some Liberal Federalists and even Conservatives, politicians like Robarts in Ontario, and Jean Luc Pepin in Ottawa. Turner was an early advocate of Quebec designating itself as a 'distinct society' within Canada, as he believed it recognized a fact that would not legally alter the balance of powers within Confederation. Trudeau believed that the designation of Quebec as a 'distinct society' would inevitably lead to new and unreasonable demands for more powers by Quebec. From his earliest days as a writer and dazzling pamphleteer, Trudeau argued that the 'compact theory' was a false reading of the origins of Confederation. The Canadian federation was 'in law' and by 'constitution' a balanced separation of powers between the federal government and the different provinces. As a result, Quebec had its different civil law, language, and education as available to other provinces had they chosen. Quebec was different as were the other provinces, but never 'distinct'. Quebec and, at times, others argued for greater powers from the Federal government - usurping some not occupied fully by the Federal government.

This fault line Mulroney brilliantly essayed and exploited, splitting the Liberal Party asunder over the Meech Lake debate. As well, with a large restive Quebec 'nationalist' contingent in his caucus, Mulroney was anxious to assuage and appease their concerns and expectations. Turner, as Leader of the Opposition, supported Meech Lake. Trudeau, then out of office, returned to the public forum only once,[156] to advocate Meech Lake's defeat, which happened.

In many ways, John Turner and Pierre Trudeau had much in common. Both were raised without fathers, by strong independent mothers; both were highly schooled here and abroad, with a liberal arts education; both were avid rugged outdoorsmen who loved to vacation, canoe and portage, in quiet northern lakes and rushing waterways; both exuded a certain grace, practiced 'old world' courtesy, and impeccable manners; both were effortlessly bilingual and facile with others; both had long held political ambitions and spent time preparing themselves for public office; both easily attracted and retained cadres of loyal friends; both had capacious recall for people and ideas; both were well-schooled skilled lawyers; both were impressively persuasive as counsel in

[156] Senators such as MacEachen, Joyal, and I believed that Trudeau, now retired, who had kept silent on the Meech Lake debate should be convinced to come out of retirement and argue against the assumptions of Meech Lake Accord at an open meeting of the Committee of the Whole in the Senate. For over two hours, Trudeau quickly mesmerized his Senate audience only occasionally referring to notes for exact quotes to support his thesis. This public transcript in the Senate Hansard, totally unedited, was a model of concision and remains an invaluable tool for future scholars to understand this era and this subject.

Court; both were voracious readers with retentive memories; both were gifted speech-writers and, on occasion, could be incandescent speakers, especially in Parliament; both were 'quick' studies who could deftly digest complex, fulsome briefing papers; both quickly cut to the heart of a political problem; both were impatient with the unprepared and with fools; both had an intense way of focusing on the issue at hand as if to wring the hidden essence of the subject matter; both diligently prepared for cabinet or public meetings; both were 'conviction' politicians; both were men of high character, a somewhat debased or overlooked dimension of politics now rarely considered in the calculus of public opinion; both respected and even admired John Diefenbaker; both cut attractive debonair athletic figures; while both were devout practicing Roman Catholics who both early had considered the priesthood as a vocation, Turner was influenced by the Basilians and Trudeau first by the Jesuits and later by Benedictines and Dominicans; both regularly attended Mass and religious retreats; both shared ideas rooted in the social gospel; both regularly consulted and held close relationships within the church hierarchy, yet never allowed their orthodox Catholicism to stand in the way of their liberal pluralistic principles.[157] John Turner and Pierre Trudeau agreed that private religious beliefs should not trump secular or temporal considerations in a liberal society, yet, each would nuance these principles in different ways with a markedly different temperament. Both were bereft of a father figure which can have an impact on sons is often left with

[157] One of John Turner's closest friends who became a valued advisor was Rick Alway who served with distinction as Head of St. Michael's College at University of Toronto. Turner had close relations with cardinals and archbishops in Quebec and met regularly and chatted with Cardinal Carter in Ontario who told me how much he admired Turner.

tangled skeins of deep-seated complex ambitions more properly left to Freudian analyses.

While both shared almost a symbiotic relationship and mutual respect for each other's skills, both were puzzled by each other and could not grasp the wellspring of the other's drives, ambitions or goals. Both Turner and Trudeau confided in me their views and I remain surprised by their reading of the other.

If there were marked differences, Trudeau as Leader, after false starts between 1968 and 1972, was able to stitch together a diverse, knowledgeable, and wide circle of capable political operatives and independent committed advisors who, for the most part, liked and respected each other that sustained him and each other in his ups and downs until his retirement. Turner's inner circle was split and divided on policy, personalities, strategy, and tactics.

When on the public stage, Trudeau was a superb actor who had an uncanny ability to observe himself and polish his techniques of public persuasion. Trudeau relished flamboyant theatrics. Turner, on the other hand, especially when he returned to public life in the early '80s to run for Prime Minister, never seemed to meld his disparate groups of advisors or forge bonds among them as a coherent circle who liked or trusted each other and to work in concert in his best interests other than to carve out their own sphere of influence. He seemed 'rusty' in his public appearances. The media said he was 'rusty' but more fairly, he was out of tune of the changing ambience and the evolving belief structures surrounding politics.

On the public stage, it was only after his electoral defeat in 1984 that Turner was able to slowly adapt and hone his techniques to match the new public environment and to become comfortable, as he once was, and restore his undoubted skills as a public advocate. It was not that Turner was 'rusty' as some observers alleged at the time; it was that the public arena itself was dramatically transformed during his decade of absence from public life, leaving him less certain and less confident in his public advocacy skills. His performance in 1988 election debates recouped his public reputation, tarnished by his earlier lack-lustre performance in the hastily called, ill-prepared 1984 election, and somewhat restored the Liberal Party membership in the Commons.

The other wrenching existential debate triggered by Mulroney that raged across Canada was about 'Free Trade'. Mulroney suddenly abandoned the age-old Conservative 'protectionist' history and jumped into the shoes of liberal 'free traders', who, like Laurier, had fought and lost an election campaign leading the Liberal Party in 1911, on the issue of North American trade reciprocity, and a more reluctant Mackenzie King who, after World War II, explored then withdrew from thoughts of 'freer' trade with the U.S.A. Louis St. Laurent's leadership on the building of the St. Lawrence Seaway with its bilateral implications was another tepid step towards 'freer' North American trade. Diefenbaker veered to the anti-American 'nationalist' protectionist perch of the classic Conservative. Pearson steered a steady moderate course to freer trade by creating the 'Autopact' with the United States. The Autopact laid the template for the FTA. Mulroney had no electoral mandate on this issue. He did not campaign on 'free trade'; rather, he took advantage of his close ties with the Reagan Administration, and surprised the country with his sudden lurch and leap to the FTA.

The Free Trade Agreement debate, the 'FTA', deeply divided the Liberal Party between classic 'Manchester' Liberals who were 'free traders' and those gradualists who, like John Turner, believed the slower erosion and gradual reduction of GATT tariffs would ultimately result in 'free trade'. Gradualism, John Turner thought, was a more coherent route forward than a sudden advance to a fulsome Free Trade Agreement that was bereft of effective dispute mechanisms or shields from the inherent protectionism, dormant yet, ever alive, in the bone marrow of the American Congress and at the state level. John Turner railed against the fact that Mulroney had not sought or obtained a public mandate for this major change and hence his use of his role as Leader of the Opposition on both principles and lack of mandate in resisting the enactment of the legislation needed to make the Free Trade Agreement effective. Mulroney obtained a public mandate in a national election and opposition in Parliament withered to the FTA.

The Canadian 'Big Banks', 'Bay Street', and the business establishments never forgave Turner for his daring to exercise a principled approach to the FTA.

Today, 'free trade' remains a resonating issue which vindicates Turner's views to some extent. The untrammeled protectionist impulses of the United States Administration and the wayward Congress continue to produce unilateral protectionist measures, measures contrary to the spirit of the FTA. Yet, the FTA has been, by any measure, a remarkable economic success of benefit to both Canada and the United States.

On both these issues, John Turner's careful 'common law' lawyer-like approach failed to unite the bubbling divisions within the Liberal Party or the avalanche of boisterous 'big' business support fomented by Mulroney, too cautious for the most part to enter the competitive entrepreneurial American market place without the threat of protectionist measures nascent in Congress diminished.

Both issues were used unfairly by divisive ambitious players within the Liberal Party to bring John Turner down, by unscrupulous power hungry operatives, who exaggerated the chasms of division and engulfed the Liberal Party in destructive flames, the embers of which still glow dimly, rather than remaining united against an aggressive politically savvy Mulroney administration.

John Turner's superbly honed advocacy and unparalleled legislative talents with clarity, accuracy, and balance were evident. What emerges from this mosaic, if still uncertain portrait, is a man of strong character, personal probity, and relentlessly consistent principles that encased him in an aura of honesty, rarely seen in public life. As Winston Churchill once lamented of his father: "*He sought to wrap himself in the mantle of Elijah.*"[158] Any flaws, failures or foibles are far outweighed by the glowing honesty, probity, and commitment to the Liberal Party, to public service, Parliament and to Canada that radiated from John Turner like a beacon to those who are interested in the good public life of Canada and in promoting Canada's vital interests.

When John Turner left politics to return a decade later to run as Leader, the tectonic shift in politics had accelerated. What was acceptable conduct in the past was now anathema. Now, 'political correctness' magnified each gender comment or contact. A new sensibility was in place. Somehow Turner had lost his groove and it took a political loss to restore his political equilibrium.

Missing from current history is the internal grammar of politics, a deeper parsing of political parties and how each Party plays a pivotal and virtual role in our political system. In that system, a Leader must immerse himself in the sinews of the Party corpus and emerge to claim political legitimacy the public's opinion of the viability and electability of the Leader. Once past the hurdle of Leadership approval in an open convention, the

---

158 Turner was deeply influenced by his elders in the Liberal Party like Louis St. Laurent, Pearson, C.D. Howe, and Jack Pickersgill.

more opaque process of working of the National Caucus, the heartbeat of the Party, takes over.

Unlike the United States, the executive branch in Canada is wholly made up of Members of Parliament, either House or then, Senate. The Ministries are responsible to Parliament. The House of Commons can refuse the money which the Government needs. This direct relationship of the Party leaders, government, and opposition in Parliament and the necessity of preserving small Caucus 'Confidence' between elections, which distinguishes these two political systems, make the Leader's constant umbilical relationship to his caucus and its trust in the Leader especially important.

The heart of parliamentary democracy is the power of the members to give or deny their leaders their 'confidence'. As John Ralston Saul points out in his concise enchanting biography of Robert Baldwin, a father of responsible government – "*such a clear principle had not yet been established in Britain or anywhere else*". Responsible government was forged in colonial Canada with 'confidence' as its pivotal principle.

In the confines of caucus that meet in secret sessions, the ordinary member may speak freely and criticize Party positions and policies. The Leader, in turn, can advance his views, and how he expresses these views is regularly evaluated to gauge his knowledge and political skills. The Leader's comments in caucus have a far greater influence on members than the addresses to the public or Parliament.

The weekly National Caucus, a gathering composed only of Liberal members of both the Commons and the Senate holds the key to 'confidence' – a paramount factor in our political system. The Leader must retain and renew 'confidence' at each weekly meeting of the Party Caucus. Party unity depends on Caucus unity.

The Caucus meeting room reverberates weekly with status of Party in government or in opposition. For example, the high-ceilinged Railway Committee Room, festooned with history, paintings, and murals, lends an element of gravitas to each meeting of a large Caucus membership.

Mastery of the Caucus, on issues large and small, achieving and retaining the confidence of the Caucus, is the defining yet little-known ingredient of political success and longevity. Pearson quit shortly after the accidental loss of a vote that shattered Caucus 'confidence' understating the importance of confidence. Nevertheless, Pearson worked assiduously to repair the damage by a new Parliamentary vote. Trudeau took his famed 'walk in the snow' and suddenly announced his resignation as Leader when he felt he had lost Caucus 'confidence'. 'Confidence' is the central and elusive, building block of our political system. Turner fought assiduously to regain caucus support after his Parliamentary defeat and became Leader of the Opposition.

It is 'confidence' that unites a party and makes it powerful within and without.

By tradition, Caucus deliberations are kept confidential and secret. No written record is kept of its deliberations or conclusions. The rule of Caucus secrecy, like that of the Cabinet, is to allow free, open, and honest debate on the issues of the day, not ripped out of context to damage or enhance any advocate on a particular issue. A breach of secrecy in the Cabinet has its consequences as should have been the case with Caucus. The 'right' to know what is decided and how issues were decided should, of necessity, have been more tightly proscribed. Of course, the national media, determined to get 'news' and inflame and inflate Party division, attempts a weekly tussle to pry loose confidential Caucus information.

The National Liberal Caucus' weekly ritual, chaired by a member of the Commons, who is elected by secret ballot, convenes after meetings of the various Regional and Special Caucuses, to hear various reports. The House and Senate Leaders and the Whip report quickly on their responsibilities, followed by the Regional and other Chairs.[159] Then the meeting is open for each member to give his 'take' on the current public agenda, to promote issues of local concern, or housekeeping matters. Members seek to capture the Chair's attention to be recognized for several minutes to air and advocate his or her grievances and national or local concerns as each struts their political 'smarts'. Applause or negative reaction is heard immediately.

Humour, self-deprecating humour or clearly articulated passion on an issue vie for Caucus acceptance.

The Caucus is a dynamic platform for mutual preening. Members seek to attract the Leader's and colleagues' attention for preferment, while the Leader seeks to convince the Caucus of his competence as the Leader and his leadership qualities. Calls for the imperative of Caucus unity, especially on contentious or divisive issues, are always on the weekly agenda. Thus, the vortex of personal ambition and public policy is on weekly display in the confines of the Caucus. By tradition, the Leader as the final speaker and arbiter then summarizes the discussions and draws a consensus setting out the action plan for the week ahead, exhorting the Caucus to renewed dedication and commitment to the tasks at hand. The Leader uses the Caucus as a forum, almost a 'focus' group, to pitch, practice, and shape his public lines of

---

[159] This was written before the current Leader of the Liberal Party, Justin Trudeau, eliminated Liberal Senators from the National Liberal Caucus. His reform of the Senate eliminating Liberal Senators from Liberal National Caucus and appointing only so-called 'Independents', remains a work in progress, too early to assess.

advocacy. The Leader himself, or he designates a spokesperson if he chooses to, makes the public summary of Caucus' deliberations at the following 'scrum'. The best practice is to allow the elected Chair of the Caucus to address the media scrum awaiting tidbits after each Caucus meeting.

Leadership is on parade in these weekly meetings matched by words, demeanor, body language, dress, mannerisms, wit, and calls to action. Machinations of the Caucus members before, during, and after Caucus in the parliamentary lobby are risible. Trudeau and Turner each in his time carefully refrained from manipulating the deliberations of Caucus by setting up sycophants to prepare their ground. Each allowed free discussion in Caucus and used their skills of advocacy to achieve coherence, enthusiasm, and team spirit if they could muster it, each week, not unlike a coach rallying his team at half time.

As a Caucus is a direct and candid exchange in the oral tradition, speaking notes or prepared statements are normally eschewed. Spontaneous reaction to individual Caucus concerns either in agreement or disagreement is spontaneously voiced by Members and then synthesized by the Leader. Whispered gossip, caustic critiques, and tart asides are parts of the normal fare.

Trudeau was skillful in startling original argumentation and analyses so as to weave together a Caucus consensus. Turner often seemed preoccupied, even episodic, at times ignoring hinted dissent and allowing unrest to fester. Both were plagued by Caucus 'leaks' to the media, as was Mr. Pearson, by unnamed Members self-seeking to curry favour for themselves or their chosen colleagues, with the media, which always is anxious to exacerbate divisions within the Party.

Of course, performance in Parliament, especially the theatre of daily Question Period, like gladiators of old, demonstrated the public persona of nimble leadership again feeding the visceral instincts of the intently watching members of the Party in this relentless, demanding task of leadership.

To be fair, only anecdotal and biased views can be scoured to gain a fuller picture of Party life within the private precincts of Caucus and lobby rooms of Parliament. It was a public letter written by twenty-two members of Turner's caucus fomented by a leadership rival that undermined Turner and instigated the startling turn in the Liberal Party fortunes.

Turner was an avid policy 'wonk', fascinated by political ideas. At University, he wrote his thesis on the Reform of the Canadian Senate. Before joining the Liberal Party, he was invited to attend, and actively participated in, the famed Kingston Conference. What would a Turner Prime Ministry have attempted? He was an early pre-political advocate of the abolition of the appointed Senate as being unrepresentative of the democratic will. The Turner-influenced 1988 Liberal Policy platform remained one unexplored avenue. Turner had distinct views on foreign policy, especially Canada's relationship with Commonwealth members, the United States, France, and Germany where he maintained a lively network of political operatives. Could Turner's highly personalized style have made a difference on the international stage? Regretfully, the wider scope of Turner's thinking remains open and speculative.

Working with John Turner on his speeches or policy statements was a delight. He was intellectual, engaged, demanding of facts to support conclusions, careful with flashes of wit, and lover of a turn of phrase. These exchanges remain a highlight of my time in politics.

Will the Liberal Party revive to play a major role in the future of Canada? The answer is a resounding "*Yes*", provided that the Turner ethics of hard work, honesty, integrity, 'grass roots' innovations, reformist ideas, diverse views, 'big tent' debate, and commitment to principles are replayed in the Party and Parliament to once again churn the engines of the Liberal Party. What seems missing during Turner's later public life was the 'politics of joy' that attracted so many young activists to the Liberal banner. Perhaps John Turner's belief in the 'Marquess of Queensberry Rules' applied to politics was outdated, but John Turner would not have it any other way. They formed a part of his basic convictions about the pursuit of politics – about the purpose of politics. His conscience was honed by his deep religious beliefs based on service to others.

In retrospect, Pierre Trudeau and John Turner represented two vital strands of Liberalism, at times running together, at times colliding. It was the combination of these two resonating strands that kept the Liberal Party in power for the longest period in Canadian history.

Was John Turner, as said of Churchill who had a thirst for public office and power, determined to make history or is this too simplistic? The restless reach, at times even the frenzy, for reputation, celebrity, and renown abounds in all ambitious politicians. In the end, the still hidden keys of John Turner's persona, like those of most senior politicians, are mixed in the valorization of political life at the core of the Liberal Party. And, like all political parties, there resides a strange, largely unchartered, reservoir in each politician, self-aggrandizement of ambition, hopes, projections, redemption and escape. Hopes to make a difference, ambitions for personal preferment, Freudian projections, internal redemption, and, at times, even escape from the humdrum confines of private life. 'Elusive Destiny', as one recent Turner biographer[160] wrote was 'elusive' indeed.

---

[160] *Elusive Destiny The Political Vocation of John Napier Turner* by John Litt (University of British Columbia Press, 2011).

John Turner, in his senior years, remains unbowed and ebullient about the future of the Liberal Party, the vital Role of Parliament, encouraging youth into public service, and optimistic about the future of Canada. He took a turn as the head of a group of Ukrainian Canadians who travelled to Ukraine to monitor a controversial election in Ukraine – split between pro-West and pro-Russian candidates and received plaudits on all sides.

In retrospect, despite all, Turner affirms that he was privileged to have played a role in the public life of the country. We shall not likely see that same unique public combination of intelligence, principles, energy, vivacity, drive, and wholesome competitiveness come our way again. His life serves as a public primer in high public purpose, the politics of purpose, genuine reform, and principles characteristic of the classic Liberal. He remains in essence an 'original' – an authentic Canadian. While institutional memory is a fading discipline, Turner and his special contributions and deep commitment to public service and public administration will survive and will not be forgotten.

For interested Liberals, let these quotes suffice:

The less a man knows about the past and the present, the more insecure must prove to be his judgment of the future.
- ***Sigmund Freud, 1927***

You cannot fight against the future.
Time is on our side.
- ***William Ewart Gladstone, 1866***

He who does not make known his own history, runs the risk that...the media and...historians will construct a

history for him, using whatever information they have, regardless of whether their information is accurate or not.
- *Osama Bin Laden in a letter to a lieutenant, Circa 2010*

Reason...is the slave of the passions...
- *David Hume, A Treatise on Human Nature 1740*

The true statesman is not one who gives orders to his fellow citizens so much as he is one who devotes himself to their service.
- *Pierre Elliot Trudeau, Vrai 1958*

John Turner - Maiden Speech

FINANCE

FOREIGN EXCHANGE HOLDINGS

Mr. John N. Turner (St. Lawrence-St. George) moved:

That an order of the house do issue for a copy of a table showing the changes in the official holdings of gold and foreign exchange, including United States dollars, held in the exchange fund account and Bank of Canada and showing "the total amount of exchange delivered to the market from the sales of foreign exchange", day by day, from April 9 to June 24, 1962, inclusive.

He said: Mr. Speaker, this being the first time I am on my feet in the House of Commons, may I use the opportunity to congratulate you on the position to which every hon. member of this house has elected you, a position of honour and responsibility unequalled in this house. Mr. Speaker, I will do my best, for my part, to abide by the rules of the house despite the pressures which may from time to time fall on me as a private member, the same pressures I have watched being applied to other hon. members in this house. I can say only that I will do my best to abide by the rules.

I should also at this stage like to recall to the memories and minds of hon. members the gentleman whom I replace in this house, Mr. Egan Chambers. Egan Chambers, as all hon. members who were in the house before the last election will agree, was a respected, a useful and a popular member of parliament. At the beginning of the campaign I knew him to be a gentleman; when the campaign was over I held the same opinion of him. I know him still to be a gentleman.

Mr. Speaker, the notice of motion before you concerns the production of documents, or the production of a certain table, and with the permission of the house I will dispense with reading it since it does appear on the order paper. Might I just say by way of explanation that what I as a private member have sought is a table showing the changes in foreign exchange reserves held by Canada on a day-to-day basis from April 9, 1962, which was the day before the last budget was presented, until June 24, 1962, which was the day on which the Prime Minister (Mr. Diefenbaker) addressed the Canadian people on television, when he announced a government program to relieve the pressure on Canada's dollar.

The Minister of Finance (Mr. Nowlan), to whom the notice of motion was addressed, under rule 47 of the standing orders had three alternatives. First he could have produced a copy of the table which I sought. So far he has not done so, although I imagine he still could. As the second alternative, on behalf

[Mr. Speaker.]

of the government he could have refused outright production of the table, in which instance I might have had the opportunity to proceed and to call for a vote for its production at that time. The minister had a third alternative, which alternative he has chosen in lieu of the other two. Rule 47 reads:

—but if on any such motion a debate be desired by the member proposing it or by a minister of the crown, the motion will be transferred by the Clerk to the order of "Notices of motions (papers)".

That is what the minister has done. He has, in effect, transferred my notice of motion from a non-debatable one to the debatable one which appears on the order paper today, and for which initially an hour's debate is permitted. The proviso to the rule I have just cited, as I understand it—and I say so with the deference of one who has been in this house for only three weeks—is of two years standing only. In other words, it was sanctioned by hon. members of this house about two years ago.

To the best of my knowledge, the transfer of a notice of motion for production of papers from the non-debatable to the debatable list has been made only on three occasions. On each of the three occasions previous to this particular instance, the motion was transferred by the private member himself, and on the basis of that transfer debate was allowed. This motion today, Mr. Speaker, represents the first instance, to the best of my knowledge, sir, of a motion being transferred for debate at the instance of a minister of the crown.

Mr. Churchill: What about 1956, the minister of citizenship and immigration?

Mr. Pickersgill: Not under the new rule.

Mr. Turner: With respect to the interjection by my hon. friend, I believe that under the new rule there have been only the three instances I have mentioned.

Mr. Pickersgill: Correct.

Mr. Turner: Mr. Speaker, if I may, for a moment, draw Your Honour's attention to the type of debate which is permitted under this motion, I should like to refer you to two of the previous instances when the question arose of a transfer of a motion of this kind to the debatable list. I would refer you to *Hansard* for February 8, 1962, volume I, at page 682. At that time the hon. member for Skeena (Mr. Howard) presented a motion for the production of certain correspondence relating to extraterritorial waters. At that time Mr. Speaker Michener had this to say:

Before the hon. member proceeds further—

The hon. member being the hon. member for Skeena—

—with that line of argument I think I should say to him that my view of the scope of the motion is that it is limited to the desirability of the production of the documents. The motion is one calling on the government to produce the documents referred to in the motion. The question in issue is whether or not they should be produced. Production of them has been objected to. It would be relevant to debate whether or not the grounds of objection were sufficient but in my view it would not be relevant to debate what the government should be doing about the breadth of international waters. That is another issue.

Words to the same effect, Mr. Speaker, were again delivered from the chair by Mr. Speaker Michener on March 22, 1962, as reported at page 2071 in volume III of *Hansard*. That instance concerned a motion for the production of papers made by the hon. member for Bonavista-Twillingate (Mr. Pickersgill) for the latest economic forecast at the time of the Department of Trade and Commerce. Mr. Speaker Michener again said:

The debate is on the issue of whether or not the government is correct in resisting the production of the documents.

In other words, I would respectfully submit that in relation to the particular question before Your Honour this afternoon the issue is whether or not the production of documents is relevant to a discussion which may or may not have taken place before the house. With your permission, I am going to define what I think is the issue.

There has been an argument in this house concerning whether the government, the present Conservative government, had knowledge of the exchange position of the country prior to June 18, which was the day of the general election and whether this position in foreign exchange was serious enough to warrant the government's advising the country before the election. Mr. Speaker, there have been two sides to the argument. On this side of the house we, the party for which I am speaking at the moment, have taken the position, through the words of the Leader of the Opposition (Mr. Pearson), that the documents perpetrated what he termed a political fraud on the country. The other side of the argument, that advanced by the Prime Minister and found at pages 109 and 110 of the current *Hansard*, is to the effect that the crisis blew up suddenly, and that on or about June 15 there was—and these are my own words—a sudden summer June storm, the crisis blew up, and it was only at that time and subsequently serious enough to draw to the country's attention. I might say, Mr. Speaker, that the Prime Minister again made that argument last night on television on the program called "The Nation's Business".

The purpose of this particular motion for the production of documents falls, I would submit to Your Honour, within the scope of that argument. I have asked for an order of the house to the affected minister, the Minister of Finance, to produce a table to show parliament, and thereby the country, what the real position was, and whether there had been a serious loss in foreign exchange reserves prior to June 18. In other words, I am seeking, on the basis of the argument I have put to you, sir, to bring the facts by way of a notice of motion for production before this house and before the people.

The Minister of Finance, when he replies to this motion, may say that the figures I am seeking are privileged because it is the custom of the Bank of Canada to publish these figures on a monthly basis only. Perhaps under normal circumstances that might be a valid argument. However, I would suggest to you, Mr. Speaker, that the Prime Minister himself broke these figures down beyond the monthly limits when he replied to the Leader of the Opposition. As found at pages 109 and 110 of *Hansard*, he produced figures for the period from June 1 to June 14 where there was a loss of $128 million exchange; he produced figures for the period from June 15 to June 22 when the loss was $270 million; and he produced figures for the period between June 25 and June 29 when the loss was $115 million.

At that time the Prime Minister said that this procedure was not to constitute a precedent. However, it is my humble submission to Your Honour that it is the Prime Minister who has broken the precedent and that in equity it is fair that the figures should be broken down not only at his choosing but also at the choosing of any hon. member of this house. If the door has been opened by the Prime Minister, then I suggest to Your Honour that the rest of us are entitled to go through and to inspect the tables and the figures in question. If the situation were otherwise the Minister of Finance, the Prime Minister and the government as a whole would be suggesting for this house a double standard, namely one standard for the government and another for the opposition and the rest of the members of this house.

If I may, I should like to review just briefly the procedure adopted by the minister in transferring this motion to the debatable list for this afternoon. The hon. gentleman might say that he has done us all a service in that he has given me and the other members of this house the right to debate the motion, whereas under the standing order without the proviso it is not debatable. I would suggest to you, Mr. Speaker, that this is the first time under this new rule, now of two years' duration, that this type of motion has been transferred by a minister. The result may be that, if this motion be talked out this afternoon in the one hour available, not only shall we not have obtained the production of the figures asked for but that we shall have lost our opportunity to vote on the measure. In other words, Mr. Speaker, I say to you that under this procedure parliament would be worse off than previously because at least previously we had the right to force a vote on the production of a document.

Some hon. Members: Oh, oh.

An hon. Member: Closure.

Mr. Howard: Getting close to the truth.

Mr. Turner: If I might do so, Mr. Speaker, I should like to examine the reason and again I do this with deference because of my lack of experience in this house.

Mr. Speaker: I might just here interject a little word of caution. Ascribing motives to hon. members on either side of the house, of course, is not in keeping with the traditions of this house. All I am doing is just issuing a word of caution to the hon. member.

Some hon. Members: Oh, oh.

Mr. Speaker: So far I have not heard anything that would infringe.

Some hon. Members: Oh, oh.

Mr. Speaker: That is all I am saying. Hon. members may be objecting now but I would point out that on other occasions they have been extremely sensitive when motives have been attributed.

Mr. Turner: May I then examine what I interpret to be the reasons behind the rule for the motion for the production of papers. As I said, I do this with the deference of one in my position. It seems to me that parliament has been so constructed over the years, by way of its traditions and the history of the parliamentary system, that it has its checks and balances. It has checks and balances so that the opposition and the individual members of the house can challenge and scrutinize what the government is doing. There are two primary methods for scrutiny, it would seem to me. The first is the method of questions with which I will not deal; it has had your attention very directly, Mr. Speaker, in these past few days. There is also the method of the production of documents whereby figures in the sole hands of the government can be demanded by opposition members, subject to the ordinary rules of public policy and privilege. What I am saying is that the procedure adopted by the minister could conceivably nullify the purpose of rule 47 for the production of papers by having the debate prolonged to such an extent that no vote could be taken forcing their production.

[Mr. Turner.]

(Translation):

Mr. Speaker, I should like to point out to my French speaking colleagues in all parts of the house that the purpose of the question now being considered is not merely to secure production of figures necessary to the public but also to protect the rights of parliament itself and of every hon. member.

If the debate is protracted, we shall have neither the figures nor the right to put the question to a vote in order to determine whether the government should produce them. To deny the production of documents is one thing, but to deny the right to vote is still worse.

(Text):

In conclusion, Mr. Speaker, if you will allow me just a minute or two minutes more, may I say this. In the alternative which the minister has chosen of opting for a debatable motion this afternoon he is entirely, I say with respect, within the rules of this house. However, if this option has the result of frustrating parliament not only by refusing production of figures but by prolonging debate beyond the time available for a vote, motions for production of documents will become a dead letter and the right of parliament to scrutinize and check the government will be infringed. I would therefore urge all members of this house to allow a vote to be taken this afternoon and to support the motion so that parliament and the public can obtain the facts with regard to our foreign exchange position prior to the date of the election and can make up their own minds as to who is right in the argument as to whether or not the government deceived the people.

Hon. George C. Nowlan (Minister of Finance): Mr. Speaker, my first words, of course, should be ones of congratulation to the hon. member who has just made a very effective speech on a very poor subject. I believe that to some extent he could have saved some of his breath, as he will understand before I sit down. I am not going to comment on the new rule. Technically he was correct in what he said about it. However, I might say that some hon. members do not have to recall to their minds the fact that in 1956, under a rule which had the same effect of transferring a debate, when a certain opposition was trying to have a matter brought forward a certain minister of the crown of that day who is now sitting not too far away from me at the moment, had a similar motion carried into debate, with only this difference. Under the old rule, that motion could not come up again during the session and parliament was frustrated. Under this rule we did this yesterday knowing we would be debating it today. That, of course, is just the difference between the two.

OCTOBER 18, 1962 675

Foreign Exchange Holdings

Mr. Churchill: Who was that member?

Mr. Nowlan: I will ask the hon. member for Bonavista-Twillingate (Mr. Pickersgill) to refresh our memories as to who that minister was at that time. Some of the remarks of the hon. member were largely technical dealing with the rule and I am not going to follow him in that course. With some of the statements of the hon. member I would agree entirely, in that banking procedures and the procedures of the Bank of Canada particularly should not be subjected to the production of detailed information such as requested in this motion.

I am glad that the hon. member said that he was speaking for his party because I thought it might be said that he was speaking only as a junior member without authority. I am glad to know he is speaking for his party when that party takes the irresponsible position of asking that this motion be brought forward and passed at this time because I suggest, as the hon. member said himself, that with regard to banking procedures, particularly those of the Bank of Canada, the central bank, in its dealings with other banks, where there are rules and limitations on confidence, the production of material, and so on, is a highly dangerous procedure and one with regard to which the bank should be protected at all times.

Although I am not entering into an argument on the point now, I would also question his statement that all information in the possession of a government should be produced at any time at the request of the house. If the house by a majority at any time ordered the government to produce such information, then that government would either have to resign or else produce the information. I would hope, Mr. Speaker, and I am confident that responsible members of the house, whenever a motion involving the ordering of the government or the bank to produce information which the government or a minister on his responsibility said was confidential and privileged and should not be produced, would accept that statement and would not order the government so to do. However, that does not arise on this occasion.

I take the responsibility for having this motion transferred from the order paper yesterday to the order paper today because I knew it was irresponsible and I knew it had many implications which should be considered. Frankly, I wanted to review it with my officials and I also wanted particularly to discuss it with my colleagues because I felt at the time that that was necessary before one took action one way or the other, knowing as I did that transferring it from the order paper yesterday to the order paper today would not in any way, shape or form delay or prejudice the house or the hon. member or the Liberal party in acquiring this information, since there was going to be a debate today.

As I said, one could argue that the bank particularly should not be put in the position of divulging the information asked for here, information which is treated as confidential between central banks all over the world. If this house should continue to put the bank in a position where it was compelled to produce information at the whim and caprice of any individual in the house requiring it, it would not be long before the integrity of the bank and its whole foundation would be shaken. On the other hand, Mr. Speaker, one can say that technically, although this is only an assumption that it is technical, the information asked for is almost four months old. The reference is to a period including part of April and extending to the latter part of June. Although I would not want my banking transactions of even four months ago revealed to the public sometimes, yet there is a little time lag there which gives some protection, in that information as to current dealings is not being produced.

More important is the fact that the hon. member very frankly put it before the house that there has been discussion and that malicious charges have been made against the Prime Minister of this country. To use the words of the hon. member, which I think I took down correctly, he said there had been charges against the Prime Minister of perpetrating a fraud on the Canadian public. The other day the Prime Minister brought forward facts and figures which I think cleared up that situation effectively but, despite that fact, if one refused to bring down the details asked for now, which supplement and add to the information given by the Prime Minister the other day, the accusation might possibly be made that there must be something about which the Prime Minister or this government is worried or else the information would be produced. There is nothing about which this government or the Prime Minister is worried so far as the facts of the case are concerned. I want the public to know that and I want this to be the end of following trails of innuendo, trails suggesting dishonour on the part of the Prime Minister and imputing motives, all of which are absolutely without foundation whatsoever.

Mr. Chevrier: Mr. Speaker, I rise on a point of order.

An hon. Member: The rug has just been pulled out from under you.

Mr. Chevrier: My point of order is, Mr. Speaker, that when the hon. member for St.

Lawrence-St. George was discussing his motion you warned him that he should be careful not to impute motives to anyone. The minister for the last five minutes has been imputing motives. I ask that he be called to order in the same manner as the hon. member for St. Lawrence-St. George was.

Mr. Speaker: With reference to what the hon. member has said, I thought I should caution the hon. member for St. Lawrence-St. George as a new member of the house with regard to approaching a line of argument or attributing to the minister—

Some hon. Members: Oh, oh.

Mr. Speaker: I trust I have the floor—any ulterior motive behind the decision and action of the minister yesterday in transferring this motion to the proceedings today. I think all will recognize that that would have been quite improper. In addition, I felt I should caution him that to attribute to parliament a motive in its determination of the rule would also be improper, and I must say that the hon. member was very careful and very proper.

Mr. Pearson: Then why caution him?

Mr. Speaker: It may be that sometimes a word of wisdom beforehand is of some advantage. With regard to the words that the hon. member for Laurier has attributed to the Minister of Finance, as attributing a motive to the Leader of the Opposition, I regret that I did not hear the name of the Leader of the Opposition from the Minister of Finance. I took it that this was a general charge that has been made, and if we go back to the debate on the speech from the throne I do not think that the hon. member for Laurier, who participated in that debate, if I recall rightly, can say that both sides did not make such statements, and without protest. Therefore unless there is a specific motive attributed to the Leader of the Opposition I do not think that the remarks call for a retraction.

Mr. Nowlan: Mr. Speaker, I do not recall that I referred particularly to the Leader of the Opposition. *Hansard* will have to speak for itself in that regard. I did say that I understood from the hon. member that he was speaking for the opposition as a party. If I referred to the Leader of the Opposition, naturally I stand on the words I used, but I do not recall doing so. However, the point on which I was basing my statement largely was the statement made by the hon. member himself when he suggested that the party to which he belongs—perhaps I am paraphrasing slightly but I think this was certainly the effect of his words—had accused the Prime

[Mr. Chevrier.]

Minister of perpetrating a fraud on the Canadian public. I think this is one statement he has made. It is because of that charge and because of the fact, if we refused to accept this motion, it might be misunderstood, and there could be some element of doubt raised with respect to the situation again, that, on behalf of the government, I am accepting the motion of the hon. member.

We could have saved 15 minutes at least, but I did not want to interfere with his speech. I assure the house that I will have this table brought down at the earliest possible date, I hope by the first of next week. When this table is brought down, sir, we will find that the statements of the Prime Minister are entirely substantiated, and I hope this will conclude this discussion. I want to make this clear, too. In doing this, as I said, we are doing it because of the unusual circumstances surrounding the motion, the charges which have been made heretofore. It is not to be construed as a precedent for producing statistics from the bank at any time in the future. So far as I am concerned, this is an end of the matter.

Motion agreed to.

PRODUCTIVITY COUNCIL

REQUEST FOR PRODUCTION OF MINUTES OF MEETINGS

Mr. Frank Howard (Skeena) moved:

That an humble address be presented to His Excellency praying that he will cause to be laid before this house a copy of the minutes of all meetings of the national productivity council.

He said: I suggest that the acceptance or rejection of motions of this type hinges upon the question of the desirability of producing a particular document. This puts one, in this instance, at a bit of a disadvantage because when the request was made yesterday to have this motion debated there was no indication from the Minister of Trade and Commerce (Mr. Hees) as to whether or not he intended to accept or reject the motion. The motion calls for the production of the minutes of the various metings of the national productivity council. I cannot, therefore, go into the question of the desirability or otherwise of producing the minutes because I have no knowledge of the attitude of the minister in respect of this motion.

Since the establishment of the national productivity council, Mr. Speaker, there have been many references to the fact that it is ineffective in its attempt to accomplish the goals which were set forth when it was established. These references have been made in this house as well. Just recently one of the appointees to that council, namely Mr. Claude Jodoin, president of the Canadian Labour Congress, resigned. The reason given by Mr. Jodoin, as I gathered, was that the council as presently constituted was an ineffective body and he saw no reason why the congress, whose representative he was, should continue to participate in a body which was relatively ineffective.

We have our own opinions as to the uselessness of the council. Perhaps a much smaller group would be more effective in attaining the goals which were set for this body. However, we are now getting into the field of the council itself. It was my thought that, having the various minutes of the productivity council produced for the public and parliament, it would be possible to make a far better assessment of the relative merits of the council and whether or not it should be maintained in its present form. I am sure the minister would like to have this matter cleared up in order that parliament, in looking ahead to the various problems confronting our economy, will be able to make an assessment on the basis of the thoughts and ideas described in the minutes themselves. I hope that we can proceed very quickly to the endorsation of the motion.

Hon. George H. Hees (Minister of Trade and Commerce): Mr. Speaker, my reason for asking that this motion be transferred to the proceedings which take place in this hour today was in order that I could explain to the house why I believe, and the government believes, that it is not in the best interests of parliament or the people of Canada that the detailed minutes of a government sponsored body such as the productivity council should be made public. I am very pleased to learn, as a result of what the hon. member has said, that his main interest is to learn of the activities of the council since its inception. I am very pleased to have this opportunity today to outline what the council has been doing since it came into being.

First of all, Mr. Speaker, I wish to outline to the house my reasons for believing it is not in the best interests of parliament or the people generally to make public the detailed minutes of any government sponsored body such as this. As the minister through which the national productivity council reports to parliament, I have been asked to provide the house with the minutes of the council. As the house knows, Mr. Speaker, the national productivity council consists of 25 persons, five of whom are chosen from the field of industry and commerce, five from the field of organized labour, five from the field of agriculture and other primary industries, five who represent the general public, four who are officers or employees of Her Majesty, and the executive director who is a permanent officer of the council.

27507-3—44

Productivity Council Minutes Requested

The people who serve on the council are outstanding representatives in the fields from which they are drawn. They serve in a purely voluntary manner and receive no remuneration whatever for the useful and time consuming tasks which they undertake as a public service. To emphasize my point, I should like to name the members of the council, and I am sure that hon. members will agree with me that Canada is very fortunate to have people of this calibre who are devoting their time and efforts to the welfare of the country. One of Canada's prominent industrialists, Mr. George De Young, president of Atlas Steels Limited, has devoted outstanding service to the council as its chairman. Other representatives from the field of industry and commerce are Mr. N. R. Crump, president of Canadian Pacific Railway Company, Mr. George C. Metcalf, president of Loblaw Groceterias Limited; Mr. W. Fraser Bruce, president of Aluminum Company of Canada Limited and Mr. J. Claude Hebert, president of Transparent Paper Products Limited. I am sure hon. members will agree that these are five of Canada's leading industrialists and businessmen.

At present the labour representatives on the council are Mr. Marcel Pepin of the confederation of national trade unions, Mr. Arthur R. Gibbons of the brotherhood of locomotive firemen and enginemen, Mr. Michael H. Nicols—

Mr. Howard: On a point of order, Mr. Speaker. What have the structure of the national productivity council and the background of its various members to do with the desirability or otherwise of producing the documents sought?

Mr. Hees: In speaking to that point of order, Mr. Speaker, the answer is simply that I am outlining to the house who are the members of this council because it is their words in their entirety, every single word that each of these men has said while the council has been in session, that the hon. member wishes to have produced verbatim; and I shall explain to the house that if we are going to ask or demand that every word, every syllable uttered by any man or woman who sits on one of these councils, who is summoned or invited to sit there by the government to help it determine policies that will be beneficial for the country in general is made available, then in the opinion of the government we will not be able to persuade people, particularly those of the calibre I am mentioning from the ranks of labour, management, agriculture and so on, to be willing to sit on these councils and give their time and energies, which are impossible to purchase with money, to the service of their country.

Autographed picture by John Diefenbaker (Nov. 6, 1974) with the inscription "*To Jerry Grafstein, The Life of the party on the Israel trip.*"

With John Diefenbaker during a trip to Israel in 1974

Autographed picture by Prime Minister Pearson circa 1963

Autographed picture by Walter Gordon circa 1963

Autographed picture by Justice Bora Laskin circa 1966

Autographed picture by John Turner with the caption "...*To a young Tiger from one of four other young tigers with warmest regards and in appreciation*" (Oct. 26, 1967). This was the date when Mr. Pearson appointed John Turner, Pierre Trudeau and Jean Chretien to the Cabinet at the same time, all of who would go onto become Prime Ministers.

Autographed picture by Pierre Trudeau
"*To Jerry, Next Year in Jerusalem*" (1968)

Surprise birthday party at Maple Leaf Gardens organized by Dorothy Petrie (later Davey) and JSG with Pierre Trudeau and the Liberal Caucus for Mr. Pearson (1972)

Kick-off of the 1974 federal campaign with Pierre Trudeau, Margaret Trudeau and Dorothy Petrie (later Davey)

Presenting Pierre Trudeau with a t-shirt at the start of the 1974 campaign

The first Red Leaf team meeting (1974) chaired by Keith Davey and JSG

Autographed picture "*Many thanks*" signed by Pierre E.T. (July 1974) with the National Liberal Campaign Committee

The 'Mad Men' of Red Leaf Communications (1980)

With Speaker of the Senate Maurice Riel on appointment to the Senate in 1984

With Keith Davey and Royce Frith who escorted JSG into the Senate with the Speaker of the Senate, Maurice Riel

Conversing with Prime Minister Pierre Trudeau at a reception after appointment to the Senate (1984)

With Keith Davey, former Prime Minister Pierre Trudeau and Royce Frith circa 1988

Anniversary of Pierre Trudeau's 1980 federal election victory circa 1990

With Pierre Trudeau commemorating 1980 election in 1996

Autographed picture by John Turner with inscription "To Jerry Grafstein, in warm appreciation of his advice and counsel during an action-packed year" (Jan. 30, 1967)

With John Turner at the federal leadership convention in Ottawa (1968) with his mother Phyllis Ross and his wife Geills

John Turner at the 1968 leadership convention refusing to join Robert Winters and Paul Hellyer on the floor of the convention with JSG on the far left.

With John Turner and wife Geills during the 1984 Federal Election Campaign

With David Smith and Lloyd Axworthy who served together as assistants to John Turner on JSG's appointment to the Senate (January 1984)

With Jean Chretien circa 1965

With Iona Campagnolo, MP and first female President of the Liberal Party of Canada circa 1982

With Jean Chretien, Keith Davey, Pierre Trudeau, Sheila Firestone and Royce Frith on the tenth anniversary of Pierre Trudeau's 1980 election

With Jean Chretien on Parliament Hill greeting volunteers travelling from Ottawa by bus to New York City for the '*Canada Loves New York*' weekend (Dec. 1-2, 2001)

With Jean Chretien after walking the streets of New York greeting thousands of Canadians and apologizing to the over 25,000 people that could not get into the rally at the Roseland Ballroom from 54th Street to 65th Street, New York City (Dec. 1-2, 2001)

With Jean Chretien in his Parliament Hill office wearing a '*Canada Loves New York*' hat and jacket

With Jean Chretien, his wife Aline & Mayor Rudolph Giuliani at the Roseland Ballroom at the Canada Loves New York weekend (Dec. 1-2, 2001)

With Jean Chretien and Mayor Rudolph Giuliani in New York City when he declared Canada Love New York Day in New York City

Being introduced by Jean Chretien to Prime Minister Blair on his visit to Ottawa

With Jean Chretien and U.S. Speaker Newt Gingrich, Washington (April 1997)

With Jean Chretien and Albert Gore, Vice President of United States (April 1997)

With Carole greeting Jean Chretien at the reception in the President of Brazil's palace in Brasilia after meeting with President Enrique Cordozo of Brazil

With Speaker Newt Gingrich of the House of Representatives in Washington during a periodic visit to Congress

From left to right, JSG, the Stones, Hon. John Manley and Dennis Mills. Dennis Mills and the JSG were key organizers of this event.

With Prime Minister Mulroney shortly after Mulroney became Prime Minister

With Pierre Trudeau and JSG's son Lawrence outside the Senate shortly after the former Prime Minister Pierre Trudeau's address to the Senate opposing Meech Lake, his final parliamentary appearance.

With Prime Minister Paul Martin

With Dennis Mills who together organized the Molson Canadian Rocks for Toronto SARS Concert to broadcast that Toronto was safe and sound after the SARS crisis of 1992 wearing two leather Rolling Stones jackets. Over 500,000 attended, a Canadian record.

With Prime Minister Harper in his Parliamentary office, daughter-in-law Rebecca, grandsons Daniel, Edward and Isaac and son Lawrence circa 2009

With Stéphane Dion, leader of the Liberal Party circa 2008

With Michael Ignatieff, Leader of the Liberal Party (May 2009)

With Justin Trudeau shortly after his election to the House of Commons

With Martha Wisdom and Justin Trudeau at a meeting for Stéphane Dion

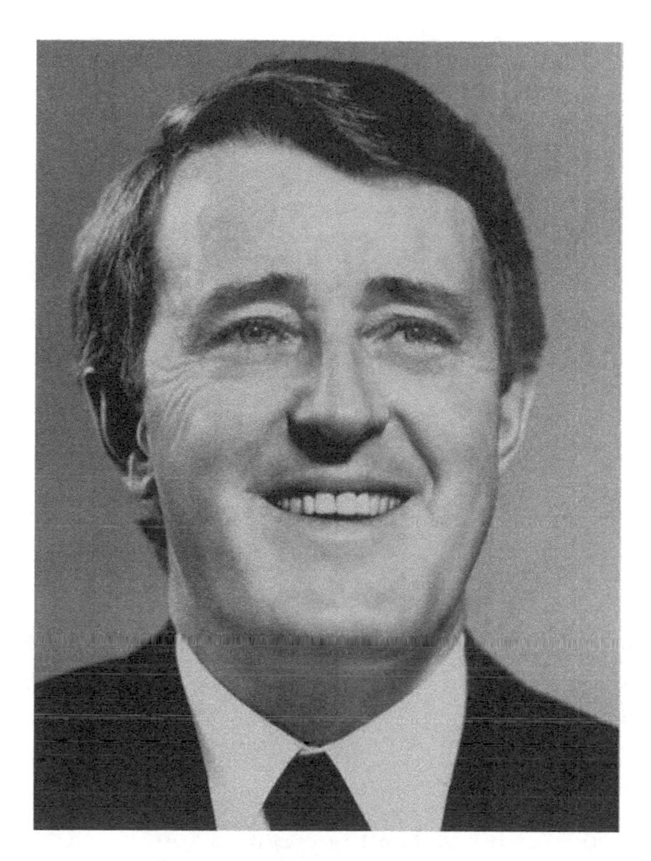

Brian Mulroney

The Brian Mulroney Charm

(18th)

Date Elected to Parliament:	August 29, 1983
Date of Maiden Speech:	September 12, 1983
Date Sworn In:	September 17, 1984
Date Left Office:	June 24, 1993

Who could fail to be charmed by Brian Mulroney in close quarters? A student and practiced practitioner of charm offences, Brian Mulroney combined the Irish charm of a 'pixie' with a hard steel edges of an old time Tammany Hall style pol. Up front and personal in all his exchanges, it was his studied charm in his academic, legal, and business careers before politics, during his public service, and after in his successful post political business career that was the alchemy that brought him success and painted over his gaffs and egregious conduct. The political and business networks he assiduously built were the mainstay of his success in all his varied careers.

Politics in Canada can be summed up in one word – 'confidence'. To gain political power in party politics, a leader must gain and retain the 'confidence' of his small coterie and more so, his political peers. The national caucus of a political leader is the key to sustain 'confidence' of its members. No modern political leader was more adept at maintaining the loyalty and the visceral support of his party caucus. Mulroney, by nature, treated his caucus as he treated each large family with patient attention to detail and respect. Every Wednesday in Ottawa, while Parliament was in session, each national party caucus consisting of Party members from the Commons and the Senate, meet to weekly coalesce around the Leader and his party to gain their inspiration and direction from the Leader who is last to speak in caucus knits together a consensus and sets the weekly political agenda.

Only in Ottawa can one learn how important 'caucus' is to hold 'confidence' and support from a Party's Members of Parliament. The Party membership, of volunteers and paid staff, is peripheral to this vital Parliamentary core. The caucus is the key of 'responsible government'. If the caucus is divided, or weakened, a leader must bend to the prevailing winds or suffer defeat.

I was curious how Mulroney maintained such high levels of avid support within his caucus despite his ups and downs. I regularly queried my Conservative Senate colleagues as well as other members of the Tory caucus to discover how he did it, week after week. These astute Senate colleagues were equally enthralled of Mulroney's techniques while maintaining their skepticism, Finlay MacDonald, a Maritimer, and Norman Atkins, key member of the Conservative Big Blue Machine for Ontario and Michael Meighan, Michel Cogger, Jean Bazin, old time friends from Mulroney's Quebec academic circle. Finlay and Norman were astute pals who each lived through a number of leaders from Diefenbaker to Stanfield to Clark and then Mulroney. Sam Wakim, never elected but a university schoolmate of Mulroney, also in brief encounters would regale me with the magic Mulroney touch out of the public eye. Most acutely analytical was Lowell Murray, a Senate colleague, school chum from their university days at St. Xavier University who astutely compared Mulroney and other Conservative leaders, especially John Diefenbaker.

Mulroney treated each caucus meeting with delicacy, preparation, patience, and careful home work. While he always arranged for a rousing welcome to each caucus meeting, Mulroney was a good and patient listener. His whips kept him up-to-date on any wavering caucus supporter. Telephone calls, illness, notes of thanks, congratulations, assistance with personal matters, especially family matters, were all part of his regular purview. He knew the mood swings of each member and he kept himself closely informed. Mulroney worked diligently at this task. He would reach out in time of need to offer solace or assistance or congratulations to friends and sometimes foes. Kim Campbell, his successor, was captivated by Mulroney in caucus yet, estimated his need to orchestrate applause on his entrance to each caucus meeting.

There is a backstory to his focus on 'caucus'. Loyalty to the leader as personified by the travails of John Diefenbaker, was never far from Mulroney's uncomfortable thoughts. He had been loyal to Diefenbaker until the Dalton Camp revolt and saga against Diefenbaker's leadership. Mulroney observed loyalty close hand, at the outset of his career as a party loyalist to Diefenbaker. He noted, with dismay, the history of divisions within the Conservative caucus, and how Diefenbaker's Cabinet turned on him and how ultimately that brought Diefenbaker down led by Dalton and other outside forces. Diefenbaker's caucus on the whole remained loyal to him. This caucus experience was seared in Mulroney's memory. He observed how Diefenbaker flagged in his efforts to deal with each Cabinet member. Mulroney was a loyalist by nature. Mulroney valued loyalty and gave it in return. He clung to loyalty to Diefenbaker until Diefenbaker's leadership was no longer tenable, still working behind the scenes keeping his views from public scrutiny. But Diefenbaker never forgot any slight or act of disloyalty. Diefenbaker's final speech at the Conservative leadership convention pitting Clark, Wagner, and Mulroney saw Mulroney, still unelected, lead in the race until Diefenbaker spoke and mentioned "*lack of experience*" that was Mulroney's weak spot. Mulroney knew he was sunk when Diefenbaker alluded to 'lack of experience'. Mulroney came back later and learned from his errors.

Mulroney was disciplined and focused, and more so due to his elegant and intelligent wife, Mila, who changed him from a party-loving rogue to the astute focused well-mannered disciplined politician he became.[161] They quickly had a large family of robust talented kids. Not much a book reader, unlike Clark, Mulroney, like Diefenbaker, would devour newspapers, relished political gossip, and endlessly worked the phone lines and kept the threads of loyalty and allegiance tied to him.

Mulroney, as each leader does, attempts to outdo his predecessors. In this case, Mulroney was in awe of Trudeau, his style and strong policies, especially Trudeau's signature legacy – the Repatriation of the Constitution and the Charter of Rights and Freedom. As a Quebecer, he envisioned a path for Quebec different from Trudeau, more in tune with his early Union Nationalist ties

Numerous efforts were made by Mulroney to outdo Trudeau. This, I believe, motivated Mulroney's Meech Lake and Charlottetown constitutional gambits. Their failure did not deter his desire to exceed Trudeau on the Constitution dossier, especially in the experience of Quebec under Rene Lévesque, the P.Q. separationist, and later under Bourassa who reneged

[161] Mulroney had an iron will. Supported by his equally strong-willed wife Mila, he overcame bouts of depression, stopped drinking to excess, and then quit smoking 'cold turkey'.

on Pearson's Victoria Accord. Constitutional reform had eluded Diefenbaker and Pearson, but Trudeau succeeded. Mulroney was a close witness to Trudeau's success. He avidly sought Quebec's support, after Trudeau had out maneuvered separatist Rene Lévesque who refused to approve Trudeau's version of Repatriation, Charter of Rights and Freedoms, and a revamped Constitution. Mulroney yearned to obtain Quebec's full-throated approval for constitutional reform. Mulroney took up the canard of Levesque that Quebec had been betrayed on Trudeau's constitutional reform – "*stabbed in the back*" was his rant. To do this required strong elements of constitutional rearrangements that would enhance provincial powers and weaken the federal central government. So, he tilted to Quebec's self-declared concerns via Meech Lake. Meech Lake would lessen federal powers and give Quebec 'special status'. The country was split in all parties on a grant that extended powers to the provinces, especially Quebec, that would weaken the federal government (already highly decentralized) along ideological lines. Mulroney argued this would resolve the Quebec separatist impulse forever.

After retiring from public office, Pierre Trudeau returned for only one time to Parliament. He had kept his silence during his retirement. Trudeau was not enamored by Mulroney less so his Constitution ideas. He spoke out against Meech Lake in an open Senate Hearing in an amazing three-hour presentation and stopped Meech Lake cold. I had a small hand in organizing that event and like Trudeau, was vitriolically opposed to Meech Lake. It went too far. Canada was already still too decentralized in the division of powers. Mulroney's Charlottetown constitutional gambit also went down to defeat. I felt we didn't even have a common market in Canada. No central market securities regulator rather a hodge-podge of provincial security authorities. Both Meech and Charlottetown would deter market efficiency and growth, especially invite more interprovincial trade barriers I concluded.

Mulroney needed another showstopper after his failure on the Meech Lake and Charlottetown Constitutional gambit. He found it in a Free Trade Agreement with U.S.A. Using his undoubtable charm and friendship to woo Reagan with open adulation and Irish persuasion, Mulroney sang '*Irish eyes were smiling*' to Reagan's delight. The FTA was his legacy and without his charm offence on Reagan, it would not have been possible.

Mulroney learned another lesson from Diefenbaker's political spiraling descent. Mulroney wanted to neutralize as best he could Liberal mandarins in the public service that Diefenbaker felt had undermined his government which had a ring of truth. So, Mulroney set up a parallel network of highly paid political appointees that reached down into each department to report directly to him and the PMO. These political appointees received the same remuneration as Deputy Ministers. And it worked for him, for a time. But their excesses and in some cases, their inexperience in government, contributed to his political demise.

Mulroney picked up Diefenbaker's lead on South Africa. He acted as well as lobbied to create an international consensus on freeing Mandela that led to his release from prison and ultimately the demise of apartheid Africa regime under the Boers. It was a sterling historic accomplishment for Mulroney and a tribute to his persistence and diplomatic skills. Without his skill and charm, it would not have happened as quickly as it did.

Mulroney decided early on as a youth in high school to become Prime Minister. Every step in his career was a step in that direction. He had a picture taken with Diefenbaker as a high school political activist which he cherished. He was ambitious and worked at developing friends especially in high places – at school and in his community. He never let up.

Mulroney was born in Baie-Comeau, Quebec, far away on Quebec's north shore, into a family of Irish origins and lower middle-class working stock. He early learned French on the streets and in lower school. His father, Ben, who he revered, was an electrician in the local paper plant owned by *The Chicago Tribune*'s owner, General Robert McCormick. It was a one company town. He lived with his family in a small company owned house. Mulroney was ambitious, quick-witted with a gift of self-promotion. He learned to network early, gaining an ever-widening circle of peers, elders, and admirers. He planned and plotted every step up the ladder. He attended St. Francis Xavier University at the early age of seventeen and became a campus activist and debater. He scored well enough in academics to apply for a Rhodes Scholarship though both his academics and sports acumen would not make him a serious contender for this revered scholastic prize.

There were other setbacks along the way. He went to Dalhousie Law School in Nova Scotia where he expanded his circle of friends; but flunked. Not deterred, he moved to Laval University in Quebec City to start on his law degree once again, enlarging his circle of friends and increasing his network as a young Conservative activist. He even joined the Union Nationale to deepen his Quebec ties. He became close friends with its leader Daniel Johnson. After graduation, he decided to make his move to Montreal as a lawyer, where he gained a position with Quebec's largest law firm on condition – that he pass the Quebec Bar. On the third try, he finally made it. His law firm admired his political activism and charm which he worked on its stodgy senior partners and who decided to point the budding lawyer and commercial litigator towards Labour Law, just becoming an area of legal specialization as labour issues plagued Quebec became front page news. Suddenly he found his niche. With his charm, network, and negotiating skills, he became an instant star and a skilled mediator. An early observer of television, he worked on his television techniques, modulating his voice and gestures to meet its singular demands.

Over and over again, his easy charm and skills won plaudits for settling contentious labour issues. Though he acted for management, he nurtured his friendship with labour leaders like Louis Laberge which allowed him to make fair and lasting settlements, a tribute to his skill and charm. He forged a tight personal relationship with Paul Desmarais, soon to be a mega mover in Quebec. Desmarais suffered a long devastating strike at *LaPresse* which lost Desmarais bundles of money. Mulroney forged a settlement that Desmarais initially disagreed with, but quickly returned *LaPresse* to profit. Desmarais, a conservative by nature and perhaps in politics, became and remained his largest booster.

When Robert Cliche was named to investigate labour issues in Quebec, Mulroney joined him in his first prolonged public exposure. He had a talent for dissecting complex issues in public.

Mulroney went on to serve as CEO of Iron Ore Company that would further enhance his business skills and broaden his network even wider.

I first encountered Brian Mulroney and Joe Clark at the 1968 Liberal leadership convention where they were both interested observers. Later at each encounter, Mulroney was friendly, witty, and charming. No matter how busy, he would pause to chat and exchange political gossip.

One episode in the Senate made me ashamed of myself in the Mulroney era. And still upsets and rankles when I think about it. The Liberals decided to slam Mulroney's Consumer Tax initiative, the GST. The NDP were more vitriolic than Liberals as they felt that a Consumer Tax unfairly taxed the poor. The NDP praised the Senate to hold up the legislation, the Senate they had heretofore detested and had called for abolishment. After a raucous debate in the Commons, the Consumer Tax bill passed, coming to the Senate for approval. NDP came over and for the first time, called on the 'hated' Senate to stop this measure.

The Speaker, Gill Molgat, a close friend of Jean Chrétien, as Allan MacEachen the leader plotted from the side lines, led the revolt in the Senate with cow bells, whistles and raucous interruptions when the legislation was introduced and debated. I participated. Afterwards, I was ashamed and I swore I would never be led to demean Parliament again. In the end, Mulroney succeeded, and this measure gave financial stability to the federal coffers allowing Parliament to expand the social net, healthcare, and aid to universities, both notable achievements - Mulroney legacies.

All and said, Mulroney will be remembered more for his accomplishments than his defeats or setbacks.

In 1988, Mulroney arranged for the G7, the economic summit of world leaders including Reagan and Thatcher, to be held in Toronto. Mayor Art Eggleton asked me to chair the Toronto Preparatory Committee to organize the world media and some side events to showcase Toronto to the world. I told Art that was not a good idea. I was a known activist Liberal and Senator and this was a Mulroney Conservative event. But I had an idea. I would co-chair a preparatory committee to liaise with Mayor of his office if I could get a well-known Conservative to co-chair to liaise with the Conservative government in Ottawa. "*Who do you have in mind?*" asked Art. I said, "*Trevor Eyton*", a staunch conservative, now a Senator, and an old friend. He agreed immediately. I enlisted Trevor who quickly accepted. We needed to fundraise to underwrite hospitality for the media which Trevor led with ease and dispatch. Our main focus was to commander a large parking lot opposite the Convention Centre on Front Street where some events would be held. We arranged for John Bitove also a staunch Conservative and restaurateur to help organize a twenty-four hours food and beverage tent composed of food stalls from every part of the globe to demonstrate the diversity of Toronto. I was the lone Liberal, other than Art Eggleton, to be invited to several of the large dinners for the world leaders organized by Mulroney and his government. At each event, which Mulroney chaired with wit and sophistication, especially with his conservative colleagues like Reagan and Thatcher, pointed out that these events were Conservative events except for one lone exception, a Liberal Senator, who he introduced with humour and gusto to the applause of his Conservative audience, and asked me to stand to demonstrate the tolerance Conservatives strived to demonstrate to their opponents.

One last anecdote. Years after Mulroney retired, he became a board member of several Fortune 500 companies in the United States. At a small luncheon in New York hosted by my friend, Gerry Tsai – a Wall Street wizard, I dined with a small group of business executives including two CEOs of major U.S.A. companies. When they heard I was a Canadian Senator, they both queried if I knew Brian Mulroney. "*Why?*" I asked. Both told me that he was the best director that they ever had on their board. Mulroney was always well-prepared, pointed in his questions, and undertook every task handed to him with skill, expertise, and conciseness. Mulroney would take the initiative on other corporate tasks. I was not surprised. Charming and effective and smart. That is Brian Mulroney. My old friend Peter Munk repeatedly told me how effective Brian Mulroney was as a board member on Barrick Gold. He took on complex tasks and settled irascible and even implacable problems for Munk who became his greatest fan.

And a final anecdote about Mila. Whenever I encountered her after Mulroney was Prime Minister and when he retired and Mila was with him, she recognized me and never failed to ask me about my wife Carole and what was her latest charitable challenge. Mila never missed a beat. Together they were redoubtable – a charming couple, a devastating duo – obviously respectful of each other's talents.

Mulroney left the Progressive Conservative Party in budget deficit after the leadership was handed to Kim Campbell who failed to meet his or her expectations. Mulroney had stayed in office too long, a flaw too often shared by most other leaders.

Yet, he left an admirable and formidable legacy on trade,[162] economic growth, reduction of outmoded Crown corporations and regulations, relations with United States, Germany, and U.K. and advocacy against apartheid in South Africa. History will treat him better than his departure from government.

Mulroney continues to be engaged in a wide range of activities, charitable business and politics, while maintaining an ever-expanding superb rolodex, especially amongst Republicans in the United States[163] and other international political and business leaders. He was called by Justin Trudeau to privately advise him on the NAFTA negotiations with the Trump administration. It seems as well that Mulroney's political DNA is alive in his daughter recently elected to the Ontario legislative, with no doubt, a bright leadership future ahead in Canadian

[162] In addition to Free Trade Agreements, Mulroney entered into a number of FIPA agreements with Poland, Argentina, Hungary, and others. FIPA stands for Foreign Investment Promotion Agreements.

[163] Brian Mulroney was remarkably popular with American Republican Presidents and Congressional leaders. He was asked to do a eulogy for Ronald Reagan, Nancy Reagan, and George H. Bush which he did with grace and eloquence.

politics. His other children are equally accomplished, poised, and fated to play roles on the public stage in some form or another. The Mulroney name is alive and well and the Mulroney charm has been inherited by all his offspring.

Brian Mulroney - Maiden Speech

26984 COMMONS DEBATES September 12, 1983

The Leader of the Opposition

AFTER RECESS

The House resumed at 2 p.m.

* * *

NEW MEMBERS

Madam Speaker: I have the honour to inform the House that the Clerk of the House has received from the Chief Electoral Officer certificates of the election and return of the following members:

Of Mr. Brian Mulroney, for the electoral district of Central Nova.

Of Mr. Gerry St. Germain, for the electoral district of Mission-Port Moody.

* * *

NEW MEMBERS INTRODUCED

Brian Mulroney, Member for electoral district of Central Nova, introduced by Hon. Erik Nielsen and Hon. George Hees.

Some Hon. Members: Hear, hear!

Gerry St. Germain, Member for the electoral district of Mission-Port Moody, introduced by Mr. Brian Mulroney and Mr. Chuck Cook.

Some Hon. Members: Hear, hear!

[*Translation*]

WELCOME TO NEW PAGES

Madam Speaker: I also wish to welcome our new group of pages who are commencing their duties today in the House.

Some Hon. Members: Hear, hear!

[*English*]

Madam Speaker: The House has already applauded the pages who are beginning service today in the House of Commons for the entire year. We hope with all our hearts that they have a good year among us and that they learn a lot from all of us.

Some Hon. Members: Hear, hear!

* * *

● (1410)

[*Translation*]

THE LEADER OF THE OPPOSITION

Right Hon. P. E. Trudeau (Prime Minister): Madam Speaker—

Some Hon. Members: Hear, hear!

Mr. Trudeau: —as you see, a spirit of benevolence pervades the House today. Perhaps you will allow me to say a few words, in addition to the welcome extended from this side of the House to the new Leader of the Opposition. I would like to address a special word of welcome to the two new Members who have just joined the House. I am told that the Member for Mission-Port Moody (Mr. St. Germain) is perfectly bilingual. Madam Speaker, I can give the Hon. Member the assurance that, in this House, all Members are on an equal footing and that we on this side intend to be as attentive to his words as to those of the other Hon. Member who has just joined our ranks.

I would like to say a very special word of welcome to the Right Hon. Member for Yellowhead (Mr. Clark). I would like to congratulate him on the duties he will be taking up at York University. However, I hope that his responsibilities there will not keep him away from the parliamentary scene, because as emeritus leader his position is a very honourable one and we intend to show him the respect he is due.

[*English*]

You will understand, Madam Speaker, if I say that, standing in this place, I feel a little bit that we are witnessing the onslaught of history. When I first came into this Chamber we on this side were faced by a very formidable Leader of the Opposition, the former Member for Prince Albert, the Right Hon. Mr. Diefenbaker. But he stood alone as leader on the other side.

On the other hand, very soon after I stood in this place, I was faced by the Leader of the Opposition who was then Mr. Stanfield. But he was flanked by his former leader, the Right Hon. Mr. Diefenbaker. It then came the turn of the Right Hon. Member for Yellowhead (Mr. Clark) to lead his Party. He was flanked not by one but by two former leaders, Mr. Diefenbaker and Mr. Stanfield, who stood by his side to assist him.

Now, as we see the Member for Central Nova (Mr. Mulroney) take on his duties as Leader of the Opposition, he is not only flanked by the Right Hon. Member for Yellowhead but also by the Hon. Member for Yukon (Mr. Nielsen) who was interim Leader of the Opposition. I dare say there is a third leader—at least his ghost is still in this place and we feel it often—the former Member for Prince Albert who, I am sure, will be here to assist the Hon. Member for Central Nova.

We are very happy to welcome the Hon. Member for Central Nova. I am sure he will forgive us if we say that we have even greater pleasure at the presence in the gallery of Mrs. Mulroney.

Some Hon. Members: Hear, hear!

Mr. Trudeau: The Hon. Member for Central Nova has come a long way from that log cabin in Pictou County. I see that he has put away his rumpled trousers and old sweaters, to be brought out again at the next election. In the meantime it is nice for us in this Chamber to be able to bask in the glow, in the benign smile, of a man who sent such shivers of pleasure down the spines of the matrons all the way from Oyster Pond to Mushaboo.

Some Hon. Members: Oh, oh!

Mr. Trudeau: I can assure him that we on this side of the House will endeavour to be every bit as helpful to him as we have to his many predecessors.

[*Translation*]

As the great André Siegfried said, if you want to harm someone, too much praise is more effective than criticism. In fact, Madam Speaker, I think there is a Machiavellian plot afoot among members of the Press Gallery who seem to be out to destroy in this way the new Leader of the Opposition—he can count on us to render the plot ineffective. We are certainly not going to praise him excessively, because he is faced with a difficult and a historic task as leader of a party that has played a major role in the history of this country, and he ought to realize that the task that lies ahead will be a difficult one. I want him to know that we wish him the very best.

[*English*]

I also want to congratulate the members of the shadow Cabinet. I think it is fair to say that never has a more vaporous group of shadows ennobled this place.

This has been an occasion to talk about the man rather than the policies, so he will understand that I have gone on a little longer than otherwise would have been possible.

Some Hon. Members: Oh, oh!

Mr. Trudeau: I can assure the Leader of the Opposition that we all wish him good luck, good health and, as they say in show business, "break a leg".

[*Translation*]

In French, the traditional expression is the "mot de Cambronne".

[*English*]

Hon. Edward Broadbent (Oshawa): Madam Speaker, in this world of constant flux I am glad to see that there are certain constants. The Prime Minister (Mr. Trudeau) has maintained his usual gracious and congenial disposition in welcoming the Hon. Member for Central Nova (Mr. Mulroney).

Some Hon. Members: Oh, oh!

Mr. Broadbent: Before I add my few words of welcome to the new Leader of the Conservative Party, I too would like to join with the Prime Minister in expressing the good wishes of my colleagues to the Right Hon. Member for Yellowhead (Mr. Clark), who is now teaching back at my old alma mater, York University—and right away I have written a warning note to all the students there not to pay too close attention. Quite seriously, though, I want to say that we do hope the Right Hon. Member for Yellowhead will continue to bring his concerns about the well being of our country to this important Chamber so that we will benefit from his views.

Some Hon. Members: Hear, hear!

Mr. Broadbent: I think the new Member for Mission-Port Moody (Mr. St. Germain) will understand that in welcoming him I have several reasons for not elaborating on the point. Again most seriously, however, I do welcome him to the House on behalf of my colleagues and I am sure he will understand my comment when I say that I hope his stay will not be too long.

I now want to turn to the Hon. Member for Central Nova (Mr. Mulroney) to say that when he has been in Chamber for some time—we do not know for how long—he will know that he should not expect again the kind of greeting that he received from all sides today. I suspect this is a one and only shot, especially for a leader of a political party. But we do welcome him and wish him well in his personal concerns and in his activities in this Chamber.

• (1420)

I have noted, and for some time knew, that the Member for Central Nova was not only a working colleague but rather close to one of our former leaders in the Province of Quebec, Robert Cliche, an old friend of mine, a distinguished Québecois and a distinguished Canadian.

I look forward to the days ahead in this Chamber, hopefully even today, when the Member for Central Nova will be just a wee bit more specific on some of his policy orientations. No doubt because of the little publicity he has had in recent weeks we have not had a detailed provision of his policy positions, but when he does reveal them I hope we will begin to note the impact on his life of Robert Cliche. I shall watch with interest.

[*Translation*]

And once more, I would like to say, very sincerely, as they say in Baie Comeau, bienvenue, bonne chance, but perhaps not too much of the latter!

Mr. Brian Mulroney (Leader of the Opposition): Madam Speaker, first of all I wish to thank the Right Hon. Prime Minister (Mr. Trudeau) for his gracious and cordial remarks. There may have been some minor political differences between us in the past, as there certainly will be in the future, but nevertheless, I have always recognized that the Right Hon. Prime Minister is a man of great distinction, and I wish to offer him my sincere thanks for his warm welcome here today.

[*English*]

The Prime Minister has always been a man of great accomplishment and distinction. I was honoured by the thoughtfulness and the generosity of his words today. I wait with bated breath for tomorrow.

Some Hon. Members: Oh, oh!

The Leader of the Opposition

Mr. Mulroney: But I want particularly to welcome the Prime Minister back from Greece, and the Cabinet back from Central Nova.

Some Hon. Members: Oh, oh!

Mr. Mulroney: I want you to know, Prime Minister, that during the summer, while you were otherwise occupied, it was a very pleasant summer for me. There was one untoward incident, only one. The Liberal candidate in Central Nova persistently referred to a candidate from Quebec who did not live in his riding but lived in a million dollar house rent free, and I defended you, Sir, regularly.

Some Hon. Members: Oh, oh!

Some Hon. Members: Hear, hear!

Mr. Mulroney: I rose to your defence with an alacrity that surprised even me.

I was also delighted and interested to read in the weekend press, Madam Speaker, the fact that the Prime Minister announced he is not a quitter. I want you to know, Sir, that we are behind you all the way.

Some Hon. Members: Oh, oh!

Some Hon. Members: Hear, hear!

Mr. Mulroney: And I say "Hang in there", notwithstanding the urgings to the contrary from some people over there. This Party, and I am sure the New Democratic Party, stands united on at least that.

Some Hon. Members: Oh, oh!

Mr. Mulroney: I am delighted as well in having an opportunity of representing Central Nova to be so close to my old friend, the Hon. Secretary of State for External Affairs (Mr. MacEachen).

Some Hon. Members: Oh, oh!

Mr. Mulroney: It is not a widely known fact—

[Translation]

—but I would like to mention it because it is quite an interesting phenomenon and one of the subjects I am really delighted to raise in the House today

[English]

—that the Secretary of State for External Affairs, the Prime Minister and I, all hold degrees from St. F.X. University, and I should point out that the President of St. F.X. is here today. On behalf of the Prime Minister and myself we want to say we did not study economics at St. F.X. under the Hon. Secretary of State for External Affairs.

Some Hon. Members: Oh, oh!

Mr. Mulroney: I only mention that because the Prime Minister asked me to.

Some Hon. Members: Oh, oh!

[Translation]

Madam Speaker, imagine my surprise and, in fact, my delight, at seeing before me, in the House today, the smiling face of the Minister of Finance (Mr. Lalonde). Before I left Ottawa for my riding in Nova Scotia, I thought that considering the tremendous and increasing popularity of the Minister in Quebec, he would have been drafted for the leadership of the Quebec Liberal Party. I am truly delighted to see that he turned down a Quebec draft, to stay in our midst. That is really good news.

[English]

I want to say a word of thanks as well to the Hon. Member for Oshawa (Mr. Broadbent). Indeed, on many occasions the Hon. Judge Robert Cliche, a truly great Canadian, spoke well and eloquently with regard to the qualities of the Hon. Member, and with good reason. Judgment, as Robert Cliche used to say, was always so important. I want you to know that we Nova Scotians appreciate your judgment, Sir, in taking your caucus down to Nova Scotia.

Some Hon. Members: Oh, oh!

Some Hon. Members: Hear, hear!

Mr. Mulroney: It did my heart good to see the socialists spending $90 and $95 a day, and then, Prime Minister, they have the temerity to say things are not going well!

Some Hon. Members: Oh, oh!

[Translation]

Mr. Mulroney: Dear friends and colleagues, Madam Speaker, I know this is a very unusual day, at least for me, but I sincerely wish to thank everyone for the warm and cordial welcome I was given here today.

[English]

My thanks to all of you for your kindness and generosity. I will try, given the magnificent example set by my predecessor, the Right Hon. Member for Yellowhead (Mr. Clark), to serve this House and to serve you with honour and distinction.

Some Hon. Members: Hear, hear!

* * *

HOUSE OF COMMONS

PRESENCE IN GALLERY OF DOCTOR BAL RAM JAKHAR, SPEAKER OF THE HOUSE OF THE PEOPLE OF INDIA

Madam Speaker: I would like to draw to the attention of the House the presence in our gallery today of Dr. Bal Ram Jakhar, who is the Speaker of the House of the People of India.

Some Hon. Members: Hear, hear!

Kim Campbell

Kim Campbell – The First Woman Who Crashed Through the Glass Ceiling

(19th)

Date Elected to Parliament:	November 21, 1988
Date of Maiden Speech:	December 12, 1988
Date Sworn In:	June 25, 1993
Date Left Office:	November 3, 1993

Brian Mulroney lingered too long in office. He overstayed his welcome and his undoubted accomplishments. His leadership was seriously questioned. Canada was anxious to get rid of him and his Progressive Conservative Party and Mulroney's personal poll numbers began to sink. His probity was openly scrutinized. Some of his closest confidants were under attack for malfeasances. Governments are not elected. They are defeated. They slip into arrogance, suffer loss of energy and purpose, and lack a sense of renewal or became careless in government. Too often, leaders cling to power. They lose public support and continue, in denial. Like a garden, politics must be continuously renewed, re-seeded, replanted with fresh foliage, and then cared for. Conventional wisdom was that Mulroney, the master politician, needed a 'Hail Mary' to change the downward narrative of his Conservative Party. Hence Kim Campbell.[164]

[164] Kim Campbell was born in Port Alberni, British Columbia, in 1947. Her given name was Avril Phaedra Douglas. She adopted the name Kim as

This was only partially true. Mulroney wanted a vigorous leadership race to regenerate the Conservative brand. Perhaps he had a preference for the talented Jean Charest. Mulroney's political breakthrough in Quebec could be preserved with a vibrant young experienced Francophone like Charest, Mulroney believed. Of course, Mulroney had cleared a path upwards for Kim Campbell with her rapid appointments to Cabinet. But the 'Hail Mary' plan backfired as Campbell's inexperience was exposed in the vigorous leadership race Mulroney encouraged. Yet, she won the leadership despite the obstacles in her path and her own gaffs. Keith Davey once opined that in a leadership race, a leadership candidate moves to reduce his flaws while in an election, the leader pivots to emphasize his strengths. The Conservative leadership race did both for Kim Campbell – exposed her inexperience and flaws and drew attention to her undoubted strengths. At the outset, she led in the polls against both her Conservative leadership competition and her main political adversaries, the Liberals and their new leader, Jean Chrétien.

Mulroney, for his part clinging to power, did not provide ample time and running room for his successor to put together a fresh team and develop a newish program that could differentiate his successor from his flawed brand. To rebrand a stale government on the run would require creating unique talent and fortitude.

Still, Kim Campbell didn't have a chance in the deep political undertow left by Brian Mulroney. Too quick-witted and inexperienced as a leader, her own flubs contributed to her swift fall. If there was one area that was a patent flaw for any wannabee leader was that she had not aggregated a loyal and skilled

---

she re-invented herself for her political career. She was married and twice divorced.

experienced entourage to aid her in her ascent up the political ladder. Most of her close advisors had never been in a national election campaign. She got swept away as did the Mulroney Conservatives when she called a quick election, sinking in the polls that she initially led. Meanwhile, Chrétien overcame his question like his age, showing youthful vigor and donning a soft sweater-clad image to warm him up to the Canadian public projecting new dimensions that added to the amiable side to the 'little guy' from Shawinigan and Chrétien borrowing a page from Pierre Trudeau's playbook, deployed sports stunts to demonstrate his agility and skills.

Kim Campbell trod an unusual path to political power. The political milieu in British Columbia is different as it oscillates to extremes from left to right ever so swiftly. Starting out as Avril Campbell, she was a bright attractive freckled face, ambitious, quick-witted young university student associated with a cluster of Liberals, especially Keith Mitchell, a pal and astute Liberal stalwart who knew BC politics inside out who introduced me to her when we first met in Vancouver in the mid-'60s. She was a wannabee politician, with a dazzling smile, strawberry-blonde hair, freckled face, and insouciant personality. Clearly ambitious, she was assertive, confident in her views, and determined to climb to the top of her peer group quickly which she did.

Astutely, she observed the political landscape and decided that her ascent to power in far off Ottawa could not be easily obtained climbing up through layered political Liberal ranks at that time. So, she moved to the right, to the Social Credit,[165] then in power in British Columbia.

---

[165] The history of the 'Social Credit' in Canada needs to be updated. Its influence on fiscal and monetary policy continues to reverberate, unnoticed.

At the University of British Columbia, she became the first woman to head the student body. On to law school where she left her mark as much in student politics as in the study of law where she made it to the prestigious Law Review. To broaden and expand her intellectual range, she gained entry to the prestigious London School of Economics, a breeding place for aspiring politicians, where Pierre Trudeau had studied under Harold Laski, the leading leftist professor of his day. She fell under the sway of Michael Oakeshott, a leading Conservative thinker. On graduation, she quickly pivoted to the Social Credit Party, running for the BC legislature where she was defeated. But she caught the attention of the Socred leadership and became the Chief of Staff to the Social Credit Premiers Bennett, then Vander Zalm, quickly gaining a reputation as a capable political operative.

When the Social Credit faltered and the Conservatives were gunning towards power in Ottawa under Mulroney, she easily switched horses to the Conservatives. She rose swiftly in Conservative ranks and in the Mulroney government, especially under the tutelage of Brian Mulroney, who helped clear her career path.[166] An activist Minister of Justice, she quickly became a favourite in the media for her brash outspoken personality and ideas. Women's issues were on the rise and she surfed that new tidal wave. She made a difference on women's issues. Her amendments to the Criminal Code made rape and assault offenses more gender sensitive by switching the onus from the complainant to the accused. She sought and obtained amendments to the Canadian Human Rights Act that broadened protection for women. She coined the phrase 'inclusive justice'

[166] Campbell had a strange somewhat distant relationship with Mulroney as recounted in her memoirs. While she admired his undoubted political skills, she questioned his need to preen before his caucus.

to broaden the justice system which critics complained was flooded with mainstream males. Her talents as a lawyer were demonstrated in her personal interest in the review of the public call for a pardon to Peter Milgaard, a convicted murderer, where she skillfully exhibited her legal talents and did not allow for a pardon. Later, when the British Columbia government painstakingly reviewed his case and refused to proceed with a new trial, she was vindicated. Milgaard, nevertheless, was released by popular pressure and his guilt remained an open question. She took her duties as Minister of Justice on issues such as these with care and diligence, a quick study with a gift for languages. She gained a fluency in French, necessary for any federal leader. Continuing to improve her French-speaking ability, she did well and was comfortable on French television.

The 1990's was the greatest decade for the advancement of women in Canadian politics and Kim Campbell rode the crest of that wave.

Campbell gained admiration and power amongst the Mulroney coterie by her wits, charm, and adept handling of the Justice portfolio. She went on to become the first female Minister of Veterans Affairs, then the short-lived first female Minister of Defense that included NATO, serving in each portfolio with verve and skill. Then, in a sudden shift, once she won the leadership, Mulroney, ever the pragmatist, realized a woman could represent the Progressive Conservative Party, to gain feminine support, and ride out the undertow of his detractors and distractions. Mulroney sought to intervene in the election while she tried vainly to separate herself without antagonizing him or part of her team who were mostly Mulroney loyalists. It was a delicate juggling act. The Mulroney brand was just too strong. Her interaction with Mulroney became public and affected her desire to differentiate herself and her policies from

Mulroney. Yet, Mulroney knew a radical change was necessary to stop the downward spiral of his Party. Campbell was unprepared for the frontal onslaught on her leadership. Leaning too heavily on Mulroney's tired palace guard and her own inexperienced cadre of loyalists who had never run a federal campaign, she was left with only two Conservative M.P.'s. She lost her own seat. She retired from public life, no worse the wear, undaunted.

Still, her political legacy was noteworthy. First female Minister of Veteran Affairs. First female Minister of Justice and Minister of Defence. First female Defense Minister at NATO. In her short tenure as Prime Minister, she reduced and modernized the unwieldy size of the Cabinet and sought to renovate Cabinet methods to make them quicker and more sensitive to public concerns. She never had the opportunity to lead in Parliament. A record of such promise was lost as she became the first Prime Minister in Canadian history to never to face Parliament.

When she was defeated, Campbell was without a job and without funds. Her Party had deserted her after her stunning loss. Jean Chrétien called to commiserate and when he heard of her financial plight, he quickly gave her an office and staff to clear up her affairs and then appointed her as Canadian Consul in Los Angeles where she did a remarkable job.

History will treat her kindlier than her precipitous brief tenure – five months – as the 19th Prime Minister of Canada and Canada's first female Prime Minister. She made it into the history books. She left fresh footprints in history on the sands of her time, waiting for the next female leader to emulate her auspicious start.

On reflection, her career path to the Prime Ministership zigzagged unlike her male counterparts who decided to become a leader early on and followed the traditional male pathways to power. As a woman, she faced a more complex series of obstacles.

Her early family life was difficult as were her early marriages, one to an older man with two siblings her age, and the second to an ambitious lawyer who left her as he was unwilling to serve as her spouse when she decided to seek the pinnacle of public power. She lacked the comfort of a strong partner to help her ride the undulating waves of public pressure.

She grasped for political power when the party structure and media was male dominated. Flora MacDonald, Cabinet Minister along with Joe Clark, supported her as did Ellen Fairclough, the only female Minister in the Diefenbaker Cabinet, but it was not enough. The woman's vote was not with her.

I served for over a decade as a Member of the Federal Liberal Women's Caucus crowded with ambitious women unlike any regular caucus I ever attended. The Liberal Women's Caucus, I observed, refused to join and unite forces to support one woman for leader as they were hotly competitive with each other. So, there were two hurdles for a female leader to overcome, the male dominated milieu and the female activists who were competing and could not find common ground to support one of their own gender.

Perhaps Campbell's curiosity, her quick wits, and her undoubted intellectual interests may have made it more difficult for her to separate the trees for the forest. Like Paul Martin, she was not able to focus on a few priorities. Her slogan of 'inclusive justice' was not clear or made relevant. The slogan itself was opaque. A thorough history of Kim Campbell's life and time is needed to better assess the challenges a female leader needs to define, overcome, and conquer. The times are ready for a female Prime Minister of strength, character, depth, and energy.[167]

[167] Canada has now elected female Premiers in British Columbia, Alberta, Ontario, and Prince Edward Island and mayors galore including Bonnie

Golda Meir proved it, so did Margaret Thatcher, one from the left, the other from the right.

- *Time and Chance: The Political Memoirs of Canada's first Woman Prime Minister Hardcover* by Kim Campbell (Doubleday Canada April 1996).

She has contributed chapters in other books:

- *Democracy and Development* by Bernard Berendsen (ed.) - Chapter: *Alternatives for a Liberal Democracy* by Rt. Hon Kim Campbell (KIT Publishers, 2008).
- *The Difference "Difference" Makes: Women and Leadership* by Deborah L. Rhode, ed. Chapter 11: *Different Rulers - Different Rules* by Kim Campbell, pp 121-126 (Stanford, CA, Stanford University Press, 2002).
- *Partnering: The New Face of Leadership* by Larraine Segil, Marshall Goldsmith, & James Belasco, eds. Chapter 21: *The Leader as Partner: the Reality of Political Power* by Rt. Hon. Kim Campbell, pp 217-222. (New York, AMACOM, 2002).

Crombie, Mayor of Mississauga, a rising star in the political firmament. Soon, perhaps not soon enough, we will have a female Prime Minister.

Kim Campbell - Maiden Speech

That Mr. Marcel Danis, Member for the electoral district of Verchères, be appointed as Chairman of the Committees of the Whole House.

Motion agreed to.

[*English*]

APPOINTMENT OF DEPUTY CHAIRMAN OF COMMITTEES OF THE WHOLE

Right Hon. Brian Mulroney (Prime Minister): Mr. Speaker, I move:

That Hon. Steven Paproski, Member for the Electoral District of Edmonton North, be appointed Deputy Chairman of Committees of the Whole House.

Motion agreed to.

[*Translation*]

APPOINTMENT OF ASSISTANT DEPUTY CHAIRMAN OF COMMITTEES OF THE WHOLE.

Right Hon. Brian Mulroney (Prime Minister): Mr. Speaker, I move:

That Hon. Andrée Champagne, Member for the electoral district of Saint-Hyacinthe—Bagot, be appointed Assistant Deputy Chairperson of Committees of the Whole House.

Motion agreed to.

* * *

[*English*]

SUPPLY

Hon. Doug Lewis (Minister of State and Minister of State (Treasury Board) and Acting President of the Treasury Board): Mr. Speaker, I move in accordance with Standing Order 81:

That this House at its next sitting consider the business of supply.

Motion agreed to.

* * *

SPEECH FROM THE THRONE

ADDRESS IN REPLY, MOVED BY MS. KIM CAMPBELL AND SECONDED BY MR. GILLES LOISELLE

The House proceeded to the consideration of the Speech delivered by Her Excellency the Governor General at the opening of the session.

Ms. Kim Campbell (Vancouver Centre): Mr. Speaker, I am honoured to have been given the opportunity to rise in this House today to move, seconded by the Hon. Member for Langelier (Mr. Loiselle), the Address in Reply to the Speech from the Throne. On behalf of the constituents of Vancouver Centre, I would like to thank the Right Hon. Prime Minister (Mr. Mulroney) and the Government for honouring Vancouver Centre in this way.

Before I begin, however, I want to take this opportunity to congratulate you, Mr. Speaker, on your re-election as Speaker of this House. I know the Members of this House will not think me parochial when I say on behalf of all Vancouverites and all British Columbians how proud we are of you, Mr. Speaker, and your contribution to this House over many years.

Some Hon. Members: Hear, hear!

Ms. Campbell (Vancouver Centre): In all the areas in which you have excelled, none has been a better showcase for the full range of your qualities as a person than has your tenure as Speaker of the House of Commons. Your warmth and caring have been reflected in your approach to the administrative as well as the ceremonial aspects of your position. A keen intellect has enabled you to master an enormous volume of law and precedent and apply it with fairness and insight. You are forward-looking in managing the business of Parliament but you have a deep reverence and respect for the history and custom without which this instrument of democracy cannot survive.

For all these reasons, Mr. Speaker, you have been freely chosen by your colleagues in this House to assume the vital role of Speaker. Your accomplishments are your own, but all British Columbians take pride in the recognition of such excellence in one of their own.

My constituency of Vancouver Centre is aptly named, including as it does the downtown core of the City of Vancouver. Much of what symbolizes Vancouver for visitors can be found in Vancouver Centre: miles of sandy beaches, Stanley Park, the Granville Island Market, and much of the site of Expo '86.

The west end, one of the most densely populated areas in North America, is an example of urban downtown living at its best, combining the privacy of big city life with the intimacy of small communities. Across the water by any of three bridges are the varied neighbourhoods of West Point Grey, Kitsilano, South Granville, False Creek, Fairview, and Mount Pleasant.

[*Translation*]

Because of changes to its electoral boundaries, the Vancouver Centre riding has lost its picturesque Chinese quarter, while preserving major parts of its Greek and French communities. As a whole, Vancouver Centre reflects rather closely the diversity of all the Metropolitan Vancouver regions, a rich diversity which expresses itself in many ways.

[*English*]

Vancouver Centre is the major business area of the city. Thousands of small businesses as well as many professional and corporate offices make Vancouver Centre an important area of employment. In addition, two great hospitals, St. Paul's and Vancouver General, are focal points for a large health care sector. Many arts and cultural organizations are headquartered in Vancouver Centre where theatres and galleries abound.

Vancouver prides itself on being Canada's gateway to the Pacific. In 1979, the Progressive Conservative Government established the Asia-Pacific initiative which has continued to play a leading role in fostering Vancouver's and Canada's pacific role. My predecessor as Member for Vancouver Centre, the Hon. Pat Carney, made dramatic advances in Canada's trade with Asia during her tenure as Minister for International Trade. Our Government has continued this thrust and has supported Vancouver's efforts to play a key role here through many initiatives including the establishment of Vancouver as an international banking centre.

Vancouver Centre is the commercial heart not only of the city but of the province. In no other area is the economic interdependence of all areas of British Columbia so clearly illustrated. Much of the wealth that builds the skyscrapers of downtown Vancouver and employs an enormous service sector there is earned in the hinterlands and small communities of our province. The people who live and work in Vancouver Centre know full well the precarious position of all in an undiversified, resource based economy. Vancouver Centre is the economic pulse of the Province of British Columbia.

From October, 1986, to October 1988, I served as as a Member of the British Columbia Legislature, during which time I travelled to all parts of the province.

• (1750)

I have come to have a deep appreciation of the energy and creativity in my province. I have come to see how often the economic aspirations of British Columbians have been thwarted by the lack of access to a large regional market. Like other British Columbians I have watched with dismay as many of our most creative and productive people have moved to Toronto or to the United States in order to find a market large enough to sustain their enterprise.

I have seen how a policy of tariff escalation in the United States has prevented the growth of value added industries in our resource based economies. As a former chairman of the Vancouver School Board I have seen how directly a recession that reduces public revenues affects the ability of a society to support its commitment to our young people without mortgaging their future.

The decision to run in this past election was enormously difficult for me requiring as it did that I resign my legislative seat. But I could not in the end stand by and watch the destruction of an agreement which would do so much to address the economic and social concerns that are so important to me.

Some Hon. Members: Hear, hear!

Ms. Campbell (Vancouver Centre): How can Vancouver retain its creativity and vitality without secure access to a large market? How can Canadian industries compete internationally from a protectionist base which discourages the qualities of efficiency so necessary to international competitiveness? Mr. Speaker, how can Canada continue to be a caring society and invest in its future human capital without a vibrant and diversified economy capable of paying the bill?

In the course of the recent debate about the free trade agreement, reference was made to the history of Canada and the supposed threat posed by the free trade agreement to the sanctity of that history. The vision of Canadian history reflected in this argument is a rather partial and myopic one. There is much in the 120-year history of our country which has engendered a deep-seated sense of grievance in the regions of Canada. No one who has studied the political history of Canada can be unaware of the profound impact that western resentment of the tariff policy has had on that history. The word "progressive" in Progressive Conservative was added when John Bracken—leader of the Progressive Party, an advocate of low tariffs—became the Conservative Leader.

British Columbia's grievances with respect to tariff policy result from two factors. First, the high tariffs on American imports to protect Canadian industries impose serious costs on British Columbia. That cost is estimated at $5.7 billion over the past 20 years alone.

Second, negotiations by Canadian Governments with the United States to reduce American tariffs have focused upon raw resources but left the tariff escalation on value added production in place. In British Columbia with a tiny domestic market, these barriers seriously limit the opportunity for diversification of the resource economy through value added production.

For example, our unprocessed zinc can pass into the United States with a 1 per cent tariff, but a zinc alloy incurs a tariff of 19 per cent. This phenomenon is not confined to British Columbia. On both coasts tariffs have made the development of a processed fish industry uneconomic.

It has been said in the free trade debate that since 1935 tariffs between Canada and the United States have been reduced by such an amount that 80 per cent of our trade is tariff free. Why then, it is asked, such a fuss over the remaining 20 per cent? Why indeed? Because the statistic itself is meaningless. The actual tariff free figure is 72 per cent and it refers to the existing volume of trade. It cannot reflect trade that might have occurred but for tariff barriers. Furthermore, if trade in automobiles and auto parts is removed from the equation, the figures for the remaining trade are very different. Of the remaining trade, only 58 per cent is tariff free. Forty-two per cent, almost half, incurs tariffs. Thus the auto pact area of southern Ontario enjoys the benefits of what the Leader of the New Democratic Party has referred to as the "continental market force" but the regions of Canada struggle with tariff barriers which distort their economic development.

The free trade agreement addresses the single most significant historical grievance of British Columbia in Confederation. The free trade agreement democratizes the Canadian economy by giving to the regions what central Canadian industries have long enjoyed, access to a significant regional market.

Some Hon. Members: Hear, hear!

Ms. Campbell (Vancouver Centre): Not only has the free trade agreement addressed the regional grievance but it has been sought by the business community in all parts of the country. Canadian businesses, large and small, have recognized that the American market can be their springboard to competitiveness on an international standard. Both the manufacturing and the service sectors have realized that the path to greater prosperity lies in removing the training wheels of protectionism.

Make no mistake, protectionism has distorted our economy to the detriment of all Canadians. In protected industries the incentives to modernize plants and engage in research and development are greatly reduced. Grantsmanship and lobbying replace entrepreneurship and good management as industries come to rely on subsidies and tariffs to compensate for an inadequate domestic market. Protectionism exaggerates the comparative advantage of the highly populated core and discriminates against the less populated regions.

Over the past five years there has been an alarming flow of corporate headquarters from Vancouver, Winnipeg, Halifax and from other regional centres to Toronto. With a population of three million—less than the population of greater Toronto—how can British Columbia hope to reverse this trend toward the centralization of the Canadian economy unless it can offer businesses a market equivalent to that of central Canada?

But it is not just our economy which is harmed by protectionism. Protectionism poses serious risks to the health of the Canadian body politic. Not only is it a major contributor to regional economic disparity, but in the ensuing competition for government spending to alleviate the effects, the sparsely populated regions cannot carry the clout of the highly populated core. From this comes the perception in the regions that they are not getting their fair share. Resentment of economic disparities feeds a sense of political impotence which spills over into other areas. Issues such as language and Senate reform come to bear an emotional colouring unrelated to their merit, a colouring derived from the deeper more fundamental problem.

[*Translation*]

Our trade with the United States has increased by 80 per cent over the past twenty years, and we have been exposed over the same period to an ever increasing volume of feature films, televised programs, music and books from that country. In spite of that, our feeling of Canadian identity has not been reduced. Quite the contrary. It is even stronger today.

As a matter of fact, over the past ten years, the production of books by Canadian authors has increased by 500 per cent. A great many of our most appreciated social programs have been implemented during the last twenty years.

Our self-knowledge and self-confidence increase as our foreign trade grows.

[*English*]

No one can define himself in a vacuum, Mr. Speaker.

In Canada we have learned to balance the onslaught of American culture with our own reality. It is that ability to balance which is one of the chief characteristics of Canadians, which is why, perhaps, a Canadian has been defined as someone who can make love in a canoe.

The greatest threat to the survival of Canada as a nation is not trade with the United States. The greatest threat to our national survival is the perception in the regions of Canada that the cost of Confederation is too high. The free trade agreement does more for regional development in Canada than any policy in our history. The time has come to tear down the tariff walls which have kept our regional economies in tutelage. It is time for the forest products of British Columbia and Québec, the minerals of northern Ontario, Alberta's gas and petroleum, and maritime fish to enter the United States in value added form.

Some Hon. Members: Hear, hear!

Ms. Campbell (Vancouver Centre): It is time for Newfoundlanders and Nova Scotians to have the dignity of secure year-round employment. The distinctive cultures of the Maritimes are not at risk, and there is nothing quaint about poverty.

I came to Parliament to speak strongly for Vancouver Centre and British Columbia. But I do not advocate the prosperity of British Columbia at the expense of Ontario or Québec or any other part of Canada. As the Prime Minister has so often said, Governments do not create wealth, people do. And if Governments provide the climate, there will be new prosperity in British Columbia and Canada. I want a Canada where all regions have a chance to grow and blossom, where no regional grievances threaten to unravel the national fabric.

• (1800)

Since 1984 the Progressive Conservative Government has been a Government of national reconciliation, but national reconciliation must include economic justice for all regions. We cannot be a caring society if our purse is empty. We cannot be magnanimous to the aspirations of all Canadians if we feel aggrieved. We cannot embark upon the federal-provincial co-operation which is essential to deal with issues of the environment, education, and the economy if we are divided by a simmering sense of injustice.

Mr. Speaker, I am proud to support the free trade agreement, and I am proud to move the Address in Reply to the Speech from the Throne.

Some Hon. Members: Hear, hear!

Ms. Campbell (Vancouver Centre): I move, seconded by the Hon. Member for Langelier, that the following Address be presented to Her Excellency the Governor General of Canada:

> To Her Excellency the Right Hon. Jeanne Sauvé, a member of the Queen's Privy Council for Canada, Chancellor and Principal Companion of the Order of Canada, Chancellor and Commander of the Order of Military Merit, upon whom has been conferred the Canadian Forces' Decoration, Governor General and Commander-in-Chief of Canada.
>
> May it please Your Excellency:
>
> We, Her Majesty's most loyal and dutiful subjects, the House of Commons of Canada, in Parliament assembled, beg leave to offer our humble thanks to Your Excellency for the gracious speech which Your Excellency has addressed to both Houses of Parliament.

[*Translation*]

Mr. Gilles Loiselle (Langelier): Mr. Speaker, I would first like to congratulate you on your election. You have earned the confidence and the respect of all those who have sat under your chairmanship and I know all the new Members join me in assuring you of our complete co-operation.

Mr. Speaker, I am well aware that, by asking me to support the Address in reply to the Speech from the Throne, the Prime Minister (Mr. Mulroney) wanted to honour the population of the riding of Langelier.

It is also symbolic that the Member from Langelier should be asked to support the Address in reply to a speech which invites all Canadians to give their country a new impetus on the road to social and economic progress.

Indeed, under various names, the riding I represent has witnessed all the great events which have marked the building of this country and has often been associated with them. It is therefore perhaps natural that Langelier should be called upon to intervene when we are about to turn a page in our history.

It is worth noting, Mr. Speaker, that Langelier is in the historic city of Québec and therefore the cradle of Canada and of much of America. It has witnessed 450 years of our history. Not only was the country founded there, but the great discoverers who opened up a whole continent used it as their base.

As a privileged keeper of our collective memory, the population of Quebec city and of Langelier, where the first Parliament of the province of Canada was established, is profoundly conscious of the place it occupies in this country, which has, with the passing decades, emancipated itself and become a modern, independent and forward-looking country.

We saw quite clearly, in the way the people of Québec participated in the national debate on the major economic issue of the recent campaign, to what extent the whole of Québec shares in the confidence we have in our capacity to meet the new challenges involved in the globalization of trade. Massively, Quebeckers joined millions of Canadians who felt free trade is the assertion of the national will to open out rather than shutting ourselves in, of self-confidence rather than fear of new horizons.

Many fellow citizens, subjected for months to the whole gamut of arguments and counter arguments dealing with free trade had an opportunity to ask themselves whether that deal should go through. But in the final analysis, at the conclusion of a campaign centered on free trade, Canadians trusted a party that embodied and still embodies free trade. Under our system of parliamentary democracy, the mandate received by this Government on that matter could not be more decisive.

The question was debated in the widest possible forum, that of a general election, and the issue was settled by the electorate. It is now incumbent upon us to ratify an agreement that we invite all Canadians to support in order that, from the day it comes into force, it may be as productive as possible, to the benefit of all groups in our society, in every area of the country.

On the eve of the 21st century, with the advent of the large trading blocks which are being formed today, this country, largely dependent on external trade for its growth and welfare, is in vital need of economic space. Such space is available with the free trade agreement, providing us as it does with the widest possible access to the American market, the most sought-after market in the world.

In that respect, free trade is the only solution within immediate reach that meets our aspirations for sustained growth. In a sense, it is also the key to doing business with the rest of the world, to the extent that safe access to the various American markets will provide our businesses with economies of scale that often cannot be derived from Canadian sales, thereby putting them in a better position to successfully meet international competition on all other markets.

Those who over these last 20 years have been closely watching the extraordinary bloom of entrepreneurship, innovation and leadership among Canadian businesses both in the industrial and manufacturing sector and in the area of services know full well we can now contemplate without any fears, doubts or reservations a free trade agreement with the United States.

What is in store is not only increased exports but also increased investments and, more generally, increased economic activity. This Agreement will benefit workers and consumers as a whole by creating jobs and increasing purchasing power.

The Agreement we are about to sign does not threaten in any way, directly or indirectly, our sovereignty. On the contrary, it specifically preserves political institutions as well as constitutional rules and regulations of each country in addition to guaranteeing full respect of the Canadian cultural identity, our way of life and our long-standing tradition of social justice.

Mr. Speaker, I will go so far as saying that the lack of an agreement would be more threatening to our sovereignty than a contract between two partners seeking together the best way to co-operate while respecting each other.

[*English*]

I would not want to conclude my remarks without a word on a most important issue for Québec as well as for Canada. I am referring, of course, to the necessary reinsertion of Québec within the Canadian constitutional family.

Some Hon. Members: Hear, hear!

Mr. Loiselle: Under the leadership of our Prime Minister the agreement that has been reached at Meech Lake represents a unique achievement in the process of national reconciliation, and probably the opportunity of this century for our country to put to rest decades of confrontation and quarrels that have mobilized the country's time and energy.

The Meech Lake Accord sets the foundation for a new and stimulating era in which Canadians, freed from counter-productive and divisive constitutional dead ends, can start building the future. The opportunity is here now. It cannot, it must not be missed.

My very deep conviction is that the conditions and circumstances which resulted in the Meech Lake consensus and the following multipartite support of Parliament and of eight Legislative Assemblies are of a rare nature. That is why I remain confident that when all is said and done the superior interests of the country and its people will carry the day.

Jean Chrétien

The Artful Juggler - The Most Remarkable Jean Chrétien

(20th)

Date Elected to Parliament:	April 8, 1963
Date of Maiden Speech:	May 23, 1963
Date Sworn In:	November 4, 1993
Date Left Office:	December 11, 2003

No recent Prime Minister in Canadian politics (save perhaps Stephen Harper) can match the unlikely, contradictory yet, remarkable career trajectory of Jean Chrétien.

Jean Chrétien was recognizable from the first moment I spied him at a Liberal meeting in Montreal at McGill in 1962, racing about. He stood out in a crowd. Tall, thin angular, energetic, restless, with an oversized forehead, topped by a fraying disheveled forelock, charming, crooked smile, unruly hair dressed in a dark narrow lapelled suit with a dark narrow tie favoured at the time. He already had a reputation as an ambitious comer gleaned from my friends in University Liberal circles. Chrétien spoke from the side of his mouth, distorted from an early physical defect, in a fractured jargon with the unmistakable Quebequois nasal twang and equally fractured English where he was obviously struggling for fluency.

From the get-go, he was friendly, endearing, quick-witted, energetic, and patently, obviously, ambitious. Always in a hurry, rushing about, never missing a beat, always amiable, quick, and witty. Every encounter was mostly about his own recent encounters. Still, you couldn't help liking him. There are leaders who are naturally amiable and those who are not. The amiable leaders possess a Teflon patina. Nothing bad seems to stick to them. Most are self-absorbed and narcissist, yet, some are more approachable and more likeable than others. Friends and foes easily forgive them for even their most egregious conduct which is overlooked in their sheen of amiability and studied mock humility.

The self-styled 'Little Guy from Shawinigan' was neither humble nor imbued with hubris. Yet, by keeping his ego in check, he appealed to a broad spectrum of the public on all sides of the deep political divisions in the country. He was shrewd, driven and believed early he was destined for great things. He overcame early challenges including a childhood disability. As a youth, he was competitive to the core in sports like hockey, skiing and swimming.[168] Able to handle himself in rough house situations,[169] he loved to compete and push himself to the limit. His childhood sweetheart, Aline, also from humble stock from small town Shawinigan Falls,[170] was tough, self-possessed, attractive, perfectly coiffed, and

---

[168] Later, when he became a Minister and then Prime Minister, he took up golf and while not a top golfer, he was hotly competitive and didn't like to lose. Chrétien liked to fish and made some spectacular catches.

[169] As Prime Minister while on a political jaunt, he was closely accosted by a young man and Chrétien instinctively grabbed him with two hands by the throat and threw him aside. Thereafter, that was known as the '*Shawinigan Handshake*'.

[170] Actually, Chrétien was born on a tiny French speaking suburb of Shawinigan called 'Begoville'.

shared his driving ambition to rise from their modest small-town roots. Both came from large working-class families with accomplished siblings.[171] They never forgot where they came from or how far up the ladder of power and fame from whence, they had climbed together. They maintained a modest residence in Shawinigan Falls and travelled there often keeping in touch with their large talented families and their working-class neighbours and voters.[172] Both had the common touch. Alene, his wife, always poised, elegantly dressed, and taciturn, was his closest advisor and critic. Any pictures taken of him to be circulated needed her scrutiny and approval. She was like Harry Truman's wife. She was 'the boss'. His often rough manners, his crudeness, and his dress came under her constant scrutiny and censorship. She never missed a detail.

When we first met in the early '60s, he was unpolished, unlike the studied urbanity of Maurice Lamontage, a favoured aide to Mr. Pearson or the powerful and articulate Maurice Sauve or the deep savvy labour roots of Jean Marchand or the quiet intellectualism of Jean Pelletier or the charisma and depth of intellectualism of Pierre Trudeau or the erudite internationally academically attained brilliance of Marc Lalonde, who after working for a conservative Minister of Justice Davy Fulton became a Cabinet Aide to Mr. Pearson or the luminous intelligent precociousness of Jean David, youthful editor of *LaPress*, or the coolness of blonde headed, handsome, suave, articulative Michel Robert later to become a brilliant judge or the polished sophistication of John Turner. Yet, Chrétien was an 'original' and authentic, never straying from his crafted persona.

---

[171] Chrétien was the 17th of 18 children and the Chrétien clan were ambitious and achievers.

[172] He even invested in a small golf club that later caused him problems.

Jean Chrétien, from small town Quebec, graduating with the help of his siblings, from college and law school with a boisterous reputation, rose through Young Liberal ranks, was easily elected an M.P. in the riding of Saint Maurice in his home region at the youthful age of twenty-nine and, slowly and steadily, like the tortoise, beat all of his early flashier Quebecois competitors, except Pierre Trudeau, to reach the highest pinnacle on the greasy pole, the Prime Ministership of Canada.

He never forgot his roots and regularly kept contact with a small circle of followers across the county to keep his finger on the public pulse. He was an excellent networker in every region of Canada.

Chrétien first burst to public attention as a young M.P. when his private member's bill changed the name of TransCanada Airlines to Air Canada – the same in English and French.

Few would imagine that he was an avid reader of history,[173] novels and yes, poetry. Or he had a fine eye for Canadian and Aboriginal art and he was an avid listener of classical music. These interests, he hid behind a mask of working man camaraderie. His hero, like others in his milieu, was Sir Wilfred Laurier. He sought the approval of his hard-working father 'Wellie' who was ever frugal with praise for Chrétien's undoubted accomplishments.

Few, including myself, could have predicted his remarkable political success. From the outset, he sought to overcome his deficits. He was disfigured from an early childhood illness. He was a rural small-town member and never part of the so-called sophisticated urbane French clique or polished elites that inhabited the inner circles of the Liberal Montreal intellectual or academic elites or Anglo-French Jewish Montreal business

---

[173] His historic muse was Sir Wilfred Laurier and he relished sitting behind Laurier's desk in the Prime Minister's office.

establishment that filled the Federal Liberal party coffers. If he had a personal connection, it was with old friends from his home region or secondary school, university or law school and it was with the Italian immigrants like Pietro Rizzuto, a wealthy self-made businessman who he later appointed to the Senate or the small town Quebec Liberal influence peddlers he befriended. An early supporter was another Italian of immigrant origin, Antonio Gagliano, who spoke fluent Italian and French and comfortable English, who went on to be a Cabinet Minister, but who later became embroiled in misdemeanors that shrank his career and tarnished Chrétien's reputation. Perhaps Chrétien owned a hidden inferiority complex that he camouflaged with his boisterous personality.

Aware of his policy deficits early on, he became an acolyte of a leading economic mandarin, Mitchell Sharp.[174] Anxious to add economic 'gravitas' to his sketchy legal experience, Sharp became a lifelong mentor and Chrétien his loyal respectful student. He acquired two bright loyalists of his own from Montreal, John Rae, and Eddie Goldenberg, both with impeccable Liberal pedigrees – John, whose father was the distinguished diplomat Saul Rae, and Eddie, whose father was the notable economist, astute mediator and clever political advisor, Carl Goldenberg. Eddie became his most assiduous and durable assistant who Chrétien labelled his 'computer'.

Chrétien enjoyed the first mark of a leader who could attract, and keep over decades, a smart ambitious loyalist group of confidents and advisors who would selflessly, whether called upon or not, give of their time and energy and in the process became longtime friends. Included was Richard Kroft of

[174] Pearson had astutely made Chrétien Sharp's ministerial assistant to hone Chrétien's economic credentials. Pearson had an early sense of Chrétien's ambitions and skills.

Winnipeg and his winsome attractive activist wife. Richard, who came from an accomplished and comfortable family, became Chrétien's first ministerial assistant, then left public life to run his family business, returned when Chrétien appointed him to the Senate for his longtime loyalty, Michel Vennat, a Rhodes scholar and a bright gregarious Montreal lawyer and business man who after a stint as Mitchell Sharpe's assistant in Ottawa and a stint as a federal bureaucrat kept in constant touch, Mike McCabe, an Ottawa operator who after time on the Hill as Mitchell Sharp's notorious assistant and operative became a skilled and knowledgeable broadcasting lobbyist and went on to an excellent stint in the foreign service. Bruce Hartley, an astute gracious understated assistant came later and assured Chrétien's schedule ran like a fine-tuned clock yet, open to sudden changes and sensitive to crucial access.

Ross Fitzpatrick from BC, who worked his way through school, an early astute laid back understated West Coast assistant who left politics to become a super successful businessman, was later appointed by Chrétien to the Senate. Kroft, Vennat and Fitzpatrick, all became lifelong friends, and my good acquaintances. Patrick Lavalle, an ebullient Liberal from New Brunswick became the head of Chrétien's two leadership drives. Former political assistants shared a common narrative and enjoy each other's war stories.

Many Prime Ministers get off to a rocky start as the leader's electoral crew morphs into the Prime Minister's staff and attempts to become acclimatized to the constant avalanche of problems, expected or surprised that assail any government leader. One key to this dilemma are the judgment and skill of the Prime Minister's Chief of Staff – formerly called 'Principal Secretary'. Chrétien's office settled down when Jean Pelletier, who was a boarding school and law school buddy, became Chief of Staff in 1993. Jean, a lawyer and former Mayor of Quebec City, political organizer, and defeated Liberal candidate was initially a member of Union Nationale. Pelletier brought 'gravitas' to the position, an ability to listen and decide quickly knowing he had the full confidence of Chrétien.[175]

The tribal aspect of Liberal politics was ever evident in the Chrétien entourage. And he was the centre of the overlap in the Mitchell Sharp loyalist circle who worked arduously for Sharp election to Parliament in the Toronto riding of Eglinton and then when Sharp, his mentor became a Cabinet Minister, Chrétien served as his assistant, first in Finance under Sharp, then went on to nine ministries of his own including Indian Affairs, Treasury Board and Minister of Finance (the first French Canadian to achieve this post), and finally Minister of Justice with a hand in constitutional affairs under Trudeau.[176] These two groups, the Sharp circle in Toronto and Chrétien's own network of assistants and Quebec friends - overlapped and bonded to support Chrétien's long drive to become Prime Minister in the late '80s after Sharp's short and abortive attempt in 1968 to succeed Mr. Pearson.

At the heart of this Sharp-Chrétien Toronto team was large shaggy good natured Toronto lawyer David Anderson from P.E.I. who came to cultivate the legal vineyards of Toronto and his wife at the time Doris, the acerbic editor and leading feminist who together gave both Sharp and Chrétien a bridgehead into

---

[175] Later when Pelletier left Chrétien, Chrétien appointed him head of Via Rail. He became embroiled in a petty scandal and was fired by Paul Martin. It took Pelletier ten years in court to vindicate his name and reputation, gaining substantial damages for wrongful dismissal, loss of reputation, and costs. He died shortly thereafter from a heart attack.

[176] No Prime Minister enjoyed this astonishing array of Cabinet posts, nine in all, with a remarkable trouble-free record of accomplishments. In each portfolio, Chrétien gained a deserved reputation as a superb administrator.

the newer Liberal and Toronto cultural and business elites, building on Sharp's earlier and older connections to the Toronto business community especially Brascan enterprise that had built commercial ties to Brazil that temporarily became a resting place for former Liberal cabinet notables like Sharp and Robert Winters. Added to this group was Bob Nixon, robust likeable farmer, son of a former Liberal Ontario Premier, who became Leader of the Liberals in Ontario. This was a minority slightly right leaning Liberal tribe divided from a larger group of so-called Toronto 'progressive' liberals led by an unlikely figure, Walter Gordon with the quiet musty-looking establishment mien, striped shirts, high pinned collars, and light greying military precise mustache who was not only an unlikely progressive, in both social policy and economic programs, but an 'economic nationalist' and a 'protectionist' in the old conservative mode who, in a perverse way, developed a singular bias against US ownership and U.S.A. banks that coloured his economic outlook.

Walter Gordon, a generous quiet spoken man of the old school, masked his deep 'progressive', 'small liberal' instincts and became an outspoken Canadian nationalist and protectionist. Thus, Gordon's opposition to 'free trade' rooted in Manchester Liberalism was contradictory to classic Liberalism to say the least. Gordon and his acolytes like Keith Davey were the architects of the renewal of the Liberal Party after the St. Laurent debacle and the Pearson missteps that led to the Diefenbaker romp in the late '50s. From a distinguished family of leading Canadian accountants, Gordon, or Mr. Gordon as we called him, became by his personality, generosity, loyalty, and self-effacing personality,[177] the natural leader of the 'progressive wing' of the

[177] Walter Gordon attracted fierce loyalty within the Liberal Party. One example. When Maurice Lamontagne got mired in a furniture scandal when a modest unpaid bill was discovered in a bankruptcy, Gordon

renewed Liberal Party just as Robert Winters and Mitchell Sharp, and to a lesser extent Paul Hellyer, were the natural leaders of the conservative wing of the renewed Liberal party under the oscillating leadership of Mr. Pearson who bent from side-to-side to the pressures of these two powerful factions who were fused in their undoubted loyalty to Mr. Pearson.

Jean Chrétien demonstrated the same split political personality that he called 'balance' – moving from one side of the ideological divide to the other pretending to be forced to govern on the 'right' where he was, as Jim Coutts once admitted, more comfortable. So, his instinctive policies were 'conservative' while his politics veered 'progressive' in a line sculptured by his mentor Mitchell Sharp. Chrétien was, at heart, a master pragmatist and a superb administrator.

Chrétien had a rocky start as Minister of Indian Affairs with a flawed 'Beige' Paper policy mandated by the policy that obsessed Trudeau and preoccupied the first Trudeau Cabinet. Chrétien quickly regained his own footing and left with a fine record, establishing ten new national parks including one park near his home riding in Quebec after a skillful negotiation with the Quebec separatist government. He was proud of his skill to avoid controversies in this accident-prone ministry. Chrétien also got off to a wobbly start as Minister of Finance. He was undercut by Pierre Trudeau and Jim Coutts, Trudeau's chief assistant. Without advising him, Trudeau announced a two billion cut in public expenditures. It was Coutts idea to insert the two billion number for greater dramatic public effort. Chrétien considered resigning, but he knew from history that quitters rarely win. His skill as Minister of Justice in the first Referendum Campaign with

---

attended his office immediately and wrote Lamontagne a cheque to cover the cost of this embarrassment.

the grudging support of Claude Ryan, the Quebec Liberal leader, showed how he could keep his temper and pride under control despite slights by Ryan and the demeaning Quebec media and some political colleagues. These slights infuriated him, but he grudgingly kept his cool.

Chrétien was anxious to emulate Pierre Trudeau, like all his successors, on the world stage. As Prime Minister, he invested serious capital into the G7, especially as it applied to Africa, the quicksand of tribalism, fragmented unity and ever-present corruption. He led in establishing a considered unified approach to Africa at the G7 Summit held in Kananaskis. This act of leadership laid the groundwork for coherent plan of increased aid from the developed world to that troubled continent.

In March 2011, I encountered Chrétien after we had both left public life in an unlikely setting. He served as Chair and Key Note Speaker at conference on water sponsored and organized by the Walter Gordon Foundation in Toronto, now headed by one of Walter Gordon's leading acolytes, the irrepressible Tom Axworthy with his ever-present smile and now ever-expanding girth. When I entered the cozy conference room on the University of Toronto campus crammed with national and international water experts, I was amazed to see Chrétien in fine form chairing a most distinguished panel of experts from the UN, France, Jordan, Canada, and an expat Canadian woman who styled herself an international legal water expert now teaching in Dundee University in Scotland. A bubbling, almost effervescent personality, she suggested that since Canada is the repository of the largest [in fact, the second largest] fresh water resources in the world and because of its leading water policies should host a world summit on water. I immediately glanced at Chrétien whose eyes were turned to the screen emblazoned with power points and seemed unaware of the irony of this proposal that met with quiet approbation except by Adele Hurley, the leading water expert at the Munk Centre in Toronto that was cohosting the event, who rolled her eyes at the suggestion and Janice Stein who had headed the Munk Centre for Global Affairs and who in part because of Canada's laggard leadership on water notwithstanding our apparent abundance of water was dismayed because much of our fresh water was polluted, had established under Adele's capable leadership an underfunded, but vibrant, program on water policy, still a work in progress.

So, the artful juggler was at it again. In Canada, two-thirds of Canada's Aboriginal communities had been earmarked by the Auditor General as continuing high risk polluted sources of drinking water. Every province had numerous boil water advisories each year that were kept local and never aggregated or collected to demonstrate how badly Canada had managed, or rather, neglected and mismanaged our drinking water where many outposts in the newly oil-rich province of Newfoundland still required to boil their water daily. Chrétien had been Minister of Indian Affairs and little had been done to fix the dire water situation on reserves during his watch.

Dear reader, before you doze off, I return to the artful juggler and my decade long crusade as a Senator to change that fundamental neglect of clean drinking water by two rather nifty private members bills that I introduced into the Senate following the disastrous small town water pollution scandal in Walkerton in South Western Ontario. I had followed that crises and hearings that followed and discovered, to my amazement, that every province and the federal government was almost criminally negligent in enforcing a strict health regulation for drinking water, lagging well behind Europe and the U.S.A. in creating a regulatory regime to protect citizen health from its most basic need of six to eight glasses of water a day. Of course, the lack of drinking water in most Aboriginal communities was the most egregious and neglected. The Federal Food and Drug Act regulated popsicles, water on planes, trains and federal parks, and soda pop, but not clean drinking water on Aboriginal reserves or elsewhere.

So after much research, especially the Walkerton judicial enquiry report into the polluted water crisis in that small community, I crafted, with the help of Mark Audcent, the most professional and skilled senate parliamentary counsel, a private member's bill to amend the federal Food and Drug Act to include a provision to cover supervision of community drinking water systems over a given size. This surgical amendment was, I thought nifty, because it overcame the biggest barrier to federal programs – Quebec. Since the Food and Drug regime was never challenged by Quebec based on the clear-cut federal crime power, I thought I had drafted a simple change to the existing regime and an end run around Quebec perennial objections to any nationwide program. As well, it replicated the American legislation passed in the early '70s that mandated the Federal Government act as an oversight of ineffective state water regulatory regimes. Clearly there was 'a clear and present danger' to Canadian health where the Departments of Health, federal and provincial, had never tabulated the costs to health from bad drinking water. But there would be a blowback, both federally and provincially, because of the estimated costs of training and infrastructure, and which estimated costs that failed to take into account the cost to the health system and provincially because of enmity to new federal oversight, the costs of which would fall to the provinces and the false provincial pride that though they failed, they were primarily responsible. Give us more dough and we will do the job, they said, and when they got it, nothing changed.

On the federal side, the power was responsible for drinking water on trains, planes, and federal parks and clearly responsible for clean drinking water in Aboriginal communities that were in crises. Chrétien, as long term Minister responsible for Indian Affairs and then as Prime Minister, with knowledge of the dire health problem in the Aboriginal communities and elsewhere in the north, had chosen, as he did, if not dodge it, not to ameliorate this egregious condition.

It came as a mild surprise that I received serious objections unstated, of course, by the Liberal leadership in the caucus and less surprise of course from Quebec and some Alberta senators from the Conservative side in the Senate who used subtle techniques of adjournments and delays in speaking in debate rather than confront the stunning facts I had assembled from the public reports, judicial enquiries, various experts articles and even auditor general reports. To my experience, I learned that persistence and repetition paid off. My private member's bills after studies and reports by Senate Committees finally were approved despite Chrétien's government's objections and several deaths, passed the Senate no less than three times, only to die on the order paper in the Commons when elections were called, and Parliament was prorogued. Alas.

My sister private bill was legislation to map the watersheds and aquifers in Canada slated to be completed in 2035 by the government but accelerated under my bill and then with restrictions on utilization without specific case-by-case approval, fared even worse in the Senate due to Conservative opposition, especially from the west farming interesting, and avoidance by repeated adjournments on all sides from the leadership and others and successive governments both Liberal and Conservative.

It was painful to experience in the slogging daily process of Parliament as an energy drainer, but more so because of ingrained opposition to needed and obvious reform. Was not clean drinking water a 'right'? I argued. Clean drinking water, it seems, had never caught public attention despite the clamour for climatic changes.

So, it was delicious irony to ask two brief questions at the Toronto seminar of the Canadian expert when Chrétien caught my hand in the air during the Q&A and called upon me at this elite seminar.

Two brief questions I rose to ask. Why are two-thirds of the Aboriginal communities in Canada still with highly polluted drinking water and secondly, why has the federal government not regulated drinking water when it regulates soda pop and popsicles? The Canadian expat expert demurred saying she was teaching abroad and wasn't up to speed on domestic Canadian law. Chrétien feigned disinterest, but there was a slight flicker of recognition of the issue in his eye as the panel was adjourned for lunch.

Immediately after, I approached Chrétien where I was warmly greeted and asked his views about the federal election about to be called because the Liberals under Ignatieff had signaled their refusal to support the Harper budget that morning and astute as ever, he pointed out the tactical and strategic shortcomings of 'Iggy' which would play out exactly as Chrétien had predicted.

But to go back in time, to the most exciting period and my initiation into Ottawa politics was 1965-1966 when I spent a year as Turner's assistant and when Pearson appointed all three on the same day into the cabinet – Trudeau as Minister of Justice after serving as Pearson's Parliamentary Secretary, Turner as Minister of State as Registrar General responsible for the Great Seal, etc. soon to be transformed into the first Department of Consumer and Corporate Affairs in North America, and Chrétien as Minister of State for Financial Affairs attached to his mentor Mitchell Sharp.

Chrétien was not considered in the first string of Francophone players but was seen as a hard-working dependable second-stringer worker, great at grass roots and capable as a Junior Minister and Minister who rarely got in trouble. He had a talent as a capable and efficient administrator, so he held nine complex ministerial portfolios some with memorable reforms, yet with many solid improvements and no political errors or patent mistakes, or singular gaffs.

He listened, learned, and improved his skills and confidence[178] in each chosen post and gained grudging success and plaudits from the ever-skeptical mandarins who he worked with and heeded their advice. Initially, he was, by nature, a Quebec conservative in his instincts married to the liberal rhetoric and reform of the day and so evolved with the times. He exceeded where his other more sophisticated Quebecers failed. There was a bevy of brilliant Quebecers that Mr. Pearson attracted to the Liberal party and to government. Of course, the most notable were Jean Marchand, Gerard Pelletier, Pierre Trudeau, Maurice Sauve, Maurice Lamontage, and public servants like Pierre Juneau and former political assistants like Marc Lalonde. In this crowd of star personalities, Chrétien was not seen as an equal player. In the end, other than Pierre Trudeau, Chrétien eclipsed them all. He was a quick study and a prodigious worker, taking on every complex task and sorting things out. His political instincts were unmatched. Jim Coutts once gave a speech separating the Prime Ministers into two categories - visionaries and administrators. Clearly, Chrétien was the top of the heap when it came to government administration. He reorganized the PMO and Cabinet making them both more efficient and quick footed. A gifted political tactician, perhaps the most gifted of

[178] Chrétien, by regular tutoring even whilst Prime Minister, became fluent in English, still with a distinct Quebecois accent that he chose not to change and even reveled in as he poked fun at himself about it. That endeared him to his followers. Chrétien always displayed a sense of humour.

modern Prime Ministers, he was a master of 'wedge politics'. He could quickly read any crowd, and especially, his opponents. He had a deep appreciation of what motivates politicians, especially those he opposed.

I got to know Chrétien and his entourage better during my first stint in the '60s in Ottawa as Executive Assistant to John Turner who represented St. Lawrence-St. George in the heart of Montreal in the mid '60s. Chrétien was seen as a rural outlier to the sophisticated lawyers and businessmen who were part of the Turner Montreal crew. Their opinion of Chrétien was condescending and I kept my opinions about Chrétien to myself who I admired for his tactical skills and never-ending energy which prepared him to undertake any party task, large or small, as he kept his bursting ambition alive. He had astutely sized up each of his competitors and one-by-one, he passed them, exceeding everyone's low expectation of his hidden grit, tactical skills, and especially his ever-present common touch with people from all walks of life.

Chrétien was loyal to Mitchell Sharp views in the 1966 Liberal Convention. The divisive issue was Medicare. The Liberal Party was divided. The economy was unsteady, and Mitchell Sharp was the Minister of Finance and Finance was hesitant. Pearson wanted party support for the immediate introduction of Medicare. Winters, Sharp, and others lined up against it. Chrétien, loyal to Sharp, supported Sharp's view, that Medicare would ultimately trigger runaway federal costs and so should be postponed before implementation until better economic conditions. On the other side was Allan MacEachen and John Munro led by Walter Gordon. David Smith, Lloyd Axworthy, and I were the three designated as floor managers for the pro Medicare vote at the Convention. We lost. Medicare was delayed with a motion added the words 'with regret'. Mr. Pearson was upset and so were we. Mr. Pearson felt the immediate introduction would help the Party's standings. In the end, due to Mr. Pearson's insistence and persistence, Medicare was introduced and funded early in 1968 as a footnote to the Pearson era and helped with Trudeau's swinging victory later in 1968.

I admired Chrétien even more when I learned that he had adopted an Aboriginal as his son when he was Minister of Indigenous and Northern Affairs where he and many of us learned about how vast and beautiful and untouched our capacious northern frontier was. Chrétien's troubled son caused him, and his wife, no end of concerns which he kept private within the confines of his family.

I saw Chrétien through the lens of a small town Jewish liberal activist of equally modest circumstances who was also on the make, but never aspired to the heights of Chrétien. Chrétien had a fiery temper, seen by his close friends and he could veer off course for any slight and, like Diefenbaker, the Kennedys, Nixon or Clintons, he harboured a disloyalty list as he had a long memory for any act of disloyalty, or worse, any hint of condescension. Later on, he began to imitate the icon he revered the most, himself and then he sounded 'tinnie' and false. But during his rise, he kept his ambitions to himself, making fast friends and allies along the way that finally came together after his loss to Turner in the leadership convention when Trudeau resigned and Turner took his short disastrous turn as Leader and Prime Minister.[179] Chrétien and I encountered each other regularly during this period. We sat on a special Joint committee of the Senate and the House on Foreign Affairs. I took committee

[179] One of Turner's key mistakes was not to choose Chrétien as Quebec leader, a job Chrétien craved. I had fervently urged Turner to appoint him, but Turner and his Montreal circle were not fond of Chrétien. This was a crucial mistake by Turner.

work seriously, attended assiduously, prepared carefully, read the materials, listened to the witnesses, and prepared succinct questions. Chrétien would burst in late, sit beside me, and ask me for a good question or two which I did for him to get on the record. After he finished his questions and listened to the answers, he left as the committee hearings continued. After doing this twice to me, I whispered to him to prepare his own questions. He laughed and raced off not before he asked another question – that I had given him. I could not help laughing to myself about his verve and 'chutzpah'. Who could fail to like Chrétien? He was a man always in a hurry.

During the 1968 leadership race to succeed Mr. Pearson, Chrétien was the first aboard the Sharp short-lived abortive run for leadership after Mr. Pearson suddenly resigned. When, as I predicted, Sharp quickly and pragmatically folded his cards and jumped aboard the Trudeau bandwagon before the formal launch of the campaign, as Sharp along with Chrétien joined the Trudeau team. One of the tasks Chrétien was assigned at the convention was to act as the conduit to the Turner campaign and I chose to be the Turner designate to the Trudeau leadership team, recognizing that the campaign might devolve into a tight race where instant action would be necessary.

Turner had agreed to stay in the race until he won, or came last on a ballot, and was dropped according to the convention rules. One exception which Turner had agreed to. If the 'right' as represented by Winters, who was late in the race, threatened to take the Liberal leadership, Turner and team would combine with Trudeau to ensure that would not happen – if Trudeau was ahead. Trudeau had agreed with me that he would do the same if Turner was ahead. This I had agreed to privately with Trudeau even before he entered the race. The convention was closer than Trudeau and his cohorts anticipated. After each ballot, Chrétien approached me and said, "*The boss wants to know. When are you coming aboard?*" One myth about that leadership was that Trudeau had the youth delegates. Due to the efforts of David Smith, Lloyd Axworthy, and myself, we had nailed down the overwhelming majority of the youth vote at that convention. Turner had rigorously attended Young Liberal and University Liberals meetings, gained their loyal support and allegiance even before Trudeau decided to enter the race. And they stayed committed and stayed loyal to the end. I urged Chrétien to remind Trudeau of our mutual private commitment. Still, Trudeau grew increasingly agitated as the balloting continued. Finally, on the fourth ballot, Turner ended his campaign still with 195 votes, mostly youth. Trudeau went on to win. Trudeau was upset with me, and when he became leader on Saturday afternoon, I left Ottawa that night, Trudeau was displeased with me and our friendship frayed until the 1972 campaign.

Meanwhile, Turner became Minister of Justice under Trudeau, an office he had long coveted. Chrétien continued on an amazing variety of cabinet postings, nine in all where his administrative skills and political instincts kept him out of trouble. In the end, he was the most prepared politician ever to become Prime Minister. Travelling often to every corner of Canada, he wanted to examine the work of each aspect of the Department minority he led at firsthand. He prided himself on his honed skills and his desk was clean and empty allowing him to concentrate at the problem at hand. He worked hard on his dossiers and his small skilled staff kept him well and concisely briefed on every issue. He didn't enjoy long briefing papers. He preferred short executive excerpts. Cabinet meetings were well scheduled and tightly led unlike with Pierre Trudeau who relished long discursive Cabinet debates. Chrétien left no paper trails conducting business orally and quickly. I experienced this first-hand on numerous occasions. Two anecdotes to illustrate. Before I was appointed Senator, I was a member of the PetroCan Board of Directors. I had checked and discovered I could continue to serve on that while a Senator, provided I did so without remuneration. Chrétien was the Minister of Energy at the time. My first act as Senator the day I was appointed was to prepare an undated letter of resignation and arrange a meeting with Chrétien in his House of Commons office. After question period, I attended his office and he greeted me warmly and congratulated me on my appointment. He asked if there was anything he could do for me. I reminded him that I was on the board of PetroCan and as a Senator, I could continue to sit provided I received no remuneration and I handed him the envelope containing my undated resignation saying he could fill in the date anytime and just advise me by telephone. Chrétien took out the letter, read it, smiled, and said, "*Fill in the date today.*" This came as no surprise to me. For Chrétien repeatedly said he did not like being trapped, caught in a situation. I laughed and dated the letter. We then had a brief but pleasant chat about my work plan in the Senate and parted as he escorted me to the door and asked to be kept up to date as I settled in Ottawa as a Senator.

Allan MacEachen once cautioned: "*Never find yourself in the way of saying no to a Leader.*" He implied it would stunt your growth in the Party and Liberal government as indeed it did for me with Jean Chrétien.

After John Turner lost the office of Prime Minister and his error prone run as Leader of the Party and tenure as Prime Minister, I decided I had had enough of electoral politics. I intended to devote all my future political efforts to be a hard-working and hopefully effective Senator. I liked and admired Paul Martin and had been approached by him, but I felt Chrétien was more experienced and deserved the job. I wanted to stay out. But it was not to be. Keith Davey called as he did regularly and asked why I had not joined the Chrétien Leadership team. While I had no negative feelings for Chrétien and rather admired him, I explained to Keith that I was burned out after the Turner experience and decided to focus on Senate work and stay away from electoral politics. "*You can't do that. Chrétien wants to talk to you. Will you take his call?*" "*Of course, I will take his call, I like Jean,*" I said to Keith.

Earlier that week, I had been sitting on the stone wall in front of the Senate commiserating about the Turner campaign with Andre Ouellette who had been a staunch Turner supporter. Jean Chrétien happened to walk by and got into a scuffle with Ouellette who Chrétien felt had betrayed him by supporting Turner in the Leadership and not him as they had been old comrades and friends. Chrétien took Ouellette's support of Turner personally and viewed it as an act of disloyalty. I parted the two who were about to slug it out and pulled Chrétien into the hallway of the Senate entrance. Chrétien said, "*I have no argument with you, Grafstein, you worked for Turner, but Ouellette was my friend and he betrayed me.*" I told him, "*That will change, so cool off, calm down, and forget about it.*" In time, frayed tempers were settled. Ouellette and Chrétien renewed their old relationship. Andre served with his usual calm professional skill in Chrétien's first Cabinet.

Chrétien called shortly after Keith rang off. In his jovial and endearing manner, he cut to the chase. "*Jerry, I want to see you. You have to be with me. I am coming to your office.*" "*No, Jean, not necessary, I will come and see you right away in your office.*" I immediately walked through Parliament hallways to his office adorned with elegant Aboriginal prints, stone sculptures, and a large clean desk. Jean rose to greet me and beckon me to sit. "*Would you like coffee?*" he graciously asked. "*No, I'm fine.*" "*Well,*" he immediately asked, "*Why aren't you with me?*" "*Jean,*

I have no problem with you but after the last election campaign with Turner, I am burned out." I explained that the last campaign with Turner "*was the toughest of my life and I needed a rest*". "*You will be fine after a little time off. But I need you to be with me.*" He emphasized the 'with me' part. "*You are a militant. You can't quit. This is an important time for Liberals, and you are a loyal Liberal.*" Jean had the Lyndon Johnson ability to sit close and not take no for an answer when he wanted something. I assumed as a staunch and visible supporter of Turner, Chrétien wanted to make sure he could unite the Party, always a challenge for any Leader. "*If you can't unite the Party, you can't unite the country*", Keith Davey regularly preached, and he was right.

"*Ok, I will join up and get motivated on two conditions that you should know.*" "*What are they?*" he quickly asked, his eyes now narrowed as he became more focused and cautious. "*First Israel. I am a Zionist and staunch supporter of Israel.*"

Relieved, Chrétien relaxed and said, "*I am a great supporter of Israel. I have good friends in Israel and, look at my staff.*" Chrétien's Chief Staff Adviser was Eddy Goldenberg[180] and his astute adviser John Rae, a selfless and brilliant political operative who served as Chrétien's Executive Assistant and a good friend was also a staunch supporter of Israel, the son of Saul Rae, leading diplomat who was one of the first Jews to climb the thin oxygen heights of the External Affairs never noted for its Israel friendly policies.

"*Second*", I said with a long pause. Again, Chrétien's smile turned grim and his eyes narrowed with intensity. "*I am a believer in One Canada. I don't believe in 'special status'. I don't believe in*

[180] Eddie Goldenberg's father was legendary Carl Goldenberg, a lawyer, mediator, law professor, and advisor to three Prime Ministers – McKenzie King, Pierre Trudeau, and Chrétien – who was appointed to the Senate by Pierre Trudeau.

'distinct society' claims by Quebec. Quebec is a special province but so is Newfoundland. In this, I agree with Louis St. Laurent and Pierre Trudeau." This was the core of my political belief and that one reason why I became a devout supporter of Trudeau's ideas – policies about a 'One Canada' and why believe it or not, I had secretly admired Diefenbaker.

Again, Chrétien's taut body immediately relaxed. "*So am I. I have always believed in One Canada. My best speech is about 'One Canada'*" – which indeed it was. "*I will never accept special status ideas for Quebec. It's not good for Quebec and not good for Canada.*"

With that, he abruptly stood up as I did. We shook hands. I knew he was always busy. Still, I was charmed that he took the time to sign me up. I helped in his leadership campaign. Afterwards, Chrétien asked me to see him. He was planning ahead. He wanted me to run Red Leaf, the Liberal advertising consortium as I had led for Trudeau and Turner. I told him that you have to know when it's time to turn over party work to younger, better people. I felt I was burned out. He was not happy. I undertook to find a replacement which I did – Kevin Shea and I promised to keep an eye on the work. I did as I promised. Shea was named Head of Red Leaf. I kept in touch, but I believe Chrétien resented my refusal to continue.

Jean Chrétien was a wonderful stump speaker in his fractured English or French. But you always knew what he wanted to say. As the title of his autobiography averred, he could speak, *Straight from the Heart.*

Stump speeches are an art form given without notes to make direct contact with the audience. A great stump speaker speaks directly – simply with repetition for emphases, always with humourous asides and a healthy dose of self-deprecation. Chrétien was the master of this political art form. His favourite topic was based on the idea of 'One Canada'. Once my longtime friend Dennis Mills, running for Parliament in the Danforth Riding in the east end of Toronto, invited Chrétien, then the Leader of the Liberal Party in the federal campaign to speak in his east end, heavily ethnic, riding of Danforth on his behalf. Dennis, whose grandfather had founded Chairman Mills where Dennis cut his teeth as an 'event' supplier of tables, chairs, china, and glasses. Dennis was an experienced event master himself amongst his other undoubted great political skills. Dennis chose a dark, dingy restaurant basement on the Danforth in east Toronto for the campaign event. Chrétien got a sense of the dismal low ceiling in the room and spoke about Canada, 'One Canada strong and free'. The room was jammed with immigrants, mostly Greek, who own small businesses on the Danforth. They were both the ethnic mix that made Toronto great and the heart of the Liberal Red Machine supporters – Toronto that Pearson, then Trudeau had so carefully cultivated and enlisted to the Liberal Party cause. Immigrants from Greece, Italy, Portugal, Korea, Hong Kong, Jamaica, and then the Mid-East and East Africa swelled Toronto's population. A polyglot group of every stripe and ethnic origin were all fervent supporters of Dennis in the Danforth.

After a simple, but successful, welcoming remarks by Dennis, culminating in introducing Chrétien as the next Prime Minister of Canada, he turned to Jean Chrétien. Chrétien leapt onto the low stage and in the darkish, dim-lit room with bare light bulbs, Chrétien started to speak with humility and humour, building on his humble Quebec roots to a crescendo in praise of 'One Canada'. There wasn't a dry eye in the room. Standing behind me was Jim Coutts, an inveterate crier, and Dennis whose bright eyes were moist, and I must confess, so were mine. Chrétien's popular touch never ceased to amaze me. I admired his ability to connect with any type of audience. He had the gift! He had the common touch. After he became Leader, I helped organize an event at a private Jewish Club in Toronto and introduced him to a tough, mostly Conservative leaning group of successful businessmen and their wives. Chrétien's charm spoken without a note won over the hard-boiled businessmen and their especially astute wives in the room. Afterwards, Chrétien shook every hand in the crowded room. Chrétien was a 'natural'.

The toughest campaign for Jean Chrétien was the second Quebec Referendum Campaign now that he was the Prime Minister of Canada. He put together a coalition of Provincial and Federal politicians of all stripes and his involvement was tightly tailored to suite each coalition partner needs. Yet, he was hamstrung in a serious way and not allowed to campaign at grass roots level where he excelled as freely as he would have liked. His coalition partners felt he was too tainted by the Trudeau federalist brush and would be counter-productive as the vote appeared to be close. Pierre Trudeau, now in retirement, but following events closely, in turn was not invited to participate. Outside of Quebec, other Liberals such as myself and others from Toronto were told to stay away.

The Referendum Campaign didn't go well. The Separatists under Rene Levesque, were well organized, well-funded, and united in message, were gaining momentum as the campaign entered the final stretch. Many of us in Toronto felt handcuffed. Brian Tobin (later called 'Captain Canada'), a populist energetic Member of Parliament from Newfoundland who enjoyed organizing events as I did, took matters into his own hands and organized a giant rally on the streets of Montreal. This rally was based on the plan and organization for bringing Canadians across Canada actually devised by Dennis Mills who first developed the idea of organizing Canadians from outside Quebec to show their passion and interest of One Canada, along with energetic

Liberals like Sheila Copps and others from across Canada that helped turn the tide or least slow the Separationist momentum. Still, I felt it was not enough! The polls were too close. It was anybody's guess.

Suddenly, I came up with a great cost-effective idea that I felt could make a difference – Pierre Trudeau – who had been the absent, uninvited, silent guest during the bitter Referendum Campaign. I discovered that the paid media campaign came to an end on Saturday midnight before the Referendum vote day on Monday. Saturday mid-morning, I went to visit Jim Coutts in his small, elegant, book-filled home in downtown Toronto to try out my 'Hail Mary' idea. Concisely put, on Sunday morning, Pierre Trudeau would go for a walk in a park near his stylish art deco house in Montreal. He would sit on a park bench. The national and local media would be notified. Trudeau could then make his pitch alone directly to the Quebec public and he would own the airways for free that weekend of the 'blackout'. Jim thought it was a great idea. I had invited David Smith to join us at Jim's small house off Avenue Road just north of Bloor. David also thought it was a solid idea. I had also figured that it would take me, along with Jim and David, to convince Trudeau, who I knew was unhappy being sidelined on the key issue of his political legacy, to participate at the last moment.

I asked Jim to contact Trudeau at his home in Montreal. Jim immediately gave me Pierre Trudeau's home telephone in Montreal. "*You can call him…it's your idea.*" It was noon on Saturday at the time – two days before the vote. I dialed immediately, got Justin and asked if I could speak to his father. Justin said his dad was not home. He had gone up to his cabin to spend the weekend alone tracking through the snow-covered woods and do physical chores around the cabin. Justin told me I could get him now because Trudeau was punctual in his habits and would come back to the cabin for lunch at noon. I got the number from Justin and immediately called. Trudeau picked up the phone. I told him I was at Jim Coutts's house (Jim had been a close trusted confidant, advisor and Chief of Staff to Pierre Trudeau since mid-1974). With me was David Smith who Trudeau knew and liked for David's political savvy and organizational skills as well. David had served in Trudeau's Cabinet and had been enlisted to lobby English M.P.'s during the Constitutional Repatriation battles. I quickly sketched out the idea. Trudeau listened quietly. There was a pause.

"*Interesting idea but the Referendum Campaign managers don't want me to participate. And if I do and the Separatists win, I will be blamed for the loss.*"

"*If we lose the Referendum, Pierre*", I quickly retorted, "*You will be blamed any way. So don't say no, just say I will think about it and we will contact the campaign managers to get their agreement.*" Trudeau said, "*Ok, let me think about it. Get back to me in an hour.*" As soon as I rung off, I called Eddy Goldenberg who was negative to the idea but said he would get back to me. After a half-hour wait and no response, at the suggestion of Jim Coutts, I called John Rae in Montreal who was also deeply involved in the campaign. John was most polite. "*We have just checked the recent polls and we are ahead*", he volunteered. I told him that Jim, David, and I disagree. Marty Goldfarb who I had spoken to regularly also disagreed. It was too close to call even though the 'No' side was ahead 20% at the start of the campaign. We, too, knew how to read polls and we thought they were close but just behind. Trudeau would be worth at least five points. John Rae, always the gentleman, said, "*Let me think about it. I will get back to you.*" There was silence for another hour. Finally, we agreed that I call Pierre who had been patiently waiting for my return call. I brought him up to speed on the calls with Goldenberg and

Rae and then the silence of no return calls. Trudeau said quietly, "*I thought so. But thanks to all there for the idea which I thought was interesting.*" We hung up. The 'Yes' Referendum Campaign beat the Separatist 'No' vote by just over 1% (49.42% to 50.8%), a squeaker if there ever was one.

To be fair to Chrétien and his team, the 'No' team had publicized a picture of Trudeau and Chrétien laughing after the first Referendum that he won comfortably that helped the 'No' side. At the start of the Second Referendum Campaign in 1995, the 'Yes' vote had surged ahead. It was even closer to call than we believed.

A last footnote to the Chrétien Referendum saga. On the Thursday before the vote, in desperation, Chrétien went on French TV to promise to support Quebec as a 'distinct society' in a vote in Parliament after the Referendum. I was aghast. Chrétien had broken his word to me. It was plain and simple – an act of desperation. I understood the pressure he was under to make his last-minute gesture, but still I felt it was unnecessary.

Some months later in Parliament, true to his word, Chrétien introduced a Resolution in the Commons, a non-binding vote of a Resolution supporting Quebec as a 'distinct society'. When the Resolution passed in the Commons by a strong vote, the same Resolution was introduced by the Liberal leader in the Senate, Allan MacEachen. After a Senate caucus that indicated all Liberal Senators supported it except me. I demurred. Immediately, Allan and Keith were on me. MacEachen quietly and painstakingly pointed out that Chrétien was pledged to make the Resolution in the Referendum Campaign and after all, it was not legally binding but just a reflection of Parliament at a moment in time. I agreed but it was not my reflection. Both urged me to reconsider. The implication was that it would hinder my career in the Senate. I called Pierre Trudeau in Montreal at his law office for advice. I recounted the background. After Pierre Trudeau had resigned, I had lunched with him in Montreal quarterly and kept in touch on contentious issues to seek his counsel. Trudeau followed everything in Ottawa assiduously and kept up-to-date but kept his silence.

In his laid-back fashion, Trudeau asked, "*What would you like to do?*" "*To make a big speech*", I reply. "*So, do what you would like to do. Make a big speech.*" So ended our conversation with the usual pleasantries.

I immediately called Allan and then Keith that I have decided to make 'a big speech'. Both tried to convince me not to. Allan suggested I not appear for the vote in the Senate. Keith, more bluntly, suggested that I should disappear the day of the vote.

At a Liberal caucus event that evening, Chrétien approached me and urged me not to attend the vote. I reminded him of our first conversation on this issue, then he turned and said, "*Look at my back. I have scars on my back for my support of a 'One Canada' in Quebec. Do me a favour, just don't show up for the vote. Besides, Trudeau is in favour of the Resolution.*" I was shocked. I didn't believe it. I had just spoken to Trudeau the day before. The following morning, I called Pierre Trudeau in his law office in Montreal. He immediately came on the phone. I told him I had heard he was in favour of the Resolution. "*Who told you that?*" he curtly asked. "*The Right Honourable Prime Minister of Canada, Jean Chrétien, told me that last night.*" "*That is not correct*" he said quickly. "*And what do you intend to do? To make a big speech?*" he queried. I was noncommittal. Again, we ended the call pleasantly.

Now I started to sweat. On one hand, my two great mentors, Allan MacEachen and Keith Davey had urged my support as had Prime Minister Chrétien. There was an unspoken menace that my Senate career would be stunted if I stood by my refusal to support a resolution that Chrétien had urged me to support or just duck.

I sought my wife's advice and she promptly answered, "*Do what you think is right.*"

In the end, I satisfied no one, not even myself. I balked. I spoke in the Senate. I made the shortest speech I have ever given. "*Canada is a distinct society. All the rest is commentary.*" Then I abstained from the vote.

Chrétien always learned from his mistakes. With the help of Stéphane Dion, he cobbled together the Clarity Bill to ensure that a proper question was sent to the electorate if separatism raised its ugly head again. While I supported his effort, I abstained because the Bill did not include the Senate in the deliberations in Parliament on framing the 'question'.

And so, it was during the balance of the Chrétien government, I never received the one appointment I craved in the Senate – the Chairmanship of the Senate Foreign Rights Committee that I had served and prepared for during my entire tenure as Senator.

I was told by Dan Hays, the Senate Liberal leader, that when the vacancy opened that the appointment had gone to Peter Stollery and I had been passed over. "*Why?*" I ask Dan. "*Why?*" I ask the Liberal leader in the Senate. Dan Hays, an honest and admirable Senator and old colleague. "*Because of Langevin Building*", i.e. because of the Prime Minister's office across the street from Parliament. Chrétien never forgot an act of what he considers disloyalty. It was loyalty to the leader he believed that kept the Liberal tribe together, a belief he himself did not always practice.

There was also bad blood between the two rivals to Liberal leadership, between John Turner (who I worked for during his leadership as a loyal supporter) and Jean Chrétien. Chrétien had lost to Turner on his first leadership run. It boiled over during

Turner's difficult period after he had lost the leadership. Turner had abruptly resigned as Minister of Finance during the Trudeau administration when Trudeau sought to set up a group of senior economic advisors that Turner took as a slap of his tenure as Minister of Finance. In the result, he resigned and returned to his successful law practice in Toronto. During this period, we kept in touch. Then Turner did something to Chrétien that deeply offended him. Chrétien as Minister of Finance was doing a credible job. John Turner supported an influential newsletter put out by his law partner Bill MacDonald that criticized Chrétien's policies as Minister of Finance. Chrétien felt Turner was behind this public act of disloyalty and unfairness. He harboured a grudge and when his turn to reciprocate came around, he did. Turner faltered in his short tenure as Prime Minister. One of Chrétien's close supporters, Ron Irwin,[181] a likeable M.P. from northern Ontario circulated a secret letter signed by twenty-two Members of the Liberal cause voicing lack of confidence in Turner's leadership. Other M.P.'s were involved including Brian Tobin and Sergio Marchi.[182] It was considered, by Turner, a near fatal stab in the back. Turner was astounded. "*Who was behind this? Why did it happen?*" he asked me. I knew nothing about it. Nothing. Chrétien had got his revenge and helped weaken Turner and Turner's weakness would catapult Chrétien to the Liberal leadership.

What comes around goes around. That letter tore up the unwritten policy of the Liberal party – loyalty to the leader. Paul Martin Jr. returned the favour as Jean Chrétien had never supported Paul's father's political aspirations. Though a good,

---

[181] Ron Irvin got his reward when he was appointed Canadian Ambassador to Ireland.

[182] Sergio Marchi also got his reward when he was appointed to a post in Europe.

loyal, and excellent Minister of Finance, Paul Martin and his tight team of loyalists, who thought Chrétien did not support him enough, began to undermine Chrétien at every opportunity to make Chrétien look inept as Prime Minister. Chrétien had reportedly agreed to resign early which he did not. Tribalism in the Liberal Party burst into the open. Both were hotly competitive and now, didn't trust each other. So, Martin's entourage attacked Chrétien's leadership in the caucus that led, in part, to the premature departure of Jean Chrétien. Had Chrétien continued to take the heat for the political scandals as Chrétien argued; Martin might have had an easier tenure as Prime Minister. Instead, Martin called a public judicial enquiry which Chrétien was compelled to attend and defend his record. Paul Martin gave evidence as well. It was awful.[183] But that was a tribal war and the Liberal Party did not recover until the remarkable rise of Justin Trudeau who reunited the Party when he won as leader and took the office of Prime Minister as a well-deserved prize. If you can't unite the Party, you can't unit the country. True today as it was then.

Perhaps the most dramatic decision Jean Chrétien took during his term as Prime Minister was not to support President George Bush's decision to invade Iraq over weapons of mass destruction. Chrétien was trapped and he knew it. Who was right remains to be seen. His instincts, perhaps buried in his Quebec genes, was against war. The repeated UN resolutions against Saddam Hussein's horrific conduct and actions, whether about human rights or weapons of mass destruction, appeared clear. International law and the UN sided with Bush. Chrétien was caught. Yet, secretly, he marshalled others to oppose the

[183] Chrétien went to court and was later exonerated from any egregious conduct.

Iraq War hoping not to offend the United States, Canada's major economic partner, involving billions in trade. It was perhaps the toughest decision he took as Prime Minister and he later surfed on public support for his stand. History has yet to be written on this chapter.

After 9/11, I was unhappy that Chrétien shrank from attending the site of devastation of the Twin Towers that the world had observed on TV. Canadians had lost their lives. Other world leaders attended, including a Prince of Japan, yet, for some reason, Chrétien hesitated to go. At the time, I was co-chair of the Canada/U.S.A. Inter-Parliamentary Group composed of all-party Canadian Parliamentarians and Members of Congress. Our group met regularly to discuss, and solve if we could, endless lists of irritants between Canada and U.S.A. As a result, I had called and written to our fellow members in both Houses of Congress, many of whom had become good friends. When I raised the question in caucus, Chrétien strangely offered that he didn't want to compound America's unease. Clearly, he felt uncomfortable attending this tragic site.[184]

His refusal upset me. When I came home that weekend, Carole said, as she usually did, "*If you can do better, go do it.*" We agreed to pull together a small group of volunteers to organize a small group to take up Mayor Giuliani's invitation rendered at the UN. "*If you want to help New York City, come and spend a weekend with us*", Giuliani implored. We decided to rent a small

[184] As Co-Chair of Canada-U.S.A. Interparliamentary Group, I attended Washington with Chrétien during one of his visits to the White House. He asked me to accompany him to Congress to introduce him to key members of the House and the Senate I knew. One memorable visit was with Speaker Gingrich. Chrétien was hesitant to engage. I started the conversation by asking the Speaker about China. Both Chrétien and I were astonished by the Speaker's knowledge and insight into China as it began to emerge as an economic power.

venue, the Roseland Ballroom, for a small event and meeting point in mid-Manhattan that those Canadians who came could meet briefly and then enjoy a weekend in New York. The idea caught fire across Canada. In the end, over 25,000 Canadians from every corner of Canada showed up at the Roseland Ballroom, lining the New York City streets of 52, 53, 54, 55, 56, 57, 58, 59, 60, 62, 63, and 64 Streets waiting to get in. So, we closed down 52nd Street beside the Ballroom (that could only hold 3,500 at best) and set up large TV screens to view the short covered and program in the Ballroom. Still inside and out, only about 8,000 people could be reached. Chrétien was visiting Los Angeles that Friday when he heard about Canadians streaming into New York. He suddenly decided to fly over night, and we agreed for him to meet me at the Ballroom side doors at 11 A.M. From there, we went up and down both streets of the New York streets crowded with waiting Canadians and apologizing to them that there would be room to get in by those who lined up. No one complained. Chrétien was cheered as he walked the lines with me and other volunteers. After a brief ceremony with Mayor Rudy Giuliani and short concert in the Ballroom, Chrétien took centre stage and his short remarks were pitch perfect. On his way out, he left to large applause. Aline, his wife, came back to say goodbye and to thank my wife and the other key volunteers graciously as always and then took her leave.[185]

In the winter of 2003, as Jean Chrétien was wrestling with Paul Martin to sustain his leadership, an epidemic of SARS broke out in Toronto and nothing was being done on the provincial

---

[185] For a fuller account, read *The Miracle on 52nd Street: Canada Loves New York Weekend* in *Parade: Tributes to Remarkable Contemporaries* by Jerry S. Grafstein (Mosaic Press, 2017) or in *Chicken Soup for the Canadian Soul* by Jerry S. Grafstein, edited by Raymond Aaron, Janet Matthews, Jack Canfield, and Mark Victor Hansen (Health Communications, Inc., 2002).

and government side to get out the message that the epidemic in Toronto was contained and the city safe. Hotels, restaurants, and entertainment venues virtually closed down.

When a small unit of the hospitality workers union visited me, they were desperate. Concerts began to cancel. Fifty percent, over 45,000 of these low-paying workers, had been laid off. I called the Mayor, the Premier, and the Prime Minister to no avail. Dennis Mills, an M.P. for Danforth, was getting the same response. Hotels, restaurants, and bars were empty. Together we decided we needed a message to send to the world that Toronto was safe and sound and open for business. At Dennis's suggestion, we contacted Michael Cohl, an old friend of both of us and convinced him to bring the Rolling Stones, who loved Toronto, and produce an all-broadcast live concert. A five-million-dollar deposit from Molson's to underwrite the preliminary costs was obtained. The concert was called *Molson Rocks*.[186]

In the event, over 500,000 people attended Downsview Park, the largest event of its kind in Canada, and the message went out over the internet and airways that Toronto was safe and sound and open for business. All this was done without government funding. Sometimes personal persistence proves more effective than government.

Finally, three postscripts to our personal relations that continue to be warm and respectful. When I retired from the Senate after twenty-six years of service, a large dinner was organized by old friends and comrades in arms Senators Serge Joyal and David Smith in Ottawa. All former Liberal leaders were asked to speak. Chrétien was out of town but sent a three-minute clip. In it, he said that I was always a great Liberal, but I

[186] For a fuller account, read *Romancing the Stones* in *Parade: Tributes to Remarkable Contemporaries* by Jerry S. Grafstein (Mosaic Press, 2017).

could also be 'a pain in the ass'. Steve Paikin, who attended, did a farewell interview with me on his Ontario TVO show and asked how I felt about that comment. I told him, "*I took that as a great compliment since Chrétien could also be 'a pain in the ass'.*"

Another Chrétien anecdote while Chrétien was Prime Minister. When the art deco American Embassy across Wellington Street was vacated, I thought it would be an ideal location for a Portrait Gallery modelled on the Portrait Gallery in London. I had visited the National Archives across the river in Quebec that stores thousands of portraits of Canada's great figures that would never be seen by Canadians. I enlisted Serge Joyal to help in the effort. We both decided the key would be to convince Chrétien, then Prime Minister. Serge came up with a persuasive idea – to put together a small brochure of great portraits. In the process, we discovered an early lively picture of Chrétien that we appended to the last page of the brochure.

We attended Chrétien in his office in Parliament Hill. As always, his desk was clear except for a small card on which some notes had been written that he would glance at, obviously a briefing note for our visit. As we made our pitch, he glanced through the brochure which he said had 'punch' when he turned to his photo, he smiled, and we knew we had his attention. We quickly plowed through the details. At the end, he said he was interested, provided we could get Sheila Copps support, his Minister of Heritage. He rose, congratulated us on our initiative and then took the briefing card, ripped it up and placed the bits in his waste paper bin. He smiled and said, "*See? No record.*" Chrétien was a careful astute politician.

In the end, true to his word, after we got Sheila's approval, his government established the National Portrait Gallery funding and set up an architectural contest only to be dismantled by Harper when he became Prime Minister as he chose to erase

Chrétien and his Liberal Party's legacy. Nothing new. It happens all the time in politics.

Chrétien attained an easy relationship with most other foreign leaders especially Bill Clinton, Tony Blair, Nelson Mandela, Jacques Chirac, George Bush, Shimon, Peres[187], Fernando Cardoso of Brazil, and especially Boris Yeltsin in Russia. Chrétien was a democratic realist in foreign affairs. He refused to publicly condemn autocratic leaders in China for human rights abuses or elsewhere believing he could be more effective in criticizing them in private, a lesson still not adequately understood by his successors.

All in all, Jean Chrétien was a unique and authentic leader, who in return, gained the lasting respect and affection of the Canadian public and his peers for his remarkable and assiduous public service to Canada.

- *Straight from the Heart* by Jean Chrétien (Key Porter Books, 1985)
- *My Years as Prime Minister* by Jean Chrétien (Knopf, 2007)
- *My Stories, My Times* by Jean Chrétien (Random House of Canada, 2018)

[187] I personally observed Chrétien with his easy camaraderie in Ottawa with Bill Clinton, Tony Blair, and Shimon Peres, when he beckoned me and introduced me to each as an active Liberal with a smile. I was also introduced by Chrétien to Fernando Cardoso, President of Brazil on a trip to Brasilia, the capital of Brazil. Chrétien demonstrated warm camaraderie with Cardoso who also became a good friend of Chrétien. Chrétien had a warm long-standing relationship with Queen Elizabeth from whom he received the Order of Merit, one of the Royal's highest honours, after he retired.

Jean Chrétien - Maiden Speech

MAY 23, 1963 185

The Address—Mr. Chretien

I have mentioned labour-management co-operation because I believe this is a field in which the maximum degree of effort is required at the present time. It is a field where such efforts will yield the greatest possible results, because management has a direct and positive interest in increasing the rate of industrial growth while the labour unions have a direct and personal interest in keeping up the supply of new jobs. This is a task which any government must set itself in moving to correct those built-in disabilities which have helped to introduce unemployment. Government can only accomplish this task by enlisting the support of labour and management in a direct and positive way. I must point out that there is a great deal of good will on both sides, good will which must be placed at the service of the economy and of the people of Canada in general.

At this time I should like to say to the new Minister of Labour that he is indeed fortunate in the calibre of those people he will find at his disposal in the Department of Labour and the unemployment insurance commission, people who have been, are, and, I am sure, will be ready and willing to carry forward the policies he may be initiating.

I have mentioned these matters at some length because I believe they are the real problems and issues which must be kept in mind when we examine the outline of government policy as it appears in the speech from the throne. It is not my intention to pull this document apart, sentence by sentence and word by word. However, there are some general remarks which I feel called upon to make at this time. While giving the government the benefit of the doubt, as we are all inclined to do, nevertheless I am forced to point out that there is very little for labour in the speech from the throne. Some of the promises which have been made by the present occupants of the treasury benches, including the Prime Minister, come to mind. I think of the measure to introduce a minimum wage of $1.25, the regulation of hours of work and a number of other things. I have scanned the speech from the throne thoroughly and have yet to find anything in it directed toward labour in this country. There is one sentence relating to automation and manpower adjustment, but it is not clear what that sentence really means. I would think it refers to a bill similar to the one we introduced in the last parliament, and setting out the same policy that was contained in that measure—one, by the way, which failed to pass.

What about the proposal to set up a new department of industry? Will the new minister be able to give direction to industry? Is that what is intended? If so, where does direction stop and regimentation begin? We should like to hear about this when the legislation setting up the new department is introduced. If the department is not going to give direction, what will be its function? We shall all be awaiting with interest the answers to these questions.

Also to be found in the speech is mention of an economic council to develop more employment and encourage efficient production. I venture to say that if this council is set up no effects will be felt in this country for at least four or five years. In fact there is nothing in this speech from the throne which would have an immediate effect. This economic council appears to be nothing more than a wrapping up of the national economic development board which we proposed and which was held up by the last parliament along with the measure to establish a productivity council. Hon. gentlemen opposite have thrown these into one basket and come up with this idea of forming an economic council.

I have no objection to this, because the measures we introduced were good measures which would have resulted in a continuation of the economic development already under way as a result of the other programs we implemented. But to try to pass these measures off as part of the bold, imaginative Liberal government program is just a little too much to swallow. I think hon. members opposite have perpetrated a hoax on the Canadian people.

They say they are going to set up a municipal loan board. What funds do they propose to make available to that board for loans? Is it $400 million? How much work is that going to provide? The municipal winter works program has seen $900 million spent in five years, giving jobs every winter to 135,000 Canadians for a period of 45 days. Yet hon. members opposite talk about solving the unemployment problem with $400 million. How is this money to be distributed? What criteria will be applied in granting loans to some municipalities and refusing them to others? Can any municipality get them? Is there to be a limit, or will Toronto and Montreal or some other large municipalities get all the money, leaving nothing for the others?

Mr. Deputy Speaker: I am sorry to interrupt the hon. member, but his time has expired.

(Translation):

Mr. Jean Chretien (St. Maurice-Lafleche): Mr. Speaker, as a new member in this house, allow me to offer you my most sincere congratulations on your appointment as Speaker of the house. I am sure that you will discharge with dignity and impartiality the heavy responsibilities that have been entrusted to you by both sides of the house.

I might be permitted also, Mr. Speaker, to congratulate the movers of the address in reply, the hon. members for Northumberland (Miss Jewett) and Lotbiniere (Mr. Choquette), for having so splendidly performed their duty in the house.

(Text):

I am very glad to be a member of a party which has a leader of the calibre of the Prime Minister (Mr. Pearson). Never has an English speaking Prime Minister had such a comprehension of biculturalism and the fact that Canada is a different nation from the United States. This is because one third of the population is French speaking and will always be so in the centuries to come.

(Translation):

Mr. Speaker, I have the honour to represent the riding of St. Maurice-Lafleche, which was set up in 1935, and which, even at that time, through the foresight of its electors, enabled a Liberal government to take over from a Conservative administration. In 1963, the electors of my riding of St. Maurice-Lafleche decided once again to help the Liberal party stop the spread of Social Credit and sound the beginning of the end for that party in the province of Quebec, and also to put in power a Liberal government to replace, once more, a Conservative administration.

Mr. Speaker, I succeed a Liberal member, Mr. J. A. Richard, who sat here for many years and served his riding and the house well. Therefore, on behalf of the electors of the riding of St. Maurice-Lafleche, I wish to pay tribute to that man who, although well in years, represented with dignity for many years the riding that did me the honour to elect me.

Mr. Speaker, since I have been elected, many of my English speaking colleagues have asked me questions on a problem of the day and wanted to know what I thought of the separatist movement in the province of Quebec.

Mr. Speaker, I believe we should not give too much importance to that situation. However, I would like, in a few words, to try and clarify the matter for the information of my English speaking friends who represent ridings in other provinces.

In the last century the province of Quebec had a population of farmers and craftsmen. It was only in the last generation that Quebec started to become an industrial province. Such a deep transformation creates a number of problems. At the present time, with the changes the premier of Quebec, Hon. Jean

[Mr. Chretien.]

Lesage, is bringing about, especially in the field of education, thousands of young French Canadians will soon make their entry on the labour market while thousands of university graduates will start their active life, and they will all ask for adequate employment.

Now, Mr. Speaker, those qualified young men want to have their due place in a French Canadian community and in the community of the province of Quebec as a whole.

As a French Canadian, I must admit that we all have a place in this house. We may speak French or English here and we enjoy complete freedom. But, unfortunately, I find that in the past French Canadians in the province of Quebec were too often left in the background, more particularly in the industrial and commercial field.

Today, we are able to carry out some functions competently. But unfortunately some industrialists and businessmen in Quebec have but too often failed to be frank and honest enough or were prejudiced against their French speaking fellow citizens, to the point of limiting their progress to a certain level. However, at this time, I have to render due tribute to various financial, commercial and industrial institutions in the province of Quebec, which offer to Canadians of French origin more and more possibilities for an advancement, to which they, indeed, have a right.

As a matter of fact, *La Presse* of Saturday, May 11, 1963, reproduced an item published in the *Financial Post* and stating that French had become the fashion in Montreal and that, if industrialists in the province of Quebec began to offer possibilities of advancement to French Canadians, it was due to a recognition of the latter's increased competence and present economic strength, which had to be reckoned with, as well as of the need to negotiate with those people. That is why many corporations in the province of Quebec now offer some possibilities of advancement to French speaking Canadians. I hope this trend will develop more and more in the years to come, so that we may live in peace within the Canadian confederation, as we trust we shall.

Mr. Speaker, we may, of course, pass some legislation in this house. However, the Canadian people in general, and more particularly the English speaking Canadians, should, in the province of Quebec as in the other provinces, give French Canadians the same possibilities of progress so that there would be no such discrimination as has been noted in the past.

Mr. Speaker, I am confident that the present separatist movement is not serious. On the other hand, I feel that at the last federal election, the people of Quebec showed their trust in the party that has always recognized the importance of the French Canadians. That explains why so many ridings in Quebec have elected Liberals to represent them in this house, even though no expert could have forecast a Liberal victory in that province. It must be admitted that Quebec, in these times of confusion, has put her trust in the Liberal party, and it is the Liberal party which will restore a climate of confidence in the province of Quebec.

Mr. Speaker, may I call it one o'clock?

Mr. Speaker: It being one o'clock, I do now leave the chair.

At one o'clock the house took recess.

(Text):

AFTER RECESS

The house resumed at 2.30 p.m.

(Translation):

Mr. Chretien: Mr. Speaker, allow me to go back briefly over some things I said this morning.

This morning I was saying that at the present time, in the province of Quebec, a peaceful revolution was being carried out by the new government. I feel it is proceeding to the satisfaction of the people of Quebec. There is no reason to worry about the events reported these days in the newspapers, because on April 8 our people gave themselves an adequate representation in the federal government, that is a Liberal representation. Nevertheless, Mr. Speaker, to give hope to those thousands of young French Canadians who are now attending university and tomorrow will be out on the labour market, I believe the federal government should pass adequate legislation. It will have to recognize the existence of the province of Quebec, which may wish to be more independent from confederation than in the past. So the government of our province must be given the means to solve its own problems. The federal government will have to adopt laws on biculturalism that are adequate and recognize, on a national scale, that during the next hundred years, Canada will be different from the United States, a country where there are two languages and two cultures.

I feel that under the present Prime Minister the government is going in that direction and I urge it to keep on going along that same path.

It will also have to study the sharing of taxes. The government of Quebec and the other provincial governments must be given sufficient financial resources to solve the numerous economic and educational problems that exist today, especially in the province of Quebec.

Mr. Speaker, I feel it is the duty of this house to give the country progressive legislation. The people of Canada will find in the Liberal program the solution to their problems.

The solutions that we have put forward shall have to be applied rapidly and, in this regard, I have a suggestion to make. I believe hon. members should be given the opportunity to take a more active part in this task, by changing the procedure of committees, so that members can really go to the root of problems and offer possible solutions. Committees should be diversified and the most competent people in this house should be appointed to work on each problem and submit solutions to the government and then adequate legislation could be enacted.

Mr. Speaker, some newspapers said that the member for St. Maurice-Lafleche perhaps had gone against his own way of thinking by supporting the government when the vote was taken on a non-confidence motion proposed by the New Democratic party. During the campaign, I took a position by saying that I was against nuclear arms but that if Canada had been committed by the Conservative government to acquire them, I did not want the Liberal government to fail to respect those commitments, or to do in public life what we do not do in private life.

Mr. Speaker, the Prime Minister told us that this question would be discussed in the house in due course; he promised us that we would have an opportunity to discuss it. We only had half a day to deal with this problem and we were called to vote that same evening without having received all the information to which we were entitled.

I believe that problem is important, and the Prime Minister undertook to give us an opportunity for a full debate, not only an afternoon sitting. That is why, Mr. Speaker, I voted with the government.

It was premature at the time to launch a debate when we were unable to discuss the NATO agreements. It was impossible to take a stand until we were made aware of the solution that would be offered at that time. That is why I voted with the government, and when the debate is really opened on this problem I shall give my opinion and shall analyse the problems honestly according to the mandate my constituents gave me.

Mr. Speaker, some members can deplore, of course, the fact I am so nervous and I understand so little English. In any case, I believe that my position is highly defensible and, as Canada has acquired a reputation in international affairs for keeping its commitments, if there were any commitments, the member for St. Maurice-Lafleche will certainly vote in favour of fulfilling them. However, I reserve a final decision until we have had an opportunity to discuss the whole problem. I will not be satisfied with only an afternoon discussion. That is the reason why, in my opinion, it should be said that this issue was raised a bit prematurely and at the wrong time.

Mr. Speaker, the member for St. Maurice-Lafleche, like all the hon. members of this house, will make it his duty, when the government raises the nuclear weapons issue before this house, to examine both sides of the coin in the most thorough manner.

I conclude my speech here. It was my maiden speech and I wish to thank the members of this assembly for giving me such kind attention. I believe that even though we occupy the government benches we must give the members of this house the assurance that we will give our point of view on every matter raised before the House of Commons.

Anyhow, it will be clear for everybody that the riding of St. Maurice-Lafleche wants a progressive representation. It made a point of ousting a Social Crediter in order to return a Liberal member. I believe that my electors gave me an extremely clear mandate.

Yesterday I heard the hon. member for Villeneuve (Mr. Caouette) say that the Canadian economy was under the control of the Americans. Mr. Speaker, I wonder how it is that the hon. member for Villeneuve, who complains of that situation, is a dealer for the Chrysler corporation, which is owned by the Americans. I hope that he will be able to give us an explanation for that situation. If he was so convinced of his opinion he would obviously endeavour to sell cars from companies other than American companies.

[Mr. Chretien.]

(Text):

Mr. F. J. Bigg (Athabasca): Mr. Speaker, this is the third time I have had the honour to represent the great district of Athabasca, the place where there are reeds; but I assure you the reeds are not shaken in the wind, except in the wind of false propaganda which recently somewhat thinned our ranks. I trust this situation will be shortly changed again. However, I do not intend to waste the time of the house in recriminations. My attitude has always been one of positive suggestion and contribution.

Last September I challenged the present Prime Minister to bring forward policies superior to those of the administration of which I was a supporter, but in the speech from the throne I see little promise to Canadians of any such change. In any member of parliament or any member of a government I as a taxpayer and as a Canadian citizen look for more than promises and empty words. I look for character, and surely one of the important aspects of character and stability. It is not enough to mouth high sounding phrases about freedom, democracy, independence and sovereignty; those phrases must be implemented and the Canadian people must be guaranteed independence, progress and sovereignty.

We are asked to believe that this new administration is going to give us this stability, but I should like to review the record. A short 18 months ago the present Minister of National Defence (Mr. Hellyer) said that nothing could be gained by having atomic weapons on Canadian soil. At that time I thoroughly disagreed with that stand. I spoke on the same day, September 12, 1961, but what I said was, of course, ignored by members of the press because they only print what they want to print. They did not report what I said. At times they refuse to cover what they know is the bald truth.

At that time I begged the Minister of National Defence to reconsider his stand. He wanted to get out of NATO. It is in the record at page 8231 of *Hansard* of 1961. He said that nothing would be gained by adding atomic weapons to our arsenal or by joining the atomic club. Why the change? Eighteen months ago the Liberals were a family of bird watchers, but now I suggest that they have been watching the eagle much too carefully. Don't try to hang "zombie" around my neck. I served my country; I made a good stand.

Paul Martin Jr.

Paul Martin Jr. – Unfulfilled Promise

(21st)

Date Elected to Parliament:	November 21, 1988
Date of Maiden Speech:	December 19, 1988
Date Sworn In:	December 12, 2003
Date Left Office:	February 5, 2006

No Prime Minister was more steeped in the travails of public life and the turbulence and unforgiving nature of politics than Paul Martin Jr. before he decided to enter public life. Well before he launched his political career, he encountered the hubris of public life.

Paul[188] was the only son of Paul Martin Sr., by far the most 'progressive' capable, accomplished, and considered politician of his generation.

Paul's aspirations and career path cannot be separated from the prolific career of his father. Born of humble circumstances and maimed early by polio with a withered shoulder and arm, Paul Martin Sr. came from working-class French and Irish Canadian Catholic roots near Ottawa. Too often, we neglect the potent role mothers play in a son's political ambitions. Such was the case with Paul Jr.'s mother. Most history should be written through the lens of a successful politician's mother.

[188] Paul Martin Jr.'s full name was Paul Edgar Phillipe Martin attesting to his mixed Irish and French-Canadian heritage.

Paul Martin Junior grew up in Windsor and Ottawa as the privileged son of Windsor's leading politician with one sibling, a sister. Not spoiled, Paul, as a teenager, sought out hard work out west in the oil patch and in the far north as a youth. Paul had a wanderlust for distant places. Early on, Paul was possessed of an independent spirit.

Any public leadership race is a pivotal event in a politician's life and that of his family, overwrought with drama and emotion – for the winner and his followers – and the losers and their desolate supporters. All believe for varied reasons their candidate was the best choice for themselves and the country. Some leadership candidates see their careers drift in despair after a loss. Others rationalize their loss as only a short-term setback and perhaps as just another building block in their path to later victory and vindication. Many seek a career in politics, invested early in leadership ambitions, to build a solid career of public service and such was the case of Paul Martin Sr. Some learn from their mistakes; others cannot adjust to the public perspective on their persona. For months in the lead up to the leadership vote, the candidates become transformed into public figures as the disinterested electorate turn their attention and begin to concentrate their mind, after the race starts, to choose their flag bearers.

After hockey, politics is Canada's national pastime. Leadership, like the Stanley Cup playoffs, is where only one team can win. The 1968 Liberal leadership convention in Ottawa was no different. There can only be one winner. At the outset, there was no clear choice. This was reflected in the five ballots it took for Pierre Trudeau to gain a majority and become Leader of the Liberal Party and Prime Minister. This was Paul Martin Sr.'s third and last futile reach for Liberal leadership.

The leading candidates in 1968, included handsome Bob Winters, slow to enter the race, Paul Hellyer, the conservative leaning Minister of Defense who had unified the armed forces and who had the master Liberal organizer Keith Davey behind him. Paul Martin Sr., the eldest and most experienced politically, with the most substantial public record, decided to make his third attempt at leadership having lost in 1948 to St. Laurent and in 1958 to Mike Pearson. Newish, untested Pierre Trudeau who after a debate amongst Quebecois leadership aspirants in the fall of 1967 in Montreal emerged as the choice amongst Quebecers when Jean Marchand demurred. The youthful dark horse John Turner, new, energetic, attractive, hopeful, and then the taciturn Alan MacEachen, M.P., former advisor to Mr. Pearson and one of the best speakers in Parliament and last but not least, Joe Green a gifted speaker in any forum. It was a full field of competent candidates. Pearson had left a talented field of capable successors. The winner, Pierre Trudeau, had eked out a win on the fifth ballot. Last minute efforts to stop Trudeau, led by a combination of Robert Winter, Paul Hellyer, and Judy LaMarch, failed when Turner refused to go along. Trudeau edged out Winters after Turner lost at the fourth ballot. Most disappointed was Paul Martin Sr. who gave up after the second ballot. Turner outlasted Martin as a flutter of Martin supporters, especially a skilled political operative, Jack Austin, joined Turner. Turner was left with 195 votes that became the seeds of his future base in the party. Most devastated of all was Paul Martin Sr. who realized that this defeat was the end of his lifelong dream in politics to reach the pinnacle of power that he craved, prepared, and practiced for his entire storied political career.

That Saturday night in April 1968 in Ottawa, I, who had been deeply involved in John Turner's leadership bid, decided to pay my respects to Paul Martin Sr. recognizing this defeat might be the last chapter of Paul Martin's productive career goals. I had been asked by Mr. Martin in the '60s to be one of his many research assistants but refused this lowly position in his office. We still kept in touch. I liked and admired Paul Martin Sr. as I learned more of his splendid record of public service as a key 'liberal' reformer during his long legislative career. I recalled that he had threatened resignation as a Cabinet Minister if St. Laurent didn't proceed to fund the beginnings of Medicare. When he was Minister of External Affairs, I knew and respected many of Martin's talented assistants especially Dune Edmonds, his brilliant top hand who knew government and was an expert in foreign affairs. Paul Martin Senior didn't quit public life after this disastrous leadership defeat. He went on to become an excellent Minister of External Affairs in Trudeau's first Cabinet.[189] Then he entered the Senate as the Leader of the Government. Retiring from the Senate, he went on to serve as High Commissioner in London. Paul Martin Sr. remained a serious practitioner of 'progressive' politics and while the younger Liberals began to make fun and imitate his speaking style, I enjoyed his company and his insight when he took time to regale me on issues large and small. No one was more attentive about his riding in Windsor where he single-handedly turned the Windsor region into a Liberal stronghold, especially against extended CCF and labour support, no mean political feat.

[189] Paul Martin Sr. was always on the look for young ambitious staffers. When he was Minister of External Affairs, he had offered me a job as a researcher which I refused. Later, when I served John Turner as his Chief of Staff, he called and wondered why I turned him down. I told him that my highest mark in law school was in international law and he hadn't taken advantage of that. Several weeks later, he appointed me Special Advisor to the Minister of Defense who was attending a NATO defense meeting in Paris. I flew to Paris to attend that meeting and met Charles DeGaulle. After that, Paul Martin Sr. could do no wrong. He kept in regular contact, calling every second Saturday morning.

I took Carole to visit him that Saturday early evening at his spacious suite at Chateau Laurier in Ottawa after the leadership race had ended. We were ushered into his elegant capacious suite. He was sitting dejected on the side of the king-sized bed in short sleeves and large suspenders, his withered left arm and shoulder noticeable. His family and key supporters were gathered about him, morose, and complaining about how Trudeau 'stole the leadership' and that he was not even a Liberal. Paul Martin Jr. was sitting beside him, eyes red and tearing, comforting his father. Suddenly Paul Sr. became aware of the grousing about Trudeau. "*We will have none of that*", he said fiercely. "*He is now our leader and we will be loyal to our leader.*"

Then he got off the bed and asked Paul to help him put on his well-tailored, double-breasted jacket that hid his withered left shoulder and arm. "*Come on, Paul, let's go out and thank our supporters.*" He thanked me warmly for my visit and we watched as, arm-in-arm with Paul Jr., all smiles and cheerful, he walked down the rich heavy carpet towards his waiting supporters. It was a scene I will never forget. And I am sure that that leadership experience was branded deep in Paul Jr.'s brain.

After that, Paul Jr. and I kept in irregular touch. I followed his career when he attended my law school at University of Toronto. I was delighted when his classmates and professors told me how well he had done. By all accounts, he was a solid student, popular with both the teaching staff and his fellow students. Paul decided to seek a business career rather than law. He worked for another good friend, the trail blazer Maurice Strong,[190] as his

[190] I became acquainted with Maurice Strong when he worked in Ottawa for Mr. Pearson. Maurice asked me to advise him on the draft CIDA legislation. Maurice wanted me to give him my views and make suggestions which I did. Pearson made Maurice the founding head of the Canadian Development Corporation. Maurice had an innovative mind and fostered

Executive Assistant in Montreal at Power Corp. and continued at Power Corp under Paul Desmarais when Strong left to build a sterling record in international development politics. When Paul Jr. decided to break out on his own, it was Paul Desmarais that allowed Paul the opportunity to acquire the moribund Canada Steamship Line, modernize it and turned into a profitable and growing international enterprise which, he did on his own with just one financial partner.

On my periodic visits to Montreal, I went to chat with Maurice Strong and John Rae and later Serge Joyal who all worked for Paul Desmarais at the Power Corp., I would drop in to see Paul, talk about his father who went on to have a distinguished career in the Senate and then as Canada's High Commissioner to England. I had visited London often on business during that period and was told by all that Paul Sr. was a notable and outstanding representative for Canada, considered by most experts as the 'best' ever. Paul Sr. did what no other Canadian High Commissioner had ever done. He astonished the staid diplomatic establishment in London. He travelled the length and breadth of England speaking and reaching out to audiences large and small, as if he were still campaigning in Windsor, Ontario.[191] When Paul Sr. left public life, he returned to Windsor to teach in the Liberal fortress Paul Sr. had created. I asked Paul Sr. to act on an advisory committee of a small cable communications company located in Windsor which I had cofounded. He did

---

a superb network of institutional and business players around the globe from China to Europe to Africa. He can be considered one of the founders of the global 'climate change' movement.

[191] During this period, the head office of a small telecommunications company I co-founded was in Reading, U.K. I was invited to visit a private men's club in Reading and several members regaled me with Paul Martin Senior's memorable visits.

so with lively interest. I spent time with him as I listened to his always interesting 'war stories' and his take on the current state of the Liberal Party.

Paul Jr.'s stories of his father were always part of our chats. Paul Sr. was fiercely proud of Paul Jr.'s business accomplishments and, though with some reluctance, I sensed he lived in high expectations of Paul entering public service.

I knew Paul Jr. was destined for politics and public service whether he knew it himself at the time. Politics was in his blood and he, I believed, wanted to vindicate his father as all sons do. Paul was not immersed in hubris. Paul initially wanted to make a difference by serving at an international organization like the World Bank. Once decided about politics, Paul's admitted political goal, if he had one, was to follow in the footsteps of C.D. Howe, the famous American-born engineer and businessman who under King became the economic czar and driver of Canada's post-war growth. Paul aspired to be Industry Minister to bring business like methods he felt so lacking in government. At the last minute, implored by his ambitious loyal circle of advisors, he changed his mind and sought to become Minister of Finance, the most powerful of all ministers, where he knew he could make a difference. Both Turner and Chrétien had served as Ministers of Finance and his entourage saw this as a prelude to the Prime Ministership.

Paul Jr., unlike his father, attracted a large, boisterous, bright, and talented entourage beyond his office, including a wide circle of financial backers, some in Toronto who I knew, who remained loyal to him from his start as an M.P., then as a successful Minister of Finance, and continued as Prime Minister. The one I knew best and respected for his work on the National Liberal executive was Mike Robinson. Robinson, unlike most of the others in the entourage who had deep experience in party politics, was open-minded and knew the innards of the Liberal Party and was well liked. Mitchell Sharp, no fan, considered Martin 'perhaps the most successful Minister of Finance' in Canadian history. Paul transformed Ottawa's deficit and debt-ridden national accounts to deficit reduction and surplus while maintaining a strong social net – a miraculous feat at the time when debt and deficit were not Canadian preoccupations either by the Party, the bureaucracy or the public.

The public rarely is concerned about the 'nuts and bolts' of the economy. Martin, when he took the reins as Minister of Finance, was aghast when he discovered that there was not one single set of public accounts in one place for all of Canada's costs or liabilities, revenues, and expenditures. Martin changed all that. He and his clever quick-witted deputy, David Dodge, worked well in harness together to make the public accounts more transparent. He set out defined restraints to reduce the deficit debt and keep the revenues in line with expenditures. He famously decided with Jean Chrétien's concurrence, that half the surplus revenues would be allocated for new spending and the other half for debt reduction. During his tight fisted yet, socially sensitive policies, all were surprised at how quickly his tough measures turned around Canada's accounts making Canada the economic leader in the Group of Seven in growth and careful management during his tenure. Martin earned an instant reputation in international economic circles. Martin's small, tight, and restless entourage urged him to run as leader against Chrétien as they felt Martin had earned his stripes to become leader and especially what they considered was Chrétien's demeaning attitude towards him. While Chrétien as Prime Minister supported Martin's major measures as Minister of Finance, there was friction on details, timing, and interventions by Chrétien and his staff that Martin found unnecessary and irritating. At times, Martin felt he was being unfairly micromanaged.

Paul, charming and relaxed in person, suffered a slight speech defect which he worked hard to overcome. As a youth, he suffered briefly from polio and worked to fully recover his health. After the urging of his wide circle of business and political friends that he regularly hosted at his pleasant farm house in rural Quebec, he finally chose to run in Quebec in LaSalle-Émard. Chrétien, who he didn't know him well, urged him to run in Windsor. Paul wisely chose a Quebec French-Canadian riding. His French grew even more fluent and he learned to speak easily in public, always with self-deprecating humour. He soon overcame his initial halting delivery.

Paul Sr., the Liberal Party's consistent progressive throughout his long career, had never been wholly accepted by the Liberal Party elites and Paul Jr., while accepted, was wary of the old party established elites as he built a young close knit, staunchly totally loyal closed mouthed team around him.

What triggered the rivalry between Chrétien and Martin was complex, but rivals they were and heated rivals they became. Both had close ties to the Desmarais hegemony.[192] At the urging of his restless entourage, Martin ran against Chrétien for leadership as a newly minted M.P. Chrétien found this action upsetting as he felt he had more than earned support for leadership due to his unstinting hard work and longtime loyalty to the Party. Chrétien felt, with some legitimacy, that he had earned the

[192] Paul Desmarais, one of Canada's most successful entrepreneurs and most powerful businessmen, who started in North Ontario turning an almost insolvent bus company around, moved to Montreal and made his mark in finance and international investment. Desmarais's scope of influence, a conservative by instinct, included Brian Mulroney, Pierre Trudeau, Jean Chrétien (whose daughter married Desmarais's son), and Paul Martin who each in their own way vied for his attention and approval and largesse. Desmarais attracted young ambitious assistants to the Power Corp. with mature political skills like John Rae and Serge Joyal.

leadership. Then, as Chrétien's problems grew, Martin ran openly against Chrétien, animated by his loyalist team while he was in Cabinet. The seeds of rivalry by then were deeply planted. While Chrétien was Prime Minister, Martin organized a tough capable circle inside the caucus and amongst the national Liberal Party Executive and plotted to dislodge Chrétien, which he did. His entourage was impatient. Chrétien had bruising encounters with Martin over his budget. Chrétien, believing Martin was disloyal and running behind his back, confronted him. Martin denied his disloyalty. It was his ambitious team that broke out ahead of Martin's own plans. It was an uncharted and difficult time for a party long accustomed to party unity. Chrétien, with his assistant Eddy Goldenberg, orchestrated Martin's resignation as Finance Minister. Martin, undaunted, continued as a Member of Parliament. He knew Chrétien's tenure was growing weaker and his time would soon come.

When Martin immediately threw his hat quickly in the ring to run again for leadership after Chrétien formerly resigned, Chrétien chose to hang on as Prime Minister before giving up the office, an old political friend and colleague, Jack Austin, now a Senatorial colleague and an early supporter of Paul Sr. – soon to be Liberal Leader in the Senate and a talented politician and businessman – urged me to support Paul Jr. A private meeting was quickly arranged. Paul opened with shared reminisces of his father. Then Paul gingerly got to the point. "*Are you with me?*" "*Yes*", I said, "*On two conditions. First, as you know, I am an unwavering supporter of Israel.*" Paul nodded with a smile and recounted how Paul Sr. was a staunch supporter of Israel as was he. He told me tales of listening to his father discuss Israel with others like 'Laz' Phillips, a Jewish Senator from Montreal. "*Second*", I told him, "*I am also an unwavering opponent to Meech Lake or the ideas of weakening the central government.*" Paul wasn't. While I respected his views, I would continue to speak out on this issue, I advised him. He understood and did not disagree. As always, he was witty, self-deprecated, and modest. "*Keep in touch*", as he warmly put his arm around my shoulder, shook hands, and led me out of his office. It was hard to dislike Paul Martin.

Paul Martin as Minister of Finance was always under the watchful eye of Chrétien as Prime Minister and his staff. Chrétien resented or at least seemed irritated by Martin's growing popularity and his economic successes at home and abroad and would subtly - and at times not too subtly, undermine him. It became more obvious when Chrétien, having promised to leave as Prime Minister, held on. The chances of Liberal continuity diminished as Chrétien became personally embroiled in the 'Shawinigate Affair' - a sordid tale of a golf course, owned by Chrétien and some old friends and whose faltering financing had been shored up from federal sources and later the Sponsorship scandal arising from the last Referendum campaign in Quebec that burst out in the public after the Auditor General's Report pointed out the use of public funds that were recycled to the Liberal Party while some stuck to the pockets of Liberal party intermediaries.

Martin, whose abrupt resignation as Minister of Finance had been orchestrated by Chrétien and his aides, quickly moved and took control of the Liberal caucus while his disagreements with Chrétien burned not far below the surface. A key Martin supporter became caucus chair and aroused Chrétien's wrath. Chrétien was criticized at the opening of a national caucus meeting. It was an unheard act of defiance. Chrétien was furious at this open display of disloyalty. He finally succumbed and surrendered his leadership. Martin, with careful organization and precision, won the Leadership race and as Prime Minister, immediately took steps to name a Judicial Inquiry to investigate the Auditor-General's Report on the Sponsorship scandal. Chrétien had implored Martin to let him take the heat alone for the Sponsorship scandal. Martin paid no heed and moved towards leadership, no longer trusting Chrétien. Few in the Party had any knowledge of this abuse of public funds. Chrétien's testimony at the Judicial Inquiry was clever, but not completely convincing. Martin, the first sitting Prime Minister in history to give evidence at a public Judicial Inquiry, was exonerated, but it was too late. Much later, Chrétien was vindicated in the courts, but by then, it was forgotten history.[193] Both suffered, Chrétien and Martin, and the Liberal Party in the process. Paul Martin had the courage to clean the deck of this lingering scandal. He never regretted this decision. Was it politically wise? This remains another question.

The Liberal Party, under the merciless onslaught of the freshly minted Conservative leader Stephen Harper who had 'united the right', failed to recover. So, Harper pushed Martin and Liberals into a minority government. In the short period as Prime Minister, Martin moved on many fronts, too many so some say. He admitted he had difficulty setting out his priorities and as a policy 'wonk' enjoyed the challenge on moving on all fronts at the same time. He manifested a thirst to make his mark on issues large and small. Endlessly curious about issues, large and small, and those that arose on the world scene, Martin's attention moved from one troubled region to another. Martin was interested in them all.

---

[193] Martin also fired Chrétien's longtime friend and former Chief of Staff, Jean Pelletier who had been appointed head of Via Rail just before Chrétien resigned. Pelletier sued in the courts. After a ten-year long legal battle, Pelletier was vindicated receiving handsome damages for wrongful dismissal, loss to his reputation, and costs. Pelletier died shortly thereafter of a heart attack.

One little known chapter of Paul Martin's skill and expertise is his unblemished reputation on the international economic front. During his tenure as Finance Minister and Prime Minister, there were uncertain economic times at home and abroad. As Minister of Finance, his austerity program worked wonders putting Canada on the road to recovery and growth. Paul Martin's leadership at the World Bank when Americans suffered economic turbulence is a chapter of history yet to be written. Historians may be surprised how expertly and modestly Martin performed on the international front as he demonstrated his understated leadership to resolve these threats to global economic security.

Martin led on the Kelowna Accord with a detailed action plan on Aboriginal issues that Harper tore up when he gained the Prime Minister's office. Martin introduced 'same sex' marriage legislation. He led on all these issues. First and foremost, he recognized the dichotomy between the growing needs of the cities of Canada and the cities' sparse tax base. The cities narrow financial base based mainly on realty taxes had been ignored too long. Martin was the first Prime Minister not only to define this disparity but moved to renovate it. The shift from farm to city was accelerating. Martin convened a meeting with the mayors of cities at a pioneering 'Conference on Cities'. He wanted provincial and federal taxes allocated to help cities. Martin reorganized the spiraling urban infrastructure deficit. Billions were needed for infrastructure renovation. A plan was developed and offered a three-part financial formula – 1/3 from the federal government, 1/3 from the provincial, and 1/3 from the cities for the infrastructure city needs – a reform desperately required.

Martin demonstrated high energy across a range of international issues, especially in the turbulent continent of Africa. He picked up and increased the influence of Canada started by John Diefenbaker, Brian Mulroney, and Jean Chrétien which he highlighted and expanded the Group of Seven efforts to reach an accord to coordinate aid and other efforts in Africa. Martin had travelled widely in Africa and had a capacious appetite to involve himself in almost intractable problems from Darfur to Somalia to Rwanda. One is left with the impression that he wanted to do so much but had so little time to make a deeper difference on the foreign front. Martin, recognizing the increasing costs of healthcare and the diminishing cost-benefit results, he shortened 'wait times'. Martin sought to rationalize and establish clear goals of costs and effects for our burgeoning health system. Once Martin gracefully resigned, his successors Dion and Ignatieff, both suffering from lingering Party divisions, underperformed. Only with the advent of Justin Trudeau were party rivalries dissolved. It was a new day. The Liberal Party was united again.

Martin's final moments as Prime Minister were disappointing to him and his devout supporters. He seemed rushed and uptight at times. One of his final private acts as Prime Minister was a farewell reception for David Dodge, his Deputy Minister of Finance. All senior bureaucrats were in attendance. I, as Chairman of the Senate Banking Committee, and few outsiders were invited. Paul was at ease, richly confident, and superb as he poked fun at himself and his time as Minister of Finance and Prime Minister. All were amazed at his relaxed mood, his warmth, ease of his remarks, humour, and self-deprecation at this event. The consensus of the attendees was that if the public saw this side of Paul Martin, he would have held his Prime Ministership.

A final vignette that exemplifies Paul Martin's great intentions and unfulfilled promises. When Paul Martin made his farewell address to the Liberal caucus, it was long and passionate with precise details and brimming with his unfinished agenda. So, he started, as he proclaimed, to set out his priorities for future of the Liberal Party. After the fulsome credits he gave to his

Cabinet and his advisors, he got to the meat of his comments, 'the three priorities' for the Liberal Party. I counted that by the time he finished to great applause, he had set out thirteen priorities. This was Paul Martin. He wanted to do so much and was afforded so little time. On the plane back to Toronto, I sat next to Navdeen Bain, a rising star in the Liberal Party and an avid supporter of Paul Martin's leadership. He turned to me with eyes still glistening, "*That was the greatest speech I ever heard*", he said quietly. "*Paul was so articulate. He set out the priorities for the Party.*" I gently reminded him that Paul had set out thirteen priorities for the Party. "*Which ones did he think were priorities?*" We smiled and reflected on the good man that Paul Martin was and is. He wanted to do so much to make a difference.

In his autobiography, '*Hell or High Water*', he listed a basketful of issues on the national and international front, all set out with equal priority – the unfinished agenda of an erstwhile, diligent leadership.

After his retirement, Martin, ever curious, ever restless, continues to devote himself to public interest projects. He takes a special interest in Africa, international financial institutions, and above all, ideas to provide a platform for Aboriginal self-development in business and good governance. He remains approachable and earnest in demeanour, never ceasing to do good works. His helpmate and supporter in all his endeavours and wise advisor is his wife Sheila whose counsel and calmness he sought and deployed all the while she raised a robust and talented family. Family counts. Paul Jr. surpassed the accomplishments of Paul Sr., a respectful and dutiful son in many ways. Paul Sr. would not have been surprised. Nothing less was expected of his only son.

- *Hell or High Water: My Life in and out of Politics* by Paul Martin (Emblem Edition, 2009)

Paul Martin Jr. - Maiden Speech

316 COMMONS DEBATES December 19, 1988

Canada-U.S. Free Trade Agreement

Such services attest to the spirit of co-operation we have been able to create in trade union circles, industry, education as well as at other Government levels.

[*English*]

Members of the House are well aware that structural problems exist in our labour market that have to be addressed. Our level of unemployment is still too high in the regions. We are still producing skills that do not match demand. The relationship between the productivity of workers and their education is a question that continually preoccupies policy makers, and particularly this Government.

We must continue to take advantage of our resources and apply Canadian know-how and expertise so that our educated workforce will be tuned in to the realities of today's labour market. It will call on the involvement and co-operation of Canadians from every sector to participate and accept some responsibility in that. This Government is totally committed to ensuring that Canadians have the best possible labour market programs. We have programs already in place that are working. We anticipate whatever advice Mr. de Grandpre and his committee will present. We are prepared to act on their recommendations.

Adjustment means change, but it also means opportunity. What Canadian workers must know is that we will draw on the resources not just of the Government but of all the communities of Canada to help Canadian workers take advantage of opportunity, to help them when they are in need of change after a lay-off and in need of assistance. All of us must be there for our workers to ensure that they can take advantage of opportunities, to ensure that, in troubled times, we are there to help them. Adjustment does mean change, but the Government must help with the opportunities that are. We intend to ensure that we will be there for Canadian workers, rather than waste time trying to decide whether an opportunity or a problem comes from free trade, comes from technological change, or comes from labour-management relations. What is important for Canadian workers to know is that whatever the circumstances, whatever their region, whatever the product their company makes, whatever future they want for themselves, this Government is there hand-in-hand with the company, with management, with the unions, with the provinces, for Canadian workers. We will continue to be there for them.

Some Hon. Members: Hear, hear!

[*Translation*]

Mr. Paul Martin (LaSalle—Émard): Mr. Speaker, on June 18, 1936, the new Member for Essex East spoke in this House for the first time. His name was Paul Martin.

I can do no better than to begin here with his words, and I quote, "I feel conscious of my responsibility and trust that my remarks will meet with the approval of my constituents."

[*English*]

My father had been in the House a year before he spoke that I have been here less than two weeks. Times have certainly changed. But as that young Member did 52 years ago, I would like first and foremost to thank the voters of my riding for their trust without which I would not be here.

[*Translation*]

The riding of LaSalle—Émard has two waterways of historic importance for our country. They are the Lachine Rapids, a unique ecological entity, from which the exploration of the North American continent began, and the Lachine Canal, which has contributed so much to the economic development of Quebec.

Together, my constituents are a microcosm of the Canadian mosaic, an enthusiastic and dynamic community. I would like to say here that I am proud to be their representative.

[*English*]

I cannot count the number of times as a young boy I sat in the galleries above and watched the debates below. In recent years I have had the occasion to visit the legislative chambers of a great number of the world's democracies. Some are older than ours; some are more famous; and many are larger. But I remain convinced that none is more representative and more true to the character of its people than this House.

• (1610)

I have worked in the corporate world where members often believe the real power over the country's destiny resides with them. I have visited the offices of the Ministers and great bureaucrats who dwell in this city. There, too, I have been told that it is there and not here that the real power lies. In both cases I have never believed it.

For me, elected office is one of the highest callings a citizen can have. As such, I deeply believe in the traditions and dignity of this House of Commons, although I sometimes wonder whether that view is as deeply held today as it was once. I hope so, for it is here over the next four years that the future of Canada for generations to come will be determined.

[*Translation*]

Mr. Speaker, we have just been through an election campaign during which, thanks to the leadership of the Leader of the Opposition, Canadians at last began the necessary process of thinking together about their economic future and therefore about the kind of country in which they wanted to live. This process is far from over.

Mr. Speaker, I am proud to be part of the new wave of Quebec entrepreneurs. This Government has nothing to teach me about the benefits of freer trade, but I tell you—

[*English*]

You want a job? Is the Minister of homelessness still talking? The Deputy Prime Minister (Mr. Mazankowski) referred to me as a free trader. I am a free trader. But we are not debating free trade here; we are debating trade disarmament.

[*Translation*]

What was the purpose of the negotiations, if not secure access to the American market? Did we get it? No. The Government's strategy failed and the results of this failure will be felt by generations to come. The resulting agreement is neither fish nor fowl, a sectorial agreement with all the advantages of a comprehensive agreement, one in which the Government has almost set aside its role in the economy for years to come. Our problem was and is that the Americans refuse to accept our subsidizing our industries, while they refuse to admit that they subsidize theirs.

[*English*]

The Government sought greater access to the American market, but in fact by failing to come to an agreement on the definition of subsidies before signing, it lost ground. By putting off that decision, the Tories have jeopardized whatever possibilities of success might have existed. Second, they have effectively negated the ability of the Canadian private sector to work with its Government as does the private sector of virtually every other modern state in the world.

Mr. McDermid: Why is the private sector supporting us?

Mr. Martin (Lasalle—Émard): Why do you not try to listen, you might learn something.

Mr. McDermid: Why is the private sector supporting us? What a silly statement.

Mr. Martin (Lasalle—Émard): Are you telling me? I have been in the business world for four years while you have been—

Mr. Deputy Speaker: Order. I would like Members to address their remarks through the Chair.

Mr. Martin (Lasalle—Émard): I am sorry, Mr. Speaker. It is hard when faced with ignorance.

[*Translation*]

The problem is that the Conservatives do not understand the mechanisms of the world economy as we near the end of the century and that is why the next four years will be decisive. That is why the Liberal Party will play a key role. That is why we will be there to see how subsidies are defined.

[*English*]

We will be watching to see if the Government fights for a definition of subsidy that simply does not protect existing programs but provides for new ones so that new opportunities can be created in Atlantic Canada and so that the western base can be diversified.

[*Translation*]

Yes, we will be there to minimize the harmful effects of this Agreement on our social programs, our agricultural sector, our cultural industries and our environment. We will watch the American takeover of our small and medium-sized businesses, because without these companies, we would lose any possibility of creating our own multinationals. We will be there to see whether the Government allows the Americans to say that our subsidies are unfair, while their billions for Star Wars, as part of their industrial policy, are not.

[*English*]

We will be watching to see if the Government allows the Americans to continue to restructure their economy by using the unique Chapter Eleven bankruptcy provisions and claim that that is not a subsidy while claiming that our modernization grants are a subsidy.

We will be watching to see if the Government allows our export subsidies to be restricted while the Americans use massive domestic subsidies to prevent our exporters from gaining a foothold in their market.

We will be watching to see if the Government adopts the American model of industrial development which works for them but which cannot work for us if we are to have any ambition beyond being enveloped in the American cocoon.

We will be watching to see if the Government has a trade agenda for Canadian entrepreneurs who want to go not just to Pittsburgh but to Panang, who want to go not just to San Diego, but to Sao Paolo.

We will be watching to see what new steps the Government is prepared to take in terms of R and D and procurement policy to ensure that Canada's manufacturing base is not hollowed out and given away.

We will be watching the dispute settlement mechanism to see if it evolves beyond the Congress' rubber stamp into a truly bi-national body that serves the interests of both countries.

We will ask that the Government not allow the Americans to simply apply American law and American practice to our exports. When Congress refuses, we will ask of the Government why it signed the deal in the first place.

Finally, we will ask about plant closings. Every day the Government denies any linkage with the Free Trade Agreement. Does it not understand that due to the rationalization of industry in the United States the burden of change will be and is being felt primarily by the Canadian subsidiaries of American companies and that this agreement has eliminated much of the protection we previously had?

During the debate the Government kept pointing to the agreement and saying nothing in it touched our social programs when the problem was that there was nothing in it to protect them. The fact is that there is nothing in this agreement that allows us to prevent closings such as Gillette's. There is nothing in this agreement that would allow us to do as the French Government did when Gillette sought to close their plant in Anec. That is the problem. Canadians have been misled in this agreement and anyone who has been in the business world more than five minutes understands it. That is why—

Mr. McDermid: Oh, come on.

Mr. Martin (Lasalle—Émard): Within two days of the signing of this agreement, chief executive officer after chief executive officer admitted that our social programs are in jeopardy—

Some Hon. Members: False.

Mr. Martin (Lasalle—Émard): —because of the need to harmonize with the United States. If Members opposite deny it then they are simply demonstrating that they may well have been clerks in the business world but never had to make a decision in their lives.

Mr. McDermid: Be careful. You are not the only businessman in the House.

Mr. Martin (Lasalle—Émard): I ask Members opposite: Why do they deny facts that the whole business world knows are true?

An Hon. Member: Get serious.

Mr. McDermid: There are a lot of business people in this House. You are not the only one.

Mr. Martin (Lasalle—Émard): I have not seen very many. I spent a long time in the business world. Let me say that I have not seen any of the Members opposite anywhere.

You do not have to be a businessman and have a lack of compassion. The business community has it and understands it. It may well be that the businessmen who do not have compassion become Tory Members of Parliament.

Where are the worker adjustment programs? Where are the policies and strategies to deal with the thousands of Canadians who have lost their jobs? The answer is that there are no such programs. If Members opposite think there are, they ought to go to the streets where the Minister of homelessness has put the people who have lost their homes to find out.

[*Translation*]

The problem will not disappear simply because the Minister or the Conservatives refuse to admit it exists. If the Conservatives think that existing programs are adequate with or without free trade, they should go to my constituency and tell it to the 2,000 people who have lost their jobs since 1984.

An Hon. Member: The employees of Voyageur!

• (1620)

[*English*]

Would you like a bus pass?

Mr. Blais: No, no.

Mr. Martin (Lasalle—Émard): Well, we wouldn't allow certain people on. We really do have standards.

Canada is not a delicate and fragile plant needing to be kept in a hothouse, but no country can survive in a globally competitive world without business and government co-operating to invest in people and in their futures.

We are entering into a new era in the international economy. Our country will not prosper in the global market-place simply because it has a captive market. It will prosper because its workers are prepared to accept change, and they will not if the rewards of change are to be enjoyed elsewhere and they are compelled to shoulder alone the burden of sacrifice.

[*Translation*]

Where does the road to our future lie, Mr. Speaker? We must, of course, continue to sell to the United States, but we must also be able to sell our environment protection technology to Japan, penetrate the European market by 1992 and sell our management techniques to the Third World.

In order to achieve these future goals, the public and private sectors will have to co-ordinate their actions. But that co-ordination requires that the Government determine the definition of the term "subsidy", thereby setting the boundaries for co-operation between the state and industry.

Mr. Speaker, this debate is about more than free trade. Indeed, in this House, there are deep philosophical differences that run deeper than the wording of any bill, even deeper than partisanship.

To my left are the NDP, who think that Canada should keep to itself, disregard major world trends and shy away from international involvement.

The Conservatives, on the other hand, Mr. Speaker, still firmly believe in an obsolete free market theory and a timid hands-off approach to the future.

The Liberal Party sees the future in another light.

[*English*]

I simply ask you in conclusion, Mr. Speaker, what would Canada have looked like if, over the last 50 years, we had had a federal Government as crippled by its own lack of will, vision and purpose, and I must say common decency, as this one? I simply ask you, Mr. Speaker, what sort of a country will we have in the future if the industrial governance of Canada is left to 10 aggressive provinces confronting a do-nothing centre with our economic policy being cabled to us from Washington?

We are at an important crossroads. We can either become an economic force with which to be reckoned, with our private sector working in concert with a strong national government, or we will die a slow death as a branch-plant economy with a central government to match. That is what this election was all about. That is why the next election will be fought on the ashes of this agreement. However, the next time, the Canadian people will not buy an illusion and a snare.

Some Hon. Members: Hear, hear!

[*Translation*]

Hon. Robert de Cotret (Minister of Regional Industrial Expansion and Minister of State for Science and Technology): Mr. Speaker, I am pleased to rise today to briefly describe the benefits of the proposed Canada-United States Free Trade Agreement and the Canadian business reality.

I think all Hon. Members will realize as well as I do the exceptional growth of the Canadian economy over these last few years, a kind of growth that brought employment to a record level, with job creation that surpassed that of any of the various countries of the European Economic Community, and which in percentage terms has been higher than in any industrialized nation, the 1.3 million new jobs created having led to a rapid decline in the unemployment rate which had become unacceptable. Also over the period Canada experienced a reasonable and above all a stable inflation rate, and in real terms growth surpassed not only that in European countries and the United States but also in Japan, which gave this country the highest real economic growth rate in the world. That is the Canadian economic reality! A reality created by the excellence, expertise and productivity of our human resources and by the abundance of and demand for our natural resources on the international markets.

Mr. Speaker, despite our achievements over these last few years, the Canadian Government cannot afford to become complacent. More and more we are dealing with a strong international market, an international market where there is daily evidence of the impact of rapid technological change on the flow of goods and even services between businesses and individuals of various countries. An international market that is constantly changing, a market that is becoming increasingly global, a market that results in the creation of larger and larger, stronger and stronger trading blocks.

And therein lies one of the basic reasons for the Canadian Government and for Canadians as they did on

Stephen Harper

The Amazing Rise of Stephen Harper and The New West

(22nd)

Date Elected to Parliament:	November 21, 1988
Date of Maiden Speech:	January 20, 1994
Date Sworn In:	February 6, 2006
Date Left Office:	November 3, 2015

No Prime Minister in modern Canadian history can match Stephen Harper's[194] spectacular rise to political power. Harper constructed his own political party in modern times as his launching pad to political power, the only federal leader to do so in the 20th century

Born of English stock in Leaside, a pleasant suburb in the east end of Toronto in 1959, he came from a middle-class Liberal family. His father was a World War II veteran and then a successful executive of Imperial Oil. When the family fortunes improved, the family moved to the more comfortable western suburb of Toronto in Etobicoke. There, Harper went to public school, joined the student Young Liberals and then onto University of Toronto where he commenced his studies in economics and political science. His passion was, and is, hockey.

[194] Stephen Joseph Harper is his full name. The name Joseph is after his father who had a profound influence in his life.

While Prime Minister, he wrote an excellent book on hockey.[195] An indifferent player, he is a lifelong fan of Canada's national pastime. An accomplished musician, he was in tune with the range of new music of his times. For relaxation, he led, played, and sang in a small upbeat band.

Dissatisfied with opportunities in Toronto, he decided to go west to seek a new start on his own. He made his way west to settle in Calgary, Alberta, where he continued his university studies in economics, perhaps due to his father's interest in accounting. He was bright, thoughtful, and made economics his specialty where he excelled. Alberta, the birth place of the radical Social Credit in the '30s, was then the hotbed of dynamic Conservatism. Unhappy with federal policies and leadership direction that tilted towards central Canada, especially Quebec, leaving the rising power and economic punch of energy-rich Alberta out of the federal power loop, Harper, a contrarian, became an avid pro Westerner whose benchmark plaint was the feeling of western alienation. The chronic western complaint was that the west was providing more than its fair share of taxes to the federal government coffers and got little in return especially respect. Disenchanted with Trudeau's National Energy policy (NEP), Harper became a deep blue conservative true believer. NEP, the hated Trudeau policy, introduced by Quebecer Marc Lalonde, was seen as arrogant and insensitive to western concerns. Quebec, Albertans felt, got an unfair share of the federal coffers especially after Alberta was contributing more than a fair share of federal taxes from its growing energy resources. It was the era of Peter Lougheed who gave rebirth to the newish Progressive Conservative Party. Pierre Trudeau's National Energy Policy (NEP) pushed Alberta further,

---

[195] *A Great Game: The Forgotten Leafs and the Rise of Professional Hockey* (Simon and Schuster, 2013).

alienating the west while disengaging with the established parties in the east. During the '80s oil crisis with gas prices escalating to new heights in the east, Lougheed declared, "*Let them freeze*"!

Harper zigzagged from job-to-job, moving with lightning speed, all geared to his rising political ambitions. Harper became Executive Director of the Canada Alliance that railed against taxes. Taxes was always a hot button in Alberta. Alberta had the lowest tax regime in Canada. Taxes, Alberta felt, benefited Canada – the rest of Canada – Ontario, Quebec and the Maritimes while Alberta got little in return. He felt after careful study that the complex transfer payments formulated by federal Liberals were tilted against Alberta. Harper served a stint as a policy assistant and speech writer in Ottawa to Jim Hawkes, an Alberta Conservative Member of Parliament who later Harper successfully defeated for the Progressive Conservative nomination and went on to win in 1993 in his Hawkes Calgary riding. Pierre Trudeau's toehold in the West, especially Alberta, was almost wiped out in 1980. Liberals never regained traction even though Joe Clark had gained the Prime Ministership in 1979 for five months before Trudeau returned to the public stage and soundly defeated him in 1980. In that campaign, it was Keith Davey's idea to 'low bridge' Trudeau whose personality was unpopular across Canada especially in Alberta, whose Liberal policies, popular elsewhere, were not exempt from the taint of the NEP. Clark's modest increase in gas taxes became, oddly, a potent point in Clark's electoral defeat in Ontario, Quebec, and the Maritimes.

A tall, pleasant, sturdy looking, soft-spoken, restrained man, Harper began to gain weight and with it, a certain gravitas. He seemed older than his age. He spoke carefully and fluently never adding an unnecessary word. Meanwhile, Harper gained an adequate fluency in French. From Executive Director of the

National Citizens Coalition, an organization aimed to reduce taxation, he joined Preston Manning in the founding of the Reform Party. Preston, son of Ernest Manning, the successful and undaunted Social Credit Leader and long serving Premier of Alberta, who upon retirement, was appointed to the Senate by Pierre Trudeau. This did little to ease the alienated west and especially Peter Lougheed who swept the Progressive Conservatives to provincial power whipping the long entrenched Social Credit. The national energy crisis fermented by the OPEC cartel that controlled international oil prices exposed east-west fissures was exacerbated by Trudeau's NEP and the endless demands of Quebec for a 'special treatment', calls for 'distinct society' and special consideration on all fronts was seen as Trojan horse for even more taxpayer dollars.

I ran Red Leaf, the Liberal media consortium, for the Trudeau Liberals in the Trudeau federal campaigns. Joe, whose stumbles as Prime Minister, were magnified. It was not a difficult task. Trudeau lost to Clark in 1979 to quickly regain power in 1980. The alienation of the West continued to simmer, and Harper was in the thick of whipping up the sources of its frustration and complaints. Even the reform of the Senate – the three E's – Equal, Elected, Effective – became a rallying cry against the power tilt to Ontario, Quebec, and the Maritimes.[196]

Manning, the son of the long serving Social Credit Albert Premier, Earnes V. Manning started the Reform Party. Preston Manning, in manner and bearing nor speaking style, was not his father's son. Harper became an activist co-founding member of this new party. Manning's aim was to gain power parity with the eastern based Liberals and Progressive Conservative Parties, both

[196] Under the BNA, Quebec was entitled to 20% of the Senate, notwithstanding change in demographics.

heavily bound to their urban voter bases in British Columbia, Ontario, Quebec, and the Maritimes. The socialist NDP were not an option in Alberta while the NDP retained resonance in Saskatchewan. Once Harper became Manning's policy advisor, he quickly sensed Manning's Reform policies and style were ineffective. So, he challenged Manning for leadership, took down Manning, and shrewdly became the Leader of the Reform Party. Ever the pragmatist and student of politics, he quickly gained entry into Parliament in 1993, on his path to national power in a Calgary riding where he had displaced Jim Hawkes, the federal Progressive Conservative Member of Parliament he had worked for. Harper quickly recognized that a marginal fringe party like the Reform with its radical far right membership and social policies was not feasible to gain federal power. He needed to tack towards centre right – 'to unite the right'. Harper skillfully engineered meetings between his Reform group and the Progressive Conservatives led by Peter MacKay. Soon after, he emerged as the undisputed leader of a merged party, the new and renamed Conservative Party in 2003. No federal political leader accomplished this swift rise to prominence from the margins of politics in so short a period while always expanding on his own political base.

As an effective Leader of the Opposition in Parliament with a dizzying number of federal elections, he finally emerged as Prime Minister in a minority Parliament in 2006 and held power with the longest minority government in Canada's history until he finally gained a majority in 2011. No doubt he benefited from the disunity within the bowels of the Liberal Party and the patent failure of the meandering NDP. He skillfully maneuvered on the right and centre and against the centre left held by Liberals and the further left socialist NDP that divided the centre left vote to gain traction and finally his majority in Parliament. Harper demonstrated a disciplined, focused deftness to overcome incursions on the far-right attacks amplified by Liberals and by the NDP to push him and his Conservative Party further right.

As the Prime Minister who came from the far fringes of the Canadian political spectrum, Harper swiftly consolidated his support of his divided caucus and slowly moved inexorably to the centre right. He tilted to right when necessary but held a steady course. Because he understood that the radical extremists in his party would block his path to the centre right of the political spectrum, a political sweet spot, Harper handled his caucus with a deft and iron fist to prevent fissures that the both Liberal and the NDP targeted to exploit. Jean Chrétien, the master of 'wedge' politics, 'framed' Harper with a 'hidden agenda' while he cleverly alluded to the influences of the 'far right' allegedly 'racist' fringe former Reform members in the Conservative caucus. Chrétien, brilliant tactician that he was, drove a stake between Harper and his plan to occupy centre right public opinion. Chrétien surgically would use his favourite word 'balance' or '*baalonce*', to keep his Conservative opposition divided hoping to drive Harper back to the far right leaving the political centre left and right open for Chrétien to hold sway. Harper, as Opposition Leader, was quiet, calm, skilled, determined, and disciplined. Pushing out right extremists in his caucus was not viable, so he contained and muffled their voices. It was a scintillating juggling act to observe.

Harper had both his supporters and detractors in his caucus, but Harper kept his caucus intact and united. Extremists were expunged from caucus. Conservative Senate colleagues I spoke to regularly during this period admired Harper's no-nonsense approach, his daily tactics and his ability to weld his Cabinet caucus in a fighting unit. His thoughtful, quiet approach won him respect, if not adulation, in his caucus. The Conservative Senate Leader, Marjory LeBreton, a Harper loyalist and hardliner, kept the sometimes-unruly Senate in check. Several Progressive Conservative senators refused to sit in the Senate as part of the National Conservative Caucus with little effect on either the Senate or the Conservatives. These 'independents' seem to marginalize themselves to keep the 'faith'.

Once in power as Prime Minister, Harper continued to maintain an iron fist over his caucus and Cabinet. Ever mindful of his right, he tacked to and from the right when necessary. He, too, had learnt the history of the Conservatives, as had Clark and Mulroney. Conservatives 'ate' their leaders for breakfast starting with John Diefenbaker. Yet, no other leader in Canada had built his own political party from scratch or constructed his own pathway to the pinnacle of political power so deftly, or so quickly and in such a methodical way. Harper tended to keep his own counsel and his cards close to his vest. Harper maintained a secret weapon that he utilized throughout his political career. He was understated and underestimated. I believe he kept his ego in rein and benefited in the process. As a result, he continued to surprise friends and foes alike as he seemed from afar to move through the icebergs of politics with quiet effective self-imposed restraint.

Harper was not a spell binder as a speaker, but he was quiet, thoughtful, rational, and steady. He attained a certain serious demeanor. Like DeGaulle, he kept to himself. His caucus grew to respect him, if not like him. His Cabinet assiduously followed his careful powerful lead.

Harper was not a showboat. Charming in private, he had a rather remote stiff public appearance. He was persuasive in caucus and on the public stage with his calmness, unruffled manner, and obvious gravitas.

After he was defeated by Justin Trudeau in 2016, he left a strong united caucus of 90 members, a large enough group, well positioned to maintain a meaningful opposition. He left his party financially sound and free of debt. This was a major Harper legacy – fiscal soundness and it transformed other parties as well as they followed his lead. This was a key component of his architecture of his new Conservative Party. While he, at times, dissipated his avowed 'balanced budget' policies on the exigencies of the vacillating economy he continued to widen his centre right wing tent. A skilled economist, he was a sound fiscal manager. When he tacked to the right, he was quickly 'demonized' by both Liberals and NDP as an 'extremist', which he was not. He was the ultimate pragmatist on most major issues.

A 'conviction' politician by nature and deliberation, Harper deeply believed in human rights. He believed in a strong military. Respect for the military and their accomplishments at wars abroad merited public support. He believed in patriotism. He believed in limited government.[197] He manifested these beliefs and principles at home and abroad. A staunch opponent of Putin's thrust into Georgia and Putin's takeover of Crimea, Harper was perhaps the most outspoken and consistent of any western leader. At first, he spoke out against human rights abuses while in China. Later, he repeated his earlier exhortations to other states with egregious human rights records. He became

[197] John Turner argued that there are cycles in government. Clearly the size and scope of government and its increasing costs need closer review and constraints with care to 'respect the tax payer's dollars'. The size of government became mammoth and always in search of value for cyclical constraints and retrenchment. Democratic governments, by nature, grow if not restrained with rational plans and careful supervision. Money is a necessary antidote to avoid cyclical austerity in lean times. Keynes was careful in this regard. Few who espouse Keynes have studied him. Harper, an economist by education, had a clear understanding of public finance and believed that public expenditures should not crowd out private investment to maintain normal economic growth.

Israel's strongest supporter, believing as he did in Israel as the sole practitioner of democratic principles surrounded in a sea of autocratic Arab nations in the Middle East.

Immigration, always a messy undermanaged portfolio with vacillating objectives mirroring beliefs of minorities who kept up public pressure, was put in the hands of capable assiduous Jason Kenney, who also came from a Liberal family. Jason planned and plotted to reform immigration, shifting from refugee concerns to economic requirements and a merit driven immigration policy, while building a Conservative base in the ethnic communities once considered a monopoly for the Liberal Party. Jason Kenney, who started as a Young Liberal, became a friend as we travelled to represent Canada at all party delegations in the OSCE-PA across Europe. He was bubbly, always pleasant company, bursting with energy and ideas. Jason, too, was a true believer in Conservatism. Jason Kenney's grandfather was Mart Kenney, a band leader from London, Ontario who had run for the Liberals, who I became acquainted with when I danced to his smooth music in front of the bandstand in Springbank Park under the stars in my hometown of London as a youth.

I encountered Harper's school time sweetheart Laureen, a warm, gracious, attractive woman who became his wife, on numerous occasions. Each time we met, she paused and asked about my wife's charitable activities and asked to send her regards. She provided a solid family environment to raise her young family, always a daunting task for a working politician – especially a leader. Harper was an attentive father, making time to spend with his children and their extracurricular activities while brushing aside uninvited publicity. The public spotlight on children is, at best of times, difficult to fend off.

Just before my retirement from the Senate, I decided to invite my American-born grandsons to visit Ottawa during Winter

Fest. It's usual to arrange a photo op with the Liberal Leader, in his office, then held by Stéphane Dion. This turned out impossible to arrange. His office seemed disorganized. I was dismayed. As I walked from my East Block office on Parliament Hill one morning, I encountered Kenny and blurted out my unhappiness. "*Would you like them to meet Stephen Harper?*" he volunteered. I thanked him, but I was not sure it could be arranged in the two days remaining before my family was due to arrive in Ottawa for a visit to Parliament Hill at Winterfest.

The very next day I received an unexpected call from Harper's office and was told that Mr. Harper would be delighted to meet with me and my grandsons, tomorrow, Friday afternoon, after Question Period. Friday afternoon at 3:15 P.M. sharp, I entered Harper's office on time with my three grandsons and the office was empty. We waited in the outer office for twenty minutes. Both the outer and inner office were empty. When a secretary sauntered in, we were told this was Dion's office; Prime Minister Harper was on the next floor. I had gone to the wrong office. We raced up the staircase to find Harper waiting. He was welcoming and charming, regaling my grandsons about hockey. "*Would you like a photo?*" he asked them. "*Probably your grandfather may not want to be in the photo.*" "*No*", I said, "*I would be delighted.*" After more than a half-hour, we took our leave stunned by his time and attention. He seemed totally relaxed during the usually busy Prime Ministerial schedule. I saw another side of Stephen Harper. Harper's ease with my young grandsons was amazing. My grandsons, all fanatic hockey fans like their paternal grandmother, were astounded with his detailed hockey knowledge. Harper seemed unhurried as he had all the time in the world – unusual for Prime Ministers. I saw a gracious softer side of him I couldn't believe.

Stephen Harper had a lifelong passion for popular music. He played, wrote, and sang as he led a small rock band. To gain a more popular image, he would surprise audiences at Party rallies, fundraising or charitable events with his catchy songs and skilled musicianship. I witnessed several of these performances, switching as he did from suit and tie to a trendy dark sweater, watching the audience surprised and enthralled with this different Stephen Harper.

There was indeed a softer side to Harper that he kept hidden from the public. He was not a narcissist.

A fairer legacy will emerge for Harper as the 'demonization' by his political foes fades. The party he created and led, the new Conservatives, after three consecutive election victories remains strong and effective. He was an early and persistent advocate of electoral Senate reform. He balanced the federal budget, returning to temporary deficit as economics demanded quickly and then back to balance. He oversaw a rise in real income for the middle-class for the first time in decades and solid economic growth. He had the lowest debt to GDP ratio in the G7 economies during his tenure in office coupled with solid economic growth. Canada came out of the recession stronger than any other of the G7 economies under his careful sound economic leadership. His 'job' policies were effective as were his immigration reforms. He increased lagging defense spending, moving more quickly towards our NATO financing commitment. He supported veterans via the new Veterans Charter. He attempted to dislodge Russia from the G7 meetings. He reinvigorated respect and support for Canada's military. He advocated human rights openly in his meetings with the Russian and Chinese leadership. He started new broader free trade negotiations, the Trans-Pacific Partnership (with Asia) and finalized the free trade negotiations with Europe - EFTA. He signed a Free Trade Agreement with South Korea. He accelerated the FTA with Israel while strengthening economic and cultural ties.

His personal probity was unquestioned. He was a man of strong beliefs and stronger convictions.

Harper distanced himself from Mulroney, concerned as he was by Mulroney's egregious conduct and some policies, he considered less than Conservative.

His policies on climate change were nuanced as he believed the carbon tax, diverting billions to underdeveloped countries, would overburden Canada economically and not have a significant impact on global warming. So, he withdrew from the ambitious goals of the Kyoto Accord that even the interested states would not attain. He supported the Lower Churchill Falls hydro project that reduced emissions equivalent to taking thousands of vehicles off the road. Harper invested $3 billion in public transit projects, especially $700 million towards the Spadina line extension to York University – long overdue. His Supreme Court appointments, while one was controversial and discarded, were sound and solid jurists. His Cabinet and caucus moved towards gender equality. Solid progress was made on Indigenous issues – on reconciliation, a key perquisite to any consensus, pushing Aboriginal education reform that faltered due to traditional Aboriginal reluctance for accountability and divided, fragmented leadership. Harper's demands for economic accountability by indigenous chiefs was not well received, but a prerequisite to any further allocation of the federal budget.

Harper's political preoccupation where he sensed he had special gifts was to safeguard the economy. In the last week of his last losing campaign, he returned to Etobicoke in the west end of Toronto where he was raised, he said in one of his final speeches, "*In the time of growing economic uncertainty, protecting the economy is the number one priority in this election.*" In a sense, he ended where he started in politics with the conviction that the Canadian economy was of paramount importance as he reminded himself and others – he was an economist.

All in all, a solid record of accomplishments. He left office without a blemish to his personal probity. The Duffy Affair tarnished his record and was a significant factor in his defeat in his last campaign. In time, history will take account of Harper's spectacular rise and solid accomplishments. He will receive better recognition as the 'demonization' wears off and his record is compared to others. He was, unlike most Prime Ministers, not in love with his own image. He was the founder of the modern Conservative Party. He left his Conservative Party with a strong base in Parliament and sound Party finances. It remains to be seen if this legacy of tilting Canada to the right will survive his laudable public service.

- *Why Chrétien Mustn't Flag* by Stephen Harper (Globe and Mail, December 2, 1999, pg. A17)
- *On Second Thought* by Stephen Harper (National Post, October 5, 2000, pg. A18)
- *Separation, Alberta-Style: It Is Time To Seek A New Relationship With Canada* by Stephen Harper (National Post, December 8, 2000, A18)
- *The Alberta Agenda* by Stephen Harper, Tom Flanagan et al. (Archived November 18, 2004, at the Wayback Machine., National Post, January 26, 2001, A14)
- *Get The State Out Of The Economy* by Stephen Harper (National Post, February 8, 2002, pg. A14)

Stephen Harper - Maiden Speech

a mainly agricultural riding where grain production has been increasing over the past few years, and given the recent developments regarding GATT and NAFTA, I would like the minister to tell me what is to become of farm income stabilization, crop insurance, and the Crow rates as they apply to western grain transportation.

Will these benefits be considered as some form of subsidy? Will they be allowed under the terms of these agreements? There does not seem to be too much of a problem for the time being. However, should this type of insurance be regarded as subsidy and should farmers be deprived of such assistance, what are you planning to do for grain producers who are presently covered?

The Acting Speaker (Mrs. Maheu): Order, please. Unfortunately the time allotted for questions and comments has expired. Will the House allow the minister a short answer?

Some hon. members: Agreed.

[English]

Mr. Goodale: I am pleased to have the opportunity to briefly respond to the question. I am sure we will have other opportunities to consider the questions raised by the hon. member in greater detail. The member certainly has touched upon some vital questions in terms of the future of Canadian agriculture.

I mentioned in my remarks that we would be reviewing the whole system of farm safety net programs and hopefully moving toward the concept of whole farm income safety nets for the future. They have a number of advantages from our domestic point of view. The whole farm income concept also has the great advantage of being largely production and market neutral. Therefore it is less likely to be subject to any violation of the new GATT. That is one of the reasons we are very interested in this concept of whole farm income safety nets. That would touch upon many of the support programs the hon. member has referred to, including crop insurance and so forth.

The area is under review. We have a conference coming up in February to begin the process of that review. Working with the provinces, the farmers and farm organizations, I think we can arrive perhaps at the end of 1994 at a much clearer understanding about how we need to adjust our programs to ensure they are doing the job properly for Canadian farmers.

• (1045)

The answer on the Western Grain Transportation Act would necessarily be long. I assure the hon. member it is a subject which is very likely to be affected at least in some way by the implications of the GATT. It is a subject matter that we will undoubtedly revisit in this House on many occasions as I consult, as I ought to do, before any changes are made.

Mr. Stephen Harper (Calgary West): Madam Speaker, this is my first opportunity to address the House at length. I am sure you are getting tired of hearing that but two-thirds of us are new members. Many of us who have been here in the past are in new roles, as are you. I congratulate you on your appointment to that role.

At the beginning of these new roles or the beginning of our careers we have the opportunity to think longer term about the problems of our country than perhaps parliamentarians have done in the past.

Many people in my constituency have built successful careers, homes and families by thinking longer term in their affairs. Now they have taken a brave step this time in electing a new MP from a new political party to represent them for the next four or five years.

I want to take a moment to say I am greatly honoured by that election. It is an overwhelming honour and I plan to do my best to fulfil their expectations. We certainly know what happens when you forget who sent you here. The Prime Minister alluded to that yesterday. I hope that I and this Parliament do not let the people of Canada down, as I feel the last Parliament did.

In my particular case I was elected from an urban riding, a riding entirely within the city of Calgary that has 100,000 people. It is in the western suburbs of Calgary. We have a large military base. We have two post-secondary institutions.

In spite of that, my riding and our city reflect largely a private sector character. We do not have a federal or provincial government. We are one of the larger cities that does not.

Of course we have experienced the ups and downs that Alberta has had in the past decade largely through and because of our dependence on the oil industry. In spite of that there is a broadening of our industry in Calgary historically from agriculture to energy, now to services. This broadening reflects our entrepreneurial spirit in the west, in Alberta and in Calgary in particular.

This growth in the view of most Calgarians, I think I am safe to say, has been not so much with the help of government as in spite of it and in spite of the federal government in particular.

I was a newcomer to Alberta when a distant government imposed policies that brought an end to the boom times that brought me to Alberta to begin with. Of course I am referring to the national energy program. No Canadian can live through an experience like that without it influencing greatly his or her thinking about government and about our country. In spite of that thinking and in spite of the drain the federal government has often imposed on Albertans, Albertans have never wavered in their patriotism or in their optimism about the future.

Today the federal government presents not hopes but obstacles to economic recovery. The obstacles are most clearly represented by the national debt and the deficits adding to it which we are experiencing and have experienced in the past number of years. I am not going to recount the statistics. I am an economist and that would be economics and that is a dangerous combination. Let me talk instead about what these numbers mean.

In the election campaign my colleagues and I in the Reform Party argued strongly about the need to understand the long-term link between fiscal mismanagement and economic recession and decline. We argued against the view that we should create jobs rather than fix the financial problem, not because we oppose creating jobs but because these are not conflicting objectives. They are the same objective.

• (1050)

Countries like companies or households that mismanage their financial affairs do not create jobs. They destroy them. Households, businesses, families and governments that mismanage their affairs do not fulfil dreams. Those who mismanage their affairs watch their dreams slowly slip away.

Many of my generation, young professionals, the backbone of the future of Canada, have left Canada, are leaving Canada or are thinking of leaving Canada because they fear the high taxes and the declining services that this mismanagement has brought about and may worsen in the future.

Let me not preach from the Reform Party policy manual. Let me quote the government itself. For members who have not read it, Canada's Economic Challenges contains a very good summary of our economic and financial situation. It lays out better than I could all the relevant numbers on the deficit and debt and the impact on our economy, such as the fact that it absorbs our domestic savings, increases our foreign indebtedness, worsening our current account, lowering national income, our potential growth, reducing our fiscal flexibility, threatening our social programs, increasing our tax burden, raising real interest costs and decreasing our competitiveness. It is all there.

Those are not short-term problems. They are not caused by the recession. A short spurt in growth or activity will not resolve them. The chapter is illustrated with dozens of statistics.

Why then would the same government that released this book also release the throne speech this week and turn its attention instead to spending priorities and in particular to the much ballyhooed infrastructure program. That is a $6 billion commitment, $2 billion sought from this Parliament to kick start the Canadian economy, as if it is possible to do such a thing as kick-start an economy.

On reading the briefing notes for the program it will be noticed there are no fewer than four program objectives and nine related criteria. There are in fact lots of objectives. There are no clear priorities. None of these objectives is new to the program spending that parliaments have passed before. We are therefore led to ask why the government believes that another $2 billion would kick start an economy in a way the first $160 billion of spending this year has been unable to do.

Let us be clear about the magnitudes involved. In the case of Alberta we are talking about $88 million against an economy of $70 billion and an infrastructure investment of at least $1 billion a year. These are hardly kick start kinds of numbers. That is the magnitude and context of the program.

I do not want to quarrel with infrastructure as a priority or even a higher priority than it has been in the past. What I want to do is simply suggest that it will not fulfil the objectives stated by the government and the raised expectations of consumers, taxpayers and investors. It is short-term thinking about jobs and activities that has long-term consequences in terms of employment and output and that has been the past generation as we have seen it.

I ask members, especially government members, to give strong consideration to this before they cast their votes on this matter and on the legislative program that will flow from the throne speech. Members opposite will be held responsible by the public for the performance of the Canadian economy in the next four years.

Possibly the infrastructure program will deliver some short-term benefits and some short-term visibility. But in the long term, by the next election—that at least we will talk about as our long term—the infrastructure program will long be passed and we will be stuck with the bills for it.

I suggest that until the government has contemplated a way to credibly finance these things and to fit these within the $153 billion spending cap that we suggest it should re-examine these priorities.

I ask government members to give strong consideration to this aspect of fiscal discipline, the subamendment we propose, to support and vote for it and to include it in the speech from the throne. On that basis we would be building a more successful government program, not just from our standpoint but also for the potential of their own re-election in four years.

• (1055)

Mr. Dennis J. Mills (Parliamentary Secretary to Minister of Industry): Madam Speaker, I would like to begin by congratulating the member for Calgary West on his maiden speech in the House of Commons. I know it will be a constructive experience over the next four or five years.

I would like to get right to my question because I know this member by reputation and I know he cares about small and medium sized businesses in this country, especially in his own community and in his own province. I noted that he did not seem to spend a lot of time in his opening remarks commenting on the difficulty that small business is having getting access to capital.

The Prime Minister said repeatedly during the campaign, in the red book and in the speech from the throne, that small and medium sized businesses would really be the engine for putting people back to work. The greatest hope for putting people back to work rests with the entrepreneurial spirit in that small business area. We all know that the banks are really not co-operating with that sector.

I wonder if the member could explain to this House if the Reform Party shares the view of our party that the financial institutions of this country really have to deal with putting the economy back on track. I wonder if the member would stand and say that the Reform Party will join with us in making sure that the banks do their job for small businesses.

Mr. Harper (Calgary West): Madam Speaker, I thank the hon. member for his question and for his congratulations. I have known the hon. member for some time and it is a delight to be able to sit with him in this Chamber.

Of course there was not time in my speech to address all of the concerns that the hon. member would like me to address. If in future the rules of the House are altered so that I can speak at greater length, I would be delighted to do so.

The member raises the question of small and medium sized business and their access to capital. My supporters, particularly my association, are predominantly people who work in small and medium sized business and they voted for our party I suspect precisely because they share our concerns.

I would suggest to the government that certainly there are problems with access to capital in the banking sector. However, I would suggest that what the government should do before it starts figuring out how to run the banks and how to run small and medium sized businesses and all kinds of other institutions that it run itself so that small and medium sized businesses have access to capital.

According to the projections of the Minister of Finance, in this financial year we will be borrowing up to $45 billion in the financial markets. Certainly some of this money, if not a large part of it, would be available to small and medium sized businesses if the government would undertake the credible program of deficit reduction that is being advanced through our subamendment. If we do not do that, it would be ridiculous to try to alter the rules of the banking system if the capital itself is being tied up by the Government of Canada which is more than absorbing our domestic savings. That is all in the book his own government has put out.

I would suggest that the way to deal with the problem of capital access for small and medium sized businesses—and the message from the people in my constituency—is to deal first with releasing those funds through deficit reduction and only then should we deal with the problems in other institutional arrangements.

The Acting Speaker (Mrs. Maheu): The hon. member's time has expired.

Mr. Mills (Broadview—Greenwood): Madam Speaker, on a point of order. Is not the question and answer period 10 minutes?

The Acting Speaker (Mrs. Maheu): It is five minutes on a ten-minute debate. They are splitting their time.

Mr. Riis: Madam Speaker, a point of order. I have listened very carefully to the very thoughtful comments of my colleague. Considering the importance and the nature of the tax system and the funding for small business, would the House permit two or three other questions in response to the hon. member's comments? Can we have unanimous consent to allow a few more questions to be put to the member?

• (1100)

The Acting Speaker (Mrs. Maheu): Is it the will of the House to allow a few more questions?

[*Translation*]

Mr. Robichaud: Madam Speaker, I thought there was a consensus and that the Speaker had been informed that we would split the time allotted, that is ten minutes for a speech, followed by a five-minute question period. I would like us to stick with this formula to give more people a chance to speak to this debate, otherwise each member could considerably exceed the time limit and I do want as many hon. members as possible to have the opportunity to speak.

[*English*]

The Acting Speaker (Mrs. Maheu): Unfortunately consent is denied.

Mr. Riis: Madam Speaker, a point of order. I appreciate the point made by my hon. friend. If the concern is to allow as many members to speak to this important debate as possible, we can always extend the hours for people to do that.

My point was that the past speaker was a very important spokesperson for the Reform Party and an obvious person of whom to ask a number of questions.

The Acting Speaker (Mrs. Maheu): There will be another chance for questions unless the next speaker is willing to cede his time.

Mr. John Williams (St. Albert): Madam Speaker, I would like to start by congratulating you on your election to the Chair of this honourable House.

I presume that while you waited with bated breath, while your colleagues took a second look before firmly ensconcing you in the Chair, but I have no doubt whatsoever in your ability to lead us in our deliberations with decorum and respect.

I would also like to congratulate the Prime Minister and his colleagues. Who would have predicted that the red book which was so long on rhetoric and so short on substance could have lead to such a stunning and upset victory?

I would also like to thank the citizens of the St. Albert constituency for the confidence they expressed in me. I spoke to them during the election campaign about fiscal prudence and sound management of the public purse. I believe it was their desire that I stand in this House and carry that message to the government.

Hon. members can be assured that I will persistently advocate the principle of fiscal responsibility during my tenure in this House.

To the hon. member for Calgary Southwest, my congratulations. Of all the particular challenges that he could have chosen, he selected a riding that was perceived to be the most daunting. Yet he triumphed in the most outstanding manner. I look forward to working with him and the rest of my Reform colleagues as we explain to all Canadians our vision of a new Canada which was so eloquently articulated by the member for Calgary Southwest "as a balanced democratic federation of provinces, distinguished by the conservation of its magnificent environment, the viability of its economy, acceptance of its social responsibilities and recognition of the equality and uniqueness of all its provinces and citizens".

I would also like to recognize the hon. member for Lac-Saint-Jean and his colleagues. Their agenda differs from ours but I hope that before the end of this Parliament the issues that currently pull this country apart will eventually pull us together to realize our hope of a new Canada.

His Excellency the Governor General spoke of his government's desire to create jobs for the hundreds of thousands of Canadians who are losing hope and faith in the economic miracle that has been Canada's until the last number of years. We have seen feeble attempts to maintain a robust economy on a philosophy of borrowing and spending our way to prosperity. That false god of prosperity without effort has taken this country into the long dark tunnel leading to economic ruin. We now have double digit unemployment, mushrooming welfare rolls, regions dependent on government handouts; in essence, breadwinners without bread. That story is repeated a million times across this land. Canadians are crying out for leadership, vision, hope, but most of all for jobs and careers. But where do they turn when their hope diminishes with each passing day? There is no plan in place for them to realize their hopes and aspirations.

• (1105)

Over 30 per cent of every tax dollar collected by this government is now paid to bankers and investors as interest on the money that we have already spent. As the debt continues to mushroom, so too does the cost of servicing that debt. On our current economic path Canadians can only look forward to a future of higher taxes and declining services while they work to fill the pockets of lenders and investors.

The Auditor General said in his report tabled in this House yesterday: "Looking at where we have been is not enough; it is also necessary to see where we are going". We are going down the road to economic ruin. He also said: "Hard choices lie ahead".

This government must choose the road to a balanced budget. That is the hard choice. That road is not paved with more social programs that destroy the initiative of Canadians to work. It is not paved with simple quick fix band-aids such as the $6 billion infrastructure program. A balanced budget means that we as Canadians accept the consequences of the follies of previous governments. The hard choice is that only 70 per cent of tax dollars collected can be returned to Canadians by way of services delivered. If we do not accept that consequence today, tomorrow we will have to live with only 60 per cent, or even less, being returned in services to Canadians.

That is the hard choice. Do we bite the bullet now or do we wait until it is too late?

During the election campaign we, as Reformers, spelled out a complete program to balance the budget. Two and a half million Canadians voted for that program. They are prepared to make that hard choice now, yet there is little evidence in the speech from the throne that the government has even heard the message. How long before the government does the right thing and makes that hard choice?

We want jobs in this country. The myth that deficit financing creates jobs was debunked long ago. If that theory worked there would not be a single unemployed Canadian today.

Where do we go from here? I ask this government to make a commitment now to balance the budget by the end of this Parliament. Business is looking for a signal that the upward spiral of government spending will come to an end. With that signal we will know that tax increases will no longer be the order of the day. Declining services will not be the way of the future. If business can believe that this government has the resolve to make these hard choices then investment will follow. That is the creator of real jobs. The private sector will pick up where the public sector leaves off.

Canada was forged by people who want to build a future for themselves and their children. I came to this country to participate in a young and vibrant nation but I have watched as socialism has wrung this vitality dry. Our economy is feeble and we must rebuild it for our children. Our heritage is free enterprise. It created our prosperity. It developed products and innovations that raised our standard of living. It was not social programs that gave us wealth but the opportunity to work hard and keep what we had made. That was the driving force that built this country.

The hard choice has a great future. If we balance the budget lower taxation will come. Jobs will be created. Horizons will be opened up. We will have the money to educate our children, look after our old, the sick and the poor and still be able to compete with any nation in the world. Jobs come from trade not from infrastructure programs.

To sum up, we must turn this country around and start anew. I look for leadership and vision from my honourable colleagues across the floor. Hard choices must be made. History has always glorified leaders who have reached beyond themselves and led their nation through the dark tunnel to the light, which in our case is renewed prosperity without debt.

• (1110)

I issue this challenge: will this government commit itself now to balancing the budget by the end of this Parliament? The first step down the hard road is to approve the subamendment by the member for Calgary Southwest to cap federal spending at $153 billion. I urge all members of this House to vote in favour of the subamendment.

Mr. Nelson Riis (Kamloops): Madam Speaker, I congratulate my hon. friend on his maiden speech in the House. One of the main points he raised referred to the fact that we have to get our deficit under control.

One of the causes of our deficit problem is the amount of money the federal government fails to collect. It is an issue that more of us should get very serious about when we consider that a major preoccupation of many Canadians has now become purchasing contraband cigarettes and illegal liquor.

We found from the Auditor General's report yesterday that tens of thousands of businesses appear to be collecting the GST and not remitting it to the federal government. This obviously indicates a clear loss of faith in our tax system, to say nothing of the underground economy that probably includes almost everybody in one form or another through cash transactions or a barter system designed to avoid paying tax.

Does my friend share the view that one of the major steps to be taken in terms of reducing the deficit would be to close off some of the more obviously unfair tax exemptions that exist in our tax system to begin restoring faith in the system so that people will again be prepared to participate in the revenue collection of the country, knowing that our system is fair and more just?

Mr. Williams: Madam Speaker, in response to the question of the hon. member for Kamloops, I mentioned in my speech that we have a feeble economy. Taxes are too high. This is why we find today that businesses are struggling to pay the taxes to keep the government afloat. Even then the government still needs another $40 billion or more to pay its bills.

If we are going to look for a vibrant and strong economy we must look forward to the day when investment overtakes spending by the government. We must also look forward to the day when taxes start to come down and affordability of taxes comes within the realm of everybody to pay their fair share.

We always agree with the need for equality but I think the focus of the government has to be toward a balanced budget. It can collect the taxes due in order to do so but we must look forward to the day when we see taxes coming down and a greater willingness by Canadian people to participate in paying for the government of this country.

[*Translation*]

Mr. André Caron (Jonquière): Madam Speaker, I listened carefully to the hon. member's words. I was surprised to hear his stand on social programs, because I understood him to say that social programs destroyed the initiative of Canadians and should therefore be eliminated.

This particular position is disappointing to me because what I heard from the voters of Jonquière during the election campaign was that Canada and Quebec have always been concerned about the weakest and the most disadvantaged. My constituents said clearly to me that they do not believe people who get rich by profiting from private enterprise will be generous enough to take care of the disadvantaged, the sick and the poor.

• (1115)

I have a question for the hon. member and I hope he will have the time to respond. I will be brief. Does he know of many cases where people who became wealthy through their work or their business were successful in setting up programs or providing health care and social services, or services to the unemployed and the disadvantaged on a scale equal to what we now have in Canada?

[*English*]

Mr. Williams: Madam Speaker, in response to the hon. member's question, I think we have to recognize that this country was born and developed out of initiative. We very much recognize our social obligations to Canadians who are old, those who are sick and those in unfortunate circumstances who are unable to look after themselves. Recognizing its responsibilities in these areas shows the maturity of any society. I would be the last to suggest that we shun that responsibility.

We also have a responsibility to those who are prepared to lead the country in its economic growth. We have to give recognition to them that prosperity comes from that direction. As I said, we do not want the government to destroy the opportunities and initiatives of people to develop the country and continue to provide the growth and the jobs we so badly need.

Mr. John Maloney (Erie): Madam Speaker, my first words in this House must be those of appreciation for the privilege and honour of representing the riding of Erie. I would like to thank its voters for their trust and confidence without which I would not be here. I am aware of my responsibility to my constituents and indeed to all citizens of this country and I hope I will be equal to this task. I will not forget where I came from or who put me there. I will advance their position from the highest government in the land. I cannot deliver perfection but I can deliver accessibility, honesty and integrity.

On a personal note I would also like to thank my wife, Sherrie, and my children, Megan, Patrick, Alanna, Andrew and Sarah, for allowing me this privilege. I will endeavour to keep their personal sacrifices as minimal as possible.

I wish to congratulate you, Madam Speaker, on your appointment to this esteemed office of which you are most worthy.

I would further like to take this opportunity to congratulate the hon. member for Welland—St. Catharines—Thorold on his election as Speaker to this 35th Parliament, a position of honour and responsibility unequalled in this House. I have enjoyed his sage advice over the years and regret the non-partisan aspect of his office now denies me the privilege of his counsel.

I further wish to congratulate the mover of the Address in Reply to the Speech from the Throne, the hon. member for Bruce—Grey, and the seconder, the hon. member for Madawaska—Victoria, on their addresses.

It is indeed a great honour for me to be in this Parliament, especially under such an honourable leader as the Prime Minister. It is a pleasure for me in my maiden address to introduce the riding of Erie to my fellow members of Parliament.

Having been born and raised in Erie it seemed only fitting that on finishing my formal education I would return to Erie. For many years I served on a great number of local committees and boards. This exposure to local issues and people made my decision to enter federal politics a little easier. I believe that Erie deserves the best representation possible in Ottawa and I hope I am worthy of that responsibility.

As some may gather from the name, Erie riding follows the north shore of Lake Erie, one of the fine Great Lakes. It extends from the border town of Fort Erie in the east to the western boundary of the regional municipality of Niagara. It is a rural-urban riding encompassing the city of Port Colborne, the southern portion of the city of Welland, as well as the towns of Fort Erie, Pelham, West Lincoln, and the township of Wainfleet.

This is only geography and does no justice to describing the heart of this riding. Erie riding was blessed with many Canadian riches. Our history, agricultural climate, economic potential and traditions in my humble opinion are unparalleled in any other part of Canada.

Many historical battles of the War of 1812 were fought on Erie soil. Erie also saw the likes of William Lyon Mackenzie during the Upper Canada rebellion of 1837 and the Fenian raids of the 1860s.

• (1120)

The early settlers of Erie were joined by the United Empire Loyalists, a group of people dedicated to what would later become the Dominion of Canada. Over the years our riding was further blessed with healthy immigration from all European countries and most recently from the Pacific Rim. There has also been lateral migration from other areas of Canada: from the west, from the maritimes and from *la belle province de Québec*, all attracted by the lushness and opportunity that Erie offered. The riding indeed reflects the multicultural heritage that makes our country so strong. I hope I may embody some of their independent, industrious and enthusiastic spirit as I work for my constituents and dedicate myself to community and country.

On the very eastern boundary of Erie riding is the Niagara River which divides Canada from our neighbour, the United States. Our proximity to the American border offers us opportunities for trade and industrial development that will help enhance and diversify our economy well into the 21st century.

Apart from the historical significance, development potential and beauty of the riding, the moderate climate and fertile soil have made Erie famous for its fresh produce, bountiful orchards and vineyards. The Niagara region is one of the best grape growing regions in the world and forms the basis of Canada's wine industry. Poultry and dairy farming represent a solid mainstay in Erie's economy as well as that of our nation.

The climate and charm of Erie attracts a great number of tourists who come to enjoy the water and beaches of Lake Erie, to browse through our heritage museums and historic sites, to marvel at the ships plying the Welland Canal, an integral part of the St. Lawrence seaway system, or just to enjoy the pleasant surroundings and chat with our friendly residents.

Due to the rural nature of my riding many Erie residents embrace a traditional way of life. This lifestyle is rooted in their heritage and must be preserved. This preservation is a goal of mine during my first term in office. I support the maintenance of

Justin Trudeau

The Justin Trudeau Trajectory

(23rd)

Date Elected to Parliament: October 14, 2008
Date of Maiden Speech: November 19, 2008
Date Sworn In: November 4, 2015
Date Left Office:

Nothing was more satisfying when Justin Trudeau (Pierre Trudeau's eldest son) chose a career in politics. He was born to politics. Trained by his father in statecraft from an early age, he often travelled with Pierre Trudeau on his domestic and foreign travels, meeting with foreign leaders. Justin developed an early, easy confidence under the public spotlight coupled with his innate grasp of good manners and graceful diplomacy. I first encountered Justin, the eldest son, blessed with a pleasant personality, as a toddler with his mother Margaret and later accompanying his father Pierre at political rallies and sports events. The most memorable early event that remains locked in my mind is when he and his brothers joined his father on the stage at Pierre Trudeau's farewell address to the Liberal Party in Ottawa at the Leadership contest to choose his successor. Justin seemed more curious than shy in the public spotlight.

No doubt the Pierre Trudeau legacy of leadership was the key to Justin's early political prominence and a material factor in his accession to party leadership. The Liberal Party, after decades of tribal infighting, was poised for a leader to unify the Liberal Party craving a return to power. The Pierre Trudeau brand was a blessing but like any son of a prominent father, a heavy collar to be lifted. Each was so different in so many ways.[198]

Justin Trudeau's first adult entry into the public spotlight was the moving eulogy he gave to the vaulting cathedral at his father's funeral crammed with the elites and foreign leaders like Castro, all under the glare of TV. At heart, like all politicians, some better than others, he relished his skills of an actor as he set sail in the sea of public opinion to shape his public persona. I sensed early that he was interested and destined for politics. His dramatic placement of a single rose on his father's coffin was moving and an elegant touch that evoked deep emotions. In his eulogy, he mentioned an anecdote about his father. Justin had criticized a political leader, a Conservative Prime Minister. Pierre Trudeau admonished him never to unfairly criticize a political leader. Lesson learned.

Early he decided, under the encouraging tutelage of his father, to become physically robust, gaining confidence in individual sports like skiing, boxing, and other forms of self-defense. Later, snow-boarding as he became a skilled teacher, was added. While not rigorous in his intellectual pursuits as his father, he quickly set a course to follow his own interests. Educated at Collège Jean-de-Brébeuf, a Catholic private school requiring high academic standards, like his father he preferred literature to more demanding intellectual courses. Like his father, Justin did not seem to relish team sports. He enjoyed solo sports that would pit his skills against himself or another. Like his father, he enjoyed

[198] Justin's full name was Justin Pierre James Trudeau named after his father and his maternal grandfather, James Sinclair, a senior Liberal Minister in the St. Laurent government in the '50s. A name can be both a blessing and an ever-present reminder of the achievements of his predecessors.

canoeing and tripping in the great outdoors. After McGill, he moved to British Columbia where his maternal grandfather had held sway decades before as a Minister in the St. Laurent government.

After a stint at McGill where he became an accomplished debater, he decided to become a teacher where he developed his skills to interact with young people in British Columbia.

Softer and warmer than his father in his interpersonal relations with both sexes, he combines a natural likeability with an attractiveness enhanced by his youthful, handsome appearance and his obvious genuine interest in people from all walks of life. Dressed in trendy, narrow suits, he was well turned out. At times, he wore colourful socks to attract attention, especially from younger voters. When he engaged with an individual, he didn't 'check the room' as some politicians do, but locked eyes with the person who engaged him. He trained himself to act, loved teaching, and travel.[199] Justine was enlisted by Jacques Hebert,[200] an old friend and colleague of Pierre Trudeau, to become the Chairman of Katimavic – an organization providing means for young Canadians to travel and work across Canada. Justin did a marvelous job travelling across Canada encouraging

[199] Justin Trudeau travelled to over fifty countries, probably the most travelled at an early stage of his career more than any other Prime Minister before attaining public office.

[200] Hebert and Pierre Trudeau were close friends. They travelled to China and wrote a book together on their experiences there. Hebert was an early capital punishment abolitionist. He influenced Pierre Trudeau to abolish capital punishment. Jacques became a good friend of mine when he was appointed to the Senate. When the federal funding for Katimavic was stopped, Jacques began a public fast in the Senate antechamber to draw attention to this issue. As the fasting continued, I worried about his health and called Pierre Trudeau in his office in Montreal. Surprisingly, Pierre Trudeau was not worried. He told me Jacques took copious vitamins – "*He will be alright.*"

young Canadians to join and become even more acquainted with our vast country. He also acquired his firsthand taste of personal politics when the Mulroney government cut off Katimavic's government funding. There seemed to be a pattern in these actions as if Justin was following in his father's oversized footprints. Yet, like any dutiful son, he aspires to outdo his father's legacy in his own way. He yearns to make his own mark on his own terms. His father self-defined himself as a 'progressive', yet, understood the conservative mainstream public was not there yet with him on some policies and issues so he tried carefully to allow the public to catch up. Pierre Trudeau was ever careful to hedge his preferred politics to gain wider mainstream support on controversial issues he wished to advance.[201]

Justin's choice of his wife Sophie was inspired. Attractive and well-spoken with a common touch, she has demonstrated that she is a quick study, a modern up-to-date advisor, and mother. A quick-witted, well-turned out, and well-travelled woman who had a professional career of her own, she and his young children add a warm dimension to his persona. It is difficult to raise children in the glare of the public spotlight, but she accomplishes this with ease. The names of their sons, Xavier and Hadrian, are instructive about both parents. Her steady partnership has given Justin added security, depth, and confidence.

I first observed Justin more closely as a toddler when he attended political events with his parents and later at small dinners at 24 Sussex. He had a special relationship with his

[201] Aware of the limitation of leadership, Franklin Roosevelt, when he attempted to move public opinion in the United States from appeasement before World War II and before as he moved to quickly legislation reforms for the New Deal at the outset of his Presidency, once opined to a close advisor that he was surprised when he looked behind him and found no one was following.

mother, Margaret, as the first born. The obvious love and pride that Pierre Trudeau had for all his three sons was manifest as they for him. Trudeau and his sons became inseparable especially after the painful 'public' separation as parents. It is trite to say that Justin inherited his softness and handsome appearance from his mother and his inner toughness and resilience from his father. Though some traits are similar, he has emerged as his own man. I recall being told how at a dinner at 24 Sussex for Menachem Begin, the Prime Minister of Israel, Justin and Sasha when introduced to Begin welcomed him with the Hebrew greeting 'Shalom' – to the pride of his father and to the surprise and delight of an astonished Begin. Justin engaged foreign leaders early with unusual poise and self-confidence. At his father's funeral, he publicly and privately, demonstrated these traits with world leaders who came to pay their final respects to his father.

Justin's facility in both official languages was based on his father's desire to ensure all his sons were fluently bilingual. Pierre conversed with his sons in French at home and as a stickler for language, he corrected their grammar. I was well acquainted with Justin's maternal grandfather, Jimmy Sinclair, an accomplished Liberal who became a Cabinet Minister in the St. Laurent Cabinet and whose easy charm, wit, and geniality made him a political favourite. Had he not lost his British Columbia seat in the 1957 Diefenbaker landslide; Jimmy Sinclair would have been considered for Liberal leadership in 1958. So, politics is part of Justin's DNA on both sides.

Pierre Trudeau started his own tragic death spiral when his youngest son, 'Miche', died suddenly in a tragic skiing accident on the snow-covered slopes of the British Columbia Rockies. At his youngest son's funeral, Pierre's normal reserve broke down at a private reception following the funeral. I approached Pierre Trudeau to proffer condolences. He reached out and we hugged.

With tears in his eyes, he whispered to in my ear, "*This is hard. Very hard.*" Pierre Trudeau loved his sons.

It was strange to hug a quietly somber Trudeau in my arms as he was not one for close physical contact. I whispered in his ear, "*You must be strong, Pierre, tres forte, tres forte!*" I motioned to Justin and his brother Sasha to take him to a side room to allow him to gather his emotions together. The two sons did so. A few minutes later, Trudeau returned to the reception under both his sons' watchful eyes, calm and in tight control once again as he slowly and quietly moved about the small crowd offering condolences. Justin never left his father's side. It was a poignant moment for me in my relations with Pierre Trudeau and his sons. I gained a quiet admiration for his two elder sons and their careful sensitivity to their father's deep bereavement, which they shared.

My next active encounter with Justin was during the leadership campaign that pitted Bob Rae against others including Stephane Dion who like me was an early Gerard Kennedy supporter. I had chosen Kennedy to support as had Justin who rigorously campaigned for Kennedy with great effort. When Kennedy dropped out and supported Dion, Justin and others like me on Kennedy's team followed suit and supported Dion. Justin got his first real taste of politics, and was good at it, and obviously enjoyed it.

Later after the unhappy, short-lived, and disastrous Liberal leaderships of Dion and Ignatieff, I, amongst many others, urged Justin, by now an M.P. to seek the leadership of the Liberal Party. The Liberal Party was deeply divided into warring camps. Tribalism reigned. Old militants felt that the Trudeau brand as personified by Justin could unite the Party, and once again, return the Liberals to power. Others were not of that view. On the contrary, some were anxious to cut away the Trudeau brand from the Liberal Party forever.

What was interesting was that Justin, when he first decided to run for Parliament, he chose to contest Outremont in Montreal. This seat held historic ties as it was where his father first logged into politics in 1942 to fight Conscription. Dion wanted him for another seat. In the end, he chose nearby Papineau with a diverse polyglot riding against a sitting member of the Quebec Parliament, a separatist, a popular female Cardinal born in Haiti. When he first sought a seat in Parliament in 1965, Pierre Trudeau ran in Mount Royal-Westmont riding in the heart of Montreal, a seat traditionally held by Anglo or Jewish Quebecers. Justin took a risky first step into public life finally deciding on Papineau.[202] Quebec remained divided about Pierre Trudeau, both hated and loved, but always respected. Justin gathered a tight cadre of loyal friends and stormed the Riding to win the nomination and then the seat by a healthy margin. He drew on the advice of others such as Andre Ouellette, a longtime Liberal, previous riding M.P., former Cabinet Minister, and a youthful Quebec organizer to advise him on the nature of this polyglot riding. Justin paid special attention to the ethnic vote in the Riding that he connected with and enjoyed. He attended mosques and churches with ease. Justin worked hard to become 'his own man' and win his own stripes. He gained a comfortable majority in his first run and surprising victory to some. Once in the Liberal caucus, he was quiet, a patient listener who hovered standing at the back of the room usually with his friend Dominic LeBlanc, spoke rarely but well. Focused on local issues, he gained the early respect of his

[202] Justin originally considered Outremont where his father had cut his political teeth working for Drapeau who ran there for Parliament against the issue of conscription in 1942 during World War II. Party politics got in the way, so he chose nearby Papineau, a tougher riding with a popular separatist sitting member but with a more working-class voter base and larger number of Francophone voters.

political peers. He worked on his speaking techniques. He took special care of his riding, diligently attending local events. It was a delight to watch him as he carefully picked his issues, mostly focused on issues in caucus that were relevant to his riding. He was careful and modest in demeanor.

His coterie of close friends included Dominic LeBlanc, with Liberal pedigree and also an M.P., jovial boisterous son of Romeo Leblanc, a longtime Liberal advisor to Pierre Trudeau, M.P. and later Senate Speaker, then Governor General. Dominic had earlier toyed with running for Leader himself and I had encouraged him to do so. Gerald Butts, a bright maritime Liberal from impoverished Cape Breton who Justin met and befriended while at McGill, who started as a youth working for the Liberal icon Allan MacEachen in Ottawa and went on to become Dalton McGuinty's chief assistant in Toronto when McGuinty became Premier of Ontario. Like his father who sought skilled Quebec operatives, he enlisted Daniel Gagnon, a shrewd experienced activist with experience in Quebec City working for Jean Charest and in Ottawa working for Dion as an accomplished political advisor, likeable and accessible. Justin attracted a small circle of diverse, loyal enthusiasts, both male and female, that would carefully plot his leadership trajectory. Pierre Trudeau's crew was more intellectually engaged with a greater diversity of opinion, interests, and age that spanned the political spectrum. Justin, however, practiced gender equality and greater ethnic diversity in his crew from the onset. His hand-picked team was young, enthusiastic, ambitious, and yearning for political experience. He was determined to earn his own way. He and his entourage rigorously studied the techniques of the social media of Obama and easily deployed them. While he took the obvious advantage of his father's name and the deep desire in the Liberal Party's DNA that asserts itself in its lust for power Justin's leadership deftly evaded Conservative efforts to frame him as 'unprepared' as he chose an achievable disciplined path to power. In his leadership campaign, he made a bold move to declare that he had no intention to merge with the NDP, a strong view I shared. Merger was a growing mood in some segments of the Liberal Party as the way back to power. It was also reflected in popular polls. A merger would mean the end of the Liberal Party. I could never envision sharing a caucus with the NDP or their extremists on the left, nor I hoped, could he.

The accusation that he was unprepared for leadership especially due to his scanty work record as a school teacher was levelled at the time. "*Not ready yet*". Early on, he was 'framed' by the Conservatives as 'inexperienced' as the Liberals had 'framed' Harper as a closet 'right wing' extremist, who harboured a 'Secret Agenda'. What goes around, comes around in politics. Justin avoided the traps set for him by his calm 'sunny ways'. In my view, few were better prepared with honed political instincts needed for modern political leadership than Justin due to his tutelage under his father, a political master – from birth to maturity and his own insights into the interests of his cohorts and his demographic. His entry on the world stage with other leaders was flawless and confident. His father's tutelage and his own preparation and confidence paid off. However, Justin was determined to blaze his own 'progressive' path to the left quickly, perhaps too quickly. He stifled dissent in his caucus to adhere to his new Party lines. He demonstrated early on that he was a 'conviction' politician that had ready appeal to the 'millenniums'.

Of course, there are material differences between father and son as there are in all families. Pierre Trudeau was the most intellectual Prime Minister in Canadian history by conviction, schooling, and by study. Pierre Trudeau's unconventional views on issues where there was not a consensus remain hotly disputed by the intellectual community to this day – especially his views on the nature of Confederation and the federal government role leading the provinces and the necessity to strengthen the federal government against the growing strength and expansion of the provincial powers.

Where father and son share one self-definition, both considered themselves fierce competitors and enjoy the cut and thrust of personal and political contests.

Justin demonstrated a deep interest in and an easy connection to people from all walks of life. One example. After he became M.P., his team asked me to assist in a fundraiser, something I had always eschewed. I preferred to make my mark on policy and politics though I had devoted most of my time and attention on political organization, but much preferred political policy development. I was never interested or involved in party fundraising. However, I was interested to see how Justin would handle himself in small intimate settings, always a mark of a leader. Carole and I invited ten couples, five Liberals and five Conservatives, friends and their spouses for $1,000 per couple. The dinner was arranged at our home in three round tables, and prepared and served by Tess, a middle-aged woman from the Philippines, our housekeeper, and our longtime family caregiver Winsome, an elderly single Jamaican who had assisted my mother and then my mother-in-law in their dotage. Justin was asked to rotate at each table to interact with each guest.

I had quickly briefed him in the background of each guest and observed how he developed an easy rapport with each, both male and female. I told him he would ask to speak informally just before dessert for ten minutes, followed by a Q&A. When the time came for him to speak, I noticed he was not in our spacious living room where the dinner was served. I ask Carole, "*What happened to Justin? Where is he?*" She looked around and said, "*I don't know.*" I searched in the living room and the reading room and every room, he was nowhere to be found. Finally, I entered our large kitchen where the doors were closed. There I found him sitting at the kitchen table deeply engaged in close conversation with both Tess and Winsome. I told him it was his time to speak. Justin nodded and said, "*The guests can wait. I want to finish my chat with these two ladies. I will be another few minutes.*" Soon thereafter, he emerged from the kitchen, took his place at his table, and after a brief intro, stood and spoke effortlessly about his policies and plans. There was a lengthy searching 'Q&A' greeted with warm applause – all were charmed. On his way out, he thanked each guest by name and returned to the kitchen, asked me to take pictures with both Tess and Winsome and graciously took his leave.

After the guests had left, I was curious. I asked Tess and Winsome what they had talked about. Justin calmly had questioned them each about their families, their backgrounds, why they had come to Canada, what were their concerns and finally to my surprise he asked how they 'got along with the Grafstein's'. Both told him we treated them as family members which we did and they always joined us at our table for meals when they are not serving guests.

Justin demonstrated a genuine interest in these working immigrant women, and they were mesmerized by him. His father, who was also our guest at our home for several meals, would be perfunctory with household assistants, perhaps to pause politely for a picture or two. Pierre was simply less interested and less engaged. Pierre wanted to wring ideas from others or contest their views. Justin had a genuine common touch which would serve him well in his years ahead in politics. He was a thoughtful listener who connected with each individual.

Justin has quickly modernized the Liberal Party and put it on strong financial footing adapting Obama-inspired fund-raising techniques via the social media. In the process, he eviscerated the dependence on Liberal Party bag men and sharply diluted their influence on the Party and politicians. He tweeted, or rather emailed, before Trump. Justin ran a disciplined campaign and avoided the jabs from Harper about his inexperience.[203] In the end, he gained a satisfactory large majority in Parliament and appointed a slew of bright, if untested, Cabinet members with a 50/50 male/female complement, a first for Canada. His first Cabinet is also racially diverse to reflect the new faces of Canada.[204] If light in experience, some will catch on and others

---

[203] Taking a leaf from Obama's political handbook, Trudeau and his team targeted the new demographic audiences – 'the middle-class'. Most people who are not in the middle-class aspire to be a member though the definition of the middle-class is problematic. The middle-class in Canada is now divided between the private sector middle-class which funds its own retirement funds and health care and the quickly growing public sector middle-class secure from inflation geared retirement funds and richer government funded health plans. Which 'middle-class' is targeted? *'Focus on the 'middle-class'* is not a new political ploy. Sometime in 1948-9, Pierre Trudeau confided to his notebook his thoughts about the 'middle-class': "*In Canada a party like the Liberal Party which moves slowly to the left can in the abstract become the vehicle leading the nation towards this popular future [of socialism]. But its laudable impulse to embrace the better elements of socialism clashes with those who represent the interests of money. I believe a great deal in the wisdom of the middles classes who are erroneously represented under the name of the bourgeoisie... Nevertheless, it is necessary for the proletariat to raise itself to the level of the middle-class. It is never better to rely on others for your own food.*" – from *Citizen Trudeau: An Intellectual Biography 1944-1965* by Allen Mills (Oxford University Press, 2016).

[204] Notably, his first Cabinet relied heavily on newcomers including four Sikhs, two Muslims, a Jew, and several with Aboriginal origins placed in senior portfolios. While a risk, it was consistent with Trudeau's campaign promises. A Canadian of Italian origin was missing in his first Cabinet and one wonders why. Justin Trudeau initiated another Cabinet reform. He wrote open letters to each Minister setting out that Ministry's priorities

will be shifted or discarded due to limited capabilities, lack of Parliamentary experience or patent failure in administrative skills. The mantra of the 'middle-class' is evoked whenever confronted by problems, self-made or otherwise. Perhaps deeper analysis beyond the focus in the so-called 'middle-class' might cast a wider net on the public front and shape a broader swath of public opinion in the nation's interest.

Daily polling by the Prime Minister's office between elections is now a reality. At times, polling is at its best to track opinion as a snapshot in time so the public can be diverted from hardening attitudes on unpopular issues of substance. Of course, polling trends appear that can reshape unpopular public policies. This is now true of the operating modality of all major political parties in Canada and elsewhere.

Well into Justin's mandate, I attended the opening ceremonies at the belated inauguration of the Holocaust Memorial located near the Canadian War Museum in Ottawa. Many spoke, including a survivor. Then Justin Trudeau was called to speak after he entered the large area led by the War Museum staff. The room was hushed in expectation. Trudeau slowly mounted the podium. All were eager to hear his comments as was I. His demeanor and his words were pitch perfect. His empathy for the Holocaust survivors present was palpable. He had matured. He easily gained control of his audience.

Leaders are not leaders until they make mistakes and demonstrate that they can handle adversity. Justin is still a 'work

---

and policies seeming to micromanage each Ministry from the PMO. The impact of open Cabinet debate and on evolving issues that differed from each Minister's mandate will await the release of the Archives of Cabinet Minutes to determine the impact of this centralization of directed power. How the unpredictable plays in each Ministry's terms of reference is yet to be measured.

in progress'. His flawless poised entry as Prime Minister onto the world stage has been purposeful and sure-footed. He is genuinely liked by foreign leaders for his modesty and friendly demeanor and his early celebrity. I live in great expectation.

The alleged conflict between 'pipelines' and Trudeau's visceral commitment to climate change is in play. Trudeau's bold move to nationalize the Kinder Morgan pipeline in the public interest is an act of leadership. While the introduction and passage of legalizing 'cannabis' nationally – the first in the western world, the consequences and political fallout across Canada is too early to opine of it – yet, it was, in its own way, an act of leadership and a cultural revolution in itself.

Canada-U.S.A. trade relations (NAFTA) were placed on the front burner by President Trump. This presented a powerful challenge to Canada's economic base. America is a complex, powerful neighbour, but a necessary ingredient in Canada's economic well-being. Over 50% of all jobs in Canada depend on our trade with U.S.A. and 70% of our exports. Canada is a trading nation by necessity and has been since before Confederation, witness the early fur trade. This dossier is the most important to Canada's continued economic growth and prosperity. Justin Trudeau and company fared well as the dossier evolved with its ups and downs, at times like a roller coaster. Trump meant what he said on revamping the NAFTA. It was clear from the outset that Trump wanted real change, change to tilt more in favour of American interests and correct some obvious protectionist measures, especially dairy products within the NAFTA. The steel and aluminum tariffs continue to present an economic challenge. The Americans, especially Trump and Co., need a careful watch. Congress is notably unpredictable. The nuances are as important as the thrust. Handle with care. This dossier remains open.

The trade barriers between provinces remain an obstacle to greater domestic growth. Recently a cabinet minister, Dominic LeBlanc, Justin's trusted friend, has been designated to sort out this pressing problem.[205] The devil remains in the details and only political will can reduce these clogs on free trade within Canada. It's estimated that billions of dollars in 'free trade' benefits within Canada await solving this national challenge. Tepid moves have been made in the past to untangle this internal paradox – 'free trade' for Canada, except within Canada. The Supreme Court of Canada didn't help in its recent Maritime decision which openly neglected express provisions in the Constitution allowing inter-provincial free trade. Alas, the courts.

The advent of a Conservative government in Ontario in the last provincial election and especially conservative leaning new party government in Quebec and Saskatchewan, New Brunswick, and Nova Scotia present political problems requiring increased attention. The erosion of the federal Liberal base in the province in Ontario pose a severe challenge both politically and economically as the Ford government moves swiftly to expunge the Federal Carbon Tax now echoed by at least three other Provincial Premiers and leaders. Once again, the Supreme Court of Canada is being asked to make a political decision. Beware.

Equally the Trump 'disruption' changed the foreign affairs outlook and western democracies consensus on issues like trade, military cooperation, and climate change. A realistic increase in NATO expenditures poses a fiscal problem. Canada has been carefully constructed on our national interests in multilateralism to expand our reach as a 'middle power'. The question of increase in military spending remains a tricky issue. Choice of expensive

[205] Just before going to press, I learned that Dominic LeBlanc had contracted cancer and voluntarily relieved himself of his ministerial duties. All wish him a speedy recovery and return to public office.

air and sea is fraught with peril.[206] Foreign policy is choppy and turbulent, and no doubt will precede change. Whether Canada can construct a new role for itself as a renovated 'middle' power abroad yet, sustain our vital interests with the Americans is not yet clear. Every former Prime Minister and External Affairs Minister has learned that Canada cannot divert too boldly from American policies and each has sought to manage this multifaceted vital vacillating relationship with special care and attention. Justin's notable and amiable reputation in Congress is an invaluable asset in this dossier.

Justin has created a remarkable space and 'celebrity' for himself on the world stage like no other Canadian leader before him. How he deploys this 'celebrity' will be a fascinating voyage. He had quickly become, as one of his key advisers confided, "a rock star". The longevity of 'celebrity' remains an open question.[207] Sometimes 'celebrity' gets worn out as the public moves on. Sustained economic progress remains the linchpin of political success.

There is an elusive dimension to Justin Trudeau. At times, it's as if he is removed from his public persona and observing his actions from afar as he invents and reinvents himself.

One caveat. The Liberal Party is deep in talent – present and past – and those who have left public life remain staunch loyal Liberals. Youth and newness have its advantages. There has been scant effort by Justin's coterie to draw on the deep past experience and expertise of Liberal party elders within

[206] In 2017, Trudeau's Ministry of Defense announced a major commitment to increase military expenditures by 70% in the next five years. The strategic plan was not broadly debated. But both are solid steps forward.

[207] In a 1975 interview, the Nobel Prize winner for Literature, the Canadian born American author, Saul Bellow, was reported to have said, "*...to be a celebrity is like picking up a high voltage cable which you can't release...*"

and without his caucus. I hope they will never need them! His abrupt disengagement with the Senate Liberals and his policy of appointing so called independents was radical. It remains to be seen if this step was in the right direction of parliamentary reform. It is in the nature of democratic institutions to form political factions and groups and to act in concert on issues of concern. The efficacy of this reform remains a work in progress.

The major challenge to Justin Trudeau and Canada was the re-negotiation of NAFTA prompted by President Trump. How Canada will ultimately emerge from this tough USCM negotiated settlement will determine, in part, Justin Trudeau's place on the next page of Canadian history. How Congress will deal with this Treaty remains an open question. Canada's growth and prosperity depends largely on international trade and most on Canada/U.S.A. trade. Justin has accelerated the negotiations of other Free Trade Agreements across the globe to his great credit and persistence. A new largely untested Minister, Jim Carr from Manitoba, has been given this targeted complex responsibility. In Asia and Europe, still developing markets for Canada await. To create these new channels of trade will take time and constant investment of time and energy to enlist the Canadian private sector. There have been stops and starts on the Asian Free Trade file, but it is still too early to assess the progress. Whether terms in the new USMC agreement will hinder this free trade effort elsewhere remains a question. But it also creates a time-consuming free trade agenda.

One visionary aspect has been Justin Trudeau's commitment to upgrade Canada's technological skills. His government recently financed commitment to artificial intelligence (AI) development was a giant stride forward. How Trudeau deals with the loss if automotive jobs in Oshawa and in the oil sector in Alberta will be a test of his leadership.

Another challenge is the costs to the economy involved in reaching the lofty environmental goals set by Trudeau. The UN has signaled Canada lags in cleaning up our own fresh water supplies, much of which is polluted, a recurring nightmare in meeting political expectations. Another pressing priority is to cleanse our domestic water environment and of course the Aboriginal communities clean drinking water policies remain to be completed and viable. Trudeau's focus on Aboriginal advancement by budget reform and to the justice system has been admirable. Yet, it is too early to judge if this focus will produce concrete results to lift the Aboriginal communities to a higher platform of economic growth and self-advancement to match the rest of Canada. So, too, his gender equality commitments which are lofty and hopefully achievable. Major progress has been made on the gender equality under Trudeau's watch.

Provincial obstacles to free trade envisaged by the British North America Act and the Canadian Constitution that called for free trade between the provinces persist and remain an economic barrier to 'free trade' within Canada. The fragmented capital markets divided by provincial jurisdiction remain inefficient, begging for a federal securities regulator to improve the costs and improve the efficiency of securities across the country.[208] A pure federal regulation, as the Americans did in the '30s would be a more constitutional appropriate policy. These issues continue as daunting challenges to the Prime Minister and his Cabinet's use

[208] I introduced a Federal Securities Act in the Senate that I drafted with Senate Counsel that I believe would have met the Supreme of Canada's constitutional objections to a national security regulator – S-214: An Act to regulate securities and to provide for a single securities commission for Canada; Sept. 10, 2009; Debate on motion for 2nd reading adjourned. Prorogation on Dec. 30, 2009 wiped out this legislative attempt to solve this problem.

of time and energy. Billions of dollars will be found in growth if Canada develops a domestic free trade zone. Provincial preferences remain intractable problems, not easy to dissolve. Of late, as mentioned, Dominic LeBlanc, an old friend of Justin Trudeau, has been appointed to resolve this decade old problem.[209] He will need the Prime Minister and his Cabinet's strong support and leadership as this topic touches every department and agency of the federal government – a public task force could speed up the process.

The Asian and especially China file presents especially complex challenges that have yet to be addressed. The China file contains complexities. China is the second largest economy country in the world. The persistent loss of Canada's patent rights to new technologies emerging on China that led to the demise of Nortel and the unfair trading diminution of foreign entities like Ericcson bear careful consideration. China is Canada's greatest challenge on the trade front. The extradition of a leading Chinese executive in this area presents a complex confrontation especially on trade relations. How this is resolved is fraught with dangers to Trudeau's leadership.

Trudeau moved sharply to cut any opposition in his caucus to women's rights to choose. The impact on free exchange of ideas, within the confines of caucus and the Liberal Party, remains an open question. The Liberal Party, constructed on a large tent of free and open exchange, seems to be narrowed.

Canada is caught up in the '*Me Too*' movement. No doubt legislative reforms in this area will be introduced into law, a delicate job at best. To retain our faith 'in due process' and the 'rule of law' is being challenged by this meritorious movement.

As well, Trudeau invested heavy political capital in the 'identity' waves of the over-heated dialectic of this complex

[209] Refer to 205 on page 400 about Dominic LeBlanc.

phenomenon. How finally the pincers of this movement will cut into concrete change remains an open question.

Promises usually are displaced by reality – always hard on campaign promises and rhetoric. Hard facts must be addressed as a Leader pivots from campaign to Prime Minister to meet exigencies of the day. The world is flooded by 'political incorrectness', an evolving and at time synthetic outlook. Political 'correctness' can take the public to confusing dead-end corners.

Where and how to stem the tide of Trudeau's ambitious electoral commitments and promises or justify necessary pivots will be a key factor in his leadership. Changing the electoral system was a step too far and correctly abandoned. The economic record to date has been satisfactory as the economy continues to grow, but not as quickly as our American neighbour. The ballooning debt and deficit need attention especially when the economy lags in growth. Increased levels of taxation and debt, both public and private, are looming as an electoral issue. Recent poverty reduction legislation is vital. Meanwhile every year, poverty in Canada increases. This, too, will require the Prime Minister's active participation to dent this file.

Sometimes it appears that Justin is trapped by his own 'celebrity'. It will be interesting to see how this evolves.

Much like Stephen Harper, Justin Trudeau is a 'conviction' politician by inclination. Trudeau's staunch support for feminism, climate change, diversity, and identity politics is self-evident. Whether politics and the art of compromise within the Liberal Party tent and compromise in Parliament is the future direction that most Canadians desire to take remains an open question.

There is nothing new in the practice of politics. Only in the face of adversity will we see what steel lies beneath the amicable handsome surface of Justin Trudeau. It is only when leaders react to mistakes and crises that a leader can be fairly measured.

I suspect Justin will do just fine. And, Canada will never be the same.

A final thought. Justin Trudeau came to power at the most momentous change – the rise of the power of cyberspace that connects individuals and corporations, instantly and digitally around the globe. History is now moving on steroids in real time. Democratic governance is being challenged. Leadership in every democracy faces this new attack on civil society! His leadership will be judged by this new political environment like none other faced by his predecessors. History is being written faster than we can read.

Justin Trudeau - Maiden Speech

24 COMMONS DEBATES November 19, 2008

The Address

Politics is a competitive business. We all know that. However, when it comes to big national projects, projects that by nature and necessity transcend traditional, regional or partisan divides, we owe it to ourselves, our constituents and future generations to make government accountable and effective.

Now our government has introduced some positive reforms to our democratic institutions that we believe are examples of positive, non-partisan reforms.

Ensuring that the House better reflects the Canadian population or introducing democracy to the Senate are concepts on which all Canadians should be able to agree. We will continue to pursue these stronger, more democratic institutions, and we will welcome any cross-party support.

We will also continue to strengthen Confederation itself. As members know, it was just last week that the Prime Minister met with the premiers to discuss the current global economic instability. Canada works best when we all work together. We will continue to respect the jurisdiction of the provinces while ensuring that federal transfers are sufficient to ensure that all Canadians can count on world-class health, education and other services close to home.

Perhaps the most important institution of all is this House. In this chamber every Canadian is supposed to have a voice through their elected representatives. Canadians do not expect us to agree on everything, but they do want our voices, their elected voices, to be focused on solutions and not on divisive rancour.

• (1605)

I am proud to second this motion, and I throw my full support behind the Governor General's remarks. May we conduct this debate, and all of our debates, with the passion and vigour of our beliefs while at the same time respecting this House, respecting each other and respecting our common obligations to all Canadians.

[*Translation*]

Mr. Justin Trudeau (Papineau, Lib.): Mr. Speaker, to begin with, I would like to take a moment to thank the people of Papineau for giving me the honour of representing them here in this House. It is a responsibility I will fulfill with grace and humility.

The government is at last admitting that Canada will, as it has under previous Conservative governments, again have a budget deficit.

[*English*]

Through this past decade Canada has faced many other crises, from SARS to BSE to currency crises in Mexico and Asia to September 11 itself and always we have managed to maintain our surplus while investing in innovation, in families and in opportunities for all Canadians.

[*Translation*]

Had this government followed the basic principles of financial administration that were in place when it took over, it could have defended the interests of Canadians, while at the same time being in a position to generate a budget surplus.

Will this government make a commitment to restore Canada to a healthy and socially responsible economy, with practices and principles similar to those it inherited two and one half years ago?

[*English*]

Mr. Bob Dechert: Mr. Speaker, I am sure all members of this august House will agree that Canada needs strong leadership and responsible fiscal management in these uncertain economic times. People's jobs and the economic stability of their savings, pensions and financial retirement incomes are of paramount importance. The initiatives laid out by the Governor General today will keep our economy and the health of our people strong and secure.

• (1610)

[*Translation*]

Mrs. Carole Lavallée (Saint-Bruno—Saint-Hubert, BQ): Mr. Speaker, I am sure you will understand that before I say anything else in this House, I want to thank the voters of Saint-Bruno—Saint-Hubert.

The Speech from the Throne made it clear that the Conservative government did not understand the message Quebeckers were trying to send. Seventy-eight per cent of Quebeckers did not vote for the Conservative Party, and there is a reason for that. They did not like this government's positions, and they did not want what it had to offer. They did not like what the government planned to do with young offenders, and they really did not like the idea of cuts to culture. In Quebec, there was an outcry against such cuts. Clearly, the government did not get it, because the Speech from the Throne had nothing to say about bringing back that funding. Yet culture is hugely important in Quebec. We not only love and respect our artists, but we also consume a lot of what they produce. Why? Because we are a nation, and our artists represent Quebec culture. We are very proud of them. Yet there was nothing at all in the Speech from the Throne for artists and the arts.

I had the opportunity, if not the pleasure, to attend the Conservative Party convention last Thursday, where I heard the Prime Minister give a speech about his election campaign to his supporters. He did not say that he understood what Quebeckers wanted, nor did he acknowledge that they were not happy with what he had to offer them. He did not suggest that the government should therefore be more conciliatory and offer something else to Quebeckers, or that it should change, or that it should reach out to them and listen carefully to what they have to say. He said nothing of the kind. He said that, basically, Quebeckers did not understand the Conservative Party, that the party was going to find some other way to get its message across, and that it was going to repeat that message as many times as necessary to convince Quebeckers that it was right.

Given the current economic context, it is understandable that the government would deliver a throne speech focused on the economy. That makes sense, and the Bloc, too, wants to act on the issue without delay. However, this raises the following question: why would the government indicate, in its throne speech, that it wants to hurt a thriving economic sector—the cultural industry—all the while seeking to create programs that will help industry in general?

Afterthoughts

What compels us to be followers? How and why do our leaders acquire our loyalty and followership while their actions may beguile us and often lead us astray? Obviously, the meandering human condition craves leadership.

From the ancient Bible, we learn of the triumphs and travails of Kings, Prophets, and their followers. From the Greeks, we learned of the conflict between mythical Gods and kings and their adherents.

After centuries of the reign of Kings and Queens who ruled by 'divine right' as witnessed in the last century, Kings like Phillip II of Belgium who made the Congo his horrendous fiefdom, or the egregious rule of the Romanovs' of Russia who rose on the plunder of feudal serfdom followed by Lenin, the revolutionary leader, who imprisoned or butchered his opponents in the name of creating the 'new Soviet man' or Mussolini who made the trains run on time, built stirring modern structures while he fecklessly invaded Abyssinia, the oldest kingdom in the world whose King begged the League of Nations to come his rescue. The world failed to answer this call and then led Italy into the Axis alliance after becoming an acolyte of Hitler to devastate his sunny nation, or Stalin whose policies massacred well over 30 million ethnic and non-ethnic Russians or Hitler who practiced ethnic cleansing infused with modern techniques all under the hopeful eye of his countrymen believing in the superiority of the so-called Aryan race and maintained the loyalty of some German people even after their devastation of their homeland, or a contrived piece of historic fiction that the Japanese Emperor was 'descended from the Gods' who countenanced all the 'rape' of China in Manchuria and Nanking and elsewhere in Asia and allowed the sneak attack at Pearl Harbour that awakened the rest of the West except South America to eradicate the Nazi Fascism ideology and Japanese idea of a divine Emperor, or the atomic bombs on Japan or the massive dislocation caused by Mao's egregious ideological lurches like the Cultural Revolution, or the fearsome leaders in the Vietnam War or the human devastation of Cambodia, or the forgotten wars of Africa or the rise of Islamic fascism under the guiding eyes of the Ayatollahs and Bin Laden and his wannabee Islamic followers incurring waste and devastation amongst true and non-believers alike. Or errant democracies that seek economic hegemony over others at every turn.

What propels rational women and men to follow these insane and inane actions concocted by deranged leaders? Who is at fault – the leaders or the followers? Perhaps we must be alert and on constant guard against egregious leaders who leave devastation in their wake, on both the small and large issues they confront or ferment, wherever and whenever they crease the surface. We should never fall in love with our leaders. We should be aware of defaulting to 'root causes' analyses as a diversion and an apologia for ill-considered actions. We should suspect power and try as best as we can to speak truth to power.

Even democratic leadership has too often defaulted to deception and deceit to maintain political power. Addiction to polling can divert from substantive, if unpopular, actions in the national interest. Are the recurring and inflating costs of the electoral cycles a democratic device worthy of constant reform?

Are democratic budget excesses by democratic governments sustainable? Can the excessive demand for 'rights' without 'responsibilities' impair democratic sustainability? Pierre Trudeau believed restraint in the use of power is the essence of democracy. Almost always, leaders and their entourages build faux echo chambers of opaqueness to divert from honesty and transparency. Is this, too, a fault line in the human condition? Was Bismarck, right? Legislating is like making sausages – not to be observed too closely. On the other hand, 'polling' can become the modern 'check and balance' on public policy when a leader veers too far along a path of egregious public policy. Still, polling reflects but a moment in time, a snapshot of opinion, that can be as misleading and harmful as it detracts from substantive debate or reforms.

The human condition is in need of constant reformation and the least we can do is to guard against its excesses. The cyberspace had brought nations together to solve common problems if we can. Science and technology are moving faster than the public can digest. Civilization is lurching forward, tacking closer to the winds of propaganda at times than truth and reconciliation.

As I reflect on our Canadian Prime Ministers, the nation needs visionary leadership for the future. Canada's riches and resources are largely untapped. The treasures awaiting along Canada's far north coastline and in the 'Ring of Fire' in northern Ontario and the Quebec Nord are barely touched. The high tide waters of Hudson Bay could provide clean energy via floating turbines is not even on the drawing board. Fusion energy or 'clean nuke' energy is not encouraged in the clamour of the pervasive climate change debate. Canada's northern sea lanes will soon be opened to shorten sea lanes to Asia and Europe while the citizenry is disinterested, and little is being done in Canada to prepare to take advantage of this coming transformation. Russia, our closest neighbour after the United States, with its much smaller economic pie has focused more time and investment on its far north with modern ports and icebreakers than Canada. Canada is beginning to catch up with a growing fleet of northern ships and ice breakers. No one is actively working with Americans or the Russians to convince them to build a tunnel under the Bering Strait that lies closer between Russia and Alaska than the 'chunnel' between France and Britain that would open rail traffic from London across Europe and Russia to Alaska down the Canadian west coast and then across Canada into the United States and to the populated American east coast and west coast. This would reduce pollution in the air and in the ocean. It's not even being debated. A tunnel would foster greater cooperation between Russia, U.S.A., and Canada. Fast trains networking all parts of Europe are now being activated. Our cities for lack of vision are increasingly inefficient. We have to still formally connect our universities with similar research efforts to work in a coordinated, collaborative fashion. Our secondary education, while leading in the world in public expenditures, lags behind in academic results. Alas, where there is no vision, the nation perishes.

We need concrete vision – 'a certain idea' of Canada. There are no limits to Canada's capabilities to grow and thrive. Interprovincial barriers clog free trade within Canada. Poverty and illiteracy continue to plague Canada. Progress on these fronts is the very definition of liberal progress. Poverty reduction initiatives remain works in progress. Lags on education standards under a provincial jurisdiction is of national concern. Canada needs an educated work force. While climate change debate rocks and occupies the political space, pollution of our lakes, rivers, and streams is shamefully neglected. As is clean drinking water in our Aboriginal reserves and in places like the Newfoundland outports where daily boiled water is still necessary for outport family use in the 21st century in Canada.

Canada is a blessed nation. Canada remains a large, and largely undeveloped, landmass rich in untapped reserves and fresh water. Our greatest asset remains our people waiting to be led. Constructed on diversity from bilingualism to biculturalism to multiculturalism to Aboriginal rights, women's rights, and LGBTQ+ rights, we live and thrive in diversity. The 'other' has become ours. Be on guard. Our leaders can, and will lead, the public astray with their errors and judgement from truth and transparency. Leaders can beguile us all. Canada, stand on guard.

Digital Democracy and 'Big Brother'

In 1949, George Orwell published a novel called *1984.* Orwell, an English author and journalist began to gather material for this novel when he was working under Brendan Bracken, then Minister of Information, in the Cabinet of Winston Churchill, for the BBC Indian Service.[210]

1984 describes the fictionalized state of 'Oceania' ruled by Winston Smith, the leader who wielded absolute power over all its citizens. Citizens were under constant surveillance via televised reminders with the repeated slogan "*Big Brother is Watching You*". Big Brother has become a synonym for abuse of government power as civil liberties were reduced and privacy diminished.

Citizen's Lab, situated in the Munk School of Global Affairs at the University of Toronto on Bloor Street West, is a dedicated organization of skilled internet experts who have been collating abuses of power via cyberspace by states and corporations around the world.

---

[210] See also *Orwell on Freedom* by George Orwell (Harvill Secker, London 2018).

Giant data collecting corporations and governments are free to invade individual privacy without legislative limits.

No doubt, cyberspace brings people closer together. Yet, this same ease of access allows states and corporations to monitor surveillance and 'hack' the daily data flow between individuals breaching their privacy, their personal data, and their communications.[211]

Without the protection of privacy, democracy withers. It limits citizens' rights and freedom to speak "truth to power" – the essence of digital democracy. Legislation is paramount to protect democracy. Caveat lector!

---

[211] For an interesting history and current assessment of the power of these digital networks, read *The Square and The Tower – Networks, Hierarchies and The Struggle for Global Power* by Niall Ferguson (Penguin Books, 2017).

"There is no room for the dilettante, the weakling, for the shirken, the salt water wavers, the fields to till, the home, the hospital the chair of the scientist, the pulpit of the preacher – from the highest to the humblest tasks, all are of equal honour all have their part to play."

- Winston Churchill, Speech to the Parliament of Canada, Dec. 30, 1941[212]

[212] From *Lincoln & Churchill: Statesmen at War* by Lewis E. Lehrman (Stackpole Books, 2018).

"...and remember the lessons of the Bible.
Even the greatest were flawed and made mistakes.
That is okay and we are not supposed to be perfect,
we are supposed to be human, and in our humanness
to become better, little by little..."

– Elie Wiesel
Lessons from Elie Wiesel's Classroom by Ariel Burger
(Houghton Mifflin Harcourt, 2018)

The Honourable Jerry S. Grafstein, J.D., Q.C.

Mr. Grafstein was a co-founder of a range of media companies, focusing on broadcasting, film, cable, communications, and publication enterprises in Canada, the United Kingdom, United States, and South America. He has served as an advisor to several key federal government ministries, including Transportation, Consumer and Corporate Affairs, External Affairs, and Justice. His legal practice was largely communications and corporate finance. He was appointed to the Senate of Canada in 1984 by then Prime Minister Pierre Elliott Trudeau. Mr. Grafstein served on all Senate Committees, especially the Foreign Affairs and Legal and Constitutional Affairs Committee. He also served as Chairman of the Senate Banking, Trade and Commerce Committee. For fifteen years, he was elected as Canadian co-chair to the all-party Canada-U.S.A. Parliamentary Group and was elected as Treasurer and then Vice President for the Organization of Security and Co-operation – Parliamentary Association (OSCE-PA) in Europe for well over a decade. During that period, he was elected Chair of the Liberal group at OSCE-PA. He retired from the Senate on January 1, 2010 and continued his law practice in corporate finance and communication law as counsel to Minden Gross LLP in Toronto until March 2015 where he is now Counsel Emeritus.

He is an author of several books including *The Making of the Parliamentary Poet Laureate: Based on Senator Grafstein's Private Member's Bill* published in 2003, *Beyond Imagination* published in 1995 and *Parade: A Tribute to Remarkable Contemporaries* in 2017. This book entitled *A Leader Must Be A Leader – Encounters with Eleven Prime Ministers* was based on observations and encounters with each Prime Minister from 1960 to the present. He is currently writing a history of the 20th century due for publication in fall of 2019.

He was named one of Canada's top public intellectuals by the National Post. He is an Honorary Commandant of US Marine Corps, Honorary Fire Chief of New York City and Honorary War Chief of the Peigan Nation of northern Alberta. He continues to serve as a director of public companies and as a key investor in several Canadian based tech start-ups. He is Chairman of the Board of The State Hermitage Museum Foundation of Canada and Chairman and President of the Board of Canadian Friends of Tel Aviv University. He is co-founder of a number of cloud-based news sites in North American, Europe, Asia, and the Middle East.

Mr. Grafstein was born in London, Ontario in 1935 and holds a Bachelor of Arts degree from the University of Western Ontario and a law degree from the University of Toronto Law School. He is married to Carole née Sniderman, has two sons, and three grandsons.

Index